Sanctuary Cities, Communities, and Organizations

Sanctuary Cities, Communities, and Organizations

A Nation at a Crossroads

MELVIN DELGADO, PhD

OXFORD
UNIVERSITY PRESS

OXFORD
UNIVERSITY PRESS

Oxford University Press is a department of the University of Oxford. It furthers
the University's objective of excellence in research, scholarship, and education
by publishing worldwide. Oxford is a registered trade mark of Oxford University
Press in the UK and certain other countries.

Published in the United States of America by Oxford University Press
198 Madison Avenue, New York, NY 10016, United States of America.

CIP data is on file at the Library of Congress
ISBN 978–0–19–086234–3

9 8 7 6 5 4 3 2 1

Printed by Sheridan Books, Inc., United States of America

This book is dedicated to all those who are actively reporting on and working to ensure that social justice is carried out to help ensure that those who are undocumented are treated fairly and are helped to realize their dreams and build upon this nation's history as a beacon for those in search of a better life.

CONTENTS

PREFACE

A preface is in order as readers begin exploring a topic that increases in importance on a daily basis. As a social worker, this identity influenced my views on the sanctuary city movement. This does not mean that readers will become immersed in how social workers do, or should, respond to this national topic. This book's goal is to reach readers with interests in sanctuary cities by drawing upon theoretical and historical information, while keeping in mind the topic's saliency for everyone in the United States, regardless of their citizenship status.

Readers are undertaking a journey that covers multiple historical periods, including the present day. One does not have to be a historian to understand how historical events have shaped the central role that sanctuary cities are playing in current national discourse and the narrative of those who are unauthorized, including how local settings have responded. A counter-narrative is offered that should resonate with readers who embrace a social justice stance on immigration laws and policies, including how they are interpreted and acted upon. In the process of addressing the unauthorized and sanctuary cities, complex issues usually not covered with these subjects are addressed, grounding this subject matter within a broader socioeconomic–political context analysis and discourse.

Readers will find ample scholarly references to pursue different aspects in greater depth related to history, economics, demography, sociology, culture, religion, and politics. My writing style is more straightforward to facilitate this reading. Readers must understand that very serious scholarship exists on this topic and the forces that led to the creation of the sanctuary city movement.

This book focuses on the sanctuary movement with extra attention on Latinos. As a Latino, this topic takes on greater saliency for me. This does not mean that the sanctuary movement has not played a role in social justice related to other groups, such as Asians and Africans. Other groups besides Latinos are targeted for deportations (Yee, 2017e).

Why write this book now? My interest was sparked due to the last presidential election and the primaries that led to the selection of candidate Trump. I followed the primaries and national campaigns very carefully because the election of Donald Trump would be challenging for this nation from a social justice viewpoint. How Latinos, for example, and specifically those who were undocumented, were addressed proved distressing. I decided to write a second edition to *Social Work with Latinos* (Delgado, 2017) book based on a visceral response to concerns raised about Latinos, which, if we are not careful, would result in the fears engendered by the statement of a "taco truck on every corner" made by a Trump surrogate.

As this book unfolded, the "Wall," with its deep and disturbing symbolism, and the need to deport several million unauthorized Latinos simply because they were "illegal," emerged as a key campaign theme. Clearly, there would not be any pathway to citizenship for millions of those who were undocumented. Rather, there would be arrest and deportation, destabilizing communities in this country and the countries to which these people would be returned, creating repercussions throughout the northern hemisphere. However, more important, the lives of those living under the threat of deportation, and the family members who may be left behind, must not be lost in the bandying about of statistics, and we must not lose sight of their profound narratives (D. Gonzalez, 2017).

Sanctuary cities have much to teach this nation. This does not mean that effort will not be made to re-examine the merits of pervasive negative counter-narratives. It is impossible to provide a counter-narrative without articulating the primary narrative, and why it has taken hold as it has during the past several years.

Scholarly literature that takes an anti-immigrant stance is found throughout this book. My emphasis is on the critical or counter-narrative. It is hoped that readers are in a position to read this book with an awareness of why I have elected to frame immigration issues in a particular way. It is my version of the "truth." I believe "sanctuaries" represent the major civil rights issue of this decade, and this should not escape attention from scholars, practitioners, and those who share these concerns.

As an academic interested in current events and issues of social justice and human rights, I have never been reluctant to use newspaper articles and other sources of information to buttress a particular point, understanding that these sources are not peer reviewed. Waiting for peer-reviewed publications on "hot" topics means waiting 2 or more years. That is very frustrating when writing on topics that are quickly unfolding. Many readers may welcome the inclusion of material from "unconventional" sources; the purest among us may take issue.

Finally, we must be prepared to learn that there is no one specific sanctuary city movement because of how sites and organizations define sanctuary in response to local sociopolitical concerns. Readers will see terms such as "sanctuary," "welcoming," "friendly," "welcoming and diversity," and "affirming" cities, with all sharing almost similar goals; readers will also see the "new sanctuary movement" alongside the "sanctuary city movement," further confusing how these efforts take hold. To make this subject even more challenging, this movement is not just about cities but also about towns, counties, and organizations that are not religious. This subject, regardless of terminology, is increasing in national significance and destined to remain in the national consciousness, with short-term and long-term consequences.

ACKNOWLEDGMENTS

I thank the external reviewers who took time from their busy schedules to review and make constructive recommendations on the manuscript. Their insights and knowledge of the subject reinforced many of the key arguments put forth in this book.

Sanctuary Cities, Communities, and Organizations

SECTION 1

Grounding Sanctuary Cities

Readers may rightly ask, if this is a book on sanctuary cities, why are there so many chapters devoted to other topics and sanctuary cities are not really addressed in detail until the second section? Sanctuary cities are best appreciated and understood when grounded within a context that identifies the role of historical, cultural, social, and economic forces in shaping this national response.

The sanctuary city movement represents a coming together of varied committed individuals and key institutions to form a social movement, be it built on ethics, morals, or civil rights, that has signaled out those who are unauthorized in this country. A moral stance, for instance, brought together activists from different backgrounds and facilitated engagement of various individuals and groups in this rights movement (Diaz-Edelman, 2014).

This movement also brings tensions and challenges that cannot be overlooked in understanding how sanctuary cities have evolved and the ultimate shape that they take when considering local circumstances and priorities, including elected political leaders. I ask the readers' indulgence in reading Chapters 1–4. Social work has always been about context; context shapes practice, and practice shapes context. In essence, context for social work is what location is to real estate. I bring the lens of a social worker in writing this book and cannot totally neglect this context.

1

Overview

INTRODUCTION

It is appropriate to start this chapter with Lazarus' Statue of Liberty quote from *The New Colussus* written in 1883:

Give me your tired, your poor,
Your huddled masses yearning to breathe free,
The wretched refuse of your teeming shore.
Send these, the homeless, tempest-tossed, to me,
I lift my lamp beside the golden door!

The United States is the primary destination of immigrants worldwide (Olayo-Méndez, Haymes, & Vidal de Haymes, 2014). The hope and symbolism of this famous quote are not lost on those seeking to make the United States their home and willing to risk health and safety to make a new life for themselves and their families (Rosenberg, 2017). The current debate on immigration, however, casts a large shadow over the Statue of Liberty and Lazarus' quote as a result of President Trump's bigoted response to Haiti and African refugees in early 2018 (*The New York Times* Editorial Board, 2018).

This introductory chapter provides the foundation and roadmap for how this book will unfold. The complexity of the sanctuary movement makes for a compelling narrative that is also controversial, which should be expected based on its highly politically charged nature.

BOOK GOALS

This book, although focused on the sanctuary city movement in the United States, provides a more nuanced, and personal, understanding of a very complex problem and the response of those backing sanctuary cities and organizations. This necessitates setting the requisite historical, political, and economic foundation to an issue that has captured the attention of the nation in a way that is as intense, if not more so, now than ever before. No segment of the country can view those who are unauthorized as irrelevant or not impacting their daily lives in visible and invisible ways.

Readers wishing to go straight to the point may be frustrated because I will take the "road less traveled" in this journey. Those reading each chapter in sequence will be rewarded when they eventually get to Chapter 5 and Section 2 of the book, although references are made to sanctuary cities throughout the earlier portions of the book. A dynamic topic experiences many twists and turns along the way. Attempts are made to predict future events, as addressed in Section 3.

This book seeks to fill a major gap in the sanctuary city movement literature. From an organizational perspective, sanctuaries can be a focus for human service interventions (capacity enhancement), as well as provision of individual assistance to those seeking refuge. Communities, too, can benefit from mezzo practice in organizing this movement. This book addresses five goals:

1. Ground the concept of sanctuary cities, communities, and organizations within the existing social science literature
2. Provide a grounding of the interrelationship between immigration, those who are unauthorized, and urban centers throughout the country
3. Identify and analyze key historical, socioecological, and political factors that have influenced this movement and can influence it in the future
4. Provide case illustrations (Boston, Los Angeles, and San Francisco) that concretize how this movement has shaped community dynamics and developments
5. Identify the implications of this movement for readers interested in translating their knowledge of this movement into practice and being involved in this human rights and social justice campaign as part of their profession, as an activist, or as a volunteer

These goals are highly interrelated and disentangling each from the others is artificial yet essential to understand and appreciate each goal, but the whole is far greater than the individual parts.

This book focuses on Latinos for good reason, although it would be foolish to ignore the broader, anti-Latino, views found in certain sections of the country because of how they feed into a particular anti-newcomer narrative, with those who are undocumented bearing the brunt of this vitriol (R. O. Martinez, 2016). Anti-immigrant rhetoric has primarily focused on Latinos, shaping the focus of who gets deported (Vysotsky & Madfis, 2016). Although this book is written by a social worker, the analysis of the issues, strategies, and tactics discussed have applicability to other professions, activists, and "ordinary" citizens who share similar social justice values.

Human service organizations have been playing, and can be expected to continue to play, a significant role in reaching those who are unauthorized in this and other countries, bringing the potential of an international movement that unites providers, religious leaders, elected officials, residents, and activists. Is this role facilitated if they function within the confines of a sanctuary city designation?

If so, how and to what extent? This book seeks to answer these "bottom-line" questions from a variety of viewpoints, with significant implications as this decade continues to unfold against a highly political backdrop concerning who "belongs" in this country.

Finally, this book has a very specific and obvious agenda. Many of us may have the conviction to act but do not know where to take our concerns and passions to make a difference in how this country treats those who are unauthorized. I hope to inspire readers to speak out, and act, for those who have not done so or support those currently playing a role in the sanctuary city movement. This movement has provided many of us with an opportunity to focus our voices and actions as part of a national, and even international, effort seeking social justice for this group during these troubling times in this country (Hall & Wang, 2017).

BRIEF STORIES OF A JOURNEY

Narratives have a powerful impact on bringing complex issues to life in a manner allowing us to appreciate and understand the stories about those who are marginalized in our society. The following stories of Alejandro and Cindy put faces and names to those who are unauthorized and the trials and tribulations that they face; the third story is about someone without a name but just a number to mark his time on earth. Each story illustrates various dimensions of a multidimensional picture concerning those desperately seeking a better life in the United States.

The irony of how this country has historically placed so much emphasis on the sanctity of the family, yet it is so willing to break up families, is not lost on me. The following story of Alejandro illustrates the tragedy of a broken family left behind in the United States and the uncertainty of what awaits those deported back in Mexico (Malkin, 2017b):

> When Alejandro Cedillo was deported to Mexico from the United States, his Florida-born son and daughter were a little older than toddlers, and it would be six years before he would see them again. Mr. Cedillo returned alone, to his close-knit family in San Simon el Alto, the hilltop farming town he had left nine years before, when he was only 17. (p. 8)

"Broken family" takes on new meaning when discussing those who are deported and leave their families behind.

Rodgers (2017) provides a story about the daily fears that those who are undocumented experience, even when they may feel more at home in this country than their country of origin, including having pride in who they are:

> Cindy and her three children live in a tiny bedroom in an apartment shared with two other unrelated adults outside a major U.S. city. Born in Guatemala, Cindy—who does not want her last name used—was brought to the U.S. when she was 5 years old. Yet she still has no legal status. "Even though I don't have

papers, I feel that I'm from here," Cindy says. She has been working at various jobs since she was 17. Now 29, she has a baby on the way and wants to stay in the only country she knows, so she can make a better life for herself and her American-born children. "Of course I'm proud of having been born in Guatemala, but I wasn't raised there. I don't know the culture, and I don't know what it's like to live there," she says. Her biggest dream, she adds, is to get residency status in the U.S. But now, more than ever, she is scared of being caught and deported.

Cindy now has a prefix as part of her identity—Guatemalan American. Her country of origin is a distant memory. Her major developmental stages have indelibly been shaped by living in this country.

The following description highlights how there are no "typical" deportations and how such an act has far-reaching consequences beyond having to go "back home" (Heyer, 2016):

> On a visit to the Kino Border Initiative (KBI) in April 2013, I had the opportunity to speak with recently deported migrants at their aid center. One gentleman had spent 26 of his 27 years in central California, brought there as a one-year-old by his uncle. He had worked harvesting pistachios and almonds to support his wife and four citizen children without trouble, even on the occasions he could not produce a driver's license for a routine stop. In the past two years, each such stop landed him in jail—with the third resulting in deportation to Nogales. He expressed dread at starting over in a country foreign to him. (p. 83)

Readers interacting with those who are unauthorized, I am sure, have heard many heart-wrenching narratives such as this one, bringing the human element to a policy that on the surface seems straightforward: "You want to be an American, then take your place in line like everyone else."

Finally, Lorber's (2013) description of the work of humanitarian aid volunteers in addressing potential deaths is heart-wrenching, highlights a dimension of crossing the border that requires greater attention:

> Walking through forbidding desert hills dotted with cacti and mesquite. I dreaded the moment when I would turn the corner and find the man's remains stretched out under the unforgiving sun. Two days earlier, another group of humanitarian aid volunteers had found an injured seventeen-year-old boy on the side of the road. His group of ten travelers had been scattered by a low-flying Border Patrol helicopter, he said, and he had wandered for days with the seventy-year-old man and a forty-year-old woman. When his companions grew too tired to continue, he tied a pair of red boxers to a mesquite tree and left them underneath, promising to return with food and water. The day after his rescue, volunteers found the body of the woman. We never found the body of the man, nor did we ever learn his name.

The prospect of dying and not even having the dignity of having a name recognized and the death recorded is unimaginable in a democracy with the resources this country possesses and the values it professes to embrace.

These narratives only scratch the surface of what it means to be unauthorized in the United States. Each story brings a different and complex dimension leading to countless outcomes that are detrimental to health and well-being.

During the past 200 years, a pervasive narrative has unfolded about how the United States has been welcoming of immigrants (Mousin, 2016). This country's "love" and "hate" relationship with immigrants is established later in this book, and its "othering" of those who are undocumented represents an extension of conflictual feelings over its history as a nation (Epps & Furman, 2016).

This nation's history of immigration has always been contested and continues to be so today. Those who are unauthorized call into question deep philosophical principles pertaining to what is meant by "citizen," "citizenship," and "nation," with the eventual answers having profound social and political outcomes (Guzmán, 2013). The argument that a nation that cannot secure its borders is not a nation comes to mind. Those who are unauthorized are often relegated to the poorest sections of marginalized urban communities, making their existence even more challenging (Openshaw, McLane, & Parkerson, 2015; Yao-Kouame, 2016).

These immigrants have received a significant amount of popular and historical coverage in the United States. It has been more than 30 years, or a generation, since the 1986 Immigration Reform and Control Act (IRCA) became law, representing this country's last widespread legalization program. The separation of families remains one of the most heartfelt symbols of this nation's failed immigration policies (Pallares, 2014). For many who left their families behind, the breakup is no less significant or dramatic, but these sentiments are difficult to capture by a camera.

It is estimated that 25 million Latin Americans have left their homeland, with the majority of them (15 million) doing so in approximately the past 20 years, in large part due to free trade agreements (Sandoval-García, 2017). Not all of these uprooted Latin Americans have moved to the United States. Immigration does not just impact this country, although one could get this impression. Cities such as Toronto, Canada, for example, have attracted a significant number of Latino newcomers (Delgado, 2016a).

Those who are undocumented do not have the luxury of belonging to the same world as their counterparts who are citizens, and this translates into seeking jobs that have low visibility, having little knowledge of worker rights or being able to act upon them, or not having a day go by in which they can enjoy life's little pleasures without also fearing arrest and deportation (Gleeson, 2012; Gui et al., 2016). These lived experiences provide a window for provision of micro, mezzo, and macro services and interventions and also the involvement of social, religious, and political organizations.

I often think that my life is "complex." However, it pales by comparison with that of someone who is undocumented and whose life is unimaginable to the average person. Readers interested in a more in-depth understanding of the lives of those who are undocumented are recommended to read Lorentzen's (2014) *Hidden Lives and Human Rights in the United States: Understanding the Controversies and Tragedies of Undocumented Immigration*, which provides a highly detailed description of the journey and lives of those who are unauthorized in this country.

Living with the "problem" of "irregular migration" requires a deliberative decision-making process on the level of tolerance a society has about who is allowed to cross its borders and how long they stay (McNevin, 2017). Those who are unauthorized in the United States were a major campaign theme during the 2016 presidential election and a topic that has garnered national attention during the past two decades and one destined to continue to do so for the immediate future, with increased deportations resulting from deportation policy enforcement (Kulish, Dickerson, & Nixon, 2017; Winders, 2016). On February 11, 2017, a nationwide sweep of cities such as Atlanta, Chicago, and Los Angeles led to hundreds being arrested for deportation (Selbourne, 2017).

Anti-immigrant sentiments can be disguised through both official and unofficial local-level policies under the guise of fairness, lawfulness, and safety (Schütze, 2016; Weissman, 2016). The sanctuary movement did not spring up overnight. It is in response to highly publicized incidents and pervasive anti-immigrant sentiments resulting in harsh immigration rhetoric and political stances, as reflected through enforcement of deportation laws and policies with long historical roots. The anxiety of living underground is very real (Becerra, 2016; Philbin & Ayón, 2016).

The deportation of Ms. Guadalupe Garcia de Rayos, a 36-year-old mother of two children who were US citizens, made national news and became the focus of concerns about President Trump's deportation policy. She went for her periodic check-in with immigration authorities while her family waited outside, and she was apprehended for the criminal act of having used a false Social Security number to obtain employment (Niles, 2017). The national publicity generated by this specific US Immigration and Customs Enforcement (ICE) deportation helped galvanized the sanctuary movement and faith organizations throughout the country.

THREAT AND ACTUALITY OF DEPORTATION

Deportation is a word associated with those who are unauthorized. Changes in immigration policies reflect increases in harshness, tone, and tactics, with severe and profound implications for the apprehended and their families. Deportation fears have always had saliency, but they have been heightened since the renewed emphasis on deportations during President Obama's second term (Amuedo-Dorantes, Puttitanun, & Martinez-Donate, 2013b).

Veterans with temporary green cards are also subject to deportation after serving their military duty and receiving honorable discharges (Jordan, 2017f). This may be surprising (Phillips, 2017):

> Indeed, deportations of veterans, which began decades ago, are often a shock
> to many who assume that joining the military has always been an automatic

guarantee of citizenship. It isn't, although previous administrations have taken steps to make it easier for foreign-born soldiers to be naturalized. Under President Trump, new regulations extend the waiting period for military green-card holders to become naturalized citizens. The Army also has stopped enlisting some immigrants who are legal permanent residents while mandating lengthy delays for others.

Threats of deportation, and the profound consequences of this act, are unimaginable to the average person, particularly those tracing their citizenship over several generations. Citizen children's world outlook has been skewed by their privileged status and the unprivileged status of their parents who are undocumented (Macías-Rojas, 2016; Mondragon, 2016).

Helping professionals are well aware of the social and psychological ramifications for these children and their parents living under the constant threat of a knock on their door and deportation (Capps, Fix, & Zong, 2016; Gulbas et al., 2016; Zayas, 2015). Families that have had a member deported suffer significant emotional and social consequences, including financial setbacks in cases in which the deported individual is the "breadwinner" (Mondragon, 2016; Muchow, 2017). Urban planners, too, must contend with dispersal patterns of those who are unauthorized to new destinations (E. R. González, 2017; Levin, 2013).

Trauma will be manifested in behaviors that can severely impact family members left behind in this country. We often talk about the trauma associated with living a life underground and fearing ICE. Immigration raids are not just traumatic for those apprehended and eventually deported; they are also traumatic for those who work alongside them, as in the case described by Macia (2016):

> José was nervous as he told me about the day his workplace was raided by police officers asking for documentation. The treatment by the officers felt abusive: They entered the company yelling "as if looking for a mass murderer," and humiliating him. The officer in charge refused to accept José's driver's license as identification and called US Immigration and Customs Enforcement. Despite receiving confirmation of José's legal status, the officer summoned him to the police station, where he dismissed his signed Social Security card and continued to ask for proof of legal status. The officer further demanded José to bring forward the coworkers who had left when the police arrived. For José this was a deeply traumatic experience. In his words, he felt less of a person after it happened and considered it a reflection of how society regarded him. (p. 110)

Discrimination becomes a major backdrop, disrupting the lives of all immigrants and reinforcing a racial narrative that brings together all Latinos regardless of citizenship status (Hopkins et al., 2016; Palidda, 2016).

Criminalization, which is further addressed in Chapter 4, has extended to "anchor" or "terror babies," insidiously feeding into fears about terrorism and denying citizenship due to birthrights (Lugo-Lugo & Bloodsworth-Lugo, 2014).

United States citizens who sponsor their undocumented spouses may also find themselves under suspicion of engaging in criminal behavior, further expanding the dehumanizing experience and alienating them in the process (Gomberg-Muñoz, 2016b). The stress (separation from family, traditionality, and language difficulties) that undocumented Latinos and other newcomers face is not unique to them, with authorized Latino immigrants also facing high levels of stress due to fears of deportation (Arbona et al., 2010).

Expedited deportations during President Obama's administration focused on those in this country less than 2 weeks and apprehended within 100 miles of the US–Mexico border. Furthermore, those without criminal histories were allowed to live with their families until deportation hearings, which could take more than a year to occur.

However, currently they are incarcerated until they have an immigration hearing (Donnatelli, 2017). As a backdrop, the delays can vary across states, and the number of delays has doubled since 2011 to more than 600,000. Recently, California had 107,419 on the wait list, with an average waiting time of 659 days; Texas had 95,242 on the wait list, with an average waiting time of 750 days; and Georgia had 18,126 on the wait list, with an average wait time of 613 days (Berenson, 2017). It takes approximately 1 year to establish a community visitation program for families to visit someone in detention, effectively adding insult to injury to these families (Fialho, 2016).

Recent events regarding national security and public safety have thrust immigration to center stage in policy debates, making immigration difficult to disentangle from national security (McElmurry et al., 2016):

> In recent years, public fears related to terrorism, refugees, and criminality have grown, raising concerns about the effectiveness of the immigration system in keeping US citizens safe. Incidents involving foreign-born individuals, crime, or weapons that have crossed borders have prompted an array of responses, the most extreme of which include calls to seal borders, end all refugee resettlement, and restrict the entry of people from areas of the world that might pose some risk. On the heels of terrorist attacks in Orlando, Brussels, San Bernardino, and Paris, for example, some voices have called for a "total and complete shutdown of Muslims entering the United States," suggesting the government should enter a "wartime lockdown" and enact a complete "immigration moratorium." (p. 4)

The challenge of balancing immigration, national security, and public safety is being tested, and the recent presidential election highlighted how difficult this goal will be in the immediate future.

Immigration, and not national safety and terrorism, is a subject that resonates for those concerned with immigration, and it is one that helping professions will increasingly address at various levels of practice, including advocacy and coalition building. The narrative that converges terrorism and immigration is highly explosive and questionable, but this argument maintains saliency in Europe and the United States (A. P. Schmid, 2016). When we interject race, and subsequent racism, it gains in saliency and explosiveness, intensifying social justice themes. Is it possible to separate "Latino" politics from "immigration" politics? Many would argue that to do so would be a "fool's errand" (Barreto et al., 2014).

Los Angeles is used to facing challenges regarding the unauthorized. However, it is facing a new existential threat in President Trump's immigration policies (Mejia, Carcamo, & Knoll, 2017):

> The chatter of Spanish serves as the backdrop of Pico-Union, where the aroma of pastries from the *panaderia* merge with the synthetic smells of an auto re-pair garage. A predominantly Latino neighborhood, it has for decades been a first stop for immigrants—both legal and illegal—coming from various cor-ners of Latin America. Over the years, this community has faced challenges, including from politicians threatening crackdowns on illegal immigration. But to many in this densely populated area near MacArthur Park, the presidency of Donald Trump poses a threat of an altogether different scale. Trump has vowed mass deportations of those here illegally, which if carried out, could fundamentally alter the rhythms of life in Pico-Union and numerous other immigrant enclaves around Southern California and beyond.

The renewed emphasis on deportations ripples throughout daily life in communities such as Los Angeles' Pico-Union (Schwiertz, 2016), with current immigration actions going beyond involving those who are undocumented and weighing most heavily upon those already marginalized (Wells, 2017).

This book discusses how anti-immigrant forces, emphasizing those who are unauthorized, have furthered the social justice agenda, as sanctuary sites increas-ingly shelter and protect them throughout the country, particularly in its cities.

It is impossible to talk about the United States' history, position in the world, and future without taking stock of how immigration currently shapes its destiny. This discussion is contentious under the best of circumstances, striking at this country's core values, including what makes it "exceptional" (Lechner, 2017). Much has happened recently that has brought out the best, and worst, in this nation from an immigration perspective.

The spontaneous public demonstrations and blocking of US airports internationalized the Trump's administration efforts to institute a travel ban on Muslims and spearheaded other mass demonstrations throughout the nation, helping bring together concerned citizens from various walks of life in protest (Adjei-Kontoh, 2017; Norton, 2017; Schulte & Bon, 2017).

Boston Mayor Walsh's reaction to the travel ban echoed that of other elected leaders throughout the country, providing an important insight from a mayor favoring a sanctuary stance (as quoted in American Geographers Association, 2017):

> Preventing people from entering this country based solely on faith runs counter to everything we stand for as Americans. Let's be clear: This is not an effective

way to combat terrorism and increase homeland security. It is a reckless policy that is rooted in fear, not substance, and further divides us as a nation and a world. It is simply morally wrong. As Americans, we must move forward together as a country proud of our diverse heritage, and find real solutions to the challenges we face.

US Muslims have the distinction of facing two wars without the possibility of these wars being "won" anytime soon—the "war on terror" and the "war on immigration" (Lamphear, Furman, & Epps, 2016). These are wars without an end.

The last two presidential elections refocused national attention on the unauthorized, but this issue, in its present form concerning citizenship, can be traced back decades and is the tip of an iceberg (Russell, 2017). Building stronger border security necessitates the cooperation of both sides of the border (Bronk & González-Aréchiga, 2011). Discussion of continuing to build a wall between the United States and Mexico, raised during the most recent presidential race, is not new in national politics. Miguel (2016) argues for an "ethics of space" when discussing those who are undocumented and being in the moment; this translates into a profound understanding of how the "border" is artificial (war zone), created by a government intent on stigmatizing, controlling, and punishing people because their skin color, language, and culture.

A number of terms have been used to name the US–Mexico border, including the "Tortilla Curtain" (Foley, 2014). This wall would have to cover a 1,969-mile stretch, including the Sonora Desert and Rio Grande. A key political point should not be lost in any fact-driven discussion of the wall: No national elected representative from this region of the country wants this project (Meckler & Peterson, 2017). Furthermore, there are many landowners who do not want to see this wall built on their properties (Hardy, 2017). For example, as of May 2017, more than 90 lawsuits had been filed to prevent the building of the wall in Texas (Nixon, 2017c).

In American film, images of the US–Mexico border, which occupies an iconic place in this genre (including Tijuana), reflect the United States' evolving and conflictual view of Mexico and the border throughout US history (Fuller, 2016). The racial dimensions of protecting the US–Mexico border must not be overlooked because of how these narratives permeate central messages and ground policies (Gutiérrez, 2016). Mexicans did not cross the border; rather, the border crossed them due to the US–Mexico War and the Treaty of Guadalupe (Burke, 2017).

Undocumented immigration brings two sides of a heated debate: how to prevent those who are unauthorized from entering and what to do about the millions in this country (Ruddell, Champion, & Norris, 2011). The building or expansion of a wall does little for those currently here. We must remember that a wall serves to both keep out and keep in. The idea of building, fortifying, or even "electrifying" a barrier with Mexico was raised during the previous two Republican presidential nomination races.

In 2012, presidential candidate Herman Cane put forth a vision for erecting a 20-foot electrified fence on the Mexican border (Chavez, 2013). Whether it is concrete, cyber, or electrified, the message is quite clear about the unwelcoming of those who are unauthorized, which translates into a psychologically and socially hostile climate. The current presidential administration's get-tough talk caused the Mexican government to provide immigration legal advice at their 50 consulates throughout the United States (Castillo, 2017).

The North America Free Trade Agreement (NAFTA), an indicator of greater globalization, signaled the tearing down of trade borders between Canada, Mexico, and the United States. This trade agreement made virtually no provisions for those wishing to cross the borders, and it resulted in lost jobs for many Mexicans living on the US side of the border (Staudt & Coronado, 2016).

"Unfair" trade agreements, such as NAFTA, have been blamed for major economic dislocation in the United States and for being a key force in bringing those who are unauthorized across US borders. Globalization generally refers to goods and finances and not human beings (Nail, 2016):

> We live in a world of borders. Territorial, political, judicial, and economic borders of all kinds quite literally define every aspect of social life in the twenty-first century. Despite the celebration of globalization and the increasing necessity of global mobility, there are more types of borders today than ever before in history. In the last twenty years, but particularly since 9/11, hundreds of new borders have emerged around the world. (p. 1)

This chapter provides a view of a subject that is expanding and immensely complex, yet how it is addressed has implications for those among the most marginalized and stigmatized. How this country handles its "undocumented problem" has reverberations throughout the Northern Hemisphere and other regions of the world, but most important, it directly affects the lives of millions of people within our borders.

SANCTUARIES: AN INTRODUCTION AND DEFINITION

A Google search of "sanctuary" will uncover approximately 55,000 entries since 2010, reflecting its saliency during the past decade. In-depth and multifaceted definitions of sanctuary cities are provided in Chapter 5. For the purposes of grounding the reader early on, *sanctuary sites* are defined as geographical entities (city, county, or state) or organizations, such as houses of worship, clinics, or schools/universities, that at minimum have openly expressed an unwillingness to cooperate with ICE when there is an effort to arrest someone who is undocumented.

This governmental definition views sanctuary cities narrowly. This definition, discussed later in this book, is broader and may not even have "sanctuary" in its title. Nevertheless, it humanizes what is means to be a city or organization that affirms the lives of those who are unauthorized and entities providing a range of expressive and instrumental services, including physical refuge from deportation.

A sanctuary designation represents much more than an unwillingness to cooperate with ICE. Having a sanctuary designation fosters individuals and community organizations coming together in sponsoring and participating in political rallies against repressive national immigration policies (Sidney, 2014a, 2014b).

Every major religion has a tradition of providing sanctuary, often a basic element of altruism and morality (Rabben, 2016). Sanctuaries are associated with sacred places and spaces, such as those found in houses of worship, bringing together individuals and families that may share only a citizenship status and making them part of a community of a like-minded gathering or congregation (Houston, 2016). When the concept is applied to a city, it is a symbol and focal point for developing a network of coalitions and individuals (see https:// patriotmongoose.wordpress.com/2016/10/04/anti-deportation-groups) seeking to meet newcomer needs, bringing together providers, the legal community, the religious community, civic leaders, and other parties (Sanders et al., 2013; Srikantiah, 2017).

The passage of laws and policies making cities sanctuaries has neither attracted nor repelled new immigration or caused an increase or decrease in reported crime (Hummel, 2016). One recent study on sanctuary city crime rates found that these policies have had no effect on crime rates, despite fears that rates would increase (Gonzalez, Collingwood, & El-Khatib, 2017).

The unauthorized are often subjected to interpersonal aggressions, and these incidents can be internalized. They must be identified and addressed through concerted interventions (Ayón & Philbin, 2017). Fears of communities being "overrun" are common and fostered by local media and elected officials, even without evidence supporting these fears (Ralston, 2016).

In 2015, North Carolina Governor Pat McCrory signed legislation banning cities and counties from declaring themselves sanctuaries, along with various other restrictions meant to curtail the mobility of those who are unauthorized (Brown, Jones, & Dow, 2016). McCrory was not re-elected in 2016, in part due to this legislation and legislation that limited the rights for transgendered individuals using the bathroom of their gender identity.

Sanctuaries have assumed a prominent place in the national immigration landscape, and they are predicated upon human rights and social justice values. Local governments can influence legislation and policies at the regional and the national level regarding immigration policy, thereby increasing the significance of a sanctuary designation (Filomeno, 2017b). Is it possible for any human being to be considered "illegal"? There are a multiplicity of views on this subject, and one would be hard-pressed to find anyone who is neutral on the subject.

One aspect that has great saliency is the emergence of sanctuary cities as safe places and spaces, yet it is a subject that has not benefitted from serious scholarly attention. The values undergirding the concept of asylum are humanistic, providing physical safety and psychological comfort (K. M. Campbell, 2012; Marfleet, 2011).

A literature search will uncover that this concept is very American, although not exclusively so, and highly reflective of this nation's unique history related to immigrants, with some periods standing out for particular importance. However, again, it is not unique to this country. In 2007, Sheffield, England, became the United Kingdom's first official sanctuary city (Darling, 2010).

THE MULTIFACETED COSTS OF THE JOURNEY

The risks and challenges of the unauthorized entering the country can be viewed from an economic perspective, such as paying someone (coyote) to transport them into the country (Sandoval-García, 2017). In the 1990s, the costs were from $200 to $300. In 2014, it was closer to $2000 to $3000, or a 1000% increase, reflecting both the desperation and the increased hurdles in making the journey, including the potential loss of life (Real Vision, 2014). It can also be marked by the increased number of deaths, injuries, robberies, assaults, and other traumas, as discussed later.

A sanctuary designation is an affirming public statement of outrage and moral indignation, followed by legal, economic, and social responses and resources. Cities, through their elected officials and key stakeholders, are well aware of the political backlash that they can expect by taking a moral or social justice stance on embracing a sanctuary city designation (A. Delgado, 2017).

The political backlash against those who are unauthorized has been fueled by two distinctive, and yet at times overlapping, contentious perspectives: (a) an economic argument that they are taking jobs away from "Americans" and that they are unlawfully receiving various forms of governmental services, which also cost money; and (b) safety concerns about individuals entering the country whose primary intent is to inflict harm and engage in criminal enterprises, most prominently gangs, drugs, and human trafficking (K. Joyner, 2016). These narratives are addressed in various depths in this book. This section sets a backdrop to the economic argument.

Papademetriou and Banulescu-Bogdan (2016) introduce a more nuanced perspective on these points:

> Broadly, immigration tends to fuel societal anxiety under five conditions: (a) when flows outpace the preparation of a country or region to receive newcomers, even if the absolute numbers are relatively small; (b) when immigrants are seen to create competition for scarce resources, particularly in poorer areas that are less accustomed to migration; (c) when newcomers (and their descendants) are perceived as isolating themselves in closed communities and challenging a host community's sense of identity; (d) when immigration is linked to security concerns (illegality, crime, terrorism); and (e) when governments are seen as unable or unwilling to control incoming flows. (p. 3)

The Great Recession of 2007–2009 had a dramatic impact on the United States' immigration policies by highlighting, and aggravating in some instances, persistent trends and preventing the moving forward of comprehensive immigration reform (Wogan, 2017; Zaun, Roos, & Gülzau, 2016). For example, 49 states had revenue decreases in their 2009 budgets, accounting for $67.2 billion in reductions.

Not surprisingly, during this period a record number of states passed newcomer restrictive or punitive laws, particularly regarding unauthorized individuals (Ybarra, Sanchez, & Sanchez, 2016). The Great Recession also witnessed outmigration of this group, such as in Durham, North Carolina, and particularly for Mexicans; there was also lower formal educational attainment (Parrado & Flippen, 2016). The tremendous consequences of the Great Recession were particularly hard-felt in urban communities of color and those home to sizeable numbers of undocumented people. It helped perpetuate the myth that "American jobs" were being filled by "illegals."

However, is this really the case? A Texas Public Policy Foundation report concluded the following with regard to Texas, a state with a strong national reputation of being anti-undocumented (Brannon & Albright, 2016):

> Undocumented workers constitute a significant proportion of the Texas labor force and it is not all clear that those jobs would be filled by Americans in their absence. Immigrants also contribute disproportionately to population growth both through migration and higher fertility rates. Additionally, even those with low levels of education and skills, immigrants have a different skill set from native workers, and so the labor market benefits from the additional specialization they bring. (pp. 9–10)

Approximately half (46%) of Texas's newcomer population is unauthorized, which translates to 1.8 million residents (Brannon & Albright, 2016). If placed into a single geographical location, this population would comprise Texas' second largest city behind Houston's 2.3 million residents. This statistic highlights the social and economic significance of this group.

An estimated 600,000 people who are unauthorized live in Houston, making it the third largest city in terms of unauthorized immigrants in the country after Los Angeles and New York City (S. Romero & Jordan, 2017). Natural disasters can spur unauthorized immigrants into the country to meet increased demands for labor. This happened after Hurricane Harvey, for example, with the prospects of employment in helping rebuild Harris County, which includes Houston (Correal & Semple, 2017).

The influence of economic concerns in combination with racist tendencies makes for a toxic mix because the moment a factory closes or a governmental benefit is curtailed or eliminated due to budgetary cuts, blame is sought to be placed on someone or some group, and those who are unauthorized make a convenient scapegoat, allowing elected officials to tap into this hatred in search of votes (Park & Norpoth, 2016). This analysis may seem harsh or simplistic. As this book unfolds, readers will make up their own mind on this conclusion.

PUBLIC OPINION, ATTITUDES, AND THOSE WHO ARE UNDOCUMENTED

Although political discourse during the 2016 national presidential election would give the impression that this country heavily favors deportation and the further building of a wall along the southern border, popular opinion is counter to these sentiments. This disconnect between the Republican national leadership and voters is both perplexing and disturbing, making a path toward citizenship arduous to achieve for those wishing to remain in this country.

For the past 20 years, the Pew Research Center has followed popular opinion on those who are undocumented and has found distinctive changes during this period (Goo, 2015). Although the overall sentiment is that there should be a path for achieving citizenship, there are significant differences between the political parties. A Pew Research Center Poll (B. Jones, 2016) provides a good perspective on current public opinion on a path to citizenship, including significant political party divides:

> Since 2013, majorities of both Democrats and Republicans have said that undocumented immigrants living in the U.S. should be allowed to stay in this country legally. But partisan differences on this issue have increased as well. Currently, 75% of the public says that undocumented immigrants now living in the U.S. should be allowed to stay legally if certain requirements are met, while 23% say they should not. Since fall, Democrats have become somewhat more supportive of a path to legal status for undocumented immigrants, while Republicans have become slightly less supportive. Nearly nine-in-ten Democrats and Democratic leaners (88%) say there should be a way for undocumented immigrants in the U.S. who meet certain conditions to remain in the country legally, up from 82% in September. Currently, 59% of Republicans favor allowing undocumented immigrants to remain in the country legally, compared with 65% in September. (p. 1)

The US public does favor some form of path toward citizenship for those who are unauthorized, if certain requirements are met, with Democrats having a distinctively more favorable view compared to Republicans.

Latinos, the largest group among those who are unauthorized, are not all in favor of a citizenship path. Latino views have increasingly been more positive, as evidenced by a 2013 poll in which 45% of adults stated that the impact of unauthorized immigration was positive, compared to 29% who said the same in 2010 (Lopez & Gonzalez-Barrera, 2013). However, when taking into account generational status, a distinct trend downward on positive views is evident, with 42% of second-generation Latinos saying it was positive, followed by 32% of third-generation Latinos.

It is appropriate to end this section with discussion of the wall with Mexico. The majority (62%) of people in the United States do not favor building a wall with Mexico; furthermore, an even greater percentage (70%) do not believe Mexico will pay for it (Suls, 2017). Not surprisingly, Republicans (74%) favor building a wall and Democrats do not (89%).

Democratic presidential candidate Hillary Clinton won the Latino vote in 2016, but support was less than that received by President Obama in 2012, obtaining 66% compared to 71% in his re-election (Krogstad & Lopez, 2016). Donald Trump received 28% of the Latino vote, only slightly higher than the 27% that Republican Mitt Romney received in 2012 and lower than Republican John McCain's 31% in 2008. Opinions on building the wall with Mexico provided interesting results. Only 8% of Latinos voiced opposition to building the wall, with 46% of White, non-Latinos and 82% of African Americans/Blacks stating opposition.

Although California is the "poster child" for the sanctuary city movement, it would be irresponsible to give the impression that everyone supports this movement. Californians hold divided views on sanctuary cities, with 56% favoring this designation versus 44% opposed. However, they strongly support (82%) a pathway to citizenship, and 59% oppose President Trump's plans for the US–Mexico wall (DiCamillo, 2017).

There are differences when taking into account party affiliation. Sanctuary city designation is heavily favored by Democrats (74%) and opposed by Republicans (80%). Pathways to citizenship are favored by 91% of Democrats compared to 68% of Republicans and 80% of those without party affiliations. Sentiments against the wall were shared among the vast majority of California's Democrats (81%); Republicans were overwhelmingly for building the wall (86%) (DiCamillo, 2017).

We generally focus on public opinion polls and discuss how views have either changed or become more solidified over time. The attitudes or views of other interested parties are generally ignored even though these influence their actions.

For instance, the views of social service providers regarding immigrants can facilitate or hinder immigrants' adjustment to their new homes. Providers have a strong moral responsibility to help newcomers, even more so when they view the immigrants as contributing important economic and cultural assets and also when they are able to provide meaningful and trustworthy assistance (Clevenger et al., 2014). The attitudes of local enforcement officials and sheriffs toward immigrants and personal characteristics also influence the degree to which they enforce immigration laws (Chand & Schreckhise, 2015; Farris & Holman, 2016).

POLITICAL BACKLASH AGAINST SANCTUARY CITIES

There have been political repercussions targeting sanctuary cities due to increasing intolerance toward these sites (Carroll, 2016). The National Immigration Law Center (2017) summarizes the legal challenges of communities that have enacted sanctuary laws and policies that will continually face legal assaults as these cities and organizations receive greater national political attention and assume unprecedented symbols in this civil or human rights struggle:

Communities nationwide embraced these policies, sometimes referred to as "sanctuary" or "community-trust" policies (because they contribute to maintaining or building trust between immigrant communities and local law enforcement), for public-safety, fiscal, and legal reasons and despite pressure from ICE to participate in the failed Secure Communities (S-Comm) program. In mid-2015, as ICE began replacing S-Comm with the Priority Enforcement Program (PEP), some members of Congress began to push harmful legislation to penalize state and local jurisdictions that have community-trust policies. Similarly, in the 2016 legislative cycle, there were no fewer than 26 attempts by states and several federal attempts to penalize "sanctuary cities." None of these efforts were successful. (p. 1)

Obviously, the 26 attempts are constantly changing reflections on the saliency of the subject. Efforts at challenging these sites have failed in the courts, and the political process is still unfolding to place sanctions on these cities.

Legislative efforts to repeal sanctuary laws and policies can also be coupled with efforts to make English the official language, an issue that has been around for several decades, as in the case of Oregon's House Bills 2921 and 2923 (Friedman, 2017). In January 2017, Miami stopped being a sanctuary city when Miami–Dade County Mayor Carlos Gimenez signed an executive order instructing the corrections department to honor all requests made by ICE to hold immigration suspects in Miami–Dade County jails (Geraghty, 2017). (This decision is addressed again later in this book.) This was done, in large measure, to address his concerns about losing federal funding ($355 billion in 2017). The political reaction was swift, as evidenced by the Libertarian Party (2017):

> For decades, the immigrant community has been one of the major driving forces of Miami-Dade County's economy and social progress. From Latin American communities in Little Havana, Hialeah, and Westchester, the Haitian communities of Overtown and North Miami, to the European businesses of Coral Gables and Coconut Grove, there is not an inch of South Florida that hasn't seen progress thanks to immigration. Yet, the federal government has been cracking down on our diversity since the launch of 2017. From President Obama's end of the Wet Foot, Dry Foot policy to President Trump's series of unconstitutional executive orders, we have witnessed hostility from Washington. This is why we are disappointed by our own County Mayor, Carlos Gimenez, who announced yesterday he was ordering county prisons to collaborate with federal authorities and end our status as a Sanctuary County. We condemn Mayor Gimenez's decision. No amount of federal grant dollars should be enough to betray the community that elected you twice. The Libertarian Party of Miami-Dade County is standing with our right to remain a Sanctuary City and we are disappointed to see our mayor flinch when the President moved. All of our party will now be focused on overriding this new collaboration.

The Libertarian Party stance is significant because of Miami's prominence among cities with large Latino concentrations, which cannot be lost on this movement, nationally and internationally. If Miami continues to embrace dropping the designation of sanctuary city, it sends a political and demoralizing message to Latinos in other cities with large concentrations of undocumented residents because Miami will be used as an example of doing "what is right" for the nation.

Soon after taking office, President Trump signed an executive order ("Executive Order: Enhancing Public Safety in the Interior of the United States," 2017) targeting sanctuary cities and counties that can result in cutting federal funding to these locales, placing these sanctuaries in the national spotlight of a political struggle on this nation's undocumented (P. A. Alvarez, 2017; A. Flores, 2017; Lee, Omri, & Preston, 2017). This order seeks to accomplish several goals. It directs ICE to hire 10,000 new immigration officers, and it instructs the Office of Management and Budget to develop an inventory of federal grant money currently allocated to sanctuary jurisdictions. In addition, this order calls for reports that would also identify "sanctuary jurisdictions," which are cities and counties in which local law enforcement authorities do not report immigration status, violating the federal government immigration laws. This task is extremely difficult in real time (Stinson, 2017), calling into question the real purpose of this threat.

Local legal questioning of the legitimacy of executive actions sets the context for localities to defy the law and seek sanctuary city designations (Chen, 2015). Cities throughout the nation have stood up in defiance against these potential cuts and have threatened to fight them in the courts (CBS New York, 2017). On March 30, 2017, Seattle sued the Trump administration over the ban's withholding of federal money unrelated to immigration enforcement in an attempt to force the city to comply; the city argued that it violates Article 1, Section 8 of the US Constitution (R. Wilson, 2017).

There is general agreement among legal scholars that *NFIB v. Sebelius*, the Supreme Court's ruling on a challenge to the Affordable Care Act over Medicaid's expansion in 2012, effectively shifted power to the states and away from agencies in the relationship (Chappell, 2017). Calling "sanctuary cities" "constitutional cities" represents an attempt at highlighting the constitutional basis on which these cities stand regarding the acceptance of those who are unauthorized (Gardner, 2014; Post, 2017). The Supreme Court is fraught with immigration doctrines that depart from conventional constitutional norms, or what has been referred to as "immigration exceptionalism" by some legal scholars (Rubenstein & Gulasekaram, 2017).

Potential federal cuts are estimated to amount to $2.27 billion annually for the top 10 US sanctuary cities; these funds do not include federal funds for law enforcement, which were specifically excluded in the executive order, and programs such as Medicaid, which are administered by state governments (Carroll, Respaut, & Sullivan, 2017). The message is clear that sanctuary cities present a social and political threat to the current presidential administration and local governments complying with federal law pertaining to ICE and police collaboration (Davis & Savage, 2017). Refusal to comply with immigration policies can go beyond sites with sanctuary designations (J. M. Vaughan, 2015).

In 2016, Texas had an estimated 1.8 million residents who were unauthorized but no sanctuary cities at the time, although in 2017 Austin became a sanctuary city, and it, too, faces federal cuts as a result (Cameron, 2017). Efforts have been made in the past to cut federal funding to sanctuary cities. For example, in 2015 the House of Representatives passed a bill called "The State Criminal Alien Assistance Program," which reimburses local government for detaining unauthorized inmates during the second phase of deportation hearings. A *Washington Post* analysis of the distribution of these funds ($165 million) for fiscal year 2016 found that the jurisdictions with policies counter to cooperating with ICE received only $18 million.

Cutting federal funding to sanctuary sites, as in the case of the Justice Department, can have a considerable financial impact on these locales, particularly because 60% of the funds are received by 10 jurisdictions throughout the country (CBS News, 2017): Connecticut: $69,305,444; California: $132,409,635; Orleans Parish, Louisiana: $4,737,964; New York, New York: $60,091,942; Philadelphia, Pennsylvania: $16,505,312; Cook County, Illinois: $6,018,544; Chicago, Illinois: $28,523,222; Miami–Dade County, Florida: $10,778,815; Milwaukee, Wisconsin: $7,539,572; and Clark County, Nevada: $6,257,951.

The federal government can be open to libel suits depending on the nature of information that it publicizes. If the government publishes a list of crimes committed by immigrants in sanctuary cities, there may be a counter-consequence, as noted by A. Flores (2017):

> I don't think the city of Los Angeles for example is going to give a rat's ass about being on a list, they may even see it as a badge of honor. . . . It's really a political issue and an opportunity to get more political points rather than actually get at the heart of the real issue.

The national debate about those who are undocumented promises to become, if it has not already, our "civil rights debate of the 21st century" (Balkaran, 2017; K. R. Johnson, 2012). Introducing a human rights perspective into this topic opens the door for a social justice stance, facilitating helping professions such as social work to engage in advocacy and social activism. The sanctuary movement has parallels with the nation's fight to protect runaway slaves, which is discussed later in the book.

There is a natural relationship between human rights and social movements, such as the sanctuary movement, attracting potential members subscribing to these principles and values (Tsutsui & Smith, 2017):

> Human rights and social movements have long had mutually constitutive relationships with each other. Many social movements have promoted human rights causes domestically and internationally since the late 18th century, elevating human rights to a guiding principle in international politics. Collective political mobilizations challenging torture, slavery, discrimination against women, and other repressive practices have played critical roles in expanding "the universe of obligations" of governments across the globe to ensure fundamental rights to every human being. Indeed, most observers

point out that social movement engagement was critical in institutionalizing universal human rights principles into international declarations and treaties, despite resistance from powerful states. (p. 2)

A human rights view of this movement opens up the possibility of gaining the support of other human rights campaigns, bringing the potential of international pressure and resources to bear on the US movement, as well as aiding such movements internationally.

The United Nation's Universal Declarations of Human Rights has provided a global perspective on this phenomenon, setting the stage for service providers and human rights advocates to reach out across borders to address this increasingly important human rights issue (Jönsson, 2014). The rise of "Human Right Cities" throughout the world ties sanctuary cities to a worldwide movement within a global movement (Oomen & Baumgärtel, 2014; van den Berg & Oomen, 2014).

Deportations have received national attention from a variety of sociolegal groups, leading to the publication of "The Forgotten Deported: A Declaration on the Rights of Expelled and Deported Persons" (Kanstroom & Chicco, 2015), again framing this issue from a human rights perspective. The framing of the "unauthorized movement" as a rights movement helps change the nature of the discourse (Bloemraad, Voss, & Silva, 2014).

In early 2017, leaked memos revealed national efforts to speed up deportations, fulfilling a campaign promise made during the presidential primaries and national election (Shear & Nixon, 2017). A national shift in deportation raid policy may be emerging. For example, in 2017, there was a raid on an Arizona desert-based organization (No More Deaths) that historically provided emergency care to those seeking refuge (Santos, 2017). Historically, the camp was not subject to raids based on an agreement with the Obama administration. This changed in June 2017, however, when Customs and Border Patrol agents apprehended four men for deportation, raising concerns about a shift in policy.

The reversal of a previous anti-sanctuary city stance by a former Bush and Obama Homeland Department administration official illustrates how the political climate has changed toward those who are unauthorized, even though it was far from sanguine during the Obama presidency (Stodder, 2017):

> Is this a good idea? It's a tricky issue, as I know from experience. I served as a senior federal law enforcement official . . . and have never been particularly sympathetic to the 'sanctuary' movement. . . . But the Trump presidency presents a different situation, one that has forced me to rethink my view. Given Trump's radical new immigration policies, I now strongly back the sanctuary states and cities. It's one thing to seek cooperation from local police departments in removing undocumented felons—that was the Obama policy. But it's another to bully cities and states into a large roundup of otherwise law-abiding undocumented immigrants—and that's exactly what Trump has proposed. That I cannot support. . . . Ultimately, Trump's executive order directs DHS [Department of Homeland Security] to execute 'the immigration laws of the

United States against all removable aliens' not just criminals. . . . In this new context, I completely understand the reluctance of state and local governments to cooperate with federal immigration authorities.

A shift in focus to deportation regardless of criminal records causes greater resistance as the narratives of law-abiding persons garner greater national media attention.

Providing the general public with the faces, if not the names, behind those who are unauthorized is considered an important step in helping change public opinion to the point where it influences legislation at the national and local levels. Developing strategies to accomplish this goal through use of film and social media has been, and will continue to be, explored (Berg & Schwenken, 2013).

Legal status invariably acts as a magnet for rumors and falsehoods, and the highly charged nature of the topic necessitates that facts be separated from fiction (Becerra et al., 2012). The fact that the unauthorized do not control the major media outlets means that they may be blamed for some of society's worst ills. With social media and citizen journalism, people have the power to craft messages and stories that can counter negative news, particularly in areas of the country where anti-immigrant sentiments are strong, with deep historical roots.

If the spirit of the executive order targeting sanctuary cities and counties is enacted, it will be challenged on constitutional grounds, raising questions of due process and the need for legal representation (Cade, 2016; Carson, 2017; Nessel & Anello, 2016; Rana, 2014). The American Civil Liberties Union (2017) provides resources that sanctuary cities can use in their legal battles with the federal government and other entities.

Legal offices will be called upon to provide pro bono legal support in filing lawsuits fighting the constitutionality of efforts to punish cities for refusing to cooperate with ICE, as in the case of two Massachusetts sanctuary cities (Chelsea and Lawrence) with sizeable numbers of Latinos and long histories of being home to immigrants (Ryan, 2017). Its impact on the families of the unauthorized within these cities, and also on the communities in which they live and the countries to which they are returned, will be devastating.

CRIME AND PUNISHMENT

Crime and punishment and the unauthorized, which are discussed in greater detail in Chapter 4, are closely associated in the current political climate. A record number of deportations have resulted from the interplay of three factors during last several years of the Obama presidency: (a) enactment of laws that expand the legal reasons for arrest and deportation; (b) increased spending on expanding immigration enforcement personnel, infrastructure, and technology; and (c) an increased emphasis on enforcing outcomes (Rosenblum & Meissner, 2014).

These forces have accelerated during the early tenure of President Trump's administration. The potential for increased deportation of those who have not committed crimes beyond entering the country without proper documents further expands the parameters of the narrative beyond a well-defined and limited group. The singling out of immigrant activists for deportation by ICE, as in the case of Ravi, the executive director of NYC's New Sanctuary Coalition, who was arrested when he went to his regularly scheduled ICE meeting, represents a new dimension to this nation's evolving deportation policy (Gottlieb, 2018).

Arrests (Siskin, 2015) can be the result of one of five types of removal orders (Koh, 2017):

> (1) expedited removal at the border, (2) reinstatement of prior removal orders, (3) administrative removal of non-lawful permanent residents with aggravated felony convictions, (4) stipulated removal orders following waivers of the right to a court hearing, and (5) in absentia orders for failure to appear in immigration court.

Each step has legal implications. The latter three have particular relevance for representation and due process, and they are open to debate on constitutional grounds (Lasch, 2012).

The act of denying a legal equality process regarding rights and entitlements for the unauthorized is a major source for creating illegalization, criminalization, and exploitation (Barboza et al., 2017; Bauder, 2016b; Burridge, 2016; Menjívar & Kanstroom, 2013; Strunk & Leitner, 2013). Providing a counter-narrative to those who are unauthorized as criminals can be advanced by helping professionals, faith and community leaders, and immigrant rights organizations enlisting allies in educating the general public, including giving testimonies before legislative bodies and social demonstrations of support (Cleaveland, 2010; Zatz & Smith, 2012).

Criminalization redirects national attention from the social–political forces that cause migration to the United States to the unauthorized themselves without consideration of why they left their homelands (Tramonte, 2011):

> Despite the facts, the existence of so-called "sanctuary cities" continues to be a hot topic on right-wing talk radio and in the conservative blogosphere. Immigration opponents point to isolated, high-profile crimes committed by foreigners to "prove" their point that immigrants are likely to be criminals. However, research has consistently shown that immigrants are much less likely than the native-born to be in prison, and high rates of immigration are not associated with higher rates of crime. (p. 12)

This narrative persists and is fueled by high-profile crimes involving those who are unauthorized and anti-immigrant sentiments, with racial overtones (Stevens, 2017). Immigration criminalization has made it easier to incarcerate the unauthorized and has created narratives that reinforce their propensity to engage in crime, although the vast majority of them do not break the law, with the only exception of being in this country without authorization (Ackerman & Furman, 2013a, 2013b; Owusu-Sarfo, 2016; Vennochi, 2017). There is a desperate call for affirming narratives to emerge to capture the nuances and experiences of being an undocumented person (Gutierrez, 2015).

The undocumented are often not welcomed in public spaces outside of their immediate community. Again, these lives tend to be invisible, or referred to as "shadowed lives," and quite vulnerable to acts of abuse and becoming victims of crime because they are fearful of going to the police to seek justice (I. R. Chavez, 2012b). Chances are good that when we go to a restaurant, the person serving us is not undocumented, but the individual bussing the tables may be undocumented, those who wash the dishes are undocumented, as are those who cut vegetables. In the evening after closing, those who clean the restaurant are also unauthorized. That dining experience would not have been possible without them, yet they remain invisible throughout the experience (Gleeson & Gonzales, 2012; Sen, 2009; Tsai, 2009).

At first glance, one may think that criminalization is highly gendered, with males being the primary threat. However, that is not necessarily the case because Latina mothers may also be criminalized due to their threat to society. M. Romero (2011) identified four views that are often used to cast them as threats to this country's basic premises and foundation: (a) They are unable or unwilling to raise loyal US citizens, (b) reproduction is used as a mechanism to garner unworthy resources, (c) the children of unauthorized mothers take away resources from those who rightfully deserve them, and (d) their children will eventually threaten the political power of White citizens. The pernicious nature of these threats speaks for themselves.

The US–Mexico border has become a "capitalism zone," opening up immense opportunities for the private sector to financially capitalize by emphasizing criminalization (Miller, 2016). How does building a wall translate into criminalization? To me, the wall conjures up images of a prison.

Deportation is big business in the United States, with the Department of Homeland Security's labyrinthine system of immigration enforcement expected to continue to expand for the foreseeable future. This country has the largest immigration detention system in the world (Snyder, 2015; Terrio, 2015).

The infusion of large quantities of funds is an impetus for attracting the private sector to this humanitarian and human rights issue, increasing the likelihood of further abuses being perpetrated upon those with compromised civil rights in the name of capitalism. Efforts to open privatized prisons to house parents who are unauthorized and their children are underway, as in Texas (Hoffman, 2017). The immigration industrialized complex has emerged, and in similar fashion to its militarized and incarceration counterparts, it is powerful, increasing in influence, and tapping into people's fears of threats (Douglas & Sáenz, 2013).

POLICE–IMMIGRATION CUSTOMS ENFORCEMENT COOPERATION

The concept of mass incarceration has gained saliency in the United States as the nation's incarceration policies have devastated millions of families of color and their communities, which invariably are urban and low-income. This concept can also be applied to the nation's incarceration of people who are undocumented and have been convicted of crimes and are facing deportation upon completion of their sentences (Guzmán, 2016; Macías-Rojas, 2016). Increased use of incarceration of both citizens and non-citizens is not race neutral (Nuño, 2013a).

Is it any better to be apprehended and then deported? How about being apprehended, incarcerated, and then deported? The evolution of this logic is a testament to how far this nation has come regarding the criminalization and incarceration of undocumented people (Waasdorp & Pahladsingh, 2017). The mass incarceration movement has finally come to this community in full force, and the introduction of the privatizing of detentions makes the parallel quite striking.

The number of unauthorized Latinos in the nation's prisons is increasing rapidly, constituting the largest portion of Latinos incarcerated among the general prison population (Velasquez, 2016). This system will only expand in the immediate future, supporting the distinction of this country having the largest incarceration system in the world. That is not a distinction that the world's "leading democracy" should strive toward.

Racial profiling takes on significance when discussing those who are unauthorized of color (K. R. Johnson, 2014). Fears of deportation have severely disrupted their lives (Yee, 2017a): "No going to church, no going to the store. No doctor's appointments for some, no school for others. No driving, period— not when a broken taillight could deliver the driver to Immigration and Customs Enforcement" (p. A1). The implications also touch upon personal concerns about coming forward, reporting crimes, and signaling out perpetrators of crime for fear of being deported if they are unauthorized (Robbins, 2017a). Many police departments do not wish to become an arm of ICE (Provine et al., 2016). This is a key issue raised by police departments in sanctuary cities. They want the cooperation of all residents in reporting crime regardless of citizenship status.

As predicted, fears of being deported when reporting a crime have resulted in fewer reports of crimes, as in the case of rape, which was a concern raised by police departments and the communities they serve (E. Lee, 2017):

> After a woman in El Paso, Texas was detained by ICE agents immediately after filing a restraining order against her allegedly abusive partner, domestic violence victim advocates have been concerned that other immigrants will be too scared to come forward to seek help. During a press conference in early April, Houston Police Chief Art Acevedo announced a 42.8 percent drop in the number of Latinos reporting rape to his department compared to the same period last year. "When you see this type of data, and what looks like the beginnings of people not reporting crime, we should all be concerned," Acevedo said at a news conference, as reported by the Houston Chronicle. "A person that rapes or violently attacks or robs an undocumented immigrant is somebody that is going to harm a natural born citizen or lawful resident."

Other cities have reported similar decreases in crimes, including Anchorage, Alaska; Los Angeles; and Washington, DC (Medina, 2017a).

Police distrust in urban Latino communities is due to a history of encounters that have been experienced as negative because of excessive force in the questioning of immigration status and unfair treatment, further socially isolating them and causing reluctance to report crimes; this applies even more so among those who are unauthorized and their fear of the police (Theodore & Habans, 2016).

Exploitation and crimes committed against the unauthorized often go unreported (Comino, Mastrobuoni, & Nicolò, 2016; Donnermeyer, 2016). Exploitation transpires in a variety of ways, such as the case of a New York state taxi cab company that charged excessive fees to transport the unauthorized to the Canadian border in their effort to flee the United States (Robbins, 2017b). Detention centers are total institutions, making it easier to violate the rights of those in these institutions; in this case, "detention" becomes an integral part of the criminalization process, with all of the negative consequences of such a status for those in detention and their loved ones (Furman et al., 2015a,b; Garcia Hernandez, 2017a; Snyder, 2016). Nationally, there are approximately 234 detention centers (Carson, 2017).

If anyone has any doubts about the convergence of the criminal justice system and immigration enforcement, one has only to look at detention centers, including the role of their privatization in cementing this partnership, which is detrimental from a physical, psychological, sociological, and spiritual standpoint (Ackerman & Furman, 2013a, 2013b; Furman et al., 2015a). The expansion of privatizing immigration using privatized detention centers has proved troubling in the past because of the violation of rights and safety concerns (Chacón, 2017). This issue bears watching under the current presidential administration.

It has been argued that imprisonment based on citizenship status, as manifested in legal doctrine, lacks a defensible justification. Latinas in immigration detention centers, for example, have been found to experience significant discrimination, physical distress, and psychological hardships that have immediate and long-term consequences (Ford, 2016).

Immigration law enforcement has historically been the responsibility of the federal government and not local authorities, so local resistance to assuming these duties is understandable in places where sanctuary designations or tendencies, as the case may be, are the prevailing ethos (Kubrin, 2014; M. A. Taylor et al., 2014; Tidwell, 2013). Stopping a car because of a broken tail light, for instance, can result in the arrest of someone who is unauthorized and driving without a license. The police will usually not stop a late model Mercedes or Jaguar with a broken tail light; in all likelihood, the one that is stopped will be an "old" car, non-vintage, that looks distressed.

Stopping a car because of a broken headlight or tail light is a pretext for checking the citizenship status of the driver. Being apprehended while driving without a license will result in arrest and eventual deportation, but also impounding of the vehicle, which has economic ramifications for a family left behind that may need it to get to work (Prieto, 2016; Robbins, 2017c; Yee, 2017h). It is not to the

advantage of the police to be viewed as an occupying force. The militarism of police departments reinforces this narrative, however.

SALIENCY OF THOSE WHO ARE UNDOCUMENTED

Readers can attest to the importance of the sanctuary movement in galvanizing
critical political support for the rights of those who are undocumented. Rarely
does a week go by that this subject does not garner major national news beyond
President Trump proclamations, highlighting the far-reaching ramifications it has
on communities throughout the country (Seltzer, 2016; Srikantiah, 2017).

The metaphor of a hotel does a wonderful job of visually stratifying citizenship
statuses in this country, illustrating the distance between the basement and the top
floor, providing a different experience, sense of self, and worldview (Wiebe, 2014):

> Drawing on property law also allows for different floors to represent different
> types of immigration status. In a nutshell, citizenship occupies the top floor
> and is akin to cooperative or condominium ownership. Legal permanent res-
> idency occupies the apartment floor, with occupants tied to leases with strict
> terms. Breaking the terms of the lease can lead to eviction (i.e., deportation).
> Traditional hotel rooms are reserved for temporary non-immigrant visa
> holders. Sandwiched on a hard-to-get-to floor between the apartments and
> the hotel rooms is the sanctuary: a place for refugees, survivors of crimes and
> human trafficking, unaccompanied children, and those stranded in the US as
> the result of natural and human made disasters in their homelands. The lobby
> serves not only as the admissions entry point, but also as a place of legal limbo
> (sort of like an easement), where people are sometime allowed to hangout for
> years on end in renewable quasi-status like parole and deferred action. Finally,
> the basement holds those without status—either they never had it, by entering
> unauthorized at an unregulated entry point; or those who entered legally but
> have violated their terms of status. The cellar or dungeon is immigration de-
> tention. (p. 41)

This metaphor is very familiar. The top floor, or concierge floor, is one that many
guests aspire to either book or get upgraded to. Invariably, those guests tend to
be White, non-Latinos, and citizens. No one wants to occupy a basement room.

In 2015, the National Council of La Raza, the nation's largest Latino civil rights
and advocacy organization, issued a statement to the US House of Representatives
Judiciary Subcommittee on Immigration and Border Security concerning its
support for a comprehensive immigration policy (Martinez-De-Castro, 2015).
Sanctuary cities can be conceptualized as stopgap localized measures until national comprehensive policies can be enacted.

The "Day Without Immigrants" campaign (February 17, 2017) symbolized one
of the latest nationwide efforts to publicize the important role that immigrants,
both documented and undocumented, play in the day-to-day functioning of

society, making the invisible visible (Knight, 2017). This "national day" protest was highlighted in a *New York Times* article (Robbins & Correal, 2017):

> But what began as a grass-roots movement quickly reached the highest levels of federal government. In Washington, the Pentagon warned its employees that a number of its food concessions . . . were closed because immigrant employees had stayed home and that they could expect longer lines at restaurants that were open. Restaurants from San Francisco to Phoenix to Washington, D.C., were some of the most visible spots affected, with well-known chefs closing some of their eateries in support. (p. 10)

This description only scratches the surface on how this day materialized throughout the country, specifically in the case of restaurants. Other sectors with high percentages of immigrants were also impacted, showing how immigrants shape everyday life in this country.

Businesses, however, can fall on the other side of the sanctuary fight. For example, Arizona's Motel 6, although not limited to that state, had employees inform immigration officials of guests who were undocumented, who were subsequently apprehended and deported (Romero, 2017). ICE raids of 98 7-Eleven stores in Washington, DC, and 17 states in early 2018, considered the largest such raid targeting an employer during President's Trump administration, also sent a stark message to employers throughout the country (Miroff, 2018). These raids of a ubiquitous business in working class communities across the country, are widely acknowledged to represent a highly public shift in dealing with employers of those who are undocumented, as well as customers with this citizenship status, to create a climate of terror in these communities (Kitroeff, 2018).

The economic cost debates regarding those who are undocumented are skewed toward the downside, ignoring local, state, and national benefits. They live in, and contribute to, their communities, and they often form a vital part of a community's social fabric, raising the question of why society has a moral and political obligation to them (McThomas, 2016). For instance, the Social Security Trust Fund receives an estimated $13 billion a year from approximately 7 million people who are unauthorized, and it received an estimated $100 billion over a 10-year period from people utilizing false or expired Social Security numbers (Germano, 2014).

The Medicare Trust Fund, too, is rarely associated with this group, even though this group was responsible for a major portion of the $115.2 billon contributed to this fund during the period from 2002 to 2009 (Zallman et al., 2013). Since 1937, there have been 333 million workers whose Social Security numbers were not valid or did not match their names (Healy, 2017).

According to the Internal Revenue Service, those who are undocumented annually pay $23.6 billion in taxes and $12 billion in state and local taxes (Healey, 2017). In Massachusetts, for example, they pay $185 million dollars annually in taxes. Another local-level example has undocumented New Yorkers contributing approximately $1.1 billion in state and local taxes (Shaw, 2015).

Virginia is another state example, with this group contributing between $200.2 million and $304.3 million in sales and excise taxes, local property taxes, and state income taxes. This estimate translates into 6.6% to 7.0% of household income for the approximately 260,000 to 290,000 undocumented immigrants in that state, which is considerably higher than the 5.1% paid by that state's top 1% of income earners (Commonwealth Institute, 2015). In Florida, they contribute approximately $588 million in state and local taxes (Chen, 2016).

What are the economic costs of deportation? There are two perspectives on these costs: physical removal and gross domestic product (GDP) costs. According to the Center for American Press, the process of deporting someone is estimated at $10,070, with $114 billion needed to remove 11.3 million people (Wolgin, 2015). It is estimated that it would take 20 years to find and deport them. Finally, as if these economic costs were not large enough, we must also add an additional $315 billion to prevent their re-entry into the country (Schoen, 2017). A citizenship path would generate $1.2 trillion to the country's GDP during a 10-year period, including increasing the earnings of all residents by $625 billion and creating 145,000 new jobs per year.

One estimate has the costs reducing the nation's GDP by 2.6%, which translates into an annual loss of $434 billion and $4.7 trillion during a 10-year period (Waslin, 2016). This figure does not include the cost of rounding them up, their detention, and their eventual deportation. Focusing on the sectors reliant (40%) on them (agriculture, construction, leisure, and hospitality) will result in losses of between 10% and 18% and countless billions of dollars to these industries. The agricultural industry will be particularly hard hit with the deportations of workers who are undocumented, with an estimated 25% of all farmhands falling into this citizenship status (E. Porter, 2017). The largest financial fallout will be in this nation's largest industries, such as financial, manufacturing, wholesale, and retail trade, because of their purchasing power.

There has been a backlash against anti-immigrant legislation and the sanctuary movement encapsulates this reaction, with California playing a leading role in these efforts (Ramakrishnan & Colbern, 2015). The overall impact of massive deportations will have a devastating impact on states such as California, where an estimated 10.2% of its workforce is undocumented. It will experience a GDP decrease of $103 billion annually, with its agricultural sector bearing a significant brunt with $8 billion in losses, along with $20 billion in manufacturing and $17 billion in wholesale and retail trade losses (Waslin, 2016). California has the distinction of having some of the earliest and the most sanctuary cities in the United States (Barenboim, 2016). These economic statistics pale in comparison to the hidden costs on the lives of those who are undocumented and their communities because as they make their important contributions, these do not come without costs (Flores-Macias, 2017).

Sanctuary cities represent an altered political state, which has been referred to as "insurgent citizenship," creating new political spaces that go beyond conventional national territorial framing of liberal democratic citizenship and in the process creating new criteria for what constitutes "citizenship" (Leitner & Strunk,

2014). Safety afforded those seeking refuge is conceptualized broadly beyond physical safety to include other dimensions, such as social acceptance and validation of experiences related to tragedy and the worthlessness that can result from forced uprootment (Hintjens & Pouri, 2014). Instrumental support is also part of this experience, helping to address daily living needs.

Sanctuary cities are a shining target for those opposed to the undocumented. A common argument is made by opponents that this designation attracts the undocumented and results in high crime rates (Houston & Lawrence-Weilmann, 2016; C. Wright, 2016). The killing in San Francisco of Ms. Kathryn Steinle in July 2015 by accused Jose Ines Garcia Zarate, an unauthorized man with an extensive history of "committing violent crimes," was used by then presidential candidate Trump to argue for stricter enforcement of immigration laws and the building of a wall separating the United States from Mexico.

The tragedy of Ms. Steinle was highly politicized (Dickerson & Stevens, 2017): "'For Donald Trump, we were just what he needed—beautiful girl, San Francisco, illegal immigrant, crime and yadda, yadda, yadda,' her mother, Liz Sullivan, told the *San Francisco Chronicle*. 'We were the perfect storm for that man'" (p. A18). Mr. Zarate, however, was found not guilty of murder and involuntary manslaughter (Yan & Simon, 2017). He would later be charged on federal grounds for possessing a gun as well as facing deportation. President Trump tweeted, "A disgraceful verdict in the Kate Steinle case! No wonder the people of our Country are so angry with Illegal Immigration."

Highlighting her murder has been referred to as "dog-whistle politics" because it taps racial sentiments regarding those who are undocumented and crime (Lasch, 2016). The undocumented as criminal threats has consistently been a focus of attention in this country (X. Wang, 2012). Media stories of this group engaged in gangs, drugs, extortion, and murder are bound to get increased attention to feed such a narrative (Donelson & Esparza, 2016; Longazel, 2013). The importance of media coverage of raids and deportations cannot be underestimated (Menjívar, 2016).

Media coverage of anti-deportation demonstrations also plays an important role in shaping public opinion (empathy), and it shapes political discourse and action. Anti-immigration demonstrations must be cast against other demonstrations that dovetail into anti-Trump ("Trumpism") and a pro human rights and social justice agenda.

The January 21, 2017, national march that brought millions of demonstrators to the streets of this nation's major cities sent a public statement that social justice activism was alive and well (Mironova, 2017):

On January 21, approximately 4 million people marched across the United States. These coordinated protests are being billed as the largest public action against a sitting president, if not the largest coordinated demonstration in United States history. The breadth of mobilization points to a real possibility for a popular resistance that can not only effectively challenge Trumpism, but also usher in broader, progressive change.

Media coverage of anti-deportation cases generally falls into three categories: (a) citizenship as acculturation; (b) citizenship as civic engagement (or "good citizenry"); and (c) deservingness vis-à-vis victim status (Patler & Gonzales, 2015).

Hing (2015) notes that engagement in disruptive acts to highlight the vulnerable status of the unauthorized encouraged President Obama's administration to undertake innovative approaches toward massive arrest and deportation of unauthorized Latinos. Readers realize the complexity of developing a comprehensive and systematic understanding of this subject.

Immigration authorities have been explicatively instructed not to conduct raids in what are referred to as "sensitive locations," such as congregations, schools, and hospitals, which are discussed later. This stance is due to concerns about raising political opposition, placing these types of organizations in a strategic position to resist immigration raids. The prospect of a raid of a school or house of worship being seen on the 6 o'clock news undermines public support for raids and deportation. It is important to note that the Reagan administration's Department of Justice never undertook a raid of sanctuary churches. However, in 1985, the Department of Justice did file criminal conspiracy charges against 16 Arizona activists, including Rev. John Fife. Eight were convicted, but none ever went to prison.

The courts are not usually associated with sensitive areas to avoid arresting those who are unauthorized. However, there is a national trend to have ICE agents conduct arrests at these settings when unauthorized individuals show up to attend to some legal matter, such as paying a parking ticket or seeking the court's assistance in deterring an abusive partner, calling for a pushback at the local level (Garcia Hernandez, 2017b)

> ICE understands its actions can paralyze important institutions. Longstanding ICE policy discourages questioning or arresting people in schools and churches. It is time to add courthouses to that list. . . . With no change to federal policy in sight, it is up to cities and states to push back. Elected officials must take seriously their legal obligation to keep courthouses accessible. In addition, the cities and states that own and operate most courthouses and ensure that no one uses their courts in a way that halts judicial business—protesters can't block the doorway, bail bondsmen aren't allowed to set up shop in the lobby—should do the same here for immigration agents. (p. A23)

Although high-profile crimes exist, there is no evidence for claiming those who are unauthorized have a propensity toward engaging in crime (Chen, 2015; Collingwood & El-Khatib, 2016). A study of immigrant integration and urban neighborhood violence found a reduction in violence, which is a counter-narrative to immigrants and violence, and it is speculated that this is due to an enhancement of trust and public social control in these neighborhoods (Lyons, Vélez, & Santoro, 2013).

Lyons, Vélez, and Santoro (2014) found the opposite of criminal involvement in a study of 9,000 neighborhoods that had a proclivity toward embracing immigrants and had an increased likelihood of reaping benefits that manifested themselves in increased safety; the opposite was the case in neighborhoods that embraced punitive policies toward newcomers. Punitive policies toward immigrants will also, in all likelihood, apply to low-income people of color in those areas. The former's neighborhoods are more likely to have elected officials and other stakeholders with a shared heritage and similar progressive values. It is critical that social workers and others in positions of influence provide a counter-argument to raise awareness of how "fake news" is undermining these communities.

The self-interests of those in power, in the case elected officials, exert tremendous influence on local law enforcement related to implementing immigration laws, highlighting the influence of local context in shaping these interests, with election and re-election having saliency (Mather, 2016). Sanctuary city elected officials, in similar fashion to their counterparts in very repressive cities, must also contend with the support of voters and their expectations.

WHY ARE SANCTUARY CITIES OF NATIONAL IMPORTANCE?

There are countless ways of answering the question of why sanctuary cities are so important to the nation. This designation has social, economic, political, and moral significance for those who are being helped and also for those helping, their institutions, and the communities in which they live.

The designation, and the political support and services that it brings, has international consequences because of the message it sends to the countries from which the unauthorized come to the United States and also the message of compassion it sends to the rest of the world and whether or not this nation can be a beacon of light in a stormy sea (Timberlake & Williams, 2012). The influence is concrete and symbolic. Sanctuaries force us to examine the prevailing paradigms and the deficit language used to describe them. When this happens, it can be quite distressing for a nation, and there lies this movement's symbolic power. A shift in paradigms provides very specific, immediate, and concrete gains and changes, with real-life consequences rather than an esoteric theoretical discussion that academics are prone to have.

The sheer number of sanctuary sites, in addition to the national prominence of several of them, makes this topic of significance for the nation as a whole and for those who are unauthorized living in sanctuary cities. It is estimated that almost 300 jurisdictions, including towns, throughout the country are either officially designated as sanctuaries or may not be so designated but have shown, based on their policies, strong proclivities toward harboring those who are unauthorized. These sites have the distinction of being identified by ICE as sanctuary sites (Vaughn, 2016). They

> have been identified by ICE as having a policy that is non-cooperative and obstructs immigration enforcement (as of September 2015). The number of cities has remained relatively unchanged since our last update in August 2016,

as some new sanctuary jurisdictions have been added and few jurisdictions have reversed their sanctuary policies.

The number of sanctuaries in the United States is dynamic, and this is to be expected. Their presence is significant enough to have been singled out for political attention from the political right and anti-immigration forces because of their location (major urban areas) and symbolism. Although the number of sanctuary sites constantly changes, they are increasing rather than decreasing in representation, reflecting a growing national movement.

SANCTUARY MOVEMENT: INTERESTS AND FORCES COMING TOGETHER

Sanctuaries have many different homes and many different histories. My first real exposure to the concept of sanctuary was in the early 1990s, and it was not related to immigrants, when I came across a book that is considered a classic in many different quarters including my own: McLaughlin, Irby, and Langman's (1994) *Urban Sanctuaries: Neighborhood Organizations in the Lives and Futures of Inner-City Youth*. Although not specifically referring to protection from legal authorities, such as the police, it outlined the role and importance of key community institutions in providing a safe (psychological and physical) space for vulnerable youth to find respite from life's daily hassles.

Urban sanctuaries were institutions in urban communities where youth could go after school, be safe, and engage in activities of meaning to them. Initially, sanctuaries focused on marginalized youth of color. Since then, they have expanded to include those who are unauthorized, reflecting the dynamic demographic changes occurring in the nations' major cities (Roth, Sichling, & Brake, 2016).

BOOK OUTLINE

This book consists of 10 chapters organized into three conceptual sections: Section 1: Grounding Sanctuary Cities; Section 2: Sanctuary Cities, Communities, Organizations, and Homes; and Section 3: Where to Now? These sections are weaved together in such a manner to unfold the story of the sanctuary city movement in this country, including integrating stories of individuals and the institutions advancing this rights and social justice mission.

WHY A BOOK SPECIFICALLY ON SANCTUARY CITIES?

Although the scholarly literature does touch upon sanctuaries and this movement, no book on this topic exists written from a human service perspective. A number of outstanding books do exist on immigrants and immigration in the United States, and there are a number of books specifically focused on sanctuary cities.

The following two books stand out because of their historical and philosophical coverage of the subject, and readers with a more in-depth interest in this particular focus will find them fruitful: Bagelman's (2016) *Sanctuary City: A Suspended State* and Rabben's (2016) *Sanctuary and Asylum: A Social and Political History*. These books broaden the coverage of sanctuaries internationally and go beyond citizenship status. My book specifically focuses on the United States, although reference is made to the history of a sanctuary designation internationally and how we can enhance this movement in the United States.

A third book is worth noting. *Deep Dive: Sanctuary Cities*, by B. P. Joyner and Voss (2017), provides an overview of the sanctuary movement by presenting both sides of the debate. It provides a "layperson" account of this movement, touching on many points and conclusions in my book but in a cursory manner.

Readers interested in what the "outsider" thinks may find C. Wright's (2016) *Con Job: How Democrats Gave Us Crime, Sanctuary Cities, Abortion Profiteering, and Racial Division* of interest. This book takes a counterview by arguing that the sanctuary movement undermines the country's social fabric by fostering the entrance of less than desirable people, and it is in line with President Trump's central argument against unauthorized immigration (Sampaio, 2016).

The focus on the unauthorized has polarized public opinion, helping reinforce fractured feelings and political alliances while making seeking a consensus opinion on how to address this issue nearly impossible at this point in time (P. Martin, 2017). Finally, although there are a number of outstanding books on immigration, this book's focus is unique by bringing this subject and sanctuary cities together to influence this movement.

Although the sanctuary movement initially focused on those who were unauthorized, other marginalized groups also facing oppression have sought the assistance of sanctuary sites. Refugees, asylum seekers, Muslims, and LGBTQ, for instance, have sought help from sanctuary sites, and this must not go unacknowledged (Fabri, 2016; Fredriksen-Goldsen, 2016). Currently, there are 58,000 Haitian immigrants in this country under the Temporary Protected Status Program who are facing increased scrutiny pertaining to criminal activity as part of the Trump administration's get tough on immigrants stance (L. Alvarez, 2017; Caldwell, 2017). Although they received a 6-month extension (Cramer, 2017b; *The New York Times* Editorial Board, 2017b), the Trump administration ended this program on November 21, 2017, so these immigrants must leave by July 2019 or be deported (Jordan, 2017d).

In addition to Haitians, 200,000 Salvadorans, 57,000 Hondurans, and 2,500 Nicaraguans have been granted Temporary Protected Status based on congressional legislation passed in 1990 (Guerra, 2017; Miroff, 2017a). Many of these individuals have been in the country since 1998 due to the destruction caused by Hurricane Mitch in their home countries. Massachusetts, for instance, is home to 78,000, with 5,300 children having parents with this status. A determination on revoking their temporary status was made in early 2018. Approximately 200,000 will lose protected status and must leave the country by September 2019 (Jordan, 2018).

Children born to Salvadorans in the United States are US citizens and can remain in this country. Thus, there is the potential for these children to be separated from their parents, who must return to Central America, while the children remain in the United States (Guerra, 2018). El Salvador, however, has one of the world's highest murder rates, so these returnees will find their country of origin more deadly than when they left it, due largely to extensive gang activity (Paulumbo & Ahmed, 2018). Deported Salvadorans have the potential to further weaken an already weak economy, and their return will mean that remittances will stop, also further weakening El Salvador's economy, in addition to breaking up families (Fox, 2018).

Salvadorans are concentrated in Florida, New York, Texas, and Virginia, and they are heavily represented in the construction industry, restaurants, grocery stores, landscaping, and day care. Walt Disney Company, for example, has hired more than 500 protected Haitians. It is estimated that the potential deportation of approximately 6,000 Salvadorans from Massachusetts represents a $400 million GDP loss to the state ("A Blow to Salvadorans," 2018).

This book takes a focused view on those who are undocumented, although it always keeps in mind that there are many others in need of sanctuary.

CONCLUSION

Unauthorized immigration is a major national issue, one with long historical ties in this country. This group's future will continue to be a topic of heated debate for the rest of this decade and longer. The complexity of the solutions this nation must employ makes it an even more difficult issue to understand. It is hoped that this chapter has captured this state of being and why a sanctuary movement is worthy of a book.

Chapter 2 provides a historical grounding of how the United States has addressed immigration and the important role cities have played in fostering immigration, in addition to why cities remain an influential setting for a sanctuary movement to take hold. Understanding immigration and the responses immigrants receive upon arrival, regardless of citizenship status, is the result of a set of major interacting social forces with deep historical roots.

2

Brief Historical Overview of Immigration in the United States

INTRODUCTION

The subject of history is rarely one that has captured the imagination and enthusiasm of many readers, and this probably has more to do with how it has been taught and the questions to which answers are sought, raising questions about relevance and bias of subjects covered, which are no small matters. History is usually written by the elites and intended to reach an audience with similar backgrounds—in other words, elites for the elites.

There is no disputing the importance of history when discussing major social phenomenon and how it shapes modern-day discourse of highly controversial topics, and immigration falls into this category (Chauvin & Garcés-Mascareñas, 2014; Gutiérrez, 2016; Tsiklauri, 2017). Current national debates on immigration are not new to this country, drawing close parallels to debates in the 1920s (Yee, 2018). The history of those who are unauthorized is not written by them and not intended for them.

A number of subjects are not recorded because they are not perceived to be worthy of attention. Municipal-focused unauthorized policies, for example, are understudied (Toussaint, 2013). The intersection of immigration and local policymaking provides a number of approaches that can emerge in response to the undocumented (Rissler, 2016). Subnational governmental entities (districts, cities, towns, counties, and states) can be laboratories of democracy or triggers for races to the bottom, which is apparent in discussing this nation's immigration laws and its incarceration policies (Hedrick, 2011).

This nation's founding was based on the implicit assumption that only Europeans would seek to settle here, and nothing could be further from the truth. Immigration, particularly when involving those who are unauthorized and of color, poses incredible ethical challenges for Western societies (Carens, 2013). An appreciation of the sanctuary movement is not possible without understanding historical immigration patterns and how national media and politics responded.

This history is highly dependent on the historians recording it. History is not apolitical, and these biases must be explicated to understand the conclusions and how they were arrived at. All students in this country have had a lesson on immigration in their American history or civics classes.

It is impossible to undertake a comprehensive and nuanced review of this nation's founding and evolution without discussion of newcomers, and particularly their contributions to this nation's prosperity and position in the world (Kennedy, 2016; Ziegler-McPherson, 2017). Immigrant contributions to this nation and its cities are evident in the names of the cities, squares, parks, and statues, many reflecting "non-English"-sounding names, drawing upon their historical contributions to these cities (Kennedy, 2016). A historical overview, and the assumptions on which major events have been based, grounds the present-day subject of this country's undocumented and the emergence of sanctuary cities nationally (Velásquez, 2017).

The study of history can prove quite informative and enlightening, bringing to fruition a quality-of-life dimension for those privileged enough to have the time, and resources, to read about history, be it immigration focused or otherwise. However, history can inform present-day actions and can have significant future consequences if the lessons learned get carried out with an understanding of the past.

Christina (2017), in discussing a resistance narrative, draws attention to the sanctuary city movement and the importance of learning history in helping us respond to challenging times, informed by historical lessons:

> We can learn history. We can learn the history of fascism, white supremacy, and extreme right-ring movements, learn how to recognize and fight them. We can learn the history of resistance movements in the past, what worked and what didn't work. We can remember history, so we won't be condemned to repeat it. (p. 34)

There is much value in embracing Christina's charge because current events have historical parallels.

The historical field has produced excellent books on immigration, particularly from a people of color and urban perspective, helping ground our understanding of present-day attitudes (Bayor, 2016; Chavez, 2013; Kurashige, 2016; McWilliams, Meier, & García, 2016; Ngai, 2014; Portes & Rumbaut, 2014). Foner (2000), for instance, examined immigration through entry in New York City, home to Ellis Island, spotlighting how a major US port of entry was transformed and set the stage for future demographic changes in New York City and, through dispersal, other cities throughout the country.

The relationship between immigrants and cities is not recent, with deep historical ties that can be traced back to the early 19th century, helping explain the significant role cities played in shaping this nation's relationship with newcomers during the past two centuries. This relationship is both "hate" and "love," and in some cities, it is more of one than the other. We cannot separate the immigrant experience from where immigrants settle, including the histories of these cities in welcoming immigrants, regardless of legal status (Jaworsky, 2016a).

This chapter is founded on the belief that the sanctuary city movement has deep roots in this nation's immigration history and, therefore, grounds readers in this country's historical relationship with this subject through a focus on several major immigration phases in our history. Such a focus presents an overview at the expense of important micro-historical events that often fade into the background. Effort is made to highlight these events to give meaning and texture to these phases in setting a context for present-day responses.

United States immigration history has included periods during which the country embraced both restrictive and expansive phases (Rodríguez & Hagan, 2016). Furthermore, this nation's immigration policies are predicated on a legacy framework and system that has historically and systematically been constructed on a foundation that is "highly racialized, transnational, exploitative, and dangerous" (Cobas, Duany, & Feagin, 2015; Jamison, 2016).

The United States no longer has commonly accepted standards of what constitutes "Whiteness." Readers may have an adverse reaction to this observation, but this stance has promoted legislation and policies that implicitly reinforce racial boundaries, with the help of media and how they cover anti-immigration legislation (Estrada, Ebert, & Lore, 2016). Racialization reinforces this narrative, and it gets manifested in who has a right to be in this country.

IMMIGRATION PHASES

Dividing this country's complex immigration history into several distinct phases is arbitrary. I struggled with various frameworks for presenting this history but kept to the goal of providing a broad overview, and one that could be covered in one chapter. Sufficient information is provided in each of the phases to allow an appreciation of the political and socioeconomic forces and significant events that were active in encouraging or discouraging certain groups from entering the country.

Immigrants are synonymous with US history, and this country's worldwide reputation has been shaped by this demographic phenomenon. Those who are undocumented can be viewed through a narrow lens of economics, which shows that they have made, and are currently making, an important direct and indirect contribution to the wealth of their communities, in addition to the economies of their homelands through remittance payments (Lewis & Peri, 2014). However, this is such a narrow view because their contributions are far greater to the social well-being of their communities and country.

A nation almost 250 years old, not counting the period leading up to its independence, has many lessons to draw upon in understanding the current state of affairs. It is often said that history repeats itself. Possibly a better saying is that it does not repeat itself, but it sure seems to rhyme, highlighting key historical parallels. The broad conceptualization and celebration of US immigration beyond a narrow focus on individual groups or historical periods is captured by the *Journal of American Ethnic History* (Varzally, 2017):

> Scholars have readily, enthusiastically answered the call—resoundingly delivered in a set of comments published in this journal in 1999—to unite previously disparate, sometimes conflicting fields of immigration history (with its roots in the study of European groups and its presumption of a singular model of assimilation and inclusion) and Chicano and Asian American history (with their origins in social revolutions and civil rights activism of the mid-twentieth century). Centering race and rethinking the forms and meanings of European ethnicities have facilitated this union. The result is a more inclusive, and analytically rigorous, if more diffuse field that better captures the complications of the past and contextualizes contemporary patterns of migration that animate discussions about U.S. foreign policy, border enforcement, memory, and ideas of citizenship. (p. 62)

An inclusive immigration historical view is essential for a comprehensive understanding of the United States in the 21st century, helping increase our appreciation of present-day social activism.

Immigration history is generally conceptualized into four distinct phases as a means of understanding its relationship with major historical events, and as presented in Figure 2.1, with immigration composition differing—with some phases having greater numbers of Asian and Latinos and covering longer or shorter periods of time.

Drawing comparisons between historical periods is tempting, but it is very difficult to draw definitive conclusions based on comparisons. For instance, between 1890 and 1920, Italians represented 24% of all newcomers, compared to 30% for Mexicans from the 1980s to 2010s (C. L. Schmid, 2017). These percentages are somewhat similar. Although both groups did not have English as their language of preference, they had different histories: One was White, non-Latino, and the other was Latino and of color. Furthermore, one crossed an ocean of water, and the other crossed an ocean of sand. In addition, the US economy was significantly different during these two time periods. This is not to say that we cannot learn from the past (Jones-Correa & De Graauw, 2013a, 2013b).

Immigration actions are never significant isolated events. As evident in Figure 2.1, there are four broad and, arguably, debated time periods or phases of immigration in the United States: Phase 1, frontier expansion (1820–1880); Phase 2, industrialization (1880–1915); Phase 3, immigration pause (1915–1965); and Phase 4, post-1965 immigration (1965 to present). Each phase consists of several shorter historical periods and events, which often overlap.

This historical view is one of many. Jaggers, Gabbard, and Jaggers (2014), for example, have taken a perspective specifically focused on immigration and conceptualized this history into five phases: (1) open door, (2) regulation, (3) restriction, (4) liberalization, and (5) a devolution phase after September 11, 2001.

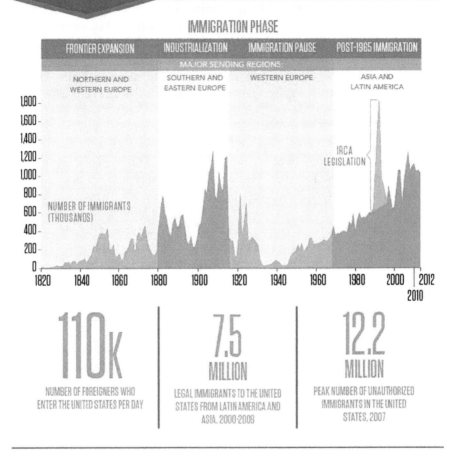

U.S. IMMIGRATION HAS OCCURRED IN WAVES, WITH PEAKS FOLLOWED BY TROUGHS

IMMIGRATION PHASE

FRONTIER EXPANSION	INDUSTRIALIZATION	IMMIGRATION PAUSE	POST-1965 IMMIGRATION

MAJOR SENDING REGIONS:

NORTHERN AND WESTERN EUROPE | SOUTHERN AND EASTERN EUROPE | WESTERN EUROPE | ASIA AND LATIN AMERICA

IRCA LEGISLATION

NUMBER OF IMMIGRANTS (THOUSANDS)

110k

NUMBER OF FOREIGNERS WHO ENTER THE UNITED STATES PER DAY

7.5 MILLION

LEGAL IMMIGRANTS TO THE UNITED STATES FROM LATIN AMERICA AND ASIA, 2000-2009

12.2 MILLION

PEAK NUMBER OF UNAUTHORIZED IMMIGRANTS IN THE UNITED STATES, 2007

Figure 2.1 United States' immigration waves.
NOTE: IRCA adjustments refer to the amnesty provisions of the Immigration Reform and Control Act of 1986, under which 2.7 million undocumented foreign U.S. residents obtained legal immigrant status.
SOURCE: US Department of Homeland Security. (2012). *Yearbook of immigration statistics.* Washington, DC: Author.

The post-September 11 phase brings this conceptualization up to the present day. For the purposes of this chapter, the conceptualization presented in Figure 2.1 will prevail because it follows most conventional views on immigration phases.

Before discussing the four immigration phases, it is necessary to address a key point regarding the post-independence period. The period after the American Revolution was marked by great expectations, but it was also marked by great injustice. The US Congress passed the Fugitive Slave Act, which made it legal for slaveholders to track and capture escaped slaves, with punishment dealt to all those who aided and abetted their escape. However, northern states refused to abide by this law and enacted safe haven legislation to counter federal legislation. The importance of the Underground Railroad, and the emergence of safe houses, parallels the current situation regarding federal immigration laws and localities resisting these laws through sanctuary designations (Loth, 2017).

An 1842 Supreme Court ruling undermined the northern states' efforts, opening the door for testing the rights of states not to cooperate with arrests and deportations of runaway slaves (Loth, 2017):

> Of course, parallels to the Fugitive Slave Act are not perfect. In 1842, the Supreme Court ruled in favor of a bounty hunter who captured and deported a slave woman who had run to Pennsylvania for sanctuary. But in an aside that opened a commodious loophole, Justice Joseph Story wrote that individual states nonetheless did not have to *help* in the hunting or recapture of slaves. "It might well be deemed an unconstitutional exercise of the power" he wrote, "to insist that the states are bound to provide means to carry into effect the duties of the national government." Congress moved swiftly by passing the even stricter Fugitive Slave Act in 1850 (eventually repealed in 1864), but the underlying constitutional principle remains.

Phase 1: Frontier Expansion (1820–1880)

This phase has its origins in the initial settlement of this country by Europeans. This country was built by immigrants, if we take aside Native Americans who were the original inhabitants and African Slaves who were forced to come to this country, creating dramatically different experiences for them, and their ancestors, that exist to this day. The year 2019 will mark the 400th anniversary of African slaves being brought to Jamestown, highlighting a disturbing period in this nation's history. This anniversary will not be marked with national declarations.

One cannot escape the parallel process of the attempted genocide of Native Americans while the nation was expanding demographically and moving westward (Rogin, 1975). There was a westward push of Native Americans during this period, but one with dramatically different motivations and outcomes. It is important to emphasize that American Indians did not achieve citizenship status until the Indian Citizenship Act of 1924, which speaks volumes about the racialization of citizenship in this country.

We can argue that those who are unauthorized have been part of this nation's history since the original European settlers stepped foot here, but we never think of the passengers on the Mayflower as immigrants or unauthorized (del Hierro, 2016). Yet, they were not invited. There are significant parallels between the American Revolutionary War and today's protests against no one being illegal

(Morales, 2016). In essence, all non-Native Americans are foreigners to this country (Tobin, 2016).

The "selling of America" was needed for this country to prosper and grow; a message was created that emphasized opportunity, hard work, and the possibility of upward mobility to attract immigrants (Ziegler-McPherson, 2017). The selling of a dream persists to this day, several hundred years later, and stands as a testament to the power of this dream for millions throughout the world.

Immigrants in the nation's cities during the late 19th century were associated with poverty, labor unrest, violence, crime, lack of cleanliness, unhealthy states of being, and resistance to American values (Tirman, 2015). Immigration controversy is almost as old as the nation, as evidenced by Benjamin Franklin's vitriol on German immigrants: "Few of their children learn English. . . .The signs in our streets have inscriptions in both languages. . . . Unless the stream of their importation could be turned away they will soon outnumber us . . . and even our government will become precarious." Thomas Jefferson, too, echoed concerns about immigrants who "will infuse into American legislation their spirit, warp and bias its direction, and render it a heterogeneous, incoherent, distracted mass."

The anti-immigrant rhetoric of both Franklin and Jefferson, two of this nation's founding fathers, can easily find a home in present-day debates about those who are undocumented, such as Latinos, and a ban on Muslims. This observation is not meant to dishearten readers. Rather, it is meant to ground the current debate historically, to understand its long reach (Epps & Furman, 2016):

> Few topics currently inspire more passion than what has been frequently termed "the immigration debate." Even within this seemingly simple phrase exists a clear message that immigration is something that must be debated, that in and of itself it is problematic.

Haensel and Garcia-Zamor (2016) provide an excellent summary of immigration laws during the 19th century, a period during which much happened regarding immigration, policies, and the expansion of the nation's cities:

> Restrictions on immigration in the US reach back to the late 19th century when the Congress voted on immigration laws such as the literacy requirement for immigrants and the exclusion of convicts and prostitutes with 85% in favor. Before that, due to political and economic circumstances as for instance the discovery of gold and the industrialization process, the United States (US) were eager to attract migrants to work in farms and factories. Between 1820 and 1840 approximately 2.8 million Irish immigrated to the US. . . . In the twentieth century, the main heritage countries of migrants shifted from European countries to Latin American and to a lesser extend Asian countries. (p. 140)

This broad-brush historical summary incorporates several major social factors that led to immigration restrictions, setting a foundation for understanding the following stages.

Yet, we must never lose sight that these overviews involved countless lives, struggles, heartbreaks, narratives, and even dreams and joys. These stories capture the imagination and motivate the seeking of social justice for those who are undocumented (Coutin & Vogel, 2016; Fuentes & Pérez, 2016; Gomberg-Muñoz, 2016a; Omer, 2015).

We often advocate for using narratives to help inform and change public opinion because of their power to bring stories forth that facilitate listeners being able to relate to the experiences shared by the storyteller. However, there are other aspects of narratives that are equally, if not more, compelling. The narratives of those who are undocumented are powerful when shared among themselves because they create a bonding experience, as well as a sense of community, and the political will for engaging in social change efforts (Gomberg-Muñoz, 2016a).

The two major Asian groups of immigrants (Chinese and Japanese) had a major presence among newcomers to the United States. The discovery of gold in California in 1848 is widely considered the key factor in initiating Chinese immigration to this county, accounted for 225,000 immigrants entering soon after this date, with many settling in California, including San Francisco (Segal, 2000). Japanese immigration significantly increased after 1910, when 72,000 entered the country.

Fears and scapegoating of racial and ethnic groups are very much a part of this nation's historical relationship with immigrants. Haines (2015) furthers the fear of certain immigrant groups by combining ethnicity and religion, which touches upon how Muslims, religion, and immigration have become explosive issues in national and international discourse, facilitating the inclusion of terrorism into anti-immigrant sentiments and policies:

> This commitment to exclude often resurfaced in the post-independence United States. Those Irish and Germans arriving at the middle of the nineteenth century were met with frequent hostility. The famine Irish were allowed in, but the "no Irish need apply" signs were common and the caricatures of the day show a ready dehumanization of the Irish and a debasement of their Catholic religion. While they helped build our modern infrastructure—from canals to railroads to new urban landscape—they were incessantly rejected on both national origin and religious grounds.

This national expansion set the stage for the expansion of industrialization and urbanization and the influential role that immigrants played in building this nation's cities.

This role has not received the acknowledgment that it deserves, and this has been a perennial theme in the nation's history, including the essential role that those who are undocumented have played. It has been argued that upon closer examination, the influx of newcomers into the nation's cities was highly influential in making cities the "lifeblood of capitalist expansion," pushing land values higher, helping expand the construction industry, and creating increased real estate values and wealth (Low, 2013). This wealth helped make the United States a worldwide power.

Phase 2: Industrialization (1880–1915)

The United States' industrialization phase cannot be separated from the urbanization phase. Industrialization served as a significant magnet for bringing immigrants into the country to fill production jobs; these manufacturing jobs, in turn, were increasingly finding a home in the nation's major cities, including major ports of entry. The convergence of three major forces (industrialization, urbanization, and immigration) fueled this nation's need for inexpensive labor and, in the process, established the country's role in the world.

The intensity of the acrimony surrounding those who are undocumented is not a recent occurrence in this nation's history, and it was intensified during this relatively short phase of 35 years, or one generation. It was not until 1890 that a national immigration agency was established in the United States. Prior to this date, states were called upon to enforce immigration laws. Ironically, not much seems to have changed during the past 100-plus years regarding states carrying out immigration policies.

In 1892, Ellis Island was established, and the image of immigrants being processed is embedded in most people's mind and been a major part of the nation's narrative (Foner, 2000). Restrictive immigration measures followed, facilitating deportations of those who were unauthorized. Prior to this period, only certain groups of people, such as the Chinese, were specifically excluded.

Race-based restrictions in the late 19th century severely limited Asian immigration. The 1882 Chinese Exclusion Act, which shamefully was not repealed until World War II, is considered a significant event in US deportation policy history. It marked what can arguably be the beginning of this nation's exclusion and deportation laws and policies, effectively serving as a "social filter," counter to the myth that this country welcomes all to its shores (Moloney, 2012). The "Yellow Peril" period was a color metaphor that originally emerged during the late 19th century to mark anti-immigrant sentiments toward Chinese immigrants, and it remerged to make an anti-Japanese stance prior to the entrance of the United States into World War II against Japan, marking shameful periods in this nation's history (Finkelman, 2014).

The period between 1900 and 1920 represents the country's first massive influx of immigrants, when 24 million entered the country. Mexican immigration experienced a dramatic increase following 1907, in response to the stoppage of Japanese immigration that year, and experienced unprecedented growth as the result of World War I and the need for labor. The US Congress had barred all Asians by 1924.

It was not until 1918 that Europeans were required to possess a passport to enter the country. There were restrictions on entering prior to this period, but they specifically focused on those arriving via ship, not on those crossing the northern and southern borders by foot (Chomsky, 2014). The irony is not lost on this author, with mode of entry restriction being the primary way of focusing on those who were undocumented back then, as it is today, with overstayed visas being more acceptable than crossing a desert.

The border with Mexico has garnered the lion's share of attention in history books. However, concerns about the US border with Canada have disappeared in any discussion of "controlling our borders." In the 19th century, the United States did attempt to control entry into the country at both Canadian and Mexican borders; at the turn of the 20th century, there were attempts to enforce the border with Canada to prevent Chinese immigrants from entering the country (Sadowski-Smith, 2014).

Phase 3: Immigration Pause (1920–1965)

This phase represents a dramatic change from the previous two phases, and it incorporates various national attitudinal shifts toward immigration and those who can be categorized as unsettling, with particular reference to criminalization and its dire consequences. In addition, criminalization and racialization must be viewed from a multifaceted perspective, although the anti-immigrant attitudes that laid the foundation for criminalization can be traced back to the previous two phases.

Criminalization of those who are unauthorized can arguably be traced back to the 1920s (B. F. Gonzalez, 2014; Ruiz Marrujo, 2014). In 1921, a quota system was developed whereby nations were limited in sending newcomers. This quota system did display favoritism toward the United Kingdom, Ireland, and Germany. It was not until 1924 (the Johnson–Reed Act) that the US Border Patrol was established, and its significance has varied according to historical period being discussed.

During the period from 1929 to 1941, there was minimal or no immigration due to the Great Depression. However, in the 1930s, the Great Depression witnessed the (repatriation) rounding up and deportation of 500,000 Mexicans, both those who were undocumented and those who were citizens. They became convenient scapegoats for the nation's joblessness and budget shortfalls (Gratton & Merchant, 2013; "Uneasy Neighbors," 2007), with strong parallels to the 2008 Great Recession period. This 500,000 figure is conservative; it is estimated that as many as 1.8 million Mexicans were deported (Wagner, 2017).

It can be argued that "repatriation" was the mislabeling of a deplorable action, and it would be better to have named it "removal," which is what we do with garbage or any other unwanted object. The racialization of these actions is undeniable. It is estimated, for instance, that 60% of those deported were US citizens (Wagner, 2017).

A more nuanced understanding of this policy is warranted because of the potential parallels with what could possibly happen under the Trump administration. Readers interested in a more detailed account of this period are referred to

Wagner's (2017) article, "America's Forgotten History of Illegal Deportations," or an even more detailed historical coverage in Balderrama and Rodriguez's (2006) book, *Decade of Betrayal: Mexican Repatriation in the 1930s.*

In an interview with Joseph Dunn, an expert on this act, Wagner (2017) states that

> back in Hoover's era, as America hung on the precipice of economic calamity—the Great Depression—the president was under enormous pressure to offer a solution for increasing unemployment, and to devise an emergency plan for the strained social safety net. Though he understood the pressing need to aid a crashing economy, Hoover resisted federal intervention, instead preferring a patchwork of piecemeal solutions, including the targeting of outsiders.
>
> According to former California State Senator Joseph Dunn, who in 2004 began an investigation into the Hoover-era deportations, "the Republicans decided the way they were going to create jobs was by getting rid of anyone with a Mexican-sounding name." "Getting rid of" America's Mexican population was a random, brutal effort. "For participating cities and counties, they would go through public employee rolls and look for Mexican-sounding names and then go and arrest and deport those people," said Dunn. "And then there was a job opening."

K. L. Hernández (2010) provides a history of the US Border Patrol and traces how it focused its attention and resources on apprehending undocumented Mexicans rather than following its mission to apprehend and deport all "undesirables," which is a category that includes many different groups deemed as compromising the nation; these groups were considered far more difficult to find. A mission focused on undocumented Mexicans was far easier to enforce, and it reinforced racist and nativist narratives.

Between World War I and World War II, Mexicans helped meet labor demands in the United States. The period from 1942 to 1956 in US–Mexico borderlands history stands out because of increased immigration law enforcement due to an immigration upsurge, which was blamed for causing the unemployment of an estimated 252,000 US domestic agricultural workers (A. E. Rosas, 2015). Ironically, in 1951, President Harry S. Truman signed Public Law 78 (the Bracero Program), which initiated the legal entry of an estimated 125,000 male Mexican immigrant laborers into the county to work in the agricultural industries and on the railroad in a maintenance capacity (Avera, 2016).

It can be argued that the basis for current immigration law can be traced back to 1952 and the passage of the Immigration and Naturalization Act (INA). Prior to the passage of INA, immigration laws existed in different pieces of legislation. The year 1953 witnessed passage of the Refugee Relief Act, which was eventually amended to grant political asylum, responding to the refugee crisis in post-war Europe and marking a humanitarian gesture in the United States' immigration history.

In 1954, President Eisenhower instituted "Operation Wetback" under the leadership of Major General Swing, which caused the deportation of 1 million undocumented workers back to Mexico that year and approximately 400,000 the following year. Ironically, the Immigration and Naturalization Service, in response to political pressure from growers, reprocessed many of these workers to be hired as braceros to work the land. This massive deportation policy left an indelible mark on this community, and it is why any talk of massive deportation has realistic, rather than symbolic, impact.

On a number of occasions during the 2016 presidential campaign, candidate Trump made reference to President Eisenhower and his efforts, and success, in deporting Mexicans, serving to highlight how this has been done in the past. Candidate Trump did not use the term "Operation Wetback" in these public pronouncements for obvious reasons. Similar to the economic upheavals of the past and that caused the repatriation of Mexicans in the 2000s, economic uncertainty caused the deportation of Mexicans to Mexico during the Eisenhower administration (J. R. Garcia, 1981; Here, 2016; K. L. Hernández, 2006).

Hyman and Iskander (2016) bring a different perspective to Operation Wetback—one that has tremendous implications for today:

> The most powerful agents for Operation Wetback were not in the border patrol but in the press corps. The operation, from its beginning, was a public relations campaign, as close to Trump's preferred medium—reality television—as was possible in the 1950s. Embedded in the border patrol crews that conducted raids throughout California and Texas, journalists wrote stories praising the professionalism of the "squads swooping down in surprise visits to farms, industrial plants, business and factories," as the *Los Angeles Times* put it. Major news outlets ran tallies of the number of "wetback captures" and noted the telephone tips flooding the switchboards at INS. Alongside these pieces, outlets ran photos, like those that appeared in the *New York Times* and the *Los Angeles Times*, of border patrol agents in crisp uniforms and helmets reviewing maps as they planned out their operations and of immigration officers and sheriff's deputies rounding up Mexican immigrants at the factories and farms where they worked. The INS celebrated the success of the program publicly.

A large number of deaths among these deportees occurred but generally went unnoticed in the United States. For example, there were 88 deportee deaths due to exposure that occurred near Mexicali because of extended exposed to 112-degree heat (Here, 2016).

Phase 4: Post-1965 Immigration

The almost 55-year period covered in this phase is quite significant even though it is a relatively short period when viewed historically, and it has the greatest relevance for those with a minimal interest in an in-depth understanding of immigration history. This period is best conceptualized as the tip of an iceberg, with the previous phases representing the ice below the water.

Strong nativism sentiments and actions can be traced back to the previous two immigration phases, reflecting the long reach of these feelings and how they have evolved over the years (Burghart & Zeskind, 2012):

> Nativism, active opposition to new immigrants and the changes they bring to the larger society, has been a part of American life since before the Anglo majority in the 1800s regarded Irish newcomers as pariahs. It was noticeably absent from most of the New Right in the mid-1970s and during the Reagan years. It was an observable element in the Klan-Aryan Nations white suprem- acist configuration during the same period, however. Within the parameters of the mainstream conservative universe, nativism owed its re-emergence largely, but not exclusively, to the Federation for American Immigration Reform (here- inafter FAIR) and the many organizations it helped spin off—particularly after Californians passed the era-defining Proposition 187 in 1994. (p. 3)

Unfortunately, hatred of newcomers, regardless of citizenship status, generally spans many different centuries and immigration phases. Future immigration historians will only extend this phase into the future, and depending on what happens under President Trump's administration, this may be a separate phase unto itself.

Unauthorized migration to the United States has been traced to the presence and interplay of four key factors, with each factor increasing or decreasing in sig- nificance depending on US policies: (1) economic crises in Mexico, (2) the ec- onomic restructuring and demand for inexpensive labor in the United States, (3) changes that have occurred in US immigration policy, and (4) the evolu- tion and corresponding maturation of migrants' transnational networks (K. L. Hernández, 2017).

Anti-Latino immigrant sentiment, regardless of citizenship status, largely derives from age-old sentiments pertaining to a "Latino threat" narrative based on their inability to assimilate ("refusing to learn English and hanging onto their cultural values") and, therefore, the view that they are undeserving of being in this country and achieving citizenship. These sentiments were also used against other immigrant groups throughout the nation's history (Estep. 2016).

It is logical to start this period with the enactment of the Immigration and Naturalization Act of 1965 (the Hart–Celler Act), passed in large part as the result of the civil rights movement and concerns raised about exploitation of Mexicans, which abolished this country's quota system based on national origin. This act established an immigration policy focused on reuniting immigrant families and attracting skilled labor to the country. The act increased the number of immigrants from Asian, African, and Latin American nations. An estimated 18 million legal immigrants entered the country, representing a 300% increase over the preceding 30 years.

The "undocumented problem" is generally traced to 1965, with primarily Mexicans and other Latin Americans entering the country, although emphasizing the former. Transnational migration is an integral topic within Mexico, and it takes on greater significance in that country than in the United States (Le Bot, 2016).

Notably, at the same time that the formerly undocumented were granted citizenship, there were also efforts to step up criminalizing the hiring of these immigrants and to increase the Border Patrol budget (Massey, Durand, & Pren, 2014). Not unexpectedly, the post-1965 period witnessed a dramatic increase in immigrants entering the United States (Massey & Pren, 2012). The "illegal" problem was crystalized as a national social problem in the 1970s when an estimated 600,000 undocumented persons entered, marking the beginning of the modern-era debate on unauthorized immigration (Gutiérrez, 2016).

In 1986, the passage of the Immigration Reform Act sought to curtail the influx of undocumented through more effective enforcement of immigration policies and opening up the possibilities to seek legal immigration. The act also created two amnesty programs and granted amnesty to more than 3 million of those who were unauthorized.

The year 1990 witnessed passage of the Immigration Act ("IMMACT," P.L. 101-649), expanding on the 1965 act and resulting in an increase of 700,000 immigrants. This act also established the category of Temporary Protected Status, which is addressed later in this book. This act provided the Attorney General with the power to avoid deportations by non-citizens to countries that are unstable or dangerous due to conflict, health epidemics, or natural disasters. This status is determined on a country-by-country and year-by-year basis (Guerra, 2017).

The 1990s witnessed a significant economic recession that fostered the growth of anti-immigrant (nativist) sentiments in the United States that continue to be experienced today, replicating previous periods in the nation's history (Schrag, 2010):

> It's hardly news that the complaints of our latter-day nativists and immigration restrictionists—from Sam Huntington to Rush Limbaugh, from FAIR to V-DARE—resonate with the nativist arguments of some three centuries of American history. Often, as most of us should know, the immigrants who were demeaned by one generation were the parents and grandparents of the successes of the next generation. Perhaps, not paradoxically, many of them, or their children and grandchildren, later joined those who attacked and disparaged the next arrivals, or would-be arrivals, with the same vehemence that had been leveled against them or their forebears.

The previous quotation summarizes the consequences of pulling the ladder up once we have climbed it, which is how I characterize this action. A global economy brings with it a global population displacement to meet increased demands for labor. The reactions to those who are undocumented are comparable to those experienced by the Great Recession of late 2007.

The 1996 signing of the Illegal Immigration and Immigrant Responsibility Act by President Clinton is widely credited for spurring the birth and rise of the

Minutemen (citizen border patrols that sought to apprehend those who are unauthorized crossing the borders) and fueling the "crackdown" on these immigrants (Becerra, 2012). Depending on one's view, Minutemen are either protecting this nation's borders or acting as vigilantes (Democracy Now, 2005):

> In Arizona, a group calling itself the Minuteman Project has stationed scores of men and women along the Mexican border in a controversial effort to track down undocumented immigrants. The Minutemen take their name from a militia group during the American Revolutionary War. The group's founder, James Gilchrist, says the project [since Oct. 1, 2004] has attracted some 450 volunteers from around the country. On Monday, Gilchirst said they aided in the arrest of 146 undocumented immigrants. The Minutemen have staked out across a 23-mile stretch of border northeast of Nogales for the month-long action. Many use binoculars and night-vision goggles. Some are armed with guns. Over 20 pilots with aircraft are also surveying the area. Organizers call their effort a peaceful protest over the government's failure to secure its borders. Both the Mexican government and the Bush administration have described them the Minutemen as vigilantes. Meanwhile, the American Civil Liberties Union has sent observers to keep tabs on the Minutemen to ensure they don't take the law into their own hands.

The militarized metaphors describing this group only reinforce the historical trend that continues to the present under the Trump administration.

Critics of this legislation, which incidentally was signed by a Democratic president, argued that it further legitimized the country's anti-immigrant sentiments and eventually led to Arizona's SB 1070, which essentially casted undocumented Mexicans into two criminalized groupings—narco-traffickers and terrorists—a highly stigmatizing and false narrative (Aguirre, 2012). It gave rise to other anti-immigrant legislation throughout the country, particularly in the South.

CIVIL WAR, DRUGS, VIOLENCE, AND UNAUTHORIZED IMMIGRATION

It is important to pause and set a foundation for this section on this country's role in creating instability in key Central American nations, which have been major sources of unauthorized migrants during this immigration phase. The dislocation of major groups of people within a nation can be the result of major events, such as natural disasters, revolutions, and other political events that result in a threat to their well-being and safety. Economic factors, such as hyperinflation and job losses, can also result in significant uprootment of people. The degree and intensity of such displacement in those situations pale in comparison to fears pertaining to physical safety (Perla, 2017; Zucker & Zucker, 2016).

Readers are warned that my view of history falls within the "left of center" political spectrum, and that influences my world view. The United States has historically played a major and destabilizing role in Latin America, with US actions causing displacement of large groups of people who eventually ended up in this country under very trying circumstances, to put it mildly (Gamso, 2014). The forces that were operating during these turbulent periods have not completely disappeared, opening up new waves of major group displacements. Current presidential administration efforts to restrict immigration of Muslims is one obvious example of these international forces.

The causes of violence have wielded tremendous influence in shaping major unauthorized movement phases to the United States and throughout the world (Bhatt, 2012):

> Equally important, for many sanctuary seekers, is the changed nature of militarism, humanitarism, war and conflict. We do not yet have adequate languages to grasp the variety of movements of people today across the globe, or the transformations of war and regional conflict since the late-1980s that have caused many of these movements. (p. 6)

Violence is a topic that everyone can understand and why fleeing these situations is a natural human response (Nazario, 2017).

Drugs, violence, and immigration are synonymous, but not for the reasons that are typically understood (Goldstein & Weiser, 2017). The influence of drugs is understood by helping professionals working in this nation's major urban centers. However, drugs, most notably cocaine/crack and heroin, have created economic opportunities in the United States with regard to their cultivation and distribution so that the world's largest market for this product has played, and is currently playing, a significant role in the uprootment and the entering of this country by those who are unauthorized.

If US foreign policies interfere in a sovereign nation's internal policies, and these actions result in people having to leave their countries due to safety fears, does the United States have a right to exclude these individuals by labeling them economic refugees versus political refugees? Labels make a world of difference. This issue is being raised because US policies in Central America have caused tremendous internal disruptions (Arias & Milian, 2013; Gorman, 2017).

El Salvador's civil war during the late 1970s and throughout the 1980s was not related to drugs but, rather, the result of a repressive regime backed by the United States. The United States' support of military dictatorships in Guatemala and El Salvador (Goth, 2013; Riosmena, 2016) made it virtually impossible for people fleeing these two countries to seek asylum in the United States, creating a no-win situation for them (S. Wright, 2017):

> By 1983, the number of Salvadorans and Guatemalans fleeing to the United States for protection had swollen, but only seven of 15,000 asylum applications had been granted. The U.S. government argued that these were not "asylum refugees" but "economic refugees," and therefore not entitled to asylum. The reality, however, was different. By the end of the first decade, more than 75,000 civilians in El Salvador and 200,000 civilians in Guatemala had been

assassinated or disappeared, for the most part victims of military regimes supported and funded by the United States. (p. 6)

Eyewitnesses and personal stories of atrocities involving torture and murder of church and humanitarian aid workers by death squads in Central American countries, with the support of the US government, helped fuel the birth of the sanctuary movement (Pirie, 2013). The US government played a significant role in siding with powerful forces in Central America to fight socialism and then turned around and blamed those seeking refuge in the United States, in essence blaming the victims. This injustice became intolerable, requiring a forceful and highly public response.

In El Salvador, a 12-year (1980–1992) civil war involving the military government fighting counter-insurgents caused the first major wave of Salvadorans to arrive in the United States during the early 1980s(Tejada, 2016). Guatemala and Honduras paralleled similar developments, which can be seen in present-day life in these countries.

Readers interested in a more in-depth coverage of this subject are fortunate because there are a number of outstanding books on the topic. The following are two examples: Jonas and Rodríguez's (2015) *Guatemala–US Migration: Transforming Regions* and Bassano's (2016) *Fight and Flight: The Central America Human Rights Movement in the United States in the 1980s*. In *The American Sanctuary Movement*, Tomsho (1987) provides a highly detailed and nuanced perspective on the social–political forces that led to the birth of the sanctuary movement in the United States. These books focus on the initial impact of violence in Guatemala, Honduras, and El Salvador, which has continued, creating a new form of push factor through the influence of drug cartels, particularly in Mexico.

In Mexico, violence and missing family members related to drug cartels are still prominent (Ahmed, 2017a; M. Fisher & Taub, 2017). Some Mexican towns have more in common with war zones than the popular images of towns associated with Mexico, creating an overall hostile climate for the country (Ahmed, 2017b):

Last year, the town [Tecoman] became the deadliest municipality in all of Mexico, with a homicide rate similar to a war zone's. . . . This year it is on track to double that figure, making it perhaps the most glaring example of a nationwide crisis. (p. A1)

Readers wishing to obtain insight into how violence, in this case in El Salvador, created an untenable climate forcing uprootment and the seeking of refuge, or sanctuary, in the United States should read the article "Killers on a Shoestring: Inside the Gangs of El Salvador" by Martinez, Martinez, and Sontag (2016), which states in part,

In collaboration with *The New York Times, El Faro*, a digital newspaper based in San Salvador, sought to pierce the secrecy surrounding the finances of the gangs that terrorize El Salvador, which is experiencing a level of deadly violence unparalleled outside war zones: 103 homicides per 100,000 residents last year, compared with five in the United States. With an estimated 60,000 members in a country of 6.5 million people, the gangs hold power disproportionate to their numbers. They maintain a menacing presence in 247 of 262 municipalities. They extort about 70 percent of businesses. They dislodge entire communities from their homes, and help propel thousands of Salvadorans to undertake dangerous journeys to the United States. Their violence costs El Salvador $4 billion a year.

It does not take a criminologist to understand how crime stifles economies and causes people to flee for safety. El Salvador and Mexico are not unique, unfortunately.

Drug cartel violence has replaced the violence from political civil wars, creating a new type of refugee fleeing the violence caused by drug activities (Correa-Cabrera, Garrett, & Keck, 2014). V. Rios (2014) provides an excellent account of this violence:

> Mexico's homicide rates have increased every year since 2004—particularly sharply since 2008—as a result of increases in territorial fights between drug cartels. From December of 2006 to 2010, 34,550 killings have been officially linked to organized crime, a dramatic increase from previous years (2000–2006) when only 8,901 killings were linked to organized crime. The major violence spike of 2008 came when drug-related homicides jumped from 2,826 to 6,837 killings, a 142% increase with respect to the previous year. In 2009, these rates increased by more than 40%, reaching 9,614 victims. By 2010, these figures had reached a record of 15,273 killings. In this last year, organized crime was officially responsible for 47% of all intended homicides happening in Mexico (Rios and Shirk, 2011). Mexico's security issues are particularly acute at the border. Drug-related homicides concentrate in border cities because US-Mexico crossing points the most profitable part of drug trafficking business chain. (pp. 4–5)

These "new" immigrants do not fall into the "typical" newcomer category as ones in search of employment and with specific goals related to economic gains.

BRIEF HISTORY OF THE WALL WITH MEXICO

Contextually, it is important to note that there is a worldwide movements toward building border walls. In 2017, it was estimated that there were 70 such structures, an increase from 20 in 2005, and in countries such as Austria, Hungary, Kenya, Saudi Arabia, and Tunisia (Nixon, 2017e). Border walls push crossers to areas that are more physically demanding and dangerous, thus increasing casualties.

Securing the border to keep out those who are undocumented has historical roots and has been the focus of attention throughout modern history, including present day, although quite intensified. Alternative media sources such as YouTube provide important alternative narratives to the criminalization themes addressed in mainstream media, including views of the wall (Lybecker et al., 2015). The majority of Americans are opposed to the building of a wall. Specifically, 61% of Texans oppose the wall.

Walls have a long history throughout the world, with some still standing long after their initial construction, such as the Great Wall of China in ancient history and the Berlin Wall in more modern times (Langerbein, 2009). One perspective of what the US–Mexico wall, or fence, means can be obtained by considering the number of deaths that have occurred in its vicinity: One estimate is that 10 times the number of deaths have occurred near the US–Mexico wall as occurred near the Berlin Wall (A. E. Rosas, 2015). Those interested in reading an in-depth history of the fence, or wall, are not at a loss to find countless books on the subject.

Initially, the wall with Mexico was not a "wall" but a fence, attempting to accomplish the same goals as a concrete wall, and its primary goal was not restricting the flow of the undocumented, which will undoubtedly be surprising to readers (Krasner, n.d.):

> As of the present day, the 1,933-mile border between the United States and Mexico is the most heavily crossed—both legally and illegally—international boundary in the world. It is armored with stretches of steel and barbed wire, fortified with infrared cameras, imposing watchtowers, and blinding floodlights, and is patrolled by over twenty thousand guards. Desire to control illegal immigration is the main impetus for the ever-expanding militarization of the border today; however, the initiating force catalyzing its development was far more modest and had nothing to do with regulating the flow of people. Somewhat ironically, fencing on the border at Organ Pipe National Monument was initiated to protect the fragile environment and livestock from the damage and disease brought by migrating animals. It was only later that several key developments in U.S. policy accelerated the expansion of the border fence and couched the problem in human immigration and national security terms.

The reasons for the initiation of this barrier have evolved in a manner that do not come close to resembling its original environmental purposes.

Casey and Watkins (2014) refer to the "dehumanizing tide of American racism" in discussing this country's views and actions toward our southern neighbors, and nowhere is this more apparent than when discussing the construction of an impenetrable wall. The border wall, too, has been cast as an act of war when grounded within the history of the Southwest and Native Americans, taking it beyond a focus on Mexicans (Tamez, 2012).

The typical media image of the wall is lifeless and sterile, but it is quite the opposite, with vibrancy and color where it exists, and it is a part of countless lives (Díaz-Barriga & Dorsey, 2016; Dorsey & Diaz-Barriga, 2010; R. Jones, 2014). "*Al muro*," which Latinos refer to in Spanish, is a barrier that cuts across social, cultural, and economic history (Thompson, 2015). A physical wall is an artifact of the geopolitical tension between these two countries. Nieto-Gomez's (2014) multifaceted chronology of the border fence's original intent and evolution may be helpful to readers.

The legal basis on which presidential administrations have used to construct a wall can be challenged in the nation's courts (Sundberg, 2015). After September 11, 2001, the building of the wall became what many consider to be a national obsession, bringing a concrete symbol to go along with a renewed emphasis on criminalization of those who are unauthorized (Correa, 2013). President George W. Bush signed the Secure Fence Act (October 26, 2006), mandating construction of 850 miles of "fencing" (double-layered). It was projected to cost $1.4 billion but was never built. In 2017, this same fence was projected to cost $4 billion (Corsi, 2016).

The Mexico border is not uniform. The area between San Diego and Tijuana consists of metal barriers, not fence, similar to the one between Nogales, Arizona, and Nogales, Mexico; other parts have double-layered fences, and yet other parts do not have any physical barrier (McGuire, 2013; Spener, 2014). It is estimated that only 5%, or 36.3 miles, of the double-layer fencing is complete (Farley, 2011):

> DHS reports that there is now fencing for 649 of the 652 miles described in the Secure Fence Act of 2006. But the vast majority of the requirement was met with vehicle barriers and single-layer pedestrian fence. The original act specifically called for double-layer fencing, and only 36.3 miles of double-layered fencing currently exist. However, the act was later amended to allow Border Security the discretion to determine which type of fencing was appropriate for different areas.

In 2007, the Department of Homeland Security was provided with an option on how to plan this barrier because it was not practical to have a double-layered fence across the 700 miles due to uneven terrain, necessitating different types of barriers.

PATHWAY TO CITIZENSHIP?

The historical context provided previously in this chapter facilitates a better appreciation of what a pathway to citizenship means for the unauthorized who wish to go this route. Not every member of this group wishes to do so. However, it is fair to say that a significant portion of those who are undocumented will take this option if provided. Mollenkopf and Pastor (2013) expressed a hopeful stance that in the mid-2010s immigration reform was possible:

> With Congress gearing up for comprehensive immigration reform, many hope that the era of growing localization of immigration policy will become a thing of the past. After all, one of the reasons given for the April 2010 legislation in Arizona—the infamous Senate Bill 1070 that required local law enforcement and public agency officials to determine the immigration status of individuals about whom they had "reasonable suspicion" that they might be undocumented

immigrants—was that local officials felt that the state needed to protect itself against a surge of "illegals" that an ineffective federal government had failed to hold back. In Alabama, Georgia, and elsewhere, political leaders were inspired to follow suit with their own attempts at what some have called "enforcement through attrition"—the notion that local authorities should make life so difficult for undocumented residents that they will willingly "self-deport." (p. 1)

The hope expressed by Mollenkopf and Pastor did not materialize, and this will most likely be the case for the next few years, at best.

There are numerous roadblocks to a citizenship path for millions of unauthorized residents wishing to remain in the United States. One barrier stands out, and it has often been referred to by Republicans in arguing against such a move for the unauthorized currently in this country—namely that they are Democrats in waiting because the lion's share of these new citizens would be expected to register as Democrats.

This political concern manifests itself in national elections and is most acutely experienced at the state and local levels. The prospect of "hordes of new Democrats" joining the electoral ranks will play an influential role in any path to citizenship legislation. This perspective is exacerbated when combined with dramatic changes in demographics and projections, such as increasing numbers of Latinos (Hong et al., 2017). An estimated 803,000 Latinos turn voting age every year, and the number of eligible Latino voters reached 27.3 million in 2016, up from 19.5 million in 2008, or an increase of 28.6% (Krogstad et al., 2016). It has been argued that the potential Latino political electoral power has not been realized (Pastor, 2016).

President George W. Bush did manage to get a sizable percentage of the Latino vote, and this was a counter-narrative to the Latino who is undocumented being a Democrat in waiting, introducing the potential of bipartisan support for a pathway to citizenship (Cisneros, 2017). While Texas governor (1995–2000), George U. Bush did not embrace an anti-unauthorized immigrant agenda, and this effectively translated into garnering political support from Latinos in the 2000 and 2004 presidential elections (Barreto et al., 2014). However, post 2004, a Republican Party anti-immigrant shift to what many considered the extreme right regarding immigration and those who are unauthorized effectively left a pathway toward citizenship to the Democratic Party.

A counter-narrative, without supporting evidence, has emerged that granting those who are unauthorized a pathway toward citizenship is unfair to those who are waiting in line and doing what is expected of them, with such a move reinforcing a narrative that hordes will continue to come in the hopes of achieving citizenship in the future (T. K. Wong & Kosnac, 2017). In the meantime, they occupy a position as "second-class citizens." This position is disempowering, leaving them vulnerable to marginalizing actions (Haas, 2017; Matis, 2016).

Going to the back of the line is often presented as ensuring fairness, using imagery to which everyone can relate. Imagine what it means for someone who is unauthorized having to go to an ICE office for an appointment. It is not a "simple" trip but, rather, can mean altering the person's life if he or she is deported, as more commonly occurs today. For those seeking to obtain legal permanent resident status (family based and employment based), there is no one line, and no one knows how long the wait is either (Bergeron, 2013).

Newcomers, particularly those of color, low-income, with low formal educational attainment, and residing in highly marginalized communities, are highly stigmatized in this society (Henderson, 2016). When imprisoned, they are also stigmatized and considered "second-class non-citizens," without the same rights as their citizen counterparts (Bosworth, 2016).

Readers have probably made their mind up about how they feel about those who are unauthorized and citizenship. In all likelihood, readers had a strong opinion before venturing to read this book, and the ending stance of this section and chapter is a foregone conclusion for them. There is intense passion on both sides of this issue. Passion equates with saliency and hope. It also equates with "strong feelings," which can interfere with arriving at a rationale decision.

Finding a middle ground is arduous. Just saying "pathway to citizenship" engenders a bitter response on both sides of the issue. The days when wanting to be a part of this country and swearing alliance to the Constitution were sufficient reason to enter, and become a citizen, are long gone. National boundaries are solidifying as economies and communications are becoming globalized. Goods and capital can move more freely, but people cannot.

Globalization, too, has meant a re-examination of what it means to be a citizen (Hoover, 2013). The question is whether citizenship is necessary to become a permanent part of a nation (Gutierrez, 2015). The quest for greater border mobility is a natural extension of a globalized society, although safety is not guaranteed for all, and greatly dependent on race/ethnicity and socioeconomic class (Milivojevic, Segrave, & Pickering, 2016).

Does the country create a stratified system of membership that falls just short of citizenship but allows those who are unauthorized to remain in the country? Critics argue that it is reminiscent of slavery, in which a major portion of the country consisted of non-voting members with limited rights. "Second-class" citizenship is a term often used for any outcome that does not grant the unauthorized outright citizenship. It is safe to say that no one strives to achieve a "second-class" status, and that is why this a term is laden with negative connotations.

The national consequences of not having a viable path toward citizenship means that localities must deal with a broken immigration system, with actions often being reactionary and dissonant with the US Constitution (Payan & De la Garza, 2014). As more sites adopt their own version of immigration laws, the country will become more fractured, and those who are undocumented will both reap the benefits and pitfalls, dependent on where they live, with sanctuary cities being such an example.

CONCLUSION

This chapter covered a vast immigration terrain, which was essential to set a foundation from which to view, and appreciate, how the unauthorized have emerged as a major population group and why the sanctuary city movement has taken on such prominence in national discourse. The United States is hopelessly tied to its past.

The multiple immigration phases this country has experienced cover an extended historical span, with each phase's dates being open to interpretation. The expansion of the nation occurred during periods in which great atrocities were committed, from enslavement of Africans to the displacement and almost complete genocide of Native Americans. The significance of immigrants cannot be debated.

Readers should have garnered an appreciation for how immigration unfolded over the country's history. It is impossible to view the unauthorized separate from the country's foreign policies in supporting dictators and its fight against communism in Latin America. This history is the result of significant social, political, and economic forces that remain even today.

Chapter 3 provides a different dimension to immigration that is often overlooked in broad discussions of this topic. We cannot disentangle negative attitudes toward cities from the characteristics of those who live in these entities. Cities have played, and continue to play, an instrumental role in the lives of immigrants. Cities, not unexpectedly, have been the focus of intense political attention in the early part of President Trump's administration, with all of the markings of continuing in the immediate future.

3

Cities, Immigrants, and the Undocumented

INTRODUCTION

Cities worldwide are destinations for immigrants, causing shifts in their composition, making them younger and more racially and ethnically diverse, and possibly unbalancing racial relationships within and between communities (Amaral, 2016; Burki, 2017). Cities, first and foremost, are places where there are employers that require a wide range of knowledge and skill sets, public transportation systems, religious institutions for all faiths, histories related to immigrants, and access to cultural institutions, thus making them attractive to immigrants.

Although the term *sanctuary* generally has very specific meaning and parameters, it is used in a different forms when addressing cities as a destination and their role in integrating newcomers, regardless of citizenship status. Cities provide opportunities for new identities for newcomers (Sassen, 2013) and space for hope to emerge and dreams to be realized.

Discussions of the United States' undocumented "problem" cannot be separated from its cities, particularly those that are major urban centers both regionally and nationally (R. Smith, 2014; Vitiello, 2014). Cities have great significance in combatting national anti-immigrant sentiments, to the point of embracing a sanctuary city label in sending a message to their states and the country that resists an anti-immigrant narrative and engaging in active resistance.

Tracing immigrant history and cities brings together scholars and practitioners interested in urban immigration history, heightening understanding of the nation's evolution and what we can expect or hope for in the future. Unfortunately, it also brings an often overlooked bias that the nation's founding fathers had toward cities (Conn, 2014), helping to create a bias against cities and immigrants that exists today. A host of terms are used to describe urban areas, such as "jungle," "violence," "decay," "crime," "decline," "drug abuse," and "poverty." Rarely does one hear "oasis" or "sanctuary" used in describing cities.

This negative close association is the result of a significant interplay of social, economic, political, and cultural factors that continue to play a role in anti-immigrant settlement and resettlement patterns (Darling, 2016), particularly in the country's 20 largest major cities. Some of these cities, particularly on both coasts, stand out in importance and are worthy of focus, offering the places and spaces that argue against humans being called "illegal" (Vrasti & Dayal, 2016).

The relationship between immigrants and cities, when taking into account the nation's love–hate relationship with cities, is in large part the result of how the founding fathers distrusted and disliked cities, based on their experiences in Europe (Conn, 2014). Urban places have resisted these negative perceptions and offered counter-narratives that are resiliency and social justice based, including the presence of hope and sanctuary from governmental forces (Nicholls & Uitermark, 2016).

This chapter grounds this rich history to increase understanding of why certain cities have embraced a sanctuary designation and how this movement owes a great debt to the nation's cities. Furthermore, Republican national polices have largely eschewed cities as major recruitment centers for voters, which has complicated efforts to find a bipartisan solution for how the United States will position itself in the immediate and distant future, particularly as it continues its march toward urbanization, which is occurring worldwide.

This chapter does not provide a highly detailed historical account because there are excellent books on this subject, which are cited. The chapter's sections are highly interrelated, setting the stage for the remaining chapters. It is impossible to appreciate sanctuaries without an urban context.

URBAN ACTIVISM AND HUMAN RIGHTS ISSUES

There is a natural relationship between activism and human rights. Immigration policies get implemented within the context of where the unauthorized live, work, play, and worship, and often as a result of social activism. Cities are home to millions of the nation's undocumented and are playing significant roles in shaping immigration law at the local level, with implications far beyond urban centers, and they can be expected to continue to do so in the immediate future (Mollenkopf & Pastor, 2016).

Cities are also a beacon for garnering media attention, magnifying events and actions that can reach far beyond their borders. A protest march in a rural county does not receive the same publicity as one in a high-profile city. The "Women's March" after President Trump's inauguration, although also including men and children, received worldwide publicity because of its presence in major cities (Sheppard, 2017). The same can be said for the "March for Science" demonstration.

The significance of the sanctuary movement is most represented in the nation's cities. This movement is not called the "sanctuary suburban," "sanctuary county," or "sanctuary rural" movement. Some would argue that cities are critical in this movement. The nation's cities have historically been gathering places for activists on human rights and social justice movements, setting the stage for the convergence of these activities and the immigrant rights movement (Nicholls, Uitermark, & van Haperen, 2016; Ridgley, 2012).

Cities have played historic roles in rights issues ranging from civil to GLBTQ, women's, environmental, and now immigrant and undocumented rights (Su, 2013). Some advocates argue that these movements would have faced even greater challenges if it were not for cities acting as vehicles for bringing major national changes. Furthermore, generally, Democrats have their base in cities, and Republicans have their base in suburbs and rural sections of the country (Davidson, Sours, & Moll, 2016). These voting patterns played out in the 2016 presidential election.

Cities have been influential in social justice movements and various civil rights-focused campaigns, and they are often home to organizations that can be mobilized to address various justice campaigns (Pallares, 2014). These places create opportunities for activists and residents to join in efforts that might otherwise be much more difficult if transpiring in suburban or rural areas.

Newcomer city integration has been facilitated by the interplay of three social–political factors or forces (de Graauw & Vermeulen, 2016): (1) local governments that are politically "left leaning" or progressive, (2) the fact that newcomer communities represent a significant segment of the voting population that vote on issues of concern to themselves and on behalf of the undocumented, and (3) an infrastructure of community organizations that can lobby for laws and policies that protect their well-being. Inner cities generally stand out as places where those who are undocumented are most welcomed, allowing the tapping of social and cultural capital in meeting their basic needs and achieving a sanctuary (Price & Breese, 2016).

Sanctuary cities bestow de facto citizenship on all residents, thus assuring residents that they are valued and have rights (Markowitz, 2015). Nationalizing the political identities of all residents generates radical and universal conceptions of rights and citizenship, essential in achieving well-being in any society (Nicholls, 2013).

URBAN INFORMAL SETTLEMENTS

The slogan "right to the city" has gained worldwide popularity because it captures a liberating stance that values urban justice and democratization of development that is inclusive driven, setting a backdrop for how cities can respond to their unauthorized residents (Katiya & Reid, 2012). The use of the term *informal urban settlements* introduced a concept that helps our understanding of the relationship between cities and the undocumented and why cities are in the foreground of embracing their worldwide presence.

Typically, informal settlements refer to city areas where housing units have been constructed on land that occupants occupy illegally. These areas can be found under bridges, in remote areas of parks, or they may be new facilitates that do not enjoy frequent foot traffic (Lombard, 2014; Nagourney, 2017; E. Sullivan & Olmedo, 2015). This concept also applies to abandoned buildings (Andrews & Caron, 2016). Durst and Wegmann (2017) challenged the notion that informal housing is a phenomenon that is not applicable to the United States. New housing modules are being proposed to provide housing in neighborhoods that have informal settlements (Kent Fitzsimons, 2017).

The emergence of urban informal settlements (residents do not possess necessary identity documents and official documents confirming their right to live there) influences the local economy and a community's social fabric (Patel & Baptist, 2012):

> There is also a lack of data about informal settlements—their scale, boundaries, populations, buildings, enterprises—and the needs of their inhabitants. This also implies their exclusion from government policies and public investments. All informal settlements exhibit some aspects of illegality, but they cannot be considered marginal or exceptional when they house between one-third and two-thirds of the population of so many cities. This also means that they provide a very large proportion of these cities' workforce. They represent important and persistent forms of urbanism that have multiple and complex links with the rest of the city. Many also have long histories. A lack of documentation about these informal settlements contributes to a lack of understanding about their importance to city economies. It serves as an excuse for public sector agencies not to provide infrastructure and services. It also means that there is no evidence to counter the inaccurate claims by politicians or civil servants that those living in informal settlements are law breakers or unemployed migrants who should go back to rural areas.

Cities are sufficiently large to accommodate informal living spaces and integrate "non-typical residents." These settlements transform their surroundings, and they in turn are transformed in the process, bringing an added dimension to this experience (M. E. Smith et al., 2015).

For informal settlements to emerge, the cooperation of key local leaders and community institutions, such as houses of worship and civil rights and human service organizations, is required; these leaders and institutions aid immigrants in making a new life in this country. The term "squatter settlement" is usually associated with informal settlements, and it has a national meaning among urban residents in this country.

CITIES AND IMMIGRANTS

Where would major US cities be without immigrants? Specifically, where would they be without Latinos? The emergence of Latinos as a major demographic group has helped transform cities (Price, 2012). Although they live throughout all areas of the country, the majority have chosen to reside in the nation's cities. Cities represent key economic and political centers in the country.

Immigrant attraction to cities was discussed previously but is worthy of extra attention. The country's ability to integrate its foreign-born population has profound implications for the future of the nation and its major urban centers, as it has in the past (National Academies, 2016). Diversity does not just relate to ethnicity and race, for example, but can also encompass generational and citizen-ship statuses.

Cities with populations that are more formally educated and ethnically/ra-cially diverse but fiscally sound, although still facing economic challenges, have been found to be more receptive of those who are undocumented (Huang & Liu, 2016). This same conclusion can be made regarding welcoming organizations. This attraction is increasingly becoming mutual. Newcomers to urban centers, as in previous centuries, bring energy, hope, and an eagerness to work in difficult and low-prestige jobs, which translates into significant positive economic benefits (Cooke & Kemeny, 2016; Kemeny & Cooke, 2017).

The unauthorized trafficking on the US–Mexico border has decreased signifi-cantly, with 65,000 arrests in fiscal year (FY) 2016, down approximately 50% from FY 2012; however, Rio Grande, Texas, did experience an increase (Associated Press, 2017a). Mexican border arrests between September 2016 and 2017, in turn, numbered 310,531, a decrease of 25%; however, arrests within the United States numbered 143,470, a 25% increase during the same period (Nixon, 2017h). The country of origin of those apprehended was Mexico in 42% of cases, with the remaining 58% coming from El Salvador, Guatemala, and Honduras (Miroff, 2017b).

Although the number of undocumented persons entering the country has decreased significantly, that is not the case in cities bordering the Texas–Mexico border (Rios, 2014):

> Even if the US as a whole has experienced a decrease in the number of Mexican immigrants, the opposite seems to be true for US cities located at the border. Mexican immigration to El Paso, McAllen, Brownsville and other cities in Texas have actually increased, increasing the price of housing and promoting the development of brand new housing complexes targeting Mexican consumers. (p. 2)

Immigration can aid cities with significant population loses, such as Baltimore (Filomeno, 2017a), representing an emerging national strategy in cities with histories of attracting immigrants (Morello & Lazo, 2012):

> After decades of seeing the city's population slide with every census count, Baltimore officials are trying to turn things around. One key strategy is embracing immigrants, in the hope they will encourage friends and family to join them. . . . The welcome mats thrown out by struggling cities and states stand in stark contrast to the reception immigrants have faced in places such as Arizona and Alabama. There, laws requiring police to ask a person's im-migration status have raised concerns about racial profiling among many immigrants, whether or not they are in the country legally, and many have left because of the stricter laws, as well as the recession. . . . Baltimore has undergone a shift in attitude. In 2004, then-Maryland Comptroller William Donald Schaefer (D), a former mayor and governor, chastised immigrants

who don't speak English well after a Spanish-speaking cashier at a McDonald's had trouble understanding his order. "I don't want to adjust to another language," Schaefer said. "This is the United States. I think they ought to adjust to us." Eight years later, Baltimore and many other cities are adjusting. The 2010 census was a tipping point. Most cities that grew had Hispanics and, to a lesser degree, Asians to thank. Cities with few immigrants lost political power and federal money as district lines and funding formulas changed to reflect new census numbers.

Although the goal is to attract immigrants who are either citizens or have permission to be in the country (green cards), these communities also accept those who are unauthorized because they want to live in communities in which there is a common history, language, values, and that are welcoming. Such efforts have faced criticism because they attract unauthorized people.

Immigrant influx has created demands for goods and services to meet their needs. Those who are undocumented, for instance, can have businesses of their own, such as cleaning services, street vendors, and food trucks. These businesses meet local needs and inject vitality into neighborhoods, increasing economic, social, and cultural capital.

Resistance to these efforts can come from city officials and Latino-owned businesses that must contend with high overhead costs, including paying local taxes (Bhimji, 2010). Increasing numbers of Latino small businesses in expanding Latino communities have been found to be indicators of communities with decreasing crime, even when there are increasing numbers of undocumented (Stansfield, 2014). These small businesses, too, have provided Latinos who are undocumented with an opportunities for employment (Delgado, 2011).

Cities have been singled out as key places where new norms and identities can be made, and playing a significant role in any discussion of immigration (Sassen, 2013). Changing the prevailing deficit narrative through economic success stories, including the undocumented becoming integral parts of their community's social well-being, helps humanize these individuals.

CHANGE LAWS BUT DO NOT BREAK THEM?

A persuasive argument can be made that a nation of laws cannot pick and choose which laws we obey or break. Rather, if we do not like the law, then we must change the law, as in any democracy. Readers can understand this reasoned approach. One law and order theme stands out in the response by critics of sanctuary cities (Crossley, 2017):

I've been thinking about the ordinary people who, throughout history, have provided sanctuary for those who would be persecuted. For example, we're *still* learning the names and true stories of the many who put themselves at great risk to protect the Jews from the Nazis. The new film "The Zookeeper's Wife" reveals the authentic harrowing tale of a Polish zookeeper and his wife, who hid hundreds of Jewish people from the Warsaw Ghetto in their home and the zoo grounds. They offered a refuge; a sanctuary. . . . These days the word "sanctuary" has taken on a charged political meaning with so-called sanctuary cities under fire as shelters for undocumented immigrants in danger of deportation. The politics may be new, but the idea of sanctuary cities is old—traced back to the Old Testament. . . . Many are infuriated that people in the country illegally in the first place are sheltered by volunteers. I understand the anger, even the fears of some who believe sanctuary cities safeguard violent criminals. Immigration experts say, however, people born in the U.S. commit more crimes than undocumented immigrants. But, I know the idea of sanctuary resonates at a gut level. Legally and practically, we can't pick and choose laws we follow, but emotionally, sometimes, it just feels wrong not to. It must have felt wrong to abolitionist Lewis Hayden and the Polish zookeeper and his wife, who both broke the law by harboring escaping slaves and hunted Jewish citizens. In the absence of comprehensive immigration policy, my gut tells me the least we can offer is refuge and sanctuary.

There is a time when a nation's laws are wrong, and this is that time. We must make up our own minds on when a law is unjust. Sanctuary cities are not in the business of harboring criminals; rather, they, at the most basic level, simply refuse to do the work of the federal government's immigration policies. The criminal narrative is emphasized by "law and order" advocates. They have been lax on policing themselves. So law and order is only applied to one side.

The close relationships of anti-immigrant presidential appointments, and even ascending into prominent positions within the current administration of reputed White supremacists, has solidified an anti-undocumented stance, making it even more difficult to address an anti-sanctuary city position without acts of defiance (Kulish, 2017a). Defiance is patriotic rather than subversive and anti-American; the nation was founded on acts of defiance!

If laws are unjust, if not immoral, it will take acts of defiance to highlight this and move elected officials to change the laws. Laws that are unfair do not change because elected officials wake up one morning and decide to make changes. The sanctuary movement has exposed the injustices of immigration laws that criminalize those whose only crime is being in this country without proper documentation.

There are hundreds of thousands here without proper documentation; they overstayed their visas and avoided the glare of public and presidential attention. At the end of 2016, there were 629,000 visa overstays (Nixon, 2017g). The sanctuary movement has rightly focused on those who crossed the border by land through the southern part of the country and who are singled out for racial reasons. That is why many in the movement view this human rights and social justice effort as the civil rights movement of our era. Shedding light on inconsistencies and injustices through acts of defiance will bring about changes in the nation's broken immigration laws and system.

SANCTUARY NEW YORK CITY AS A CASE IN POINT

As someone born and raised in New York City, although in a different part of the city from that of President Trump, I point out some fundamental misconceptions pertaining to newcomers that must not go unchallenged. Readers can take issue, and a healthy debate is always essential in democracies, and this goes back to the origins of democracy in Athens, Greece.

Any form of federal governmental threat directed at sanctuary sites must be seriously deconstructed, as we have done with criminalization of those who are undocumented. Putting aside the legality of stopping funding, it can be considered ludicrous that Attorney General Sessions would stop grant funds from going to New York City, considering the city's role in the history of dealing with terrorism and in addressing present-day threats. The nation's cities are targets for terrorism because of their symbolic value and potential to generate global publicity. Terrorists attacking a small rural town, although tragic, will not generate worldwide publicity. Regardless of our views on large cities, this point can be considered as an axiom.

The prospect of cities, such as New York, being punished through withholding of federal funds defies logic in order to fulfill a campaign promise made by President Trump in support of his voter base, the majority of whom do not reside in cities. These anti-urban sentiments cannot get lost in these actions and draw us back to Chapter 2. President Trump is a New Yorker, having spent almost all his life in that city. One would guess that such a distinction would make him acutely aware of his surroundings regarding business opportunities and issues related to crime and safety. I recall when he took issue with Senator Cruz during the presidential campaign and the dog whistle statement he made about "New York values." Trump's response was on target then, counteracting the underlining message that Senator Cruz was attempting to make to the nation, at the expense of New York City.

Without delving too much into data, New York City does not stand out for being "crime ridden" or "crime infected." In 2016, New York City's major crime rates fell to the lowest levels in recorded history (Kanno-Youngs, Calvert, & Gay, 2017). Its immigrant population, regardless of citizenship status, has remained very constant throughout its long history as a port of entry, including present day.

CONCLUSION

My bias toward cities is rather obvious. I am sure readers raised in suburban or rural America also share a similar passion for their birthplaces. These experiences have a profound impact on our world view growing up and currently, and sometimes we are not even aware of this information.

Cities that have achieved greater autonomy because of their political and economic capital are in a better position to craft responses to repressive or reactionary immigration policies, including enlisting the support of key organizations in these campaigns (Zorn, 2014). Any effort by the current presidential administration to "punish" Boston, Chicago, Los Angeles, New Orleans, New York City, or San Francisco, for example, will result in a no-win situation that will further polarize the country.

When major religious groups in these cities join this human rights and social justice struggle, they, too, will galvanize support from congregations throughout the country, including those in "red" and "purple" states. Cities are a vital part of this country, and some would argue that this country would not be "exceptional" without the power and symbolism of its cities. Those who are foreign born, authorized and unauthorized, are vital parts of these cities, as they have been since the nation's beginning.

4

Who Are the Unauthorized?

INTRODUCTION

Readers recognize the pitfalls of sweeping generalizations of any group of people and the immense power of labels in shaping popular opinions, and this is the case when discussing newcomers. Labels convey a great deal of information and sentiments, either explicitly or implicitly.

Labels of "alien," "illegal," or "undocumented," for instance, bring strong emotional responses on both sides of the political spectrum, necessitating that we take a moment to inform ourselves of the lives behind these labels. We must never forget that we are talking about human beings who are vulnerable psychologically, socially, economically, and politically because they are in a country that is not their own, they speak a non-English language, and they must cope with a set of values foreign to them (H. Hernandez, 2015).

This chapter develops a portrait of those who are undocumented, and it seeks to capture their voices and humanize a subject that desperately warrants humanization. Humanization occurs by pulling back labels and numbers and capturing their stories, which uplift their sacrifices, dreams, struggles, and injustices suffered (Ochoa, 2016; Reed-Sandoval, 2016).

Urrea (2015) addresses the invisibility of those who are undocumented:

> Undocumented immigrants have no way to tell you what they have experienced, or why, or who they are, or what they think. They are by the very nature of their experience, invisible. Most of us pass them by—some of us might say a prayer for them, some of us wish they would return to their countries of origin. But nobody asks them what they think. Nobody stops and asks. (p. 5)

Their invisibility dehumanizes them, and if we were to engage and really listen to them, they have a story to share that we can relate to.

Their stories bring statistics to life and reinforce why those interested in this subject must never take a back seat in national discussions. Each life impacts countless other lives and their communities and countries of origin. Eliciting their stories requires a commitment to do so and the time to listen and ask questions, as well as being prepared to have questions asked of us because we, too, have narratives to share.

The displacement of millions of people is a worldwide phenomenon, with no indications that it will subside anytime soon (Nail, 2015):

> The twenty-first century will be the century of the migrant. At the turn of the twenty-first century, there were more migrants than ever before in recorded history. Today there are over 1 billion migrants. Each decade, the percentage of migrants as a share of total population continues to rise, and in the next twenty-five years, the rate of migration is predicted to be higher than in the last twenty-five. More than ever, it is becoming necessary for people to migrate due to environmental, economic, and political instability. In particular, climate change may even double international migration over the next forty years. What is more, the percentage of total migrants who are nonstatus or undocumented is also increasing, thus posing a serious challenge to democracy and political representation. (p. 187)

This phenomenon will be addressed differently in each receiving country (Koca, 2016), but there will be overlapping themes. The United States will not be exempt from these influences while concomitantly making its own contribution, with the sanctuary movement being one prominent example.

LABELS AND IMMIGRATION

It is impossible to separate "labels" from the topic of "immigration." The term "citizenship," too, brings discussion points that are open to debate and, therefore, controversy (Rosenbloom, 2013). Labels of any kind frequently wrap up a range of factors and emotions into a "neat little package." Labeling the undocumented, such as "criminal aliens," brings together two emotionally charged and deficit-centered identities, making it easier to consider them not human (Kubrin, Zatz, & Martinez, 2012).

While seeking the 1988 Democratic presidential nomination, Reverend Jesse Jackson remarked on the problem of "illegal aliens." Although I did not know it at the time, his remarks would stay with me to this day. Simply stated, "illegal" brings a connotation pertaining to criminal behavior; "alien," in turn, elicits images of E.T. (extraterrestrial), which was a popular movie at that time. Those who are unauthorized are not criminals, although that narrative is well established, and they are not from other planet either.

Lakoff and Ferguson (2017) address the power of language in framing immigration in this country:

> Framing is at the center of the recent immigration debate. Simply framing it as about "immigration" has shaped its politics, defining what count as "problems" and constraining the debate to a narrow set of issues. The language is telling.

The linguistic framing is remarkable: frames for illegal immigrant, illegal alien, illegals, undocumented workers, undocumented immigrants, guest workers, temporary workers, amnesty, and border security. These linguistic expressions are anything but neutral. Each framing defines the problem in its own way, and hence constrains the solutions needed to address that problem.

The terms "people without documentation," "migrants with undocumented status," and "people in motion," for example, capture this social phenomenon without using derogatory labels (Ryer, 2014).

Van Horn (2016), too, addresses the importance of immigration labels:

> Advocates have long fought over the terms used to describe the people most affected by antiimmigration policies. Progressives have preferred the use the term "undocumented" instead of "illegal," arguing that the latter influences public opinion on policy fights in favor of white supremacists. Conservatives, however, have long insisted on using the word "illegal," saying that any alternative terms mask the fundamental "legal violations" committed by those who overstay their visas or enter the country without one. Policy analysts, demographers, and federal agencies have tended to use the term "unauthorized immigration" in a supposed attempt to use a more descriptively accurate and politically less laden term to refer to those eligible for deportation. Most importantly though, those competing claims share the belief that framing has an important consequence in shaping public opinion toward the undocumented and policy. (pp. 4–5)

Terms describing a social phenomenon are very telling of its sensitivity, as was the case with the Japanese "internment camps" versus "imprisonment camps" and "camps" versus "concentration camps" during World War II. The term "prison camps," too, has been part of this landscape and can be traced back to the Civil War, during which 56,000 soldiers died while in captivity.

For most Americans, the connotation of "camp" engenders images of summer camp, games, swimming, fun, and so on. These types of camps are nothing like any camp that I have attended. The term "detained" is another example that emerges in communications on what constitutes "arrest" and "imprisonment." The same can be said of "deportation" versus "removal" (Golash-Boza, 2015). The latter term brings a range of negative associations to "soften" the reality of what it really connotes. The term "deportation" is bandied about to describe a mundane and not a forceful event, which in reality is far from mundane or violence free.

The following description of "illegal" immigration, which seems to be the preferred term used by those opposed to people without authorization, puts the discussion in a historical and highly criminalized light (American Immigration Council, 2016):

> As laws were passed to keep out Asians and Eastern and Southern Europeans, immigrants from those countries—as well as others who could not pass literacy

tests, pay the head tax, or enter through the quota system—began to enter outside of the legal system. In 1925, the Immigration Service reported 1.4 million immigrants living in the country illegally. A June 17, 1923, *New York Times* article reported that W. H. Husband, Commissioner General of Immigration, had been trying for two years "to stem the flow of immigrants from central and southern Europe, Africa and Asia that has been leaking across the borders of Mexico and Canada and through the ports of the east and west coasts." A September 16, 1927, *New York Times* article describes government plans for stepped-up Coast Guard patrols because thousands of Chinese, Japanese, Greeks, Russians, and Italians were landing in Cuba and then hiring smugglers to take them to the United States. Many immigrants were also violating the laws of their home countries, which required them to get permission to migrate, complete military service, or pay off debts prior to leaving.

More than 100 years after Lazarus' Statue of Liberty quote marking the beginning of this book, the quote illustrates the impact of undocumented immigrants on the receiving and sending countries.

The derogatory term of illegal seems to be forever tied to those who are unauthorized in this country (Hartelius, 2016; Merolla, Ramakrishnan, & Haynes, 2013). Chomsky (2014) questions the meaning of legality within the context of immigration and its symbolism for this nation:

> Most of us think we know what the word illegal means and why some people fall into this category. It seems right and natural to us that people should be divided by citizenship, and by documents, into different categories with differential rights. . . . So we rarely question the idea that countries should be able to decide who can cross their borders and treat people differently under the law depending on statuses that these same countries assign them. But there is nothing natural about this state of affairs. Countries, sovereignty, citizenship, and laws are all social constructions: abstractions invented by humans. What's more, they are all fairly recent inventions. (p. 22)

Chomsky goes on to undertake a historical review of how immigration became illegal in this country, drawing attention to the close relationship between national citizenship and race, which is inescapable in the case of those who are undocumented.

Resettlement must never be narrowly viewed from an economic perspective; it must be expanded to include an emotional investment point of view on the part of immigrants and on the part of the receiving community. An analysis of the emotional responses on both sides is far more powerful than any economic analysis, although economics cannot be totally ignored.

Confronting social injustice entails having a profound understanding of the close interrelationship between various forms of oppression (intersectionality), such as those who are unauthorized of color and the emotionally charged environment they face (Hemish, 2017; D. L. Johnson, 2017). We cannot separate race from deportations.

A more impenetrable border with Mexico can also mean that asylum seekers, too, can get caught up in the frenzy to keep out those seeking this status (Kulish, 2017a, 2017b). Those seeking asylum must be allowed to argue their specific circumstances, but they are increasingly being turned away without an opportunity to plead their case, violating US and international laws (Dickerson & Jordan, 2017): "Asylum seekers who spend weeks preparing documents to prove their cases often return within hours because they are rebuffed at the border" (p. A9). Asylum is virtually impossible to obtain for those fleeing violence in Central America (Yee, 2017c). Being unable to obtain asylum in the United States has had a bottleneck effect, with Mexico experiencing an upsurge of Central Americans seeking asylum in that country, threatening to overwhelm their asylum system (Semple, 2017).

The journey for immigrants with "green cards" can also be trying because they must contend with backlogs and waits entailing many years, thus compromising their chances for upward mobility and more extensive incorporation into society (Obinna, 2014). Individuals with green cards are also subject to deportation raids and detentions and having their rights violated if they are in the wrong place at the wrong time (Matis, 2016). President Trump's immigration policies have caused an upsurge of individuals with green cards making the move toward citizenship (Jordan, 2017c). Permanent residency can be revoked, placing them at risk for deportation.

The number of undocumented people in the United States is debatable because of their movement across the border in both directions. It is estimated at 11.3 million, of whom 75% are Latinos and 25% non-Latino; 50,000 are Irish, for example, and they can generally be found in New York City, Boston, Chicago, and San Francisco. It is difficult to develop a sensible rationale as to why Latinos are bearing a disproportionate impact. There is no disputing that deportations have targeted Latinos because only a very low percentage of Asian and European immigrants are deported, even though they comprise approximately 25% of the total immigrant population (Voekel, 2016).

An estimated 4.2 million persons have been deported during the period from 2000 to 2016, with people from Latin America accounting for more than 93% of all those deported (Price & Breese, 2016). In 2014, almost 177,000 Mexicans were deported, and only 33 Irish were sent back to Ireland (Burnett, 2015), illustrating the racialization of this phenomenon (Kiss & Asgari, 2015): "While there are similarities between the experiences of undocumented immigrants from Eastern Europe and Mexico or Central America, the added component of race poses an additional challenge for undocumented Latino/a immigrants compared to that of Eastern European immigrants" (p. 58). This racialization has continued to the present day (Kawashima, (2017).

In discussing the Irish on St. Patrick's Day, O'Toole (2017) casts the response they are getting with that of other immigrants in the current political climate:

Is it right to applaud the legacy of mass migration from Ireland because the Irish are white and Christian? The question is especially pertinent because so many of the people who have been devised, defended and attempted to carry out Mr. Trump's policy of identifying immigrant communities with criminality and terrorism are themselves Irish-Americans. (p. A25)

Students of immigration history can point out the anti-Irish sentiments in this country, particularly in East Coast cities such as Boston and New York.

It is difficult to obtain an accurate number of undocumented people from Eastern Europe; estimates placed the number at 300,000 as of January 2011 (Kiss & Asgari, 2015). There are almost 400,000 Africans/Blacks who are undocumented, mostly from the Caribbean or Northern and sub-Saharan Africa (Hsi Lee, 2016). Finally, the second largest group of those who are undocumented is claimed by Asians with 1.4 million (Nguyen, 2014). India currently ranks fourth, behind Mexico, El Salvador, and Guatemala, with 500,000 (Singh, 2016).

Dick (2011) provides a detailed historical analysis of two major narratives in which "Mexican immigrant" and "illegal alien" have become conflated in US discourse, criminalizing and racializing them. This national narrative has been racialized with an emphasis primarily on Latinos. A comprehensive understanding of who is undocumented will reveal White Europeans, too, as in the case of the Irish, as noted previously (Carswell, 2016a; Tharoor, 2016). The Irish, it is fair to say, did not cross the southern border but arrived in the United States via modern transatlantic transportation or crossed the country's northern border with Canada, as in the case of Gerry (Burnett, 2015):

Gerry is one of them. A 40-year-old Irish bricklayer who lives in a Chicago suburb, he sneaked into the country 21 years ago, crossing at the Canadian border with a fake driver's license. For that reason, he doesn't want his last name used for this story. Now he's married, with a 5-year-old son and a small masonry business with six employees. One is a Mexican man who is also in Chicago illegally. Gerry says he feels a kinship with the undocumented Mexican worker on his crew. "He's got family, and he's worried about his family," Gerry says. "He's traveling from into the city to the job. He's probably worse off than me, because he probably doesn't have a license." Chicago has been good to Gerry: He owns a house and a company. He's taken his wife on vacation to Las Vegas and New Orleans. If he'd stayed in County Tiperrary, Ireland, he probably would have taken over his parents' milk delivery business. Gerry says he's speaking out because he wants people to know that the immigration system in this country is so broken, it affects him and his Mexican employee alike. Gerry may feel more accepted and less of a target because he's Irish, but when he talks about his life in America, he sounds like many Latin American immigrants.

Gerry's story is similar to that of many others in this country. These narratives are often racialized so that those who are White, non-Latinos escape the glare of attention; yet they, too, live in fear of deportation. This topic conjures up images of a Juan or Maria rather than a Gerry, and there lies the racialization process (Leyro, 2017).

A second label, not as derogatory as illegal, is that of "Dreamers," which is addressed in Chapters 7 and 10. In 2014, this label emerged when President Obama signed an executive order titled Deferred Action for Parents of Americans (DAPA), granting protection against deportation to children of those who are undocumented who are either American citizens ("birthright" because of being born in this country) or lawful residents. This action does not provide full legal status and has a 3-year, renewable work permit, safeguarding against deportation; it is discussed in-depth later in this book (Singer, Svajlenka, & Wilson, 2015).

CRIMINALIZING THOSE WHO ARE UNDOCUMENTED: A PERILOUS PROCESS

The eminent philosopher Bertrand Russell said, "Collective fear stimulates herd instinct, and tends to produce ferocity toward those who are not regarded as members of the herd." There is little dispute that those who are unauthorized are viewed in many different circles as not part of the herd, and we do not have to treat them in the same manner as those who are part of the herd. Criminalization was touched upon earlier but warrants more in-depth attention.

This treatment can be manifested through criminalization, even when an unauthorized person is put forth as a model of being a hard worker, respected, and worthy of being a member of society (Escobar, 2016). The emergence of these Latinos as being "disposable," by racializing and criminalizing them, has made it easy to create an anti-immigrant narrative and actions (Rocco, 2016).

It is important that these narratives not focus on providing sympathetic portrayals of immigrants, which can have a deleterious effect on broader perceptions because these lives can be reductionist and stereotypical representations (Sowards & Pineda, 2013). Feeling sorry loses sight of profound rights issues and the role the government plays in causing their uprootment. A charity view is never empowering and does not take into account strengths and capabilities (Gallo, 2016; Pérez Huber, 2017).

The criminalization of those who are unauthorized accelerated post-September 11, 2001 (Kanstroom, 2003; D. Martinez & Slack, 2013). It is estimated that the United States has spent $109 billion in US–Mexico border security technology, which includes video equipment, ground sensors, fencing, walls, and infrared cameras (Nixon, 2017a). Interestingly, due to the rough terrain, the Border Patrol uses horses for many of their apprehensions.

The belief in immigrant proneness to crime has deep roots in the nation's history, and this narrative has survived and evolved into different forms since the beginning of the nation (Simes & Waters, 2014). Criminalization was addressed in previous chapters. No one associated with this group escapes the criminalization process.

The criminalization process also involves smugglers who are often portrayed as "violent, greed-driven, predator racialized, and gendered as a male from the global

South" (Sanchez, 2017). Minimal attention is paid to descriptors of humanitarians and their organizations in addressing border crossing.

Criminalizing those who are unauthorized makes it much easier to dehumanize them, making them unworthy of being treated like everyone else in society (Ackerman, Sacks, & Furman, 2014; Rumbaut, Ewing, & Martinez, 2015; C. Taylor, 2016). Citizens are human beings, and those who are unauthorized are "others" and non-human. This stance can be taken to various lengths. However, the basic premise remains that those who are unauthorized "are not like you and me," including being prone to breaking the law and being untrustworthy.

Ewing, Martínez, and Rumbaut (2015) summarize the central "truth" about crime and anti-immigrant sentiments in this country:

> For more than a century, innumerable studies have confirmed two simple yet powerful truths about the relationship between immigration and crime: Immigrants are less likely to commit serious crimes or be behind bars than the native-born, and high rates of immigration are associated with lower rates of violent crime and property crime. This holds true for both legal immigrants and the unauthorized, regardless of their country of origin or level of education. In other words, the overwhelming majority of immigrants are not "criminals" by any commonly accepted definition of the term. For this reason, harsh immigration policies are not effective in fighting crime. Unfortunately, immigration policy is frequently shaped more by fear and stereotype than by empirical evidence. As a result, immigrants have the stigma of "criminality" ascribed to them by an ever-evolving assortment of laws and immigration-enforcement mechanisms. (p. 1)

This conclusion leaves little doubt that anti-immigrant worries about how crime rates have increased, or will increase, in this country are not based on facts.

This criminalization, also referred to as overcriminalizing, has been conceptualized in some circles as state sanctioned violence (Chacón, 2012; Menjívar & Abrego, 2012). Hate crimes directed at those who are unauthorized have been compared to a present-day version of a lynching, tapping into a horrid period in American history (Johnson & Ingram, 2012).

In discussing those who are unauthorized, Tanaka (2014) draws upon the classic work by Piven and Cloward, *Regulating the Poor* (1971), in this case raising important parallels between state use of public assistance in the 1960s and 1970s to control labor supply and the use of day laborers in the present day. Unlike the earlier period when welfare recipients were not criminalized but simply "thrown off the roles," today's version has undocumented workers being labeled criminals and facing deportation.

Many forces came together over several decades to criminalize those who are unauthorized, and it is not restricted to the United States (Coté-Boucher, 2014; H. Jones et al., 2017; Woude, Leun, & Nijland, 2014). G. Rosas (2015) refers to the increased emphasis on border enforcement as the "thickening of the border" to capture how these actions draw attention to the "dark legacy" of the passage of the

US Immigration and Nationality Act (INA), with criminalization being the most obvious consequence.

The Illegal Immigration Reform and Immigrant Responsibility Act (IIRIRA), signed into law by President Clinton (1996), made conviction of a crime, even a minor one such as shoplifting, grounds for deportation. It also authorized the training and use of local police departments to enforce deportation orders (Provine & Varsanyi, 2012).

Arizona's SB 1070 sought to create local and national support for enforcement of immigration laws criminalizing the undocumented (Park & Norpoth, 2016; Torre Cantalapiedra, 2016; Wallace, 2014). Alabama, Georgia, Indiana, and South Carolina followed Arizona's lead with this punitive legislation (Campsen, 2013; C. E. Wilson, 2011).

Arizona's legislation was also considered dangerous (Tramonte, 2011):

Laws like SB1070 are not only unnecessary, they are dangerous. State and local police already have the authority to arrest anyone suspected of criminal activity, including non-citizens, and police regularly work with the Department of Homeland Security (DHS) to identify foreign-born criminals, detain them, and transport them for eventual deportation. However, most police do not arrest immigrants solely for being undocumented. (p. 2)

Alabama's HB 56 (the Beason–Hammon Alabama Taxpayer & Citizen Protection Act), which has the dubious distinction of being the nation's most restrictive immigration bill, went into effect in September 2011 (Giagnoni, 2017).

A number of outstanding books capture narratives about those who are unauthorized. For example, Orner's (2015) *Underground America: Narratives of undocumented lives*, Lamphear, Furman, and Epps' (2016) *The Immigrant Other: Lived Experiences in a Transnational World*, and Caminero-Santangelo's (2016) *Documenting the Undocumented* provide profiles and narratives that vividly illustrate their dehumanizing and disenfranchising experiences while seeking refuge in the United States and throughout the world. These profiles cannot be separated out from national immigration policies exploiting their precarious situation, furthering marginalization.

This process of "otherization" is an alternative way of thinking about how those who are undocumented have been dehumanized (Vasquez, 2014). Local media, for example, plays a critical role in shaping public narratives about newcomers, particularly in new destinations, and whether these new residents are cast as "others" or welcomed (Sohoni & Mendez, 2014).

These individuals are invariably of color, low income, and low wealth, do not have English as their primary language, and may not share dominant cultural values, making criminalization easier to carry out. For example, Sean Spicer, White House Press Secretary under President Trump, tied Chicago's crime and violence problem to its sanctuary designation and the welcoming of those who are unauthorized into its midst, illustrating the broad reach of a criminalization stance (Skiba, 2017).

The term "crimmigration" has emerged to capture the phenomenon of criminal-ization (Arriaga, 2017; Dingeman et al., 2017; Koulish, 2016; Kubrin et al., 2012). The term "crimmigration complex" is also finding saliency (Fan, 2013). Political ideology is a strong influence on perceived criminal threats from immigrants, with those having more conservative leanings having greater fears of criminal ac-tivity (Stupi, Chiricos, & Gertz, 2016).

In late 2017, an estimated 20% of all federal prisoners were foreign born, with 92% being undocumented, but no breakdown of crimes committed was provided (Yee, 2017i). The commission of crimes is often used as an overriding rationale for deportation. A breakdown of these crimes is necessary because accepting this premise gives the impression that we are talking about drug dealers and gang members, facilitating their criminalization, which is not the case (Hester, 2015):

> Unlawfully entering the United States after a deportation is a felony. Remaining in the United States after the expiration of a visa is a felony. Passing a bad check when undocumented is an aggravated felony. Each punishable by at least one year in prison, these immigration-related crimes today constitute the leading cause of imprisonment in the federal penal system. Drug offenders, in other words, no longer constitute the majority of federal prisoners. Over the past decade, immigration offenders have consistently equaled or outnumbered drug offenders in the federal penal system, although the margin is relatively slight. In 2011, for example, drug offenders made up 29.1 percent of all federal convictions compared to immigration offenders who represented 34.9 percent of all convictions. Together, however, immigration and drug offenders were the majority of all prisoners in the federal penal system, making both immigration control and the war on drugs cornerstones of the carceral state.

Presidential candidate Trump said that he would focus on those who are unau-thorized who had committed serious crimes, or "bad hombres." As noted previ-ously, the "war on drugs" met the "war on the unauthorized." Many Latinos, in this case Mexican, have pushed back on this narrative and eschewed adopting the identity as drug pushers (M. Ramirez et al., 2016).

This is not to say that crimes are not committed by those who are unauthorized or that they avoid engaging in drug trafficking or gang membership (Dingeman-Cerda, Burciaga, & Martinez, 2016). However, the percentage of those engaged in criminal activity is far lower than that of their native-born counterparts.

Although these criminalization forces are quite powerful, there is hope, with the sanctuary movement symbolizing this hope. Identifying this deleterious pro-cess is immense and should not be minimized. States are making important efforts at decriminalizing these immigrants, as in the case of Washington state (Cházaro, 2012). Cities, too, are part of this movement, by their actions and reactions to the latest threats by President Trump to strike back at sanctuary cities.

I end this section with a discussion of the criminalization of smuggling because it has not received much attention but is an essential component of the experi-ence of those who are unauthorized. Watson (2015) argues that this narrative is shaped by three categories that bring ambiguity and complexity to undocumented entry into the country: smugglers/humanitarians, legal/illegal entry, and agents/victims:

> The criminalization of migration, for instance, has rendered a wide range of activities and people subject to criminal penalty, from crossing borders, use of false identity documents, and harbouring migrants, to marrying, renting property to, and employing undocumented migrants. . . . Criminalization also renders forms of non-criminalized but "equally injurious acts," usually those perpetrated by the state against those criminalized, as appropriate and necessary. . . . Criminalizing smuggling, which is often the sole means of escape for those facing violence and endemic poverty, justifies numerous "equally injurious acts" against vulnerable populations and those who assist them. The process by which these acts are rendered appropriate and necessary requires increased attention.

The broadening of criminalization casts a wider net entangling numerous people, organizations, and immigration enforcement processes.

Immigration criminalization and militarization go hand-in-hand, and this bears addressing. Increased criminalization also parallels the increased militarization of the police in the nation's cities (Mummolo, 2016). The growth in policing budgets during the period from 1980 to 2010 was largely the result of President Clinton's crime bill and the creation of the US Department of Homeland Security; policing budgets have particularly increased in cities with increasing African American and foreign-born populations, most notably Latinos (Vargas & McHarris, 2017).

Readers who doubt the militarization of immigration have only to turn to how the US–Mexico border has been turned into a "war zone" (I. Johnson, 2015). Border militarization has been evolutionary, but September 11, 2001, marked an intensification of this drive (G. Rosas, 2015):

> In the wake of tragedy of September 11, 2001, the militarized policing of the US–Mexico border region intensified. To reiterate, September 11, 2001, marks not a rupture but an intensification of border control. . . . The militarization of the border, or the high intensity militarized policing which is now a routine part of everyday life in the border region, has augmented longstanding practices in the actual border region. Unauthorized crossings at "the border" in such conditions thus became increasingly difficult, increasingly life-threatening. Yet they continued, in spite of the growing spectre of thousands of corpses discovered in "the killing deserts." (p. 127)

We often think of wars as transpiring in other areas of the world, not within our borders, with the exception of the Civil War.

Unfortunately, an urbanized population has little appreciation for what happens in the nation's border deserts. There is a war going on, and it is happening in our deserts where the media cannot provide the images associated with war correspondents and for which photo journalistic prizes are awarded.

Increased use of drones and other surveillance equipment is but one small aspect of this militarization. The emergence of paramilitary groups, as well as counter-humanitarian groups, on the border highlights how border enforcement has taken on the elements of war, with requisite deaths and injuries. Although it has been proposed that the National Guard should guard the border, this has not gotten great traction in national discourse. However, use of the National Guard has gotten traction in discussions of Chicago's "crime problem," which is racialized, including by those who are unauthorized, as playing a prominent roles in resolving the city's "gang problem."

Post-traumatic stress is usually associated with soldiers and rarely with those who are undocumented. However, it is very prevalent among many of those who were "successful," if we can call it that, in crossing the desert. Traumatic experiences are usually associated with the crossing of the border and the events leading to undertaking the journey. These events become narratives that are shared within the communities where they settle and work, and they are even passed on to children and grandchildren.

ELECTRONIC ANKLE MONITORS

The increased emphasis on arrests of those who are undocumented is reflected in the proportion (50%) of all federal arrests (unauthorized entry and smuggling others into the country) ending in fiscal year 2014, the most recent data available, almost doubling the 28% in 2004 (Gramlich & Bialik, 2017). The Department of Homeland Security has evolved into the nation's leading arrester, replacing the Department of Justice, signaling a dramatic focus on immigration-related offenses.

The increased use of electronic ankle monitors, called "alternatives to detention" (ATD), which can also entail telephone check-ins and home visits, further criminalizes those who are undocumented and raises Fourth Amendment rights concerns (Suárez, 2016). ATD has generally gone unreported or unresearched, even though it is a profound intrusion into the lives of those who are required to use them (Gilman, 2016; Gómez Cervantes, Menjívar, & Staples, 2017).

In 2015, 12,000 undocumented immigrants wore monitors, with the expectation that the number would increase to 50,000 in 2016 (Bishop, 2015):

> Immigrant advocates say the ankle monitors aren't a true "alternative to detention," but rather a way to expand the scope of detention and to further punish immigrants living in the US illegally. They point to evidence that more humane tools—like providing legal help to immigrants—are just as effective at getting people to show up to their hearings. And they question how appropriate is it to strap ankle monitors on mothers seeking asylum with their young children, one of the groups that has been seeing more and more use of the monitors.

The use of ankle bracelets is closely associated with having to post a bond and paying a monthly fee to a private company (Nexus), which can ultimately wind up costing thousands of dollars before a case can be resolved in the courts (Fisher, 2016). To post this bond and pay the monthly fees, family members must often borrow money, causing financial stress. If these fees are not paid, "licensed recovery agents" ("bounty hunters") may be employed to apprehend the immigrants.

Furthermore, psychological and physical consequences can be quite severe (P. Wilson, 2016):

> The use of GPS devices on ankles is often criticized by the immigrants who are forced to wear them. There is frequently a feeling of degradation. There are also practical issues. Ankle monitors are hot and can cause irritations to the skin. Above all, perhaps, is the feeling that there is an invasion of privacy. This ankle device stays on at all times, thereby removing any feeling that the individual is ever by themselves.

The stigmatizing of family members is obvious.

DEPORTATION RAIDS: A BRIEF GLIMPSE

Highly publicized raids generate publicity and send a national and international message that discourages future influx of those who are undocumented and also encourage self-deportations. Voluntary return involves detailed planning and execution, whereby deportation is greatly disruptive (Roberts, Menjívar, & Rodríguez, 2017).

It is estimated that 8 million people have been targeted for potential deportation. President Trump's failure to erect a wall, limit immigration, and punish sanctuary cities does not mean that his foiled efforts have not translated into seismic consequences across the nation because of the numbers and threats of deportations, as evidenced by the 116,337 deportations in the United States during September 2017 (Viser, 2017). The Atlanta ICE office, for example, made 80% more deportation arrests during the first 6 months of 2017 compared to 2016, representing the largest increase of any US field office (Yee, 2017h). Bennett (2017) addresses the magnitude of this number and puts it into a unique perspective:

> Up to 8 million people in the country illegally could be considered priorities for deportation, according to calculations by the *Los Angeles Times*. They were based on interviews with experts who studied the order and two internal documents that signal immigration officials are taking an expansive view of Trump's directive. Far from targeting only "bad hombres," as Trump has said repeatedly, his new order allows immigration agents to detain nearly anyone they come in contact with who has crossed the border illegally. People could be booked into custody for using food stamps or if their child receives free school lunches. The deportation targets are a much larger group than those swept

up in the travel bans that sowed chaos at airports and seized public attention over the past week. Fewer than 1 million people came to the U.S. over the past decade from the seven countries from which most visitors are temporarily blocked.

It is impossible to fathom the meaning of 8 million potential deportations. It is almost the equivalent of the population of New York City or the states of Massachusetts, Vermont, Rhode Island, and most of Maine combined! That view brings a perspective on what this means for the country to be missing this group from a social, economic, and political stance.

The act of being arrested for eventual deportation is often not covered in any great detail by the media, with some rare exceptions (Rodgers, 2017). The experience of being arrested for deportation has been compared to the roundup of Jews by the Nazis during World War II (Hayoun, 2017):

It usually begins with a startling knock at the door before dawn. Most people in Los Angeles are asleep at around 4 or 5 am. But in the undocumented community, many are already awake, preparing for longer-than-average workdays, making breakfast for their children. This is also typically when immigration authorities arrive on doorsteps—often in predominantly Latino neighbourhoods. . . . Sometimes undocumented people on the other side of the door assume there's a burglar or rapist in the neighbourhood, or perhaps a fire—and that the police are there to protect them, not to ship them back to their country of origin. So, they open the door. And legally, that's when the agents are allowed to enter, apprehend the suspected undocumented person, potentially have them make declarations revoking their residency and eventually repatriate them to their country of origin. . . . When ICE comes knocking, agents rarely break down the door unless the undocumented person behind it is considered armed and dangerous, activists say. Many undocumented people do not know that they don't need—by law—to open the door at all. "I know of cases of people who happened to answer the door when ICE showed up to their house. They describe it as the most horrifying moment of their life. Nowhere to run to, no one to scream to for help," said an undocumented young woman, who asked to remain anonymous. . . . "The raids target large neighbourhoods, particularly neighbourhoods with large amounts of Latinos." . . . . "We see people answering the door and although [ICE agents] are not there for that person, they end up taking them also."

This description provides a glimpse into a situation that few people in this country have experienced, with the possible exception of Jews who survived concentration camps and shared these experiences with relatives and friends.

It is fitting to end this section with a vignette that provides a view of the panic that spreads as news of raids travels throughout the country's cities (Kulish, Dickerson, & Robbins, 2017):

In Austin, Texas, unauthorized women working in a laundromat cowered in the back of the room, petrified after seeing a video and a photograph of apprehensions outside a local grocery store and burger joint. A day laborer and mechanic in Staten Island, New York, told his 17-year-old son where the list of emergency contacts were, including the name of the guardian who would take responsibility for him and his two younger siblings. In Savannah, Georgia, un-authorized restaurant workers were asking for rides rather than walking home, afraid they might be stopped and questioned.

It does not take a vivid imagination to understand the level of anxiety and out-right fear that raids cause and how they impact those who are vulnerable to de-portation and those who are not but still experience the fallout. The after-effects of raids reverberate in a community long past the actual event. A raid on a home is a raid on a community, violating basic beliefs about living in this country.

OVERSTAYS

There is a propensity in national discussions to use the label of undocumented as an all-encompassing term that fails to differentiate how those who are unau-thorized arrived in this country. How a person arrives in this country has a great deal to do with whether he or she is a high priority for arrest and deportation or escapes the glare from immigration authorities.

The number of undocumented persons in the country who overstay their visa expiration date is considerable. Of the estimated 45 million people whose visas expired in fiscal year 2015, approximately 416,500 were still unaccounted for during that year (Wilkins, 2017). This figure is comparable to the 415,816 Border Patrol arrests at the US–Mexico border. Between 2013 and 2015, 1.6 million foreign visitors overstaying their visas (Dinan, 2017a). Canada had the highest number of overstays (H. I. Wang, 2017). It is speculated that a significant number of these overstays in the United States are highly skilled workers who entered the country under its H-1B program or are foreign students, groups not labeled as potential threats to the nation (Nixon, 2016).

During the same period, immigration agents investigating approximately 10,000 overstays (approximately 0.2%), with fewer than 2,000 (less than 0.04%) being arrested (Dinan, 2016). During the first quarter of fiscal year 2016, an addi-tional 66,000 persons overstayed their visas (Gomez, 2016). These statistics raise serious questions about whether the fiscal and political price of building a "Great Wall" on the US–Mexico border is worth the effort. Florida's undocumented overstays arriving via airports, for example, account for 70% of that state's unau-thorized population (Sherman, 2017). Building a wall, it is important to empha-size, is symbolic in addition to being a physical act (Carter & Poast, 2017).

Visa overstayers can adjust their status within the United States, but those who are undocumented border crossers are required to leave the country to change their status. When this happens, they "trigger" a 10-year ban, which has been called "el castigo," "the punishment" (Gomberg-Muñoz, 2015).

There is a consensus that voluntary or "self-deportation," a concept raised during the 2012 presidential race by Republican candidate Mitt Romney, is not attractive or feasible, yet it persists to this day in various forms. This stance refuses to recognize the powerful forces that led to uprootment in the first place. In the current political climate, the stressors of being undocumented have introduced the subject of self-deportation once again, and it is increasingly finding its way into communities with high numbers of those who are undocumented, which is a dimension of immigration that has generally escaped national attention (Healy, 2017). Self-deportation went from a campaign slogan to a reality today.

WHO BELONGS IN THIS COUNTRY?

The question of who belongs in this country is laden with values and strong feelings that get translated into actions both for and against those who are undocumented, striking at the heart of the sanctuary city movement. Developing a systematic assessment of who are the unauthorized is only possible when there is a common understanding of who belongs in this category. This consensus is arduous to arrive at, making it even more difficult to derive a definitive number, because they blend into society and often do not traverse the same spaces as the general population.

Answering this question often involves philosophical, political, and sociological perspectives because the subject is difficult to grasp from a unidimensional viewpoint. Many of us are used to having "difficult" conversations, but discussion of those who are unauthorized brings up much that touches upon the basic core of who we are, or at least how we perceive and identify ourselves.

Basing our knowledge on what is reported in the popular media, which has emphasized Mexico border crossings, the sizable number and percentage of those entering this country through overstaying their visas, either as students or as tourists, will be overlooked in any discussions. The image of entering this country on a jetliner and picking up baggage at the carousal, instead of carrying possessions in a bag, is counter to stereotypes and limits our understanding of the many facets of this phenomenon (Chávez, 2011).

The prevailing portrait of a person who is undocumented feeds into racial and socioeconomic class stereotypical narratives, and it would be reckless not to challenge these images. No two persons who are undocumented are similar, unless viewed from a very broad perspective such as "Mexican." Furthermore, these individuals can be well integrated into the social fabric of their communities, as in the case of Juan Carlos Hernandez Pacheco in West Frankfort, Illinois, and not on the "margins" of society (Davey, 2017):

> Juan Carlos Hernandez Pacheco—just Carlos to the people of West Frankfort—has been the manager of La Fiesta, a Mexican restaurant in this city of 8,000, for a decade. Yes, he always greeted people warmly at the cheerfully decorated restaurant, known for its beef and chicken fajitas. And, yes, he knew their children by name. But people here tick off more things they know Carlos for.

How one night last fall, when the Fire Department was battling a two-alarm blaze, Mr. Hernandez suddenly appeared with meals for the firefighters. How he hosted a Law Enforcement Appreciation Day at the restaurant last summer as police officers were facing criticism around the country. How he took part in just about every community committee or charity effort—the Rotary Club, cancer fund-raisers, cleanup days, even scholarships for the Redbirds, the high school sports teams, which are the pride of this city. (p. A1)

The case of Carlos is not isolated. Having these individuals as vital parts of their community's social fabric presents a strong counter-narrative to those who are criminally involved, making the subject of deportation even more complex.

Those who are undocumented are expected to occupy low-wage and highly undesirable jobs (status, pay, and safety). The fact that many of them may occupy the bottom rung of the employment ladder makes it easier to scapegoat them (Durand, Massey, & Pren, 2016). Why is a group working in jobs that are not worthy of being performed by "honest citizens" being scapegoated? Chomsky (2014) provides a compelling answer to this question:

Illegality is a way to enforce a dual labor market and keep some labor cheap, in a supposedly postracial era. Illegality uses lack of citizenship—that is, being born in the wrong place—to make workers more exploitable. Once naturalized, the status neatly hides the human agency that forces workers into these marginalized status. It is not just coincidence that illegality has burgeoned in the postindustrial societies of the Global North at the end of the twentieth century. It serves a crucial role in their economies and ideologies. (p. 39)

Those who are undocumented cannot be separated from the labor market and the prevailing ideology in some sectors of our society, bringing an economic perspective to a political issue, although at times controlling the nation's borders is cast from a national defense perspective.

The unauthorized crossing the southern border enter another world—one that is not safe for them (Chavez, 2012a). In essence, "beware that crossing this border may be hazardous to your health and well-being." Then why cross? The odds of survival are higher on this side of the border.

Viewing those individuals through an intersectionality lens is not new. Derby (2015), for instance, argues that having an unauthorized status is much more than not meeting administrative requirements associated with being a non-citizen, and it is best to think of being unauthorized as a critical factor alongside other factors that marginalize groups in this country. Citizen status is best thought of as an integral dimension of intersectionality, dictating worthiness and unworthiness in society.

Marginalization of this group can take its place alongside other forms of marginalization, bringing intersectionality into our understanding, as well as other aspects related to intersectionality (Rajaram, 2015). This marginalization has far-reaching implications for the self-identity of those who are unauthorized, and those seeking to aid them, and adopting a "second-class" identity that undermines their sense of well-being (Quesada, 2011).

Not all unauthorized persons are created equal or face similar challenges. For example, undocumented transgendered persons face a very different reception in their countries of origin compared to those who are heterosexual, where discrimination and physical safety concerns exist (Moreno, 2014). Those who are LGBTQ or HIV positive face challenges to their safety and are even more vulnerable to being apprehended and deported than their counterparts who are not LGBTQ or do not have HIV (Gruberg, 2014):

> Although undocumented immigrants account for less than 3 percent of the total adult LGBT population in the United States, they represent nearly 8 percent of LGBT hate violence survivors. Violence against LGBT and HIV-affected undocumented people rose by almost 50 percent between 2012 and 2013, though this increase may be attributed to better reporting and local organizations' increased outreach to this community.

Intersectionality places certain groups at greater risk for health and safety, which is contrary to the popular practice of lumping together disparate groups under the umbrella of "undocumented" (Arriola, 2015; Seif, 2014).

WHO WANTS TO STAY AND WHO WANTS TO EVENTUALLY LEAVE?

The question of who among the undocumented wants to stay or eventually return home is not an academic question. It is a question that is appealing to practitioners, politicians, residents, and academics, too, by providing insight into the reasons for seeking a new life in this country, be it temporary or permanent. This motivation cannot be ignored in discussing the sanctuary city movement.

History books have generally focused on those who are undocumented from a unidimensional perspective, with an emphasis on those staying in this country. An understanding of the factors influencing those planning to return or stay presents an often overlooked perspective in developing a more complete understanding of this population (Efstratios, Anastasios, & Anastasios, 2014; Ravuri, 2014). This type of analysis has tremendous implications from a policy and services perspective.

Not all unauthorized individuals wish to remain in this country, contrary to popular opinion. Being in the country is a means to an end. Whether their dream to return home will become a reality or an impossible dream remains to be seen. My experience has been that the level of communication with those back home is a reliable indicator of whether or not they hope to return.

Understanding the forces that led to departing their native homes is important. These forces can be conceptualized as either "push" or "pull," although there is a great deal of overlap between them. D. E. Martinez (2016) provides a succinct but effective definition of push–pull factors:

In the most parsimonious sense, *push* factors consist of circumstances that lead people to leave their communities of origin, while *pull* factors include circumstances that attract people to receiving communities. Push and pull factors can operate independently of one another, or they me interdependent. Moreover, push and pull factors may act on multiple levels (e.g., global, national, regional, community, household, or individual). (p. 100)

Pull factors attract immigrants to a country and are reflected in desires for a better life, such as better educational opportunities, health care, and living conditions. These immigrants have minimal or no desire to return home, although they may often have responsibilities back home that require sending money. Nevertheless, their future is here. However, even those who aspire to return may never be able to do so. Their dream becomes impossible.

The push factors are generally forces related to a desire or desperate need to leave to make money and send it back home or to achieve other concrete goals. The home situation may be quite arduous, but unlike those who are seeking a better environment and intend to stay in this country, home conditions are still tolerable for those wishing to return after certain goals are achieved, most likely related to funds. A major economic recession can be considered a significant push factor that contributes to a decision to leave a home country (Becerra & Kiehne, 2016; Davila & Saenz, 1990).

There is considerable debate concerning this conceptualization of uprootment because it is a complex phenomenon, and these "push–pull" factors are invariably obtained post facto to explain an existing immigration flow (Portes & Rumbaut, 2014). The "tipping point" between push and pull represents an understudied area on immigration, and more so in the case of those who are undocumented. The push–pull conceptualization has remained attractive because it simplifies our understanding of the forces at work, although a more nuanced appreciation is needed.

Although raids and deportations garner considerable publicity, the strength of the host economy and that of the sending nation economy may still be stronger indicators of unauthorized migration patterns and the primary motivation for entering the United States (Amuedo-Dorantes, Puttitanun, & Martinez-Donate, 2013a). Physical safety concerns are not tied to economics and are often sufficiently important to put aside severe host country policies if it means safety for the unauthorized and their families. Not all border enforcement strategies have the same impact on restricting crossings (Coleman & Stuesse, 2014; Massey, Durand, & Pren, 2015; J. Slack et al., 2013).

Finally, uprootment occurs when someone leaves his or her country of origin; it also occurs after a person has been in this country for an extended period of time and is then deported. Deportations always involve at least two countries— the sender and the initial receiver—and may potentially involve a third if the individual is being deported from a country other than the initial receiver. Deportations to Mexico or Central America are a case in point.

Deportations invariably are viewed from one side of an equation—deporting. The second part addresses the country receiving those who are deported. Mexico plays a significant role in this part of the equation. However, it has publicly stated that it will not cooperate with the United States on this action. Mexico's Foreign Secretary vowed that Mexico will only admit Mexicans who are deported, but the trend is to admit non-Mexicans, primarily from Central America (Agren & Stanglin, 2017).

REMITTANCES

Recently, the topic of remittance has generated considerable attention among scholars, and there is even a journal specifically devoted to this subject (*Remittances Review—An International Peer-Reviewed Journal*). It is a topic that I have paid close attention to in my scholarship on Latinos. The subject of remittances has received a small degree of attention in the past, and it will likely receive increased attention as federal authorities seek to curtail the transfer of funds from those who are undocumented to their homelands in order to encourage voluntary departure from the United States.

This subject has rarely been viewed from a systematic and comprehensive perspective that incorporate economic, political, social, and foreign relation considerations. The international nature and message of this topic is quite clear to the nations from which those who are unauthorized originated and are the beneficiaries of these funds.

Remittances are a form of foreign aid with all of the benefits and consequences tied to these monies as if they involved government-to-government assistance. Remittances are not restricted to the United States, however (Schoen, 2016). More than 250 million migrants worldwide send $601 billion back to their home countries on an annual basis, with developing nations being the primary beneficiaries with $441 billion, or 73% of all remittances worldwide. The United States ranks first on the list with $56 billion annually, followed by Saudi Arabia ($37 billion) and Russia ($33 billion).

President Trump has threatened to tax remittances to Mexico as a way of paying for the wall he promised to build. There is general agreement that the money generated from these taxes, if ever enacted, will not be sufficient to pay for the wall, which if built to the specifications outlined by President Trump would cost between $25 billion and $31.2 billion (Howrasteh, 2017). There are numerous ways to bypass this proposed tax, including getting citizen relatives and friends to transmit the funds or finding informal ways of smuggling currency back home.

Remittances to Mexico are estimated at $25 billion per year. Most of the funds going to Mexico originate in California, further tying this state's long relationship with Mexico dating back to when this territory belonged to Mexico. Mexico's economy, it bears noting, is estimated to be $1.3 trillion, so on the surface the estimated $25 billion in remittances may appear to be minimal. The amount of remittances to Mexico increased dramatically in January 2017—representing a 6.3% increase from January 2016—after Trump's election, reflecting concerns about increased difficulty sending funds in the future (Bernal, 2017). For readers interested in this phenomenon, remittances tend to be highest in May and lowest in January.

The estimated $25 billion in remittances is the largest single source of income for Mexico, even higher than the $23.2 billion income generated from exported oil (Gillespie, 2017):

> The average remittance from Mexico is about $300. Essentially, Mexico's most lucrative natural resource are the people who leave home. Remittances help drive Mexico's economy, from paying for new home construction to schools, especially in low-income areas. The cash transfers from the U.S. have also been growing faster than wages and inflation. And it's a critical time for Mexico's economy, which is showing signs of weakness.

This total of $25 billion also surpassed the income generated through foreign investment, tourism, and exports of manufactured goods (Bernal, 2017). Remittances are considered "big business" for Mexico because of the amount of funds that are transferred to the country, and this significance is often lost when the focus is on individuals rather than population groups (Pew Research Center, 2016).

Readers may question why I discuss remittances when this book is about sanctuary cities. There are numerous facets of remittances that play a critical role in why those who are unauthorized are in this country. In a very informative study of remittances to Mexico and Central America, Held (2017) draws implications for those working with immigrants on this issue and their motivation for entering the United States:

> In particular, social workers can assess not only the settlement-related needs of immigrants, but also remittance goals to meet the needs of their families back home and how clients perceive their responsibilities to meet those needs. For example, recognition that immigrants with undocumented status are more likely to remit, despite their greater vulnerability and job insecurity, can inform assessment and treatment planning. . . . Social workers can inquire about immigrants' degree of worry or stress related to family who remain back home. Assisting with coping skills to manage this stress may be a step toward improving immigrant well-being. Further, social workers can assess immigrants' ability to remit to their family back home and assess the family's urgent needs (e.g., medical conditions) as elements of better understanding their clients' goals. Immigrants' ability to remit may impact the well-being not only of family in the home country, but also of immigrants themselves.

Held's view is that social workers and other helping professionals must be cognizant of the impact that remittances can have which can lead to a better understanding and the creation of interventions that are responsive to immigrants' unique position.

DO WE COUNT THE UNDOCUMENTED DEAD?

This section heading is deliberately provocative because it focuses on one of the most severe consequences of unsuccessful entry into this country. The material in this section is disturbing, and this subject is addressed from a multiplicity of views. Rubio-Goldsmith and colleagues' (2016) book, *Migrant Deaths in the Arizona Desert: La Vida No Vale Nada*, is highly recommended for readers wishing to obtain an in-depth and nuanced understanding of migrant deaths that occur during attempts to enter the United States through Arizona's Sonora Desert. It is difficult to fathom the extent of this tragedy, but when an entire book is devoted to the subject, it sheds the light that this topic deserves and adds a much needed, although extremely sad, perspective on this nation's failed immigration policies.

When discussing crossing the southern border, a desert, in its simplest form, can be thought of as a large unmarked grave, with all of the horrid symbolism and images that such a statement elicits. Markers signifying the death of migrants crossing the desert have emerged (Auchter, 2013). Using a mass unmarked grave metaphor is gruesome but effective in conveying an injustice and indignity that, in many ways, is indescribable. There is no national monument to African Americans who were lynched; there is no national monument to those who have died attempting to enter this country either.

Mass unmarked graves are never unintentional and are often associated with war crimes for good reason (Reineke, 2016):

> The deaths and disappearances along the border are part of a strategy of state control within the United States. . . . Disappearances have been at the core of many regimes of terror where they were used to salience and intimidate the opposition. In the border context, the physical disappearance of migrants as they attempt to travel through the desert borderlands is a continuation of the disappearance of personhood effectuated by the current international neoliberal market, which exploits workers as "bare life." (p. 147)

The indignity of being assigned a number, rather than having one's name on one's final resting place, sums up the tragedy of trying to enter this country (Fernandez, 2017a):

> Case 0435 died more than a mile from the nearest road, with an unscuffed MacGregor baseball in his backpack. Case 0469 was found with a bracelet, a simple green ribbon tied in a knot. Case 0519 carried Psalms and Revelations, torn from a Spanish Bible. Case 0377 kept a single grain of rice inside a hollow cross. One side of the grain read Sara, and the other read Rigo. The belongings are part of a border-crossers' morgue at a Texas State University lab here—an inventoried collection of more than 2,000 objects and 212 bodies, the vast majority unidentified. All 212 were undocumented immigrants who died in Texas trying to evade Border Patrol checkpoints by walking across the rugged terrain. Most died from dehydration, heatstroke or hypothermia. Even as the number

of people caught trying to illegally enter the United States from Mexico has dropped in recent months, the bodies remain a constant, grim backdrop to the national debate over immigration. "When we get them, we assign them a case number because we have to have a way of tracking cases, but no one deserves to be just a number." (p. A22)

The quote "no one deserves to be just a number" uplifts the untold narratives of these individuals and the joining of the narrative on this national issue—namely these are just numbers (dehumanized) and not lives.

The Arizona desert has been referred to as a "war zone" because of the causalities it has claimed (Torres, 2015). The concept of "undocumented border crosser deaths" (UBCDs) has emerged to capture this phenomenon (Fleischman et al., 2017). In 2016, the Arizona Maricopa County Office of the Medical Examiner had more than 200 unidentified individuals. More than 100 were believed to have died while trying to cross the border; the majority of these individuals were males ranging in age from 15 to 60 years. Those who are undocumented have a choice of possibly dying in the dessert or drowning attempting to cross the Rio Grande, which, incidentally, has not received much publicity in discussions of these deaths (K. Martinez, 2015):

Mission Fire Chief Rene Lopez Jr., of the fire department's dive-and-rescue team responsible for recovering bodies from the river, told the Associated Press (AP), "It used to be one a month. Now it's one a week." He added, "You just feel for them, they are young, in their 20s and 30s, even teenagers." The expanded patrols and surveillance have caused immigrants to cross the river in more dangerous and secluded areas, including murky canals that are 50 feet wide with debris and currents that make it hard to climb out. Capt. Joel Dominguez, part of the rescue team, also told the AP, "They get tied down and it's hard to get away from that in black water. And they are often panicking, running from agents." According to officials, dead bodies take a few days to surface but without ID it is very difficult to identify the deceased, mostly young immigrants from Mexico and Central America.

This vivid description does not begin to capture the reactions family members will have if they ever to find out what happened to their loves ones.

Border crossing deaths, many of which occur in this country's deserts and the dead suffer the indignity of not having a funeral, must be recognized in discussions of those who are undocumented (Parks et al., 2016). Their numbers must be counted in any comprehensive discussion of those who are undocumented in this country, as casualties are counted in any of this nation's wars. They are a casualty of a war in similar fashion to how we count our dead in wars. Unlike the more than 400,000 soldiers buried at Arlington National Cemetery or the approximately 59,000 names of soldiers etched on the Vietnam War Memorial, there are no national memorials to those who are unauthorized who died seeking to fulfill the American Dream.

Deaths of border patrol agents, however, do get national attention even when they are suspicious, as in the case of Rogelio Martinez, who died under mysterious circumstances (Dickerson, 2017b). President Trump and Senator Cruz both used this death to highlight the dangers of security along the Mexican border.

Deaths while attempting to enter a country are not unique to the United States, and neither is the quest for a memorial for them. A German newspaper (*Der Tagesspiegel*) attempted an accounting of those who died during the period from 1993 to 2017 fleeing their homelands and seeking to enter Europe. The paper published "The List," a 48-page monument in print to the 33,293 lives lost in this desperate endeavor (Cowell, 2017).

The deaths of those attempting to cross the desert often go unnoticed and unrecorded. Generating publicity acknowledging desert deaths takes on great symbolic and political prominence in the US–Mexico border debate, bringing attention to how state-sponsored violence is fostered and condoned (B. J. Martinez, 2017; Nienass & Délano, 2016).

Although these deaths have started to receive increased attention, unfortunately, injuries and humiliations suffered have not, bringing a different perspective on being a victim (Comino, Mastrobuoni, & Nicolò, 2016; De León, 2013; Michalowski & Hardy, 2014). Those injured while entering this country are further compromised in their efforts to seek employment and a better life, while hoping to eventually return to their countries of origins. Rapes, too, fall into the category of invisibility when discussing border crossings (Falcón, 2016).

The media can portray the trip across the border as dangerous, with death being the ultimate price, and the promise of a better future for those who succeed. However, even those who manage to achieve "success" in crossing the desert can experience tremendous indignities with a lifetime of negative memories (O'Leary, 2016):

> The name bajadores comes from bejar, the Spanish verb that means to "pull down," and refers to the tactics these bandits use of forcing victims to pull down their pants at knifepoint or gunpoint in order to keep them prostrate and to facilitate body search for valuables. (p. 83)

To make matters worse, those "lucky" to enter the country will face incredible challenges to their well-being. Employment often means difficult or unsafe work conditions, below minimum wages, and a high likelihood of injury on the job, without the recourse of seeking assistance (Abrego, 2015).

DEMOGRAPHIC SNAPSHOT OF THOSE WHO ARE UNAUTHORIZED

It is appropriate to provide a demographic snapshot of those who are unauthorized in this country and an important picture of who constitutes this group. However, it is a unidimensional picture and devoid of any narratives that bring these numbers to life. This is not to take away from the value of such a perspective because it grounds a statistic within the broader context.

In 2014, there were approximately 11 million persons in the United States who were undocumented. A profile of them, according to country of origin, reveals very few surprises based on the material covered in Chapter 2, Phase 4 (Migration Policy Institute, 2016): Mexico, 6,177,000 (56%); Guatemala, 723,000 (7%); El Salvador, 465,000 (4%); Honduras, 337,000 (3%); and China, 268,000 (2%).

A focus on urban demographics and the unauthorized would be foolish without due attention to the Asian American community, which represents 13% of this immigrant group. Asian Americans have often taken a back seat to Latinos in discussions pertaining to the unauthorized and national demographics. In 2015, the Asian American community numbered 20.7 million, with 94% having origins in 19 different countries (Lopez & Patten, 2017). It grew 72% from 2000 to 2015 (11.9 million to 20.4 million), which is the fastest rate of growth of any group in the country. Almost one-third of the Asian American community lives in California, with San Francisco and Los Angeles standing out as home for this group.

Developing an understanding of the distribution of sanctuary cities is but one dimension of any equation that helps enhance our understanding of these sites, as addressed in Chapter 6. The geographical distribution of those who are undocumented, and where are they concentrated, is the other aspect of this equation and of sufficient importance to increase our understanding. Patterns of geographical destinations have gone through different phases, including an increased prominence of urban cities (Massey, Rugh, & Pren, 2010).

In 2014, 61% of the nation's unauthorized lived in 20 metropolitan areas, and these areas accounted for 36% of the nation's overall population; their percentage has remained consistent over the past decade. Those who are unauthorized are overrepresented in certain cities compared to the immigrant population in those cities (Passell & Cohn, 2017a):

> Unauthorized immigrants account for about one-in-four foreign-born US residents. They make up a somewhat higher share of immigrants in the Houston (37%), Dallas (37%), Atlanta (33%), Phoenix (37%), Las Vegas (35%), Denver (37%) and Austin (34%) metro areas. They make up a somewhat lower share of all immigrants in the New York (19%), Miami (18%), San Francisco (17%) and San Jose (17%) metro areas.

The number of Mexicans who are unauthorized has declined from a peak of 6.9 million in 2007 to 5.8 million in 2014, which is counter to the pervasive narrative that they are only increasing in number and will increase even more in the immediate future if this country does nothing about the "illegal" problem (Barrera & Krogstad, 2017).

Those who are unauthorized have shown a propensity to embrace residential stability, increasing the likelihood of having children who attend schools. In 2014, for example, 66% of all adult unauthorized immigrants had lived in the country for at least one decade, an increase from 41% in 2005. A view of age breakdown in 2014, with a focus on school-age children, revealed that children of those who were unauthorized represented a significant cohort in this nation's schools, with 3.9 million kindergarten through 12th-grade (K–12) students, or 7.3% of the total (Passel & Cohn, 2016).

It is important to note that the number of births to a parent who was unauthorized declined to 275,000 in 2014 from 330,000 in 2009. Not surprisingly, K–12 students of unauthorized parents tend to cluster in six states: Nevada (17.6%), Texas (13.4%), California (12.3%), Arizona (12.2%), Colorado (10.2%), and New Mexico (10.1%). Six states at the end of the continuum, in primarily the Midwest and Northeast, had less than 1%.

Demographically projecting into the future should not be limited to demographers. The demographic picture of those who are unauthorized remaining in this country is fairly predictable. It does not take a crystal ball to see the potential challenges for those in human services, for instance, when those who are undocumented and who remain in the United States increasingly age and face serious challenges in receiving services typically associated with this life stage, such as hospice care (N. A. Gray et al., 2017). These potential ramifications, however, can be applied across the age spectrum.

Based on the statistics presented in this section, we can understand why the Mexican community in the United States is particularly alarmed about ICE and the president's deportation strategy. Any discussion about instituting increased vigilance and deportation policies will have a disproportionate impact on this group. In 2015, almost 250,000 undocumented Mexicans were deported, an increase from 169,000 in 2005 but a reduction from almost 310,000 in 2013 (Gonzalez-Barrera & Krogstad, 2017). The significant increase during the past decade has been attributed to a shift in policy traced back to 2005.

The decline in border crossings continues to the present day, with their number decreasing in 2015 below that at the end of the Great Recession and Mexicans representing a declining share of this population (Passel & Cohn, 2017b). Thus, this decline predates Donald Trump's campaign for the presidency.

THOSE WHO ARE UNDOCUMENTED AS RESILIENT

Readers may be at a point of mental exhaustion based on the emotionally draining nature of the material presented in Section 1. It is therefore appropriate to reshift and focus on the positives as we transition to Section 2 and the promise of the sanctuary movement. Advocates and activists are often called upon to be grounded in the operative reality of those who are undocumented without losing sight of their strengths, the power of their dreams, and their hopes (Garcia, 2015).

It is easy to lose sight of the strengths and resiliency of people who are unauthorized because of negative news and actions taken against them, including their criminalization. It is essential that we do not get into a reactionary stance that very easily overlooks their many attributes. The challenge is how to focus on resiliency, strengths, and assets without losing sight of vulnerabilities, needs, and challenges (Aysa-Lastra & Cachón, 2015).

Capturing and publicizing the emotional intensity of the experiences of those who are unauthorized, starting from the day they left their homeland and made their way through often dangerous checkpoints and eventually settled in the United States, including documenting their daily lives and struggles, is essential to fully comprehend their tenacity and resourcefulness (Bailey, 2013; Marquardt et al., 2013). Also, they are not totally devoid of dignity, a component that must be present in resiliency and strengths (Kim, 2009).

Urbana's (2014) book, *Illegal: Reflections of an Undocumented Immigrant*, focuses on their success and his, rather than their, trials and tribulations. This type of scholarship does not lose sight of resiliency, while grounding the journey within a lived experience perspective that does not minimize barriers. These self-narratives are rare, but they give voice where voices are rarely sought, particularly when stressing hard work, pride, dignity, perseverance, and even good or bad luck.

Those who are undocumented are resilient and draw upon knowledge and skill sets that help them navigate difficult living circumstances (Gleeson & Gonzales, 2012). I am very fond of saying that the ability to survive should never be minimized, and that applies to those who made it to this country. Some may say that they are not resilient but lucky. I agree that there may be an element of luck, but that is insufficient to explain the outcomes of those who have managed, under the most arduous and even unimaginable conditions, to succeed in achieving the goals they had upon entering this country.

The concept of resilience is complex, particularly when discussing this group, and needs to be deconstructed beyond an individual and to take into account families, communities, and even the organizations serving this community. W. S. Campbell (2008), for example, addresses the importance of more attention being paid to immigrant strengths, in this case focuses on women but not restricted to them.

Shaikh and Kauppi (2010, p. 155) view this community's resiliency as consisting of eight types, clustering into two major modes of thinking and two major perspectives (psychology and sociology). Psychology covers six key themes that are very familiar to readers: (1) individual personality traits, (2) positive outcomes/forms of adaptation despite high risk, (3) factors associated with positive adaptation, (4) processes, (5) sustained competent functioning/stress resistance, and (6) recovery from trauma or adversity. Sociology encompasses (1) human agency and resistance and (2) survival. Survival should never be overlooked, regardless of circumstances.

Evading increased policing is not just luck but the convergence of excellent urban navigational skills and support (Stuesse & Coleman, 2014). Due to intense scrutiny and increased threat for arrest and deportation, those who are unauthorized have, in some cases, become "model" members of society—spotless workers and invisible, taking an even lower public profile, particularly in cities that are non-sanctuary designated (Harrison & Lloyd, 2012):

> The stress and financial debt of the migration contribute to workers' willingness to work long hours, take few vacation days, and do monotonous work at low pay. As one worker stated, "We paid $3000 to get across the border. I went to work to repay the money that they lent us so we could come here, because it takes a lot of money to come here. The most important thing was we had work, and we needed work." One worker explained that the cost of the border crossing prevents him from taking any days off or returning home to visit his child: "I can't afford to go back to Nicaragua (to visit) and I can't take that risk. It cost me too much just to get here."

Anti-immigrant laws serve purposes that go far beyond the most obvious reasons of encouraging immigrants to return home (Harrison & Lloyd, 2012):

> Critical geographers have played a crucial role in identifying how these increasingly militarized and spatially expanded immigration policy enforcement practices are not just oppressive but also tremendously "productive" in that they serve two key functions of the state: ensuring capital accumulation in industry and maintaining the political legitimacy of the state in the eyes of the public.

The emergence of an "immigrant revitalization perspective" offers a counter-narrative that resonates among those embracing an asset or capacity enhancement paradigm, which identifies and mobilizes indigenous strengths within highly marginalized communities (Ramey, 2013).

CONCLUSION

We cannot discuss those who are unauthorized in a dispassionate manner. This is a subject about human lives, living under demanding circumstances and struggling for survival. This chapter addressed belonging and worthiness, core aspects of human life. Furthermore, the forces fighting against their presence in this country are formidable. These forces, including countervailing forces, have a long historical existence serving as a basis for present-day social change efforts. It is appropriate to end this chapter and section with the following quote (Ochoa, 2016):

> Like all people, they have dreams and sometimes even make mistakes. Their lives are much more than the potent images and broad claims circulating the media and popular discourse. When they are not being detained or deported, abused or dehumanized because of their status—they are (like you and me) working hard every day to provide and keep their families safe. Their story is a testimony of the unified struggle of what it means to be an illegal immigrant within this country. Undocumented immigration is not solely an issue tied to

corrupt foreign governments and policies, but a humanitarian one. Until then, we cannot begin to understand the issue of unauthorized immigration, unless we begin listening to these "illegals" directly. (p. 63)

Those who are undocumented are first, and foremost, human, regardless of their nationality; they are also individuals who have uprooted due to extreme circumstances.

Sanctuary Cities, Communities, Organizations, and Homes

It is hoped that readers have developed an appreciation for how the sanctuary city movement emerged in response to the convergence of major historical, economic, political, and social forces. The "perfect storm" is still active and gaining strength, to continue the metaphor. This section focuses on a multidimensional view of the sanctuary movement and its various manifestations that are continuing to evolve in new and exciting ways for readers interested in immigration and, specifically, those interested in immigrants as a focus of activism, volunteerism, practice, research, and scholarship. The forces outlined in Section 1 set the stage for appreciating why sanctuary cities are so important to this nation at this point in time in its history.

5

Definition, History, Demographics, and Boundaries of Sanctuary Cities

INTRODUCTION

Section 1 provided readers with a more firm grounding of important social, political, historical, and economic factors setting the foundation for examining the origins, role, and complexity of sanctuary cities, including a brief definition of sanctuary cities in Chapter 1. Providing sanctuary has been framed as a human rights and social justice issue associated with mass migrations and expulsions (Daiute, 2017). Sanctuary cities have become a beacon of light guiding the nation through a dense fog or very turbulent storm, or if you wish, our North Star.

No academic profession stands out as paying much attention to the sanctuary city movement, with academic disciplines being slow to study it, as in the case of anthropology (Mancina, 2016). Social work, other professions, and closely allied academic disciplines have also been slow to focus on it.

As the movement gains greater traction throughout the nation, and with increased publicity, increased scholarly attention will bring greater understanding, as well as scrutiny, to how this movement will consolidate gains and evolve during this and future presidential administrations. Immigration is a phenomenon that will continue for many decades. The sanctuary movement gained traction in the 1980s; it is not a knee-jerk response to the current presidential administration. All social movements are expected to evolve as they mature and respond to changing social circumstances, and this movement must also be expected to do so.

This chapter further defines and establishes the nuanced parameters that make cities sanctuary cities and their roles and effectiveness in this movement. This movement goes far beyond cities. Context brings together a variety of terms, viewpoints, tensions, and relevant perspectives. There is no disputing that this movement has empowered a group that has faced incredible challenges throughout the years and that continues to face even greater challenges. The sanctuary city designation encourages those who are unauthorized and who have been invisible or underground to come out and be counted.

There is no fanfare or an "official signing" ceremony whereby an entity, such as a city, town, county, or organization, becomes a sanctuary. In fact, it has been argued that the closest we can get to obtaining a sanctuary designation is at the county level with a sign-off on a 287(g) agreement. This agreement makes reference to section 287(g) of the US Immigration and Nationality Act and outlines a relationship between the federal government and counties that deputizes local police to aid immigration enforcement and become an extension of ICE.

These agreements differ significantly from the 2009 Secure Communities program, which allowed law enforcement to determine the immigration status of those arrested for committing their first non-immigration crime: "1. Identify criminal aliens through modernized information sharing; 2. Prioritize enforcement actions to ensure apprehension and removal of dangerous criminal aliens; and 3. Transform criminal alien enforcement processes and systems to achieve lasting results."

This program broadened the "net" for deportation (Clause, 2017):

"A 287g agreement is more, 'We are going to do your job for you and help you round people up, or help identify people for you.' So that's more of an affirmative agreement between a state or locality with ICE," says Mary Holper, director of the Immigration Clinic at Boston College Law School. "The true [area] where people can make a difference is going to the state, the locality, and just saying, 'Don't do this. This is a bad idea, on lots of different levels.'"

As discussed in Chapter 6, a significant number of counties are listed as sanctuaries. Having a county designation does not bring the same publicity, or cachet, as a city, for reasons addressed previously. A "sanctuary county movement" does not have the cachet as the "sanctuary city movement." County designations, however, are tremendously important and indicators of major national anti-immigrant sentiment.

The following Massachusetts sheriff's comments on the liabilities of signing a 287(g) agreement, in a county designated as a sanctuary, highlight the concerns typically raised by law enforcement officers throughout the country (Clause, 2017):

"This is not our job, so it shouldn't be our money," Ryan says. "The fact that we're even discussing it or the fact that the president is trying to take away resources from the state because they're not doing what [ICE] should be doing is silly. And also, it's not possible." According to Ryan, 287(g) agreements further expose municipalities to the liability of a potential breach of the Fourth Amendment, which protects against unwarranted search and seizure, just as Secure Communities had. Conversely, the federal government stands to violate the 10th Amendment, Holper says, by mandating how local law enforcement conducts it's policing, a power vested in the state government. "Not only are we putting ourselves at risk of being sued for violating people's rights if we embrace the 287(g) agreements," Ryan says, "but we will also be paying to do the job of the federal government—while at the same time, making our local and state police forces less effective because they won't be able to engage in community policing because the communities that they police will be afraid of them."

A sanctuary designation can have many different meanings for an organization, county, town, city, or even a state such as California. This "fluidity" does not diminish the symbolic and practical values of such a designation. Refusal of counties to sign a 287(g) agreement is one way of achieving a sanctuary designation.

There are numerous ways of labeling a city a sanctuary. The official designation can best be thought of as the tip of an iceberg, with the vast mass of this iceberg below the water. Rarely is there a consensus as to their origins, boundaries, and latent and manifest purposes. Understanding and accepting this ambiguity goes a long way toward understanding the sanctuary city movement in the country.

CONCEPT OF SANCTUARY

The concept of sanctuary is both ancient and modern—a testament to its importance in the lives of individuals in desperate need of a new life—setting the stage for involvement of religious leaders and congregations, including the use of the Bible and religious doctrine, in establishing a rationale for social activism on immigrant rights (Ahn, 2013a; Avalos, 2016; Bagelman, 2016; Coutin, 1993; Schewel, 2016).

The Hebrew Bible makes mention of six cities in biblical Israel where sanctuary was possible for those fleeing retribution for murdering someone. Myers and Colwell's (2012) book, *Our God Is Undocumented: Biblical Faith and Immigrant Justice*, captures the religious origins of unauthorized immigrants and the concept of sanctuary, highlighting a moral imperative on active resistance.

The religious origins of the concept of sanctuary are strong, but this concept is no longer exclusively associated with religious beliefs and institutions, representing an important evolutionary step beyond having a moral stance (Rabben, 2011). The concepts of asylum or sanctuary can be found in various forms throughout all cultures and have been codified across countless societies (Kendall, 2014).

I do not possess the philosophical acumen to engage in an erudite discussion of sanctuary as a state of mind or virtual environment. For example, a sanctuary of the self is often referred to as a space that is conducive for an individual to reflect on his or her life and current circumstances (Poputa, 2016). A sanctuary does not have to have a physical space. It is wise to pause and take a moment to touch upon various aspects of what it means for a sanctuary to be viewed from this standpoint.

A sanctuary is often associated with a locale with clear boundaries, is duly and publically designated, has expressed values and principles, and explicitly states that what transpires within its boundaries can create feelings of safety while other instrumental needs are met (de la Torre, 2016). Casting sanctuary in a different light—for example, as a state of mind—makes this concept more elusive and difficult to measure but no less important than its place counterpart. Nostalgia has been referred to as a sanctuary for immigrants regardless of their legal status (Parveen, 2017). The longing for the homeland often becomes an important narrative within immigrant communities.

Readers may question whether we are about to enter into a profound philosophical discussion on a topic that is complicated enough. The simple answer is yes and no. Sanctuary, as a state of mind, is not possible if one is physically or psychologically threatened, as in the case of fearing deportation.

An opportunity for renewal provides a moment to reflect and take stock of where one has been and where one wishes to go. The quest to enter this country, and the challenges associated with the journey, does not provide a moment to reflect. Conversely, just because a place is called a sanctuary does not guarantee that interactions transpiring within that space create this state of being for those fleeing persecution.

The *Oxford American Dictionary* traces the origins of "sanctuary":

Middle English (in sanctuary (sense 3): from Old French *sanctuaire*, from Latin *sanctuarium*, from sanctus "holy." Early use in reference to a church or other sacred place where a fugitive was immune, by the law of the medieval Church, from arrest, gave rise to sanctuary.

Governments have been less embracing of this designation. England, for example, abolished sanctuary laws in the 1620s (Emanuel, 2017). Sanctuaries are not limited to European or English-speaking nations. The religion of Islam and the countries in which it is the main religion have a long tradition of embracing this concept (Zaman, 2016).

Tracing the origins of sanctuary can start with asylum being considered the precursor, with roots tracing back to ancient Egyptian and Hebrew civilizations and the Greek city states, where it was possible to seek protection against extradition for a variety of acts. With the advent of the early Christian era, sanctuaries further evolved. They usually occurred in churches, eventually leading to the political right to asylum being granted by a sovereign state (Peters & Besley, 2015).

Sanctuary's evolution throughout the centuries has been codified by key institutions and governments, illustrating a state of being for those entities embracing this designation. Cadman (2014) provides a historical overview of sanctuary's evolution:

Ever since men have bonded together into civil societies, two notions have been present in those societies in one form or another: exile and sanctuary. Exile generally involved someone being cast out of society for conduct or expressions of thought contrary to that society's norms. Sanctuary represented its obverse, someone fleeing the reach of a society for crimes real or perceived,

usually to another land. Oddly, though, sanctuary in the ancient world sometimes consisted of flight to a particular, acknowledged spot physically within
the society's boundaries, but nonetheless deemed outside of its reach—usually
a site held to be sacred to the gods, and thus not subject to man's rules. Concepts
of the inapplicability of civil law within the religious realm, however, continued
well into the development of European nations, with the Mother Church not
only enforcing its own set of laws, at times with terrible effect (witness the
Inquisition), but also providing in its churches, monasteries, and elsewhere
places of refuge from the monarch's sometimes inflexible and arbitrary appli-
cation of law. Modern notions of sanctuary have come down to us from those
ancient origins, and are now embedded in a variety of international laws and
treaties. (p. 2)

Sanctuaries have persisted over time because they fulfill important functions
throughout the world. Sanctuaries in the United States have taken center stage,
increasing in number and significance because of the millions of unauthorized
persons in this country.

Sanctuaries in modern US history have not been restricted to immigrants. In
1971, Berkeley, California, declared itself a sanctuary city for American soldiers
refusing to be deployed to Vietnam (Ridgley, 2012). Canada, too, provided sanctuary to US Vietnam War resisters during the 1960s and 1970s (Squire, 2011).
Groups in Canada emerged in response to the moral or ethical dilemma posed
by the Vietnam War, making it easier, although no less challenging, for sanctuary
seekers (Lawrence, 2015).

The following description provides critical boundaries on a subject that often
defies conventional boundaries (Litemind, n.d.):

How about using your imagination to create a place that you can go to at any
time to generate or recreate any feeling, emotion or memory you feel like? This
place can serve as a relaxing place for meditation, a place to feel energized, to
bring good memories or feelings, overcome fears, solve problems or perform
any change in your mood. In fact, how about creating a place that can achieve
all of this and more?

Sanctuaries are meant to disrupt everyday business, as are most acts of resistance,
and interject thorny ethical and moral points of view that are not easily dismissed
without serious efforts to do so.

Readers have probably found themselves in very vulnerable positions that required the assistance of others. This situation may have been episodic, meaning it
was time limited, or over an extended period. This vulnerability required emotional
and social support. A sanctuary is predicated on meeting the instrumental (concrete), expressive (psychological), and even spiritual needs of those who are unauthorized, which translates into them feeling safe and valued—critical aspects of
well-being for anyone, and more so for those who know they can be apprehended
and deported without a moment's notice and even possibly as their family watches.

DEFINITION OF SANCTUARY CITIES

There is a challenge in writing this section, and part of that challenge has to do with the various definitions of a sanctuary city and the level of depth in covering this material. For most readers, a broad definition will suffice, as provided in Chapter 1; for the avid reader, getting into the "tweeds" is necessary. I take the middle ground and run the risk of disappointing both audiences.

Bauder (2016a) presents a compelling argument that the concept of sanctuary cities is highly ambiguous, particularly when viewed from an international perspective, because it seeks to capture a wide range of policies and practices, local circumstances, variable population groups, and different national contexts. A formal definition of sanctuary city is in order, although it seems self-evident in its meaning and central purpose (Kopan, 2017):

> The term "sanctuary city" is a broad term applied to jurisdictions that have policies in place designed to limit cooperation with or involvement in federal immigration enforcement actions. Cities, counties and some states have a range of informal policies as well as actual laws that qualify as "sanctuary."

Most of the policies center on not cooperating with federal immigration law enforcement policies. Many of the largest cities in the country have such policies. This definition brings flexible boundaries, and that is to be expected when the concept embraces such a broad geographical territory and is highly politically charged.

A layperson's definition of sanctuary cities is captured well in the following statement (Aguilar, 2017): The term "generally refers to municipalities that have established policies prohibiting police officers from enforcing immigration laws or cooperating with federal immigration officials." This definition highlights how this concept has no federal legal meaning but still brings immense symbolic and instrumental consequences for entities adopting it. The term is closely intertwined with cities, and this association brings an added dimension to the debates because of how this nation has historically taken an anti-urban attitude. This view has been shaped because of the historical attraction cities have had for immigrants.

Sanctuary cities have often been defined by relationships between the local police, immigration authorities, and those who are undocumented; such a focus emphasizes law enforcement. Sanctuary cities and organizations, as discussed in Chapter 7, go beyond this focus, although it is an extremely critical position regarding safety from deportation, which must not be minimized in the current political climate.

The imagery of the "shining city on the hill" places cities squarely in the center of the immigrant rights movement in this country. Note that it is not a "shining rural or suburban setting on the hill." It is no mistake that the image is about a city. Unfortunately, most images of cities tend to be negative. Rarely does one hear about the city as an "oasis" or even a "sanctuary." It is not uncommon for negative or stigmatizing terms to be associated with the city, such as "urban blight," "urban wasteland," "urban jungle," "urban poverty," "urban crime," "urban drug abuse," "urban decay," and "urban degeneration."

Developing a standardized approach toward understanding the initiation of a sanctuary designation is important in developing an understanding of the primary sources for achieving this distinction. Due to the influence of local circumstances, any framework that seeks to classify these forces must be sufficiently general, or flexible, and not lose sight of key local factors that were operative to increase the chances of this designation taking hold.

Sanctuary city designation can be obtained through one of three major sources: legislation through passage by a city council, bureaucratic initiative by a police department, or mayoral order. However, as noted by Hedrick (2011),

> Obviously, the vast majority of sanctuary policies do not come from bureau-cratic innovation. Instead, they are largely the product of legislative resolutions and ordinances that direct local law enforcement not to "inquire about the immigration status of crime victims, witnesses, or others who call approach or are interviewed." In short, nationwide sanctuary cities seem to be a case of the principals, the local legislature, exerting direct control over the activities if their agents, the police departments. (pp. 9–10)

The possibility of achieving an agreement between city councils, mayors, and po-lice departments requires active communication and cooperation between these entities and a general embrace of shared values regarding social justice.

Laman (2015), in turn, identifies three critical elements in defining sanctuary cities that bring a nuance to the previously mentioned factors: (1) It specifically refers to a group of individuals who are undocumented; (2) it refers to a setting with specific spatial qualities that protect those who are undocumented; and (3) it brings to the fore social and political manifestations through mobilizations and movements with specific goals of non-cooperation with federal authorities, with intents to raise national consciousness concerning the plight of those who are un-authorized. These three elements bring social, cultural, and political forces to bear on the definitional process.

Reconciling the ideals embedded in the nation's Constitution and Bill of Rights, with practices that have been fostered by a reactionary political system we find in this country today, has resulted in the emergence of sanctuary cities, with religious-inspired activists playing leadership roles in this movement (Bilke, 2009; Freeland, 2010; Houston & Morse, 2017). Pro-immigrant legislation targeting those who are documented and unauthorized, as manifested through the sanc-tuary city movement, coexists alongside stricter, regressive legislation seeking to foster greater immigration enforcement cooperation with local governmental entities (Hedrick, 2011).

The sanctuary movement goes beyond cities, encompassing towns, counties, states, and even organizations. Although a geographical and political entity can declare itself a sanctuary, this does not mean that every institution within the en-tity subscribes to this designation to the same degree, if at all. Furthermore, the period leading up to an official sanctuary designation can last several years, as in the case of San Francisco. After 4 years of pressure from the board of supervisors, Mayor Diane Feinstein, who eventually became a Democratic senator to the US Senate, signed legislation making San Francisco the first sanctuary city in the country (Abraham, 2011). This point is revisited again in Chapter 8, but it is worth pursuing further here.

Conflicts regarding sanctuary city status generally get overlooked, as in the case of San Francisco, a city with a national and international reputation for being progressive. The tendency to overlook conflicts does a disservice to this movement because when resistance is encountered, it is viewed from a local and isolated perspective, making it unique to that setting (Gregorin, 2015; McKinley, 2009). McKinley notes,

> In the debate over illegal immigration, San Francisco has proudly played the role of liberal enclave, a so-called sanctuary city where local officials have refused to cooperate with enforcement of federal immigration law and undocumented residents have mostly lived without fear of consequence. But over the last year, buffeted by several high-profile crimes by illegal immigrants and revelations of mismanagement of the city's sanctuary policy, San Francisco has become less like its self-image and more like many other cities in the United States: deeply conflicted over how to cope with the fallout of illegal immigration.

Tensions can remain long after a city achieves a designation as a sanctuary site (Villazor, 2010). Tensions can emerge between residents and officials who favor, or do not favor, having their city embrace this designation.

Some religious institutions not only embrace this designation but also may conduct outreach and provide social services to those who are unauthorized, whereas others ignore this group, and yet others fall somewhere between these two extremes. An evolutionary perspective lends itself to viewing levels of organizational efforts at embracing a sanctuary designation, allowing a more nuanced and multistage approach, with each phase bringing its own set of dynamics, rewards, and challenges.

In summary, I subscribe to the belief that the attraction of sanctuary cities is largely due to the interplay of employment opportunities, local activists, local histories, key community institutions such as houses of worship and human service organizations, and the belief of those who are unauthorized that this designation captures a state of well-being that they can expect will make living there better for them as well as safer from arrest and deportation (Cebula, 2016; Quesada et al., 2014).

Finally, it would be irresponsible to move on without addressing financial costs. Enlisting the support of local law enforcement to perform immigration actions can also be viewed as a means of shifting costs from the federal government to local governments, raising important financial questions and concerns with regard to county and city budgets.

It is appropriate to end this section with the following quotation by Clause (2017):

The term "sanctuary city" distills one component of the exceedingly complex debate over immigration policy into a convenient buzzword, and for this reason, it will likely remain part of the continued debate. But the final battles could very well play out on the state and county level.

The following history of the sanctuary city focuses on the movement from a conceptual rather than a legal perspective.

IS IT OR IS IT NOT A SANCTUARY CITY?

The posing of the question is not intended to be provocative but, rather, to highlight a key consideration for readers in need of exactitude on defining this movement. Readers may wonder out loud whether their city, for those who live in cities, is a sanctuary city. They may find contradictory information regarding this question and think it is unique to their particular locale.

Some cities and towns may function as sanctuary sites without embracing this designation. Others may use different terms that are less politically charged but function as sanctuary sites, and some may use a different label such as "welcoming." Yet, there are others without a unanimity of opinions one way or the other. For example, some lists label Seattle as a sanctuary city, whereas others label it a welcoming city.

The following examples of Detroit, Michigan, and Tacoma, Washington, are illustrative of the challenge of compiling a comprehensive listing of sanctuary cities and counties throughout the country. Detroit is an example of a city that appears on both "not a sanctuary city" and "sanctuary city" listings, and the Tacoma is an example of a city that does not have such a designation but is functioning as one. There is no "official" stamp that can mark a city as a sanctuary (Boscarino, 2017):

> The conflicting declarations arise from the fact that "sanctuary city" has no precise legal definition, referring instead to a variety of policies that may describe a stronger stance in some jurisdiction or a less openly defiant one in others. Detroit's ordinance, adopted in 2007, is among the latter. While it does instruct city employees to provide equal services to all residents regardless of citizenship and generally instructs police not to ask about immigration status, there are exceptions—police *may* ask when conducting an arrest or when cooperation is requested by federal authorities. Moreover, Detroit does not use "sanctuary city" or any similar phrase in its legislation.

The threat of losing federal funding is serious enough to halt efforts to seek a sanctuary city designation, as in the case of Tacoma (King5 News, 2017):

> Mayor Marilyn Strickland asked the City Council Tuesday night to not declare Tacoma a Sanctuary City, although the city already engages in many similar practices. Strickland asked the council to not declare Tacoma a Sanctuary City in order to protect federal funding. "I applaud cities that don't need federal

funding, but Tacoma is not a tax rich city," Strickland wrote in a Twitter message, "And we depend on federal funds for transit, social services and economic development that often helps under-served communities." Strickland said that Tacoma already engages in many of the actions of Sanctuary Cities without the label. Tacoma Police do not ask about immigration status when interacting with the public, and city services are available to all, regardless of immigration status. "Actions are more important than words," Strickland wrote.

Reference to actions speaking loader than words will stand out for some readers, whereas others may wish to have actions and symbols regarding a sanctuary designation, bringing a more nuanced perspective on the topic.

Those seeking exactitude will feel uncomfortable with such fluid boundaries on such an important designation; others can accept the murkiness or ambiguity of this designation and instead focus on how those who are undocumented in their midst are able to go through the average day with minimal fear of arrest and deportation.

No city, regardless of designation, can guarantee residents who are unauthorized that they will be free from arrests and deportations. The question is how closely local authorities will work with ICE in cases in which those who are unauthorized have been victims, or perpetrators, of a major crime. Nevertheless, having this designation helps diminish anxieties.

With California recently becoming a sanctuary state, which is discussed further in Chapter 10, those who live in the state and are undocumented feel safer going about their daily living activities (Adler, 2017):

> But Romulo Avelica-Gonzalez, a Los Angeles immigrant who was detained earlier this year while taking his daughters to school, says the governor's action made him very emotional. "There will be a lot more tranquility in our community," Avelica-Gonzalez said at De León's news conference. "We're gonna be able to take our kids to school, go visit the doctor, go to courts, with the confidence that we won't be detained."

This movement's history is influenced by this designation. Regardless of the delineation of sanctuary city definitional boundaries, there is no denying the legal and social significance of this movement over time and its potential evolution in the future.

HISTORY OF THE SANCTUARY MOVEMENT

Tracing the etiology of a social movement is never for the faint of heart because so many different factors must come together, and this is dependent on the historian's bias in writing the history. This history must be put against a backdrop of "historical neglect" of immigrant rights social movements in this country in general, even though the sanctuary movement embraces many of the same values and language used in other movements (Bloemraad, Silva, & Voss, 2016; Bloemraad, Voss, & Silva, 2014).

The New Sanctuary Movement is focused on enlisting and supporting houses of worship, which may or may not be located in sanctuary cities. The sanctuary city movement has essentially focused on local government. These two movements are separate but can, and often do, overlap and reinforce each other. One emphasizes the moral while the other emphasizes the social and political. When both converge, they emphasize human rights and social justice.

As previously noted, the origins of the sanctuary movement have been traced to the ancient Judaic tradition of Sanctuary, which takes this value thousands of years back (Houston, 2016). The sanctuary movement, in essence, is an urban movement although not restricted to cities (Bagelman, 2016). The failure to achieve a comprehensive immigration policy, and the localization of immigration policies, has thrust local communities into the role of immigration brokers, fostering the emergence of sanctuary cities and other anti-immigration sites (Rodriguez & Sider, 2013).

Jaworsky (2016b) advances the notion that values held by these sites are similar to the ones that newcomers embrace and also the American values of freedom, fairness, and equal opportunity. Ironically, these same values served as the inspiration for leaving their home countries and crossing hostile terrain into this country. These values unite those who share an undocumented status but not necessarily countries of origin.

"Sanctuary" is not the only term used to capture this movement; it can also be referred to as "hospitality" (Balch, 2016a; Darling, 2014). Hospitality is not possible without sharing space in an affirming and noncontested manner (Calvo & Sanchez, 2016; Phelan, 2017). If immigration is consistently presented as an existential threat to a country, with fear winning out over hospitality, a nation is bound to respond in a militaristic fashion (Balch, 2016a).

"Cities of refuge" has also been used to capture this social–political state of being (M. J. Gray, 2016; Walker, 2014). "Welcoming cities" is yet another term that captures the sentiments associated with sanctuary cities and is gaining popularity but not to the same political degree. This term is used in Winston-Salem, North Carolina, which seeks to convey a welcoming environment for immigrants and refugees by stressing the importance of diversity to the city (DiPazza, 2017).

A "welcoming "designation does not have the same political significance as "sanctuary," although it functions in much the same manner, and this may be an attempt to depoliticize a term with strong political connotations, as in the discussion of Boston in Chapter 8. It remains to be seen if a welcoming designation can be viewed from a politically developmental perspective signifying a "pre-sanctuary" designation. In other words, is this a specific destination or a stop along the way toward eventual sanctuary status for some cities?

Activism and mass demonstrations have helped mobilize formal and informal support, playing a critical role in channeling this support into political actions that lead to the creation of sanctuary cities (Bauder, 2016a). Social demonstrations that are considered "unconventional," as in the case of sanctuary city demonstrations, attract participants who are at ideologically extremes compared to participants in more "conventional demonstrations" and are considered more alienated from conventional political systems (DiGrazia, 2014).

Pro-immigrant demonstrations serve the role of promoting progressive immigrant legislation and blocking anti-immigrant legislation (Steil & Vasi, 2014). These demonstrations provide opportunities for participation from all sectors of society, from the "average" resident to celebrities and elected officials (Medina & Yee, 2017).

A study of newcomer participation in immigrant rights demonstrations (Texas and Indiana) addressed the important question of who among newcomers actually engages in public protest, with findings strongly indicating that this movement initially focused on individual grievances and discontents but has evolved and become more conventional regarding mode and level of involvement, with many being older, in this country longer, and with higher levels of formal education (McCann et al., 2016).

Immigration activists must not be viewed solely from an individual perspective but, rather, from a family perspective consisting of many different members, drawing upon collectivistic values (Pallares, 2014). These demonstrations are far from monolithic in composition, and there are few events that can accomplish bringing attention to this issue, as evidenced in Texas and throughout the country (Montgomery & Fernandez, 2017).

A shift from attempting to reform existing laws to radically alter them can be found in some mass demonstrations, although this phenomenon is seriously understudied (Abrams, 2016; Weffer, 2013). Community organizing is a form of civic engagement, and more so in a democracy. Some would argue that public protest is the most fundamental form of civic engagement, and one has only to read about this country's struggles to achieve independence from England to understand this point. Historically, foreign-born Latinos, particularly those who are undocumented, are highly reluctant to participant in mass social demonstrations, yet in 2006 almost 4 million participated in mass demonstrations throughout the country (Zepeda-Millán, 2016). This number is significant because it represented more than 30% of all those who were undocumented in this country.

Mass demonstrations on unauthorized rights have taken on transnational activities by having participants share organizing tactics and materials with other similar-minded groups throughout the nation (Mena Robles & Gomberg-Muñoz, 2016). It is important to note that mobilization for immigrant rights can occur online, representing the advantage of social media and a challenge for activists who prefer the "old-fashion" way of coming together and carrying out civic engagement (Jaworsky, 2015). National immigration organizations are in a propitious position to generate national and international support for immigrant rights.

Public demonstrations are an integral part of democracies, channeling and conveying important social and political values that can influence legislation and the implementation of policies that are detrimental to those who are unauthorized. Participation in social movements, such as the sanctuary city movement, is important because when one initially gets involved, it is an excellent indicator of future involvement in other social movements (Corrigall-Brown, 2013).

There is no one sanctuary movement, which can lead to confusion. One sanctuary movement can be traced to the 1970s, with a significant upsurge in sanctuary designations during the 1980s, which was a period of tremendous violence in Central America, particularly El Salvador, Guatemala, and Honduras, causing displacements of thousands seeking safety in the United States (Laman, 2015; Perla & Coutin, 2012).

In 1985, San Francisco became the first city in the nation to officially declare itself "a non-cooperation governmental entity." There was a dramatic increase in this designation soon afterwards, and by 1987 there were more than 440 sanctuary zones in the United States (Lippert, 2006), including 20 cities and the states of New York and New Mexico (Ridgley, 2008). Caminero-Santangelo (2012) documents the origins of the religious-initiated New Sanctuary Movement to May 2007, in major cities such as Chicago, Los Angeles, New York, San Diego, and Seattle, and with more than 50 cities by the end of the year, providing refuge and a counter-narrative to the prevailing blaming the victim discourse on those who are unauthorized. The New Sanctuary Movement effectively tied religion and immigrant rights in a moral and political manner (Yukich, 2013a).

It can be argued that initially, cities in which the sanctuary movement took hold, such as Los Angeles, had significant numbers of Latinos, refugee organizations, and Latino-dominant religious institutions to merge religious beliefs with social activism (Bhimji, 2014; Stoltz Chinchilla, Hamilton, & Loucky, 2009). These "perfect storms" galvanized public and political support to create this designation, serving to unite within, and across, and communities throughout the country.

Bagelman (2016) provides a very erudite philosophical discussion of the concept of sanctuary throughout the ages and its influence on the present-day sanctuary movement worldwide. The sanctuary movement is international, but no country has explicitly embraced this movement more than the United States (Bagelman, 2013; Darling & Squire, 2012). A chronological review of the international sanctuary city movement is beyond the scope of this book. Laman (2015) focuses on the United States and traces this movement to 1980 and Arizona, a state with a well-recognized history of being unwelcoming to those who are unauthorized:

> The first US declaration of sanctuary that occurred was in 1980 when members of the Southside Presbyterian Church came to the aid of Salvadoran nationals wandering the Arizona desert. Granting sanctuary proved difficult as church members were threatened with indictment for housing "illegals" by the then Immigration and Naturalization Service (INS). Faced with an ethical dilemma and not wanting to submit to INS threats, church members rallied public support. They launched a public relations campaign that drew on biblical references of refuge cities to assert moral obligation in aiding asylum seekers. . . . Soon after, on March 24, 1982—the second year anniversary of the assassination of Archbishop Oscar Romero—Southside Presbyterian and other churches across the United States declared themselves as "sanctuaries" for asylum seekers. This marked the unofficial beginning of the 1980s American sanctuary movement. (p. 9)

The March 24, 1982, date was very symbolic because it marked the second anniversary of El Salvador's Archbishop Romero's assassination. Two banners were erected outside of the church that read "This is a Sanctuary for the Oppressed of Central America" and "Immigration: Do not profane the Sanctuary of God" (M. Davidson, 1998). Remarkably, there is consensus on the importance of Arizona's Southside Presbyterian Church as being at the epicenter of the sanctuary movement in the United States, as well as the critical date that marked this movement's beginning.

Kotlowitz (2016) also traces the "birth" of the sanctuary movement to Tucson, Arizona, and President Regan's administration in 1982:

> The American movement to provide sanctuary to undocumented immigrants dates back thirty-four years, to the Southside Presbyterian Church in Tucson, Arizona, where the Reverend John Fife announced that his church would protect refugees fleeing the civil wars in El Salvador and Guatemala. Because the Reagan Administration supported the regimes in those two countries, it was difficult, if not impossible, for Salvadoreans and Guatemalans who felt persecuted by government forces to gain political asylum in the U.S., and harboring them was done in open defiance of the federal government. Between fifty and a hundred people stayed at the church each night, sleeping on foam pads on the floor, or on the carpet in the chapel. Volunteers provided meals, legal assistance, medical care, and English-language classes. Over ten years, Southside Presbyterian harbored thirteen thousand refugees, and some five hundred other congregations across the country ultimately joined the effort. These churches and synagogues physically protected refugees in an act of open civil disobedience.

Historical beginnings and interpretations are often open to debate, and it has gotten even more complicated and contentious with regard to the sanctuary movement.

There is general acknowledgment that enforcement of immigration laws is difficult under the best of circumstances; this is an even greater challenge when communities refuse to cooperate with immigration authorities (Saunders, Lim, & Prosnitz, 2014; Thi Nguyen, 2014). Some states have taken on enforcing immigration laws and have even passed very reactionary legislation. The previously outlined history of Arizona, which is one of the nation's most reactionary states regarding those who are unauthorized (Teixeira, 2016), illustrates the role and significance of religious institutions in galvanizing local and national support.

Soon after the Southside Presbyterian Church and other churches throughout the country declared themselves sanctuaries, the city of Madison, Wisconsin, do so too (Collingwood & El-Khatib, 2016):

> On June 7th, 1983 the Madison, Wisconsin city council passed Resolution 39,105, officially commending churches in the city that were offering sanctuary to Central American refugees, many (if not most) of whom had arrived

illegally. The Madison city council followed this with Resolution 41,075 on March 5th, 1985, officially declaring the entire city a sanctuary for Central Americans fleeing violence in El Salvador and Guatemala.

The turmoil in Central America has played a significant role in the uprootment of Latinos, and it continues to do so today. The presence of Latinos from Nicaragua, El Salvador, and Honduras reflects this historical shift in migration from Mexico (Cohn, Passel, & Gonzalez-Barrera, 2017):

> One metric—the number of new immigrants arriving in the U.S. each year— illustrates dramatically how immigration trends from Mexico and the three Central American nations, known collectively as the "Northern Triangle," have diverged in recent years. According to US Census Bureau data analyzed by Pew Research Center, about 115,000 new immigrants arrived from the Northern Triangle in 2014, double the 60,000 who entered the US three years earlier. Meanwhile, the number of new arrivals from Mexico declined slightly from 175,000 in 2011 to 165,000 in 2014.

Deportation back to these countries will only exacerbate social, economic, and political tensions in these countries.

Sanctuary cities emerged in response to harsh national immigration policies and narratives that were arbitrarily imposed with a specific focus on Latinos and other groups of color (Bell, 2010). Initially, the sanctuary movement was organic, without the centralized coordination seen in other social movements seeking to address social justice issues in this country. These efforts shared similarities, as well as differences, taking into account local circumstances. Such a stance makes analysis difficult, but it is essential to understand that "one size does not fit all," although the central organizing principles remained very similar.

HISTORY OF SANCTUARY CITIES IN URBAN AMERICA

The historical context that led to the establishment of sanctuary cities during the Bush and Obama presidencies, covering a 16-year period, was summarized by Boston College professor Kari Hong, a specialist on immigration (as quoted in Irons, 2017):

> Yes, unfortunately. It is not an official designation. Its use started under President George W. Bush's Secure Communities Program, which asks cities and states to work with the federal government on deportation enforcement by running background checks on those they arrest and then detain until Immigration and Customs Enforcement authorities determine if they are deportable. The federal government's effort was renamed the Priority Enforcement Program under President Obama. The reason why cities began to decline helping the federal government is because the federal authorities told them they were going to get all the bad guys—the drug dealers, rapists, and murderers—out

of cities and towns. But what was happening was that about 40 percent had no criminal record and 16 percent had minor crimes, such as undocumented immigrants who were driving without a driver's license on the way to drop their kid to school. The states and cities were also stuck detaining immigrants for years and were not being reimbursed by the federal government. The effort ended up costing millions.

Humanitarian concerns, combined with fiscal considerations, converged to create a condition that could not be ignored by local governments, and a sanctuary city designation united these sites across the nation in pursuit of a common social and political national justice agenda.

Although those who are unauthorized can be found throughout all regions of the country, there is no denying that the concept of sanctuary is deeply embedded in the nation's urban centers. This is due to the historical and current attraction of cities for those who are undocumented. Cities have played an influential role in attracting newcomers to countries (Bauder, 2017):

Cities have always attracted migrants. The European medieval saying "city air makes you free" (*Stadtluft macht frei*) describes how moving to the city once enabled people to shed feudal bonds and become free citizens. Like in the past, people today move to cities to take refuge, seek freedom, and pursue opportunity. However, many migrants and refugees today are not free citizens. In fact, those who crossed an international border before settling in a city are often denied legal status and thus criminalized. These "illegalized" migrants exemplify marginal populations that are denied equal participation in urban life. In this article, I use the case of illegalized migrants to explore the practical and utopian possibilities of all inhabitants belonging in the city.

Cities have emerged as critical geopolitical entities in the nation's struggle to address human rights and achieve social justice for various marginalized groups, such as those who are undocumented (Su, 2013), with police departments poised between local elected officials and federal immigration authorities (Stockman & Goodman, 2017).

Cities allow those who are unauthorized to blend in with minimal public attention, particularly in communities with high concentrations of Latinos and other people of color, while still tapping into social networks that can help them obtain employment, find housing and places of worship, and even engage in mass demonstrations (Negrón-Gonzales, 2016). Cities are places where those who are "different" are welcomed and have opportunities to create a new life. Small-town America has developed a mystique throughout the years, and the nation has romanticized it. However, if one is different, such as being LGBTQ, it is far from romantic because standing out can be hazardous to one's health, psychologically and physically.

Local networks play a very influential role in helping shape how local movements begin and evolve, including to what extent they draw upon local issues when there is an effort made to be inclusive, as in the case of Los Angeles and the Occupy Movement and pro-undocumented movement uniting to aid each other (Uitermark & Nicholls, 2012). A sanctuary city designation also serves to attract major media attention due to the national interest in this issue.

A mass public demonstration in a city brings forth visual images that a similar demonstration in rural America does not. In other words, "it makes good press." This makes these cities highly visible targets for the political right to fight against the "illegals" in this country. The Japanese saying, "The nail that sticks out gets hammered down," is applicable here. Thus, these cities must be prepared to have both positive and negative attention bestowed upon them.

Yukich (2013b) introduces an often overlooked dimension concerning sanctuary cities and their focus on the "model minority" and separating them from the "less desirable" unauthorized, in addition to the media emphasizing families and children as opposed to men. Men, honorable and hard-working, are also part of this community, but they represent too much of a threat to society.

Sharpless (2016) raises awareness of the pitfalls of using a conceptualization of those who are unauthorized as deserving and undeserving, which is often the case with immigration reformers, introducing the "politics of respectability" into the discourse. This view draws a sharp contrast between "favored groups" and those that are "degenerate, deviant, or less deserving." Sharpless understands the attractiveness of putting forth these "model" persons rather than arguing for a racial justice perspective that places attention on hyper-incarceration and how those who are unauthorized have been swept up with this movement because of their racial and ethnic backgrounds.

The nation's cities are home to 6.8 million unauthorized immigrants, or 61% of the nation's total unauthorized, with New York, Los Angles, and Houston accounting for 2.75 million or almost 40%. Viewing these immigrants within the context of the foreign born provides a more contextualized perspective of them in the nation's cities (Passel & Cohn, 2017a).

In early 2017, Austin, Texas, became a sanctuary city, joining Houston, which reaffirmed its welcoming city designation soon afterwards. Both Austin and Houston have become a focus of intense political pressure from the Republican governor and the Republican legislature to rescind the welcoming city designation and policies (Barajas, 2015; E. Rios, 2017; Tallet, 2017). Governor Abbott withdrew $1.5 million in funding. This move will be watched very carefully nationally as an indicator of how national and local policies move an anti-immigrant agenda and also of the resolve of this movement politically and legally, including its ability to draw support from national immigration and civil rights organizations, in addition to concerned citizens. The law has been referred to as "legalized racial profiling."

Incidentally, a federal judge blocked the governor's order to punish sanctuary cities in Texas (*The New York Times* Editorial Board, 2017, p. A20):

The judge's [San Antonio Federal District Court Judge, Orlando Garcia] ruling . . . is temporary and the state will appeal it, but it did not seem at all disconnected from the powerful display of America projected before the nation. Houston and five other major sanctuary cities and counties sued to block a Texas law's attempt to reinforce the nativist political gospel of President Trump and the strong-arm tactics of former Sheriff Joe Arpaio, who pioneered the use of local police officers as enforcers of federal law in abusive dragnets across Latino communities in Arizona. Judge Garcia (94 page order) concluded: "There is overwhelming evidence by local officials, including local law enforcement, that SB 4 will erode public trust and make many communities and neighborhoods less safe."

This decision is expected to be appealed.

The topic of undocumented immigration and sanctuary cities is best viewed from a pre- and post-September 11, 2001 (9/11), perspective and a renewed interest in "controlling the borders" to ensure national safety against terrorists. The USA PATRIOT Act, in response to the September 11 terrorist attacks, further marginalized the undocumented by making it legal to detain them without a hearing, marking the war on terror turning into a war on those who are undocumented (Hing, 2012b).

Crime and terrorism threats, it is necessary to emphasize, do not have to be real but only perceived to be real to achieve political ends, as in the case of Texas's Republican Party and its stance on "illegal aliens" within that state (J. D. Kincaid, 2016). The heighten militarization and policing of immigrants has brought a different perspective on crossing the border from Mexico to the United States (Balch, 2016b; Coleman, 2007; Coleman & Kocher, 2011; Gupta, 2014). Readers are well versed on border militarization, a key element of geography and violence, and how it has increased abuses and violence by immigration enforcement agents (Slack et al., 2016).

Joyner's (2016) assessment of the federal government's budget targeting those who are unauthorized post 9/11 crystalizes a long and close relationship between these two subjects and why it is necessary for the federal government to substantiate major investment of public funds into arrest and deportation activities:

> The U.S. government contributes more to the budgets of the agencies responsible for immigration enforcement (i.e., Customs and Border Protection and Immigration and Customs Enforcement) than to those of all other law enforcement agencies combined (e.g., the Federal Bureau of Investigation and Drug Enforcement Administration). Funding for immigration enforcement in the decade following the September 11 terrorist attacks increased considerably as a consequence of policies and programs that the Department of Homeland Security (DHS) implemented to deter illegal border crossings and identify those who were illegally residing in the U.S. (p. 2)

Local efforts integrating immigrants translates into supporting all newcomers regardless of citizenship status, generating an intended or unintended spillover effect (de Graauw & Bloemraad, 2017). These efforts have been framed as threats to national security.

The fact that no known unauthorized terrorist has crossed the southern border and been apprehended speaks volumes about the merits of this strategy. Yet, it persists and has gathered momentum since the 2016 presidential election. The visual images of people crossing the border caught on cameras reinforces this focus.

Post 9/11, there has been an increased use of formal identification, making it even more difficult for those who are undocumented to secure needed documents that facilitate day-to-day activities, including driving (C. L. Schmid, 2017). This period has also witnessed the growth of organizations specifically targeting those who are unauthorized and advocating for stricter immigration policies that reinforce deficit narratives of newcomers from certain racial, ethnic, and religious backgrounds (Bloch, 2016).

Burghart and Zeskind (2012) found a decline in the number of anti-immigrant organizations prior to the inauguration of President Obama:

It should be noted that IREHR [Institute for Research and Education on Human Rights] is not arguing that these organizations have disappeared altogether. Neither does IREHR contend that such organizations have ceased to be a danger to human rights. Rather, the data suggests that their size and power have fallen relative to the strength they had achieved at their height during the period 2007–2008. (p. 1)

Unfortunately, this decline has been followed by an increase in anti-immigrant activities by Tea Parties (Burghart & Zeskind, 2012):

This re-articulation of the Nativist Establishment into the Tea Parties changes both the shape and strength of the anti-immigrant impulse in American life. Mixed into the activities of multi-issue organizations (the Tea Parties), it will be harder to delineate and counter by immigrant rights advocates. Further, the Tea Party movement by itself is larger and more significant than the Nativist Establishment ever was, even at its height. Anti-immigrant activism has a bigger immediate constituency and is likely to be stronger. (p. 2)

Those who are unauthorized having the right to drive takes on greater significance in circumstances in which public transportation is very limited or employment opportunities necessitate use of a motor vehicle (Campos, 2014). We should not lose sight of counter unauthorized movements active prior to 9/11. One study found that between May 2006 and September 2007, 131 cities and counties in 30 US states passed or proposed laws that increased sanctions against renting housing to those who are unauthorized, in addition to other sanctions, such as those on employers (Hannan & Bauder, 2015).

The emergence of "immigration federalism," which has expanded state and local law enforcement of immigration laws, has created controversy and tension at the local city level, fostering racial profiling and arrests for minor infractions (Armacost, 2016). Localities with Democratic Party control of government have better police–community relationships and higher policing efficiency rates (Ciancio, 2016).

Increased enforcement of immigration policies has thrust local police in sanctuary cities, such as Denver, Colorado, into the middle of this national debate (Stockman & Goodman, 2017):

> In Denver, Sheriff Patrick Fireman, who runs the local jail, has long received one set of instructions from the Democratic-run city government and local advocates. The city attorney warned him against detaining anyone without a warrant. The American Civil Liberties Union threatened to sue him if he did. Immigrants' rights groups applied the added deterrent of local political pressure. When the federal Immigration and Customs Enforcement agency wants to deport one of his inmates, the jail sends a fax notifying ICE before the inmate is about to walk free—leaving it to federal agents to show up and make an arrest. But the fax is not necessarily sent with a great deal of advance notice. (p. A10)

Sanctuary city critics have framed their arguments on law and order, portraying local law enforcement's lack of cooperation with ICE as condoning breaking the law and being un-American.

Mexico shares a 2,000-mile border and a long history with the United States, and it is not surprising that the border has been a focus of national attention throughout the years concerning unauthorized immigration (Krogstad & Keegan, 2014). Part of this shared history also has much to do with the fact that major sections of the Southwest were once a part of Mexico and were acquired by the United States after the US–Mexican War.

Any history of Texas and the United States, for example, requires examining the naturalizing of Mexican immigrants, which has largely gone unnoticed in Texas and national history textbooks (Menchaca, 2011). Since 1965, an estimated 16 million Mexicans have entered the United States, with a significant number remaining as a permanent part of this nation's expanding Latino community, particularly in states such as California (Krogstad, 2016).

It must be noted that just because a city has a sanctuary designation does not automatically mean that deportations cannot transpire within its boundaries, although deportations can be made considerably more difficult to conduct (Armenta & Alvarez, 2017). Local law enforcement and ICE involvement can transpire through three different avenues: (1) actively enforcing immigration law, (2) cooperating with federal immigration entities, and (3) active everyday policing of newcomer communities (Armenta & Alvarez, 2017). Each of these can be conceptualized on a continuum, particularly when taking into account local enforcement policies (Ross, 2015):

> The policies and practices differ in the estimated 60 sanctuary cities around the country. . . . But generally, when someone has been, for instance, arrested for driving without a license and then identified as an illegal immigrant at a jail in a sanctuary city, they must serve jail time for state charges or pay related fines.

Then, they are let go. Most of these cities have identified some set of guidelines or conditions under which federal immigration officials must be alerted before the person's release. Usually they are connected to what's on the person's rap sheet. But some either don't have them or don't follow them.

Cities and states with strong Republican elected leadership and legislatures are less likely to have sanctuary designations (Tsiklauri, 2017). This declarative statement may not come as any great surprise to readers, and it is worth pausing and discussing this observation or conclusion. Changes in state legislatures and leadership from Republican to Democrat, as in the case of Colorado, facilitate a shift from anti-immigrant to pro-immigrant legislation, including fostering the embrace of sanctuary city designations, such as in Boulder and Denver (Berardi, 2014).

In the 2016 presidential election, immigration was a campaign theme that was larger than life: It had less to do with facts or research and more to do with feeding into the anti-immigration hysteria of the political right. Readers can take a less controversial perspective.

Cities and states do not need to have a sanctuary designation to carry out the functions associated with this movement. A case in point is Vermont, a state with a long liberal tradition and home to Senator Bernie Sanders, whose Republican governor recently took a highly unusual action by someone from the Republican party—enacting legislation that specifically prohibits state and local police departments from carrying out immigration laws without his approval. This measure prohibits the collection of personal information on immigration status and religion for any governmental registry that could be used by federal officials (Medina & Bidgood, 2017):

> Immigration advocates say Vermont's law is largely symbolic, because the Trump administration has not tried to collect information for a registry and because departments there do not currently enforce immigration law. But the bill, which passed unanimously in the State Senate and overwhelmingly in the House, has raised alarms in the northern reaches of the state, where small-town police officers frequently turn to federal officers, like the Border Patrol, for help in emergencies. The law "sends a message that could be construed to imply that local law enforcement shouldn't be working with our federal partners," said Chief Leonard Stell, of the Police Department in Swanton, a community of about 6,400, eight miles from the Canadian border.

The "symbolism" of this act should never be minimized. Although the sanctuary cities can only provide physical space to a limited number of people seeking refuge in local institutions, its symbolism far exceeds its practical impact.

SANCTUARY AS A PLACE AND SPACE

"Space naming," in the case of sanctuary cities and organizations, takes on great social and political importance in creating a national narrative of defiance, resistance, and moral outrage at the local level, and this goes far beyond symbolic value. Fletcher (2017) poses a number of important questions pertaining to the sanctuary city movement and space:

> While each space may declare itself as an advocate for undocumented immigrants, the ways in which various institutions uniquely identify themselves within this movement raises several questions. Why there are different names to spaces that seek to protect undocumented immigrants? Why do some institutions align themselves with sanctuary beliefs and ideals, but refuse to call themselves "sanctuary"? How important are the ways in which institutions identify themselves in the Sanctuary Movement? (p. 1)

Unfortunately, answering these questions cannot be done by using a broad stroke, with each city and organization requiring their specific voices to be solicited, recorded, and analyzed. There are broad generalizations that can be made on whether or not a city or organization embraces a sanctuary designation.

A sanctuary concept is multidimensional, and this is to be expected of a concept with such a long and distinguished history. There are multiple layers when discussing sanctuaries (Mironova, 2017):

> There are multiple layers to this declaration: a symbolic one, creating a welcoming space for undocumented students, parishioners, and community members; one related to information and data, where a campus may decide not to share information about its students' legal status with federal authorities; and a physical one, where a space can choose to actively shield a person from unjustified persecution, including deportation.

Each layer brings unique rewards and risks.

Communities are continuously in search of places and spaces that are considered safe and validating, and sanctuary cities and organizations represent this state of being for one group desperately needing an opportunity to be themselves. The example of Bushwick's (Brooklyn) Mayday website, as quoted by Mironova (2017), highlights how certain community places actively promote people and groups coming together in search of a common social justice agenda:

> [M]ovements and organizations need sustainable and supportive infrastructure to maximize their impact. There are few inviting spaces in NYC that serve as both organizing hubs and social venues to promote solidarity across a wide range of groups and communities. . . . By coming into a shared space, disparate activists and organizations will feel connected to a broader social-justice community, allowing for the cross-pollination of ideas and relationships. As many of our organizations are unable to effectively advance a policy agenda on our own, the trust and cooperation engendered between activists, community-based organizations, labor, and other progressive institutions will strengthen the coalitions needed to win meaningful reforms.

These places and spaces can be labeled sacred, sanctuaries, safe, welcoming, affirming, or some other label. Their role is well recognized, fulfilling important concrete and symbolic functions within their respective communities, in similar fashion to sanctuary cities and organizations.

SANCTUARY SYMBOLS

Another perspective on sanctuary cities and organizations views their hospitality from an examination of community visual signs. Outward symbols of a welcoming environment can transpire in a variety of ways. The use of murals, for instance, is one example that captures critical values and messages that show the community within, and without, in an affirming and welcoming manner (Crimaldi, 2017; L. A. Flores, 2016; Welch, 2016). Those who are unauthorized bring with them cultural talents related to music, art, and storytelling of various kinds.

Sponsoring community-based art exhibitions by newcomers is one way of tapping their voices and narratives, but it also allows attendees to share theirs as well (Rubesin, 2016). Opportunities for the unauthorized to share their narratives can also transpire through community-sponsored events focused on storytelling, with active audience participation (Cabaniss, 2016).

Community gardens can be conceptualized as sanctuary spaces and symbols that allow immigrants with agricultural backgrounds and histories, regardless of citizenship status, to reconnect with these histories and with others to have a sacred space where they feel safe, valued, and part of a community (Guerlain & Campbell, 2016). Community gardens can also be transformed into religious sanctuaries (Nix, 2016).

Hondagneu-Sotelo (2017) points out the immense instrumental and expressive benefits of community gardens in the lives of newcomers: These gardens help newcomers create new homes in this country and serve to bridge the old world with the new, increasing bonding and bridging social capital. In addition, these gardens allow them to grow food that has historical roots, helping them connect with their past while forging a new life in this country.

WELCOMING CITIES

Readers may wonder out load: "Welcoming cities? Wasn't this chapter devoted to defining sanctuary cities?" Passing local legislation with the term "sanctuary" can prove quite difficult, even when all the provisions associated with that designation can be obtained without a sanctuary designation (Parker, 2017). Becoming a welcoming rather than sanctuary city is such an example.

In 2011, the question, "What is possible if Dayton became a city that intentionally welcomed immigrants?" led to an active campaign in Dayton, Ohio, to shift the narrative at the local level. The campaign, "Welcome Dayton—Immigrant Friendly City," typifies efforts to localize and counteract national immigration law and policies, based on extensive collaboration between organizations sharing similar concerns about newcomers (Housel, Saxen, & Wahlrab, 2016; Majka & Longazel, 2017).

The designation of "immigrant friendly" has also emerged in an effort for cities to stand out in welcoming immigrants through special initiatives seeking multiple goals, such as "urban regeneration strategy" in Rust Belt cities such as Dayton, Ohio; Indianapolis, Indiana; and Utica, New York (Filomeno, 2017a,b; Shepard, 2016). A "welcoming" designation does not have to be publicly affirmed or restricted to cities, complicating the ability to obtain a comprehensive picture of the sanctuary movement. Places such as rural Iowa (Storm Lake), for instance, have become very dependent on immigrants (African, Asian, Central American, and Mexican) who have been able to meet local labor demands (pork, egg, and turkey factories) that are low paying (Cohen, 2017).

Planned efforts to attract newcomers are far wider nationally, with several cities in the Rust Belt, for example, standing out for their initiatives and indicative of systematic and planned efforts (Preston, 2013):

> Other struggling cities are trying to restart growth by luring enterprising immigrants, both highly skilled workers and low-wage laborers. In the Midwest, similar initiatives have begun in Chicago, Cleveland, Columbus, Indianapolis, St. Louis and Lansing, Mich., as well as Detroit, as it strives to rise out of bankruptcy. In June, officials from those cities and others met in Detroit to start a common network. "We want to get back to the entrepreneurial spirit that immigrants bring," said Richard Herman, a lawyer in Cleveland who advises cities on ideas for development based on immigration. The new welcome for immigrants reflects a broader shift in public opinion, polls show, as the country leaves behind the worst of the recession. More Americans agree that immigrants, even some in the country illegally, can help the economy, giving impetus to Congressional efforts to overhaul an immigration system that many say is broken.

However, regardless of the goal, there is no definitive definition of what being an immigrant friendly city means or actually entails. These and other efforts have gone under the radar as anti-immigrant efforts receive greater attention, creating a narrative that supporters of these anti-immigrant efforts hope encourages immigrants to leave, particularly those who are unauthorized.

CONCLUSION

There is no disputing that sanctuary cities bring an exciting and highly social and politicized dimension to immigration and cities—one that is evolving to include new manifestations and arenas. It is hoped that readers have developed an understanding of this concept and how it is evolving as it receives more national attention.

Chapter 6 grounds sanctuary cities from a geographical perspective, providing readers with a rare national, regional, and localized snapshot. Such a view helps ground the narratives that are emerging from local sites, making them a part of a national movement and increasing the significance of their presence. Unfortunately, a similar listing of sanctuary organizations is not presented, or possible, at this time. Such a listing would prove impressive and illustrative of this movement's influence.

6

Geographical Location of Sanctuary Designations

INTRODUCTION

As discussed in Chapter 5, there is no universal definition of what constitutes a sanctuary city, and this is a major source of contention among policymakers and law enforcement officials. This translates into numerous sites that may function in a sanctuary capacity but are unnamed as such, making the exercise of geographically locating sanctuary cities and counties difficult. Nevertheless, despite this limitation, there is much knowledge to be obtained by undertaking this exercise.

Geographically locating sanctuary cities is an art rather than a science because of the dynamic and designation factors outlined in previous chapters. This statement is not meant to denigrate the process or importance of the topic. Sanctuary sites, depending on their regional and national image and reputation, can wield influence beyond their geographical location and include an international reach.

Readers will no doubt be surprised by the list of geographical cities and counties in this chapter. Many of them are in states where this should not come as any great surprise; others will be surprising. Sanctuary counties provide an often missing perspective on this movement. It is important to state the obvious that cities are located within counties. Cities take on great significance in some areas of the country and are geographical markers in others areas, without any great significance.

Although it is quite clear that sanctuary sites are expanding throughout the United States, including counties, states, and other entities, because of the current political climate regarding those who are unauthorized and the continual political and economic threats on the part of elected officials toward these sites, the the number of sites can fluctuate either as an act of defiance or an act of self-preservation. However, the fundamental principles and values guiding these efforts do not change. This chapter provides a statistical portrait of sanctuary sites with some observational commentary to help guide readers.

A caveat is needed, however, because the number of designated sanctuary sites is dynamic, increasing almost on a weekly basis but occasionally decreasing due to some cities dropping the designation (e.g., Miami), and thus subject to change. For instance, in Massachusetts, the city of Newton voted to become a sanctuary city in February 2017 in response to President Trump's declaration against sanctuary cities, and the cities of Salem (famous for its witch trials) and Acton are seriously considering joining ranks with Boston, Cambridge, Chelsea, Lawrence, Northampton, and Somerville (Acitelli, 2017).

Furthermore, there are geographical locations that are not cities but, rather, towns, which are often overlooked in attempts grasp the national, regional, and local sanctuary picture. Last, there are cities, and even states, that have not officially embraced this designation but still functioning as sanctuary sites. For example, at least five states on both coasts have some form of state-level legislation preventing police from cooperating with ICE unless there is a warrant: California, Connecticut, Oregon, Rhode Island, and Vermont (J. C. Lee, Omri, & Preston, 2017). Readers may ask, Why then attempt to do such an inventory? Such an inventory has merit because it provides a numerical grasp of the significance of this movement, including where sanctuary cites cluster and where they do not exist, highlighting why there is such a significant political divide on this subject.

NATIONAL EXPANSE OF SANCTUARY DESIGNATIONS

The early sanctuary city movement period consisted of four cities (Cambridge, Massachusetts; Chicago, Illinois; San Francisco, California; and St. Paul, Minnesota), and since then it has expanded exponentially. Because of their national profiles and histories involving progressive causes, it is not surprising that these cities, with the exception of St. Paul, became the original sanctuary cities. As previously noted, but still worth emphasizing, the number of sanctuary cities and counties is dynamic and currently increasing. In February 2017, Jersey City, New Jersey's second largest city, joined Newark, its largest city, in becoming one of the latest cities to vote to have a sanctuary designation (McDonald, 2017). In late January 2017, Cincinnati, Ohio (the third largest city in Ohio), also joined the movement.

Anti-immigrant attitudes generally cluster geographically, with major areas of the country having few, if any, sanctuary sites (Hopkins et al., 2016). Restrictive state or local anti-immigration legislation and policies are expensive because they are often litigated and difficult to enforce (de la Vega & Steigenga, 2013). The publicity generated by these policies serves to further politically divide communities (Møller, 2014). Therefore, sanctuary designations can unite as well as divide communities and organizations.

Readers will see in the lists presented in this chapter major gaps supporting this conclusion. It is worth noting that Montreal, Canada's second most populous city, became one of the latest cities in North America to declare itself a sanctuary, illustrating its international appeal (Eleftheriou-Smith, 2017).

As of April 2017, 24 states had no sanctuary designations within their borders, which means that more than half of the states have such a designation within their borders. These numbers can be misleading due to the fact that "high-profile" states draw greater attention compared to other states. Any effort to institute federal penalties on these sites will effectively split the country in half and set in motion a political civil war regarding those who are unauthorized.

A listing of the states in which sanctuary sites (cities and/or counties) have been designated illustrates the scope of this movement: California, Colorado, Connecticut, Florida, Georgia, Illinois, Iowa, Kansas, Kentucky, Louisiana, Maine, Maryland, Massachusetts, Minnesota, Nebraska, Nevada, New Jersey, New Mexico, New York, North Dakota, Oregon, Pennsylvania, Rhode Island, Texas, Virginia, Washington, and Wisconsin. In addition, Washington, DC, is also a sanctuary site.

Some of these states, such as California, have many sanctuary counties and cities, whereas other states have few designated sites—for example, Georgia, Maine, and Wisconsin each have one site. The "Deep South" has a long and disturbing history related to civil rights, and this legacy has carried over in various forms until the present day and manifested itself in anti-immigrant policies and laws.

In 2010, for instance, Alabama's Republican Party won control of the state legislature (the first time since the Reconstruction) and the following year passed, and its Republican governor signed, HB 56 (known as the Citizen Protection Act), which at that time had the distinction as the "harshest immigration law in the country" (Ferreti, 2016). Alabama's HB 56 resulted in Latinos withdrawing their children from school, even in circumstances in which the children were citizens, and fleeing Alabama to states such as Tennessee, Texas, and Florida (Vasquez, 2014). The passage of this law is considered a critical event in helping frame immigration as a civil rights issue and drawing increased support from African Americans/Blacks (Williams & Hannon, 2016). For example, South Carolina, another southern state, is arguably one of the most restrictive states in the nation for those who are undocumented and, not surprisingly, does not have any sanctuary designations (McCorkle & Bailey, 2016).

Using a broad stroke to understand this phenomenon is not advisable, although significant conclusions can still be made about how sanctuary cities and counties emerge and thrive and why this is not the case in other cities one would expect to be part of this movement. Understanding the trends, in many ways, is significant for deepening our understanding of this movement.

GEOGRAPHICAL DISTRIBUTION OF SANCTUARY SITES

Sanctuary Designation Regional Distribution

Although sanctuary cities are a national movement, there is a strong bicoastal presence that cannot be ignored, which is addressed later in this chapter. A number of organizations have attempted to maintain a current list of sanctuary sites, and some of these are discussed here. Each organization brings its own set of biases and reasons for maintaining these lists. Three organizations are presented here for readers to stay abreast of changes in sanctuary designations.

The Center for Immigration Studies provides an interactive map of sanctuary cities and counties throughout the country (https://cis.org/Sanctuary-Cities-Map). The Center, it is fair to say, does not take a "progressive" view toward sanctuary cities. The Ohio Jobs and Justice Pac considers itself the first nongovernmental organization to track sanctuary cities throughout the country, and it provides an updated listing (http://www.ojjpac.org/sanctuary.asp). This listing is similar to the one provided by the Center for Immigration Studies, but it has more information on the sources for claiming the designation, which the avid reader may find of interest. Finally, the Immigrant Legal Resource Center (https://www.ilrc.org) represents a formidable progressive counterpart to the two other sources, and it also publishes a list of sanctuary sites that overlaps those of its more conservative counterparts but also has differences (B. P. Joyner & Voss, 2017).

Depending on their political leanings and interests, some readers may skim the lists presented in the following sections, whereas others may delve deeply into them. These listings are presented in a variety of configurations to illustrate key clustering of sanctuary sites and also their absences.

West Coast

The Pacific Coast has the potential to form a political "blue wall," with profound implications for national politics (Burns & Johnson, 2017). The West Coast has a large number of sanctuary counties and city designations, with California having 18 cities and counties, Oregon having 33, and Washington having 19 (Griffith & Vaughan, 2017):

California: Alameda County, Berkeley, Contra Costa County, Los Angeles, Los Angeles County, Monterey County, Napa County, Orange County, Riverside County, Sacramento County, San Bernardino County, San Diego County, San Francisco, San Francisco County, San Mateo County, Santa Ana, Santa Clara County, Santa Cruz County, Sonoma County

Oregon: Baker County, Clackamas County, Clatsop County, Coos County, Crook County, Curry County, Deschutes County, Douglas County, Gilliam County, Grant County, Hood River County, Jackson County, Jefferson County, Josephine County, Lane County, Lincoln County, Linn County, Malheur County, Marion County, Marlon County, Multnomah County, Polk County, Portland, Sherman County, Springfield, Tillamook County, Umatilla County, Union County, Wallowa County, Wasco County, Washington County, Wheeler County, Yamhill County

Washington: Chelan County, Clallam County, Clark County, Cowlitz County, Franklin County, Jefferson County, King County, Kitsap County, Pierce County, San Juan County, Seattle, Skagit County, Snohomish County, Spokane County, Thurston County, Walla Walla County, Wallowa County, Whatcom County, Yakima County

Other Regions of the Country

The East Coast does not have the same distinction as the West Coast, with major gaps, particularly in the South. Northern Florida has two sites (Alachua County and Clay County), with Virginia being the next eastern seacoast state with one sanctuary designation (Chesterfield County). Miami and Miami–Dade County withdrew their designation and are discussed later in this chapter. Georgia, South Carolina, North Carolina, Delaware, Maine, and New Hampshire do not have sanctuary designations.

The Southwest, too, is generally absent in the sanctuary movement, with notable exceptions:

Colorado: Arapahoe County, Aurora, Boulder County, Denver County, Garfield County, Grand County, Jefferson County, Larimer County, Mesa County, Pitkin County, Pueblo County, Routt County, San Miguel County, Weld County

New Mexico: No county jails will honor ICE detainer; Benalillo, San Miguel

Nevada: Clark County, Washoe County

The northwest states of Idaho, Montana, South Dakota, North Dakota, Wyoming, and Utah have none. The southwestern states of Arizona and Utah also do not have any sanctuary designation. However, Texas does have sanctuary sites (Austin, Dallas County, Houston, and Travis County).

The Middle Atlantic states are well represented in the sanctuary movement:

Maryland: Baltimore, Montgomery County, Prince George's County

New Jersey: Jersey City, Middlesex County, Newark, Ocean County, Union County

New York: Franklin County, Ithaca, Nassau County, New York City, Omondaga County, St. Lawrence County, Wayne County

Pennsylvania: Bradford County, Bucks County, Butler County, Chester County, Clarion County, Delaware County, Eerie County, Franklin County, Lebanon County, Lehigh County, Lycoming County, Montgomery County, Montour County, Perry County, Philadelphia, Pike County, Westmoreland County

Virginia: Arlington County, Chesterfield County

The Midwestern region, too, is well represented:

Illinois: Chicago; Cook County

Iowa: Benton County, Cass County, Franklin County, Fremont County, Greene County, Ida County, Iowa City, Johnson County, Jefferson County, Marion County, Monona County, Montgomery County, Pottawattamie County, Sioux County

Kansas: Butler County, Harvey County, Sedgwick County, Shawnee County, Story County
Minnesota: Hennepin County
Nebraska: Hall County, Sarpy County
Wisconsin: Milwaukee

The following New England states are participating in the sanctuary movement:

Connecticut: East Haven, Hartford, New Haven
Massachusetts: Amherst, Boston, Cambridge, Lawrence, Northampton, Somerville
Rhode Island: Providence, Rhode Island Department of Corrections
Vermont: Montpelier, Winooski

Maine and New Hampshire are absent from this list. New England's place in this nation's history and how it has shaped the nation's views of immigrants cannot be overlooked.

Finally, Louisiana (New Orleans) has the distinction of being one of two southern states (along with Florida) with a sanctuary site. Hawaii does not have a sanctuary designation, but it essentially functions as one.

Readers can take issue with how the states have been regionally clustered. For example, Connecticut can easily fall within a Middle Atlantic or New England category. Regardless, the national patterns within and between regions become apparent, highlighting where this movement is well represented and where there is room to grow.

CALIFORNIA SANCTUARY DESIGNATIONS: THE GLARE OF TWO CITIES AND THE SHADOW OF ANOTHER

California, with a special focus on Los Angeles and San Francisco, receives considerable attention in this book for many good reasons (Medina, 2017b). Chapter 8 crystalizes why California is a beacon in the sanctuary movement. This state, for instance, is considered to have the world's six largest economy, ahead of France, and this economic power makes it a force to be reckoned with, including the national political influence that goes with this designation.

As shown by the distribution of sanctuary sites listed previously, California has many sanctuary designations, and it is consistently in the news with regard to both official and unofficial actions it takes to support its unauthorized residents. For readers who live in California, the information presented here may be "old news."

However, for the rest of the country, it should be revealing and inspirational, with lessons learned for expanding and shaping the unfolding of sanctuary sites. There is no disputing that Los Angeles and San Francisco have received the lion's share of attention in discussions of sanctuary cities, and their prominent position in the national landscape has added to the narratives on this movement.

Immigration laws are no longer the exclusive purview of the federal government, and a sanctuary designation attests to how immigration law is modified, or ignored, at the local level. California is a prime example of this phenomenon (Karthick Ramakrishnan & Colbern, 2015):

> Immigration law is no longer the exclusive domain of the federal government. That was certainly clear in the mid 2000s, with restrictive laws on immigration enforcement in many states and localities. Starting in 2012, however, momentum shifted away from these restrictionist laws, and towards a growing number of state laws that push towards greater immigrant integration, on matters ranging from in-state tuition and financial aid to undocumented students, to expanded health benefits and access to driver's licenses. California has gone the furthest in this regard, both with respect to the number of pro-integration laws passed since 2000, and in their collective scope.

California, specifically Los Angeles and San Francisco, stands out in how it has responded to national immigration laws (Papazian, 2011). This state and its cities have stood out historically and do so currently with regard to how they conceptualize those who are unauthorized and their contributions to the well-being of their neighborhoods.

The following is a summary of the sanctuary church movement and its reintroduction in California and why it is expanding (Werman, 2016):

> There's been a history in California of churches offering sanctuary to undocumented immigrants. Back in the 1980s, several hundred churches became sanctuary churches, primarily for Salvadorean refugees. "(The churches) saved the lives of a lot of these people and then after that war was declared over and people stopped coming in large number the sanctuary movement sort of unwound," Pastor Morris said. But now it's winding up again. Many Mexicans come to the US from rural places where there are no jobs to go back to if they're deported. So they're desperate to stay. And Central Americans even more so. Gangs—especially in El Salvador—are ravaging their towns. Gangs that . . . ironically got their start in Los Angeles and then exported their brutality back to Central America when the LAPD began getting them deported them in the 1990s. "And so they deported hundreds if not thousands of Salvadorans, Hondurans and Guatemalans gang members back to their country," Pastor Moris said. "Well these kids got off the airplane, they had no skills, they hadn't finished school, the only thing they knew how to do was to run a gang, and they were very good at that. So they got guns and they began a protection racket. Most people in El Salvador now even the lady on the corner selling bananas off of a cart has to pay a gang $20 a week to keep her store going." That's why so many unaccompanied minors have been fleeing Central America and making their way to the US. ICE has targeted a lot of them since the beginning of this year. The organization has said it wants to send a message that they cannot come here—and just stay. But for a

lot of Central America, going back is an option that's too dangerous. It's also why Pastor Morris gave his church in North Hills sanctuary status. "I don't feel we're at risk here at all because I don't think ICE is going to want to break down the doors of the church on camera for Telemundo and Univision," he said. "I think that's too heavy for them. They're not going to do it. They didn't do it in the 80s to any of these churches that were holding people, I don't think . . . so I'm not losing any sleep over that possibility, but . . . we are waiting now."

California, as a symbol of freedom, has taken a place alongside the Statue of Liberty in national discourse because it has played such an important role in the sanctuary city movement and can be expected to continue to do so in the immediate future.

Interestingly, San Diego and San Diego County are widely considered to be sanctuary sites and have not received the attention they deserve, particularly because San Diego is near the Mexico border and a northern neighbor of Tijuana. As addressed again in Chapter 10, San Diego is not officially a sanctuary city.

There is a broader political context that has been touched upon in this book and that is worth mentioning again. The Democratic Party is increasingly building a larger political base in California, and there are concerted efforts to increase their hold on local and national elected offices, including the US Congress, making it easier to resist federal efforts to enforce immigration policy (Nagourney & Martin, 2017).

MIAMI AND MIAMI–DADE: AN EXCEPTION OR THE START OF A TREND?

As discussed in Chapter 1, Miami's decision to stop being a sanctuary city bears more attention because of its significance within the constellation of cities with large Latino populations and other groups, such as Haitians and African Americans. Miami's decision to stop being a sanctuary city proved quite controversial in early 2017 (Mazzei & Hanks, 2017a). This decision to withdraw being a sanctuary city created considerable protest (Mazzei & Hanks, 2017a):

> After becoming the first big-city mayor to appease Trump, Gimenez drew weeks of protests at County Hall from activists who said revoking the county's sanctuary stance represented an unacceptable rebuke to deeply blue Miami-Dade's immigrant identity. More than half of the residents are foreign-born. "This is a day that will define Miami-Dade County for the future," said Monestime, the board's first Haitian-American member. "Today cannot be about money, Mr. Mayor. It must be about justice. It must be about dignity."

The arguments made to counter the decision to withdraw set the stage for a decision made by Miami–Dade County, which soon afterwards dropped its sanctuary designation. This, too, proved controversial (Mazzei & Hanks, 2017b):

County commissioners rejected hours of impassioned testimony from residents who implored the board to stand up to the mayor and the White House. More than 150 people spent the day at County Hall delivering an often eloquent defense of immigration and South Florida's vaunted diversity; only a small number supported Gimenez's action. "Shame on you!" members of the crowd cried after the 9-3 vote, hurling bits of paper and white carnations at the dais and standing up to stomp out of the chambers. "May God have mercy on your soul," one woman hollered.

Readers can sense the tension and political climate at this meeting and how this decision sent shivers through the unauthorized community and their allies in this area of the state.

The ultimate impact that these decisions will have on the elections of mayor and county commissioners remains to be seen. In other words, is there a political price for this decision? The ripple effect of these two sites has yet to be felt in other sanctuary sites, making Miami and Miami–Dade County stand out. Therefore, is this an isolated instance or the start of a trend?

CONCLUSION

Developing a demographic picture of sanctuaries throughout the country is arduous. At best, we can take a snapshot knowing that this picture is frozen in time and will likely change in the next week or so. However, there is value in taking this snapshot of a "movement in time" because it is an indicator of how the movement may evolve, and it provides a deeper understanding of why the movement took hold where it did. Whether this inventory is expanded or contracted is debatable, but there is no denying that it is national in scope, with significant "holes" in between. Development of a comparable map of "welcoming cities" would add a missing and valuable perspective and an even more nuanced understanding of how localities are responding to increases in those who are undocumented in their midst.

Chapter 7 introduces a new dimension pertaining to a sanctuary designation—the emergence of sanctuary organizations. It is hoped that this dimension will prove exciting for readers who are in states and cities where there is no official sanctuary designation, bringing this movement more deeply into communities in which the unauthorized live, work, play, and even worship. Religious organizations have a prominent place within the movement, but they are not the only game in town, with other types of organizations playing visible or invisible, yet important, roles. These organizations must be acknowledged and supported if we hope to have this movement take hold more deeply in communities.

7

Sanctuary Organizations

INTRODUCTION

The sanctuary world is broad and goes beyond what we typically think of when discussing sanctuary sites and even when it involves "unofficial" designations. It is an expanding universe and full of surprises. Historically, states and localities have played critical roles in interpreting and establishing immigration laws (M. R. Slack, 2013). Local organizations can also be called upon to interpret immigration laws, a topic that has not received needed attention. Taking it to this extension places organizations in a position to assume sanctuary status, even more so if we entertain unofficial designations, with them serving de facto sanctuary roles without a highly visible designation to the external community but recognized locally.

As noted in Chapter 6, the sanctuary movement goes beyond a specific focus on cities and includes towns, counties, and even states. It can include places not normally associated with this movement. Urban transportation systems, such as San Francisco's Bay Area Rapid Transit (BART) system, have instituted specific instructions to "limit collaboration with Immigration and Customs Enforcement and other federal agencies" (Carcamo, 2017).

Sanctuaries include organizations beyond houses of worship, which undisputedly play a central role at the local level and will receive due attention in this chapter. Other forms of sanctuary organizations exist, enriching this field, including opening up options for all forms of practice as well as complicating our understanding of what is meant by a sanctuary site. The sanctuary movement is a magnet bringing together individuals and organizations that, on the surface, may not share very much in common beyond a set of guiding values making them act in response to an injustice being perpetrated on immigrants regardless of citizenship status (Squire, 2011).

A guiding principle of the sanctuary movement has been "access without fear," which translates into embracing the undocumented into a community's social fabric and facilitating their access to a range of services under difficult circumstances. Access brings instrumental, expressive, and symbolic benefits.

Broadening our understanding of sanctuaries to include organizations beyond religious institutions helps us operationalize what it means to have such a designation that is accessible to everyday life in a community (Bhuyan, 2011). This enriches our understanding and appreciation of what it means to be a sanctuary. This chapter defines the sanctuary organization, and it discusses how these institutions have operationalized the concept and values of sanctuary sites, including identifying potential tensions inherent in embracing this movement.

WHAT IS A SANCTUARY ORGANIZATION?

Discussion of a sanctuary concept has invariably been relegated to cities or other geographical entities such as towns, counties, or states. The concept of "sanctuary organization," however, calls for an assessment and mapping of these institutional resources and their importance in any sanctuary designation. Schools, for instance, can be sanctuary organizations when they actively attempt to thwart immigration efforts to apprehend undocumented adults as they drop off their children, which is more common than one might realize (Crawford, 2017): An "all-American" activity becomes an immigration enforcement opportunity.

Although the term "sanctuary" has been applied to cities and houses of worship, for example, it is important to differentiate between these two entities. The latter are engaged in a public act of subversion or resistance, whereas cities are engaged in "non-cooperation" by instructing local enforcement authorities to refuse to provide assistance to federal immigration authorities. Organizations are often called upon to provide instrumental and expressive services to those who are unauthorized.

Thinking of citizenship requirements based on social justice organizations being at liberty to interpret, or devise, their own immigration policies makes a sanctuary designation desirable and feasible (Jovanovic, 2017). Cities can facilitate those who are unauthorized being integrated into everyday workings. For instance, provision of municipal identification (ID) card programs in New Haven, Connecticut, followed by San Francisco, integrated immigrants into city life affairs, creating an avenue for urban citizenship that is counter to federal efforts to marginalize them (de Graauw, 2014).

In late 2012, the Los Angeles City Council passed a law (by a 12–1 vote), signed by Mayor Antonio Villaraigosa, approving ID cards for city residents. These cards allow unauthorized city residents (approximately 400,000) to switch from a cash economy to use the banking system, borrow library books, and even pay utility bills. A separate debit card feature allows users to preload their cards with cash (Saillant, 2012). In late summer 2016, the Phoenix City Council passed a measure to create a city photo ID that undocumented residents and others who face barriers obtaining valid government identification can use in conducting daily business (Gardinar, 2016). Phoenix has steadfastly refused to be designated a sanctuary city (Goth, 2017). In 2015, nine counties throughout the country issued ID cards regardless of resident immigration status (A-Wan et al., 2017). In 2017, Trenton, New Jersey, followed suit in issuing cards.

There is a different experience in using ID cards when taking race and ethnicity into account, with Latinos, more often than their White, non-Latino counterparts, having to share their ID card and experiencing other forms of micro-aggressions (Ditlmann & Lagunes, 2014; Lagunes, 2011). Municipal ID cards do not grant legal residency or a right to work (Costantini, 2011; Guttentag, 2012).

There are privacy concerns that lists of names of people issued ID cards (through the Freedom of Information Act) can be obtained for the purposes of turning them in to ICE, although these efforts have been unsuccessful. A sanctuary city designation without requisite change in policies to help ensure greater integration and access for those who are unauthorized is doomed to fail, as evidenced in Toronto, Canada (Hudson, Atak, & Hannan, 2016; Villegas, 2017).

The sanctuary city movement gained momentum under President Obama's administration in response to the extensive use of deportations, which proved controversial throughout his administration. In early 2008, Congress passed the Secure Communities Program, which authorized the fingerprinting of anyone charged with a crime; these fingerprints are entered into a national database that can be accessed by ICE (Kotlowitz, 2016).

The Personal Responsibility and Work Opportunity Reconciliation Act (PRWORA), enacted by Congress in 1996, officially prohibits those who are unauthorized from receiving most federal benefits. The fingerprinting and sharing of this information facilitates deportations of undocumented health care patients, raising important ethical issues (Hamel, Young, & Lehmann, 2014):

> Drawing on the ethical dimensions of informed consent, equality, distributive justice, transparency, and trust, we assess the tension between medical repatriation and the ethical duties of health care providers. At this time of great change in health care and immigration policy, clarity about our ethical obligations to undocumented immigrants is crucial if we are to create systems that are not only efficient, coordinated, and technologically sophisticated but also equitable for those who are vulnerable. (p. 669)

Health care organizations are in positions to either reinforce the law and cooperate with immigration authorities or resist facilitating the arrest and eventual deportation of these patients.

Unfortunately, the prospect of universal health care, regardless of citizenship status, is but a fantasy (Fernández & Rodriguez, 2017). Accessibility is severely limited without linguistic accessibility for newcomers, regardless of citizenship status, but more so among those who are undocumented because of the limits to socially navigate different organizations (Roth & Allard, 2016; C. E. Wilson, 2013a, 2013b). Equal access is not possible if citizenship status becomes a barrier (Bloemraad & Gleeson, 2012).

Those who are unauthorized have specifically been excluded from receiving medical services under the American Affordable Care Act, otherwise known as "Obama Care," severely limiting their care-seeking process. States such as Massachusetts were able to use hospital funds to provide coverage to this population group (Joseph, 2016). Philadelphia's Puentes de Salud stands out as a sanctuary organization because of the focus of its mission to meet the health needs of those who are unauthorized. This organization depends on contributions and civic engagement. Advocating for the right of the undocumented to have their basic human needs met in a humane and safe manner can be conceptualized as an ethical duty in health settings (Berlinger & Raghavan, 2013).

Holding meetings to discuss how a city should respond to harsh immigration rhetoric and policies can make a significant difference in how the discussions unfold and the eventual outcome of these meetings, as in the case of New Haven, Connecticut, and the Fair Haven branch of the public library (DeStefano, 2016; Resnik, 2016). Libraries, too, can be considered sanctuaries where all are welcomed regardless of citizenship status.

Human service organizations can also develop policies and reputations either as safe places to turn to for assistance or as places that can be hostile to the undocumented (Gast & Okamoto, 2016). Sanctuary organizations can fulfill key roles in meeting the needs of these immigrants and can facilitate referrals to other organizations embracing sanctuary values and principles (Diaz-Edelman, 2014).

An understanding of the "bottom-up dynamics in the politics of immigration," such as those in sanctuary city designations, provides important insight into street-level bureaucracies (informal) and how localities interpret and implement their policies (Gravelle, Ellermann, & Dauvergne, 2012). For instance, federal prosecutors have historically had discretion as part their responsibilities, a subject not often discussed.

Federal discretion in prosecuting those who are unauthorized, not surprisingly, may also vary within district offices, highlighting that even at the federal level there is local discretion, allowing local sentiments regarding those who are unauthorized to influence decision-making (Apollonio, Lochner, & Heddens, 2013). P. G. Lewis et al. (2012) studied police enforcement of immigration law and found that local departments headed by Latinos displayed a greater likelihood of not cooperating with federal authorities, bringing an added, and much nuanced, dimension to this discussion.

Ohio Jobs & Justice PAC (2017) addresses informal sanctuary policies, with applicability to governmental and nongovernmental entities and, in the latter case, organizations:

> An informal sanctuary policy is an "unwritten" policy that exists but is not documented on paper. None-the-less, an informal sanctuary policy is sanctioned by a local government authority and implemented by its public employees (administrative, service, and or safety forces). Informal sanctuary policies are more difficult to document since no public record exists. Informal sanctuary policies however can be evidenced in other ways.

A network of partnerships between individuals, organizations, and elected officials has been identified as essential to advancing a progressive and social justice agenda targeting immigrant rights (de Graauw, 2012). Developing an understanding of why sanctuary cities are constitutional is instrumental to the advancement of the movement in the future as efforts to impose legal consequences increase in type and frequency (M. J. Davidson, 2014; Hing, 2012a).

Independent lawyers, law firms, and law students have joined the sanctuary movement in an increasing and highly publicized fashion. A sanctuary network can provide a range of services that would otherwise not be available in a coordinated fashion. This perspective on the sanctuary movement is less well known and has not garnered the scholarly attention that it deserves.

The New Sanctuary Movement has played a critical moral and social role in being the focal point for community organizations interested in immigrants coming together. Although religious organizations play a pivotal role in fostering this movement, nonreligious organizations can be a vital part of this coalition.

The Boston New Sanctuary Movement, for example, consists of various organizational partners: Brazilian Immigrant Center; Centro Presente; The Chelsea Collaborative; Jobs With Justice; Massachusetts Coalition for Occupational Safety and Health; Massachusetts Interfaith Worker Justice Matahari: Eye of the Day; and Student Immigrant Movement. Boston's New Sanctuary Movement, similar to other New Sanctuary Movement organizations throughout the country, has three congregations that are prepared to physically house unauthorized families and approximately 12 local synagogues and churches that offer logistical and political support (Wangsness, 2017). This support falls within symbolic and practical realms, as is usually the case when discussing this movement.

The following description of a local coordinated attempt in Austin, Texas, to defend those who are undocumented in that city illustrates how organizations come together under a coordinating body (Lauer, 2017):

> The Austin Sanctuary Network has broadened in the last year from a handful of churches and advocates to more than two dozen congregations and religious groups, three labor unions, several nonprofit groups and dozens of individual volunteers. This mirrors the loosely organized national sanctuary movement that has grown to more than 800 churches and congregations, with a good portion of those joining since Trump was elected.

Sanctuary organizations, such as schools, may not have an official designation but still manage to subscribe to the values and principles shaping this movement and "get the word out" to those who are undocumented in their communities, including an embrace of Spanish language in English-only systems (Newcomer & Puzio, 2016). The provision of Spanish language instruction must be viewed not only as symbolic but also as a political and identity affirming step in reaching out to those who are unauthorized who speak Spanish in those districts.

Collaboration is essential in bringing about inclusion of disempowered groups, including those who are unauthorized (Rongerude & Sandoval, 2016). The development of an extensive organizational network that comes together to develop a systematic, if not comprehensive, network to assist takes on even greater importance in the case of unaccompanied children (S. Schmid, 2017). This nation's effort to integrate newcomers conflicts with a similar, if not more powerful, force that undermines their existence and minimizes, if not erases, their contributions to their communities and cities (Eaton, 2016).

de Graauw (2015) addresses the increasing need to integrate newcomers into the basic social fabric of communities and where these efforts must be focused, which is clearly at the local level and among neighborhood institutions:

> In the absence of a federal integration program, much of the government re-sponsibility to advance immigrant integration has rested with cities and in-creasingly states. This was true historically, when urban political machines helped with the social, economic, and political integration of the large wave of European immigrants, though they often did so coercively and for self-interested political reasons. While political parties today are less willing to fulfil this role, state and local governments—and big city mayors in particular—have stepped in to fill the integration policy void. (p. 1)

Integration of newcomers requires local elected officials to play an instrumental, if not leadership, role in advancing the causes associated with immigrants, and more so when they are unauthorized.

Sanctuary sites have emerged in defiance of laws that were considered illegiti-mate and counter to the basic values that this country was founded upon (Reddon, 2016). Sanctuary educational institutions are becoming an increasingly impor-tant part of this movement (M. Porter, 2017). Sanctuary universities/colleges, for instance, are but the latest major institutions explicitly embracing this iden-tity, bringing into the movement formidable institutions (Dinan, 2017b): "Forget sanctuary cities: The next heated congressional battle on immigration could be over 'sanctuary campuses'—the dozens of colleges and universities that say they will resist any cooperation with federal immigration agents, unless they are forced to by law."

The emergence of the sanctuary university movement parallels many of the efforts undertaken by sanctuary cities. Interestingly, many of the same considerations or issues emerge with this movement concerning officially labeling universities/colleges "sanctuary" or "welcoming" institutions, with some officials arguing that there is no difference between these two designations.

Freedom University (Athens, Georgia) brings together key elements and so-cial forces associated with educational institutions responding to anti-immigrant sentiments, which, incidentally, parallel those associated with the sanctuary movement. Freedom University was created in response to the 2011 Georgia Board of Regents' passage of an educational policy denying unauthorized students entrance to the state's five selective institutions of higher education. This anti-immigrant stance was recognized for its reactionary and racist sentiments.

This response represents an overt act of resistance, providing students who are unauthorized with an opportunity to continue pursuit of post-secondary educa-tional goals (Muñoz, Espino, & Antrop-Gonzalez, 2014): "Their mission statement proclaims, 'We believe that all Georgians have an equal right to a quality education.

Separate and unequal access to higher education contravenes this country's most cherished principles of equality and justice for all' " (p. 3). Again, a rights agenda and message resonates in this mission statement.

Muñoz et al. (2014) arrive at a conclusion about Freedom University that should resonate with those putting faith in sanctuary organizations:

> We believe that the creation of Freedom University is indeed a sanctuary in the sense that, like the Freedom schools, it provides a safe physical and psychological space for students without documentation to engage in a learning process with teaching that honors them as "fully human." And it does so without vilifying and framing them as undeserving. (p. 24)

The historical connection with the civil rights freedom schools grounds their latest response upon the legacy of those southern institutions (Hale, 2014).

Finally, local service organizations provide opportunity for civic engagement focused on immigrants because these institutions often enjoy consumer legitimacy: They are trusted, speak the same language, embrace similar cultural values, and are engaged in active outreach to immigrants (Gast & Okamoto, 2016). In essence, immigrants feel welcomed and valued, which are critical elements in achieving well-being (M. Delgado, 2017).

THE HOLY ALLIANCE OF ORGANIZATIONS

Development of an appreciation of sanctuary sites requires that they include a wide array of community organizations that bring the spirit of this movement to life and also that they tap into highly cherished values that are often taken as a given and, therefore, unmentioned. Immigrants threaten essential core values in this country, with this threat often manifested in economic or political ways rather than the role that immigrants can play in the country's transformation and future (Cooper, 2015).

It is much easier to think of immigrants as cheap labor ("outsiders") and "lucky" to be here rather than living in their own countries. But how does their presence threaten, or make us question, our most fundamental beliefs about a democracy and the role we play within the constellation of other democracies throughout the world?

Sanctuary organizations provide critical space for the education of activists and the planning of resistance actions that can go beyond those who are unauthorized, encompassing other marginalized groups and thereby serving a critical focal point in neighborhoods (Mironova, 2017):

> Resistance movements become visible in traditional public spaces. However, they gain strength just below the surface, in community centers, faith-based institutions, bookstores, and other spaces that serve as local hubs for the development of oppositional discourse. In New York City, older spaces like Judson Memorial Church in Greenwich Village, as well as newer hubs like the

Mayday Space in Bushwick, Brooklyn, provide a safe environment for people to meet, build trust, and organize, offering the stability necessary for long-term movement-building.

Although most urban service organizations come into contact with newcomers, immigrant-focused organizations stand out in importance for reaching this group. These organizations provide services, such as helping with the process of integrating newcomers into communities, but also embrace an activist function (C. E. Wilson, 2011).

Legislative advocacy and community organizing can play instrumental roles in making valuable resources available for those who are unauthorized, as well as providing a counter-narrative for prevailing views that are criminalization focused (A. B. Gates, 2017). For example, providing assistance and advocacy for Dreamer eligible applicants and advocating for comprehensive immigration reform can be part of these efforts (Hardina, 2014).

The children of undocumented Latinos face the challenge of an uncertain future but still only really knowing one life, and that is in this country (Burciaga, 2016). It is estimated that there are 840,000 Dreamers (DACA), many of whom are no longer young children and in their 20s and 30s (Hirschfeld Davis & Steinhauer, 2017). The immigrant rights movement has embraced the narrative of the "perfect Dreamer," but no human being is perfect, including the children of those who are unauthorized (Lauby, 2016).

A sanctuary designation can be associated with inter- and transcommunity goals, bringing a city or community into a national movement, such as the sanctuary movement. The following six types of organizations have been selected for attention in this chapter, reflecting how this sanctuary designation can unfold at the local level: sanctuary schools, hospitals and health clinics, sanctuary libraries, sanctuary homes, houses of worship, and nontraditional settings.

Sanctuary Schools

Schools can be thought of as sanctuaries without officially embracing the designation because these institutions can be conceptualized as places where students can feel physically, emotionally, and psychologically safe and part of a caring community (O'Gorman, Salmon, & Murphy, 2016). The need for this sense of well-being is enhanced when their families are undocumented.

The term "sanctuary" can be found in literature related to elementary and high schools, which are sometimes referred to as sanctuary schools. Sanctuary schools are institutions of learning that are welcoming of all students regardless of their backgrounds and citizenship status. Not surprisingly, there is a greater push to turn schools into sanctuaries in response to the Trump administration's anti-undocumented policies (Leonard, 2017).

These schools, although not able to prevent local law enforcement and ICE from entering and detaining students who are undocumented, can still refuse to cooperate. Symbols have emerged to signify schools as sanctuaries, as in the case of Chicago, where a symbol of a monarch butterfly serves this purpose. These schools provide workshops and other forms of assistance to the parents of students. The argument is well made that a student who is worried about losing his or her parents due to an immigration raid is not able to focus on learning. In 2017, Chicago's Mayor Rahm Emanuel launched a media campaign (One Chicago) welcoming all immigrants regardless of their immigration status and sued the Department of Justice over threats to stop funds to that city (Byrne & Dardick, 2017; M. Smith, 2017).

Typically, a sanctuary school designation means that immigration agents are not permitted on school grounds without explicit permission from a district's law department and the school superintendent (Born, 2017). It bears noting that schools do not have the legal right to question a student's immigration status.

In 1982, the Supreme Court issued *Plyler v. Doe* (5 to 4 vote), a landmark decision prohibiting states from denying students a public education based on their citizenship status (American Immigration Council, 2012). The Court ruled based on the Fourteenth Amendment of the US Constitution, which states in part, "No State shall . . . deny to any person within its jurisdiction the equal protection of the laws." This ruling was instrumental in striking down California's infamous Proposition 187 that prevented children who were unauthorized from attending public schools.

This sanctuary identity also helps draw and unify disparate groups of people behind this social justice movement. The sanctuary movement in higher education has a long history in this country, dating back to the Underground Railroad and the refusal to embrace fugitive slave laws, particularly in the north, which required that runaway slaves be returned to their "masters" (Ngai, 2017). There are significant parallels between these two civil rights movements (Villarruel, 1986).

Readers may encounter the concept of "sanctuary model," causing even more confusion with regard to sanctuary cities and organizations. The sanctuary model can trace its origins to the 1980s and efforts to build upon the therapeutic community model, seeking to develop an organizational culture that actively identifies the importance of an affirming and safe enviornment, counteracting the consequences associated with trauma and constant exposure to adverse circumstances (Esaki et al., 2013).

Hospitals and Health Clinics

The importance of health and health services is universal, regardless of citizenship status. Thus, it is important that there be health care organizations that can function as sanctuary organizations and be a part of a sanctuary network. This network makes and receives referrals. Unauthorized immigrants are often forced to use emergency rooms when requiring medical attention and when they fear discovery (Maldonado et al., 2013). Not surprisingly, local politics and circumstances will dictate the level of comfort and options that are available to meet their health care needs (Page & Polk, 2017; Portes, Fernández-Kelly, & Light, 2012).

Hospitals and health clinics are also considered "sensitive settings" where raids and deportations are discouraged, and these settings have generally escaped attention in the media, although stories of arrests and eventual deportations by ICE are legendary (Kline, 2017). The case of 10-year-old Rosa Maria Hernandez made national news because she was undocumented, having entered the United States as a baby and lived in the border town of Laredo, Texas. Rosa, who had cerebral palsy, had to undergo emergency gallbladder surgery in Corpus Christi, Texas. On route to the hospital, the ambulance in which Rosa was being transported was stopped by agents at a Border Patrol checkpoint (Yee, 2017g). After determining that she was undocumented, she was followed by the Border Patrol, and her hospital room was guarded with the intent of deporting her upon her release from the hospital. Upon discharge, she was taken to a shelter that housed undocumented juveniles, and she was separated from her mother. The American Civil Liberties Union filed suit in this case (Ugwu, 2017). This case raises serious questions about past immigration policies of avoiding sensitive settings.

Free health clinics and emergency departments can also function as sanctuary organizations (Akincigil, Mayers, & Fulghum, 2011; Ameringer & Liebert, 2017; Appold, 2015). These settings are more frequently used by undocumented Latinos compared to medical service facilities (Chavez, 2012b). As noted previously, Philadelphia's Puentes de Salud (http://www.puentesdesalud.org) is an example of a sanctuary health center.

Does a sanctuary designation translate into increased access to services and a reduction in health disparities? The answer to this question is yes, and this is critical for helping professionals (W. D. Lopez et al., 2017; McEwen, Boyle, & Messias, 2015). For example, a study of diabetes conducted in Chicago and the San Francisco Bay Area found that at least in some settings, being Mexican and undocumented did not alter clinical outcomes compared to those of Mexicans who were documented or were citizens (Iten et al., 2014).

Sanctuary Libraries

Libraries must be open to all people in a community, and this access is increased when there is an acknowledgment that they can only be viable when they are responsive to their communities (Pateman & Williment, 2013). This statement may be considered bold. In reality, the history of public libraries is one that is quite democratic and inclusive, even more so when they are located in communities that are highly marginalized and in which residents have very limited access to their materials and space.

Libraries have a multifaceted role to play as sanctuary organizations, drawing upon a long and deeply held belief that everyone is welcomed regardless of their background, including citizenship status. Readers can easily see how such an affirming and inclusive stance translates into libraries becoming sanctuary sites, and why they often can constitute the heart of a community, or part of a constellation of organizations serving those who are undocumented.

Libraries have played important community organizational roles in this movement, as evidenced in New Haven, Connecticut, and the role a library played in providing space and support for that city's efforts to achieve sanctuary status. When conceptualized as "safe spaces," libraries translate into sanctuaries for all, including those who are unauthorized (Wexelbaum, 2016). Houses of worship can provide services normally associated with libraries, such as a minivan library, increasing accessibility to services (Cruz, 2016).

The concept of sanctuary has even been applied to medical school libraries because of the space they provide for mindfulness and because they can be stress-free environments (R. S. C. Wong et al., 2016). The inclusion of libraries within the sanctuary movement should not be surprising in light of the role they have historically played within immigrant communities (Fleischaker, 2017; Kipton, 2016). Libraries as sanctuaries are not limited to this country, as witnessed in Sweden (Lundberg & Strange, 2016).

Some would argue that this institution has always had a special role that is sanctuary driven, even when the label was not used (I. Saunders, 2017):

> Libraries have a huge role to play in sanctuary cities. In fact, public libraries could be considered the ultimate sanctuary space: Public libraries are free to all people, at all times. Anyone, regardless of any race, color, creed, or immigration status, can enter a public library and use their resources, spaces, and services for free. They can receive one-on-one research and assistance from a librarian, and participate in programs and training sessions. No one is asked to identify themselves to enter the library and use their resources on site, and most public libraries (not all, I know, but many) have policies that aim to enable, rather than inhibit, access to a library card.

A library can provide safe spaces for meetings to transpire that can eventually lead to having a city declare itself a sanctuary, providing critical political space within an immigrant community and city. Daza (2017) continues this sanctuary library theme:

> There is a powerful, effective and meaningful way to uplift and protect immigrant New Yorkers right now: Support public libraries, institutions that proudly wear the sign of "everyone is welcome here" each and every day. These sanctuaries without our sanctuary city need our investment now and more than ever. Libraries are often the first stop for new Americans. In diverse communities like Corona, Queens . . . we want to help our neighbors adjust to a new country, language and culture, while also equipping them with the skills they need to succeed.

Librarians can engage in acts of resistance (Flock, 2017):

> But protests against the new administration by librarians only began popping up in large numbers around the country after Mr. Trump signed two executive

orders on immigration, one which could lead to the stripping of federal funds of so-called "sanctuary cities" for illegal immigrants, and the other which temporarily banned all refugees as well as travelers from seven Muslim-majority countries from entering the U.S.—an order that's been halted by the courts, but is still at the center of a legal battle.

Libraries must respond to their communities, and as these urban communities undergo demographic changes and the influx of those who are undocumented, it entails reaching out to them (Pateman & Williment, 2013). Social work practice, for instance, has a place in public libraries for conducting outreach, holding group meetings, and providing training and workshops, including a specific focus on immigrants and their needs (Kelley et al., 2017). Public libraries provide those who are unauthorized with ready access to computers and the internet for communication back home (R. Gomez, 2016).

Sanctuary Homes

The metaphor of a "home" is not difficult to understand. Applying this metaphor to sanctuary cities brings an important dimension to this movement (Boccagni, 2017). Although their impact is limited by the sheer number of people they can actually house, as in the case of the Underground Railroad and Safe Houses, at the same time, they are fulfilling important resistance functions that can easily be overlooked in any broad discussion of sanctuary cities and organizations. These homes are sanctuaries now, as they were during the 19th century for African slaves, fulfilling critical expressive and instrumental functions within their respective communities and nationally.

The Los Angeles Rapid Response Team, which conjures up an image of a military operation, captures how homes represent the evolution of one element of the sanctuary movement (KTLA5, 2017):

A hammer pounds away in the living room of a middle class home. A sanding machine smoothes the grain of the wood floor in the dining room. But this home Pastor Ada Valiente is showing off in Los Angeles, with its refurbished floors, is no ordinary home. "It would be three families we host here," Valiente says. By "host," she means provide refuge to people who may be sought by US Immigration and Customs Enforcement, known as ICE. The families staying here would be undocumented immigrants, fearing an ICE raid and possible deportation. The purchase of this home is part of a network formed by Los Angeles religious leaders across faiths in the wake of Donald Trump's election. The intent is to shelter hundreds, possibly thousands of undocumented people in safe houses across Southern California. The goal is to offer another sanctuary beyond religious buildings or schools, ones that require federal authorities to obtain warrants before entering the homes. "That's what we need to do as a community to keep families together," Valiente says. At another Los Angeles neighborhood miles away, a Jewish man shows off a sparsely decorated spare bedroom in his home. White sheets on the bed and the clean, adjacent full bathroom bear all the markers of an impending visit. The man, who asked not to be identified, pictures an undocumented woman and her children who may find refuge in his home someday. The man says he's never been in trouble before and has difficulty picturing that moment. But he's well educated and understands the Fourth Amendment, which gives people the right to be secure in their homes, against unreasonable searches and seizures. He's pictured the moment if ICE were to knock on his door. "I definitely won't let them in. That's our legal right," he says. "If they have a warrant, then they can come in. I can imagine that could be scary, but I feel the consequences of being passive in this moment is a little scary."

The parallel of Los Angeles' Rapid Response Team with the Underground Railroad and Safe Houses is striking. This city will arguably emerge as a beacon and laboratory for how sanctuary cities can evolve.

Houses of Worship

In any word association with sanctuary sites, houses of worship will emerge as the most popular response. There are few institutions that have a closer association with this movement than houses of worship. Houses of worship, specifically those designated as sanctuaries, have a moral role to help settle those who are uprooted, as well as to unsettle the political climate to create more welcoming policies and laws (Gallet, 2017; Snyder, 2011). The religious concept of "forgiveness" has also emerged with regard to those who are undocumented (Ahn, 2013b; Ahn, Chiu, & O'Neill, 2013). It is important to emphasize that although this book focuses on the sanctuary city movement, it is impossible to separate this movement from the religious-based New Sanctuary Movement.

Houses of worship can function as sanctuaries with regard to other causes, as in the case of the Philippines. The Catholic Church in the Philippines has opened its doors as a sanctuary to those fearing for their safety from vigilantes and the police addressing that nation's drug epidemic (Almendral, 2017).

There are no "typical" stories of those who are undocumented and their quest to avoid deportation, and the case of Ingrid Encalada Latorre is such an example (Turkewitz & Heisler, 2017):

Ingrid Encalada Latorre, 33, spent the last six months living in a red brick Quaker meetinghouse in Denver, one of hundreds of religious communities in the United States offering refuge or other help to immigrants facing deportation. Supporters of these churches say they keep families together. . . . Ms. Latorre came to the United States from Peru in 2000 at age 17. She took a nursing home job, and in 2010 authorities arrested her for using a Social Security number that belonged to someone else. She pleaded guilty to a felony,

spent two and one half months in jail, completed four and half years of pro-
bation and paid $11,500 in back taxes. Then facing deportation, she sought
refuge in the church in November. . . . She has two children, both citizens. In
the meetinghouse, she lived in an upstairs bedroom, exercised on a stationary
bicycle and cooked in a kitchen by the pews. (p. A11)

The case of Ms. Latorre splendidly illustrates the complex lives that many who are
unauthorized live and the sacrifices that they make to remain in this country, including the role that sanctuary houses of worship play in their lives.

Tomsho (1987) published a listing of sanctuary churches throughout the
country. It consisted of 193 churches in 35 states and the District of Columbia.
With 63, or almost one-third, California had the most sites . A comparable list is
currently not available. However, more than 30 years later, California still leads
the nation in sanctuary sites, both religious and non-religious.

According to estimates provided by the Church World Service, which has
actively offered immigrants legal assistance and helps organize the sanctuary
movement, the number of sanctuary houses of worship doubled from 400 to 800
after Donald Trump was elected president (Religious News Services, 2017). The
sanctuary movement has focused important scholarly attention on religiopolitical
activism of faith-based and community organizations, bringing together those
persons with moral and ethical concerns (Kotin, Dyrness, & Irazábal, 2011).

New York City's Sanctuary Coalition and Faith in New York, for example, have
attracted houses of worship that can physically house undocumented people for
both short and extended periods of time (Zimmer, 2017). Unfortunately, fears of
arrest can translate into avoiding workshops specifically meant to help immigrants
protect their rights, even when offered in houses of worship.

Legal clinics can be found in cities such as New York City, where they provide training to volunteers to accompany those who are unauthorized to ICE
appointments (Zimmer, 2017). In Massachusetts, congregations are establishing
physical shelters to house those who are unauthorized, based on the example of
a church in Denver that took in a mother and three of her children (Wangsness,
2017). This family left after 89 days after they were granted a 2-year extension
by ICE, which was largely due to political lobbying in Colorado (Winsor, 2017).
These efforts are largely symbolic because there are an estimated 210,000 unauthorized individuals in that state.

On March 31, 2017, the board of trustees of the Union for Reform of Judaism,
the nation's largest Jewish denomination (approximately 900 congregations),
voted to join the New Sanctuary Movement and provide sanctuary to the unauthorized in danger of deportation (Jenkins, 2017):

The Board's resolution, which also called on Congress to pass comprehensive
immigration reform and for President Trump to maintain pro-immigrant
executive orders enacted under Obama, rooted its support for sanctuary in
the scriptural example of Nathan, a Jewish prophet. Nathan challenged King
David for committing adultery, a move that board members described as "an

exemplary biblical model for confronting a state authority that wields its power unjustly and abusively."

The resolution went on to offer shelter, legal assistance in resisting deportations, and material, financial, and educational support.

Rabbi Jonah Dov Pesner (Religious Action Center of Reform Judaism) made an impassioned charge to the membership (Jenkins, 2017):

> "Today, we urge congregations to protect undocumented immigrants facing deportation by adopting a plan for providing resources, temporary shelter, legal assistance, or other forms of support to those in need," Pesner said in a statement. He noted that many synagogues have already offered sanctuary, which he said was in keeping with the Reform Jewish tradition: "The Reform Movement has a history of providing support in the form of advocacy and sanctuary for undocumented immigrants and refugees fleeing persecution in their home countries, and now we will do so for those fearing deportation from our own."

I cannot help but have a profound appreciation for how the persecution of Jews by the Nazis, and the importance of providing sanctuary during that time, can have significant moral and ethical meaning in extending a welcome and protection to another group trying to escape deportation by ICE, even at potential personal cost regarding safety.

Sanctuary churches that hold prominent positions within their respective communities generate political capital and apply pressure on local human service and community organizations to provide services to the unauthorized. This action enhances their power. These institutions occupy a very special place in our society, with a long history of supporting social justice rights.

Seeking sanctuary in houses of worship is not ideal for undocumented families because these places were not set up to physically house families. For instance, showers, a basic feature of a home, are generally not found in these institutions (Duin, 2016):

> I spent time with people who didn't dare leave the square block on which their sanctuary church sat for fear of ICE snapping them up. They were going mad with boredom and cabin fever; they had cleaned the church basement a zillion times for something to do, yet they were the lucky ones who had gotten from there to here.

Seeking sanctuary in a house of worship entails providing much more than a physical home. It also involves seeking and coordinating a range of social and legal services, as noted by a California minister (Werman, 2016):

> Pastor Morris and his congregation declared their church to be a sanctuary church in January. "We are waiting now for a family to come in here and be

our guests until we can appeal their deportation order and get it reversed," he said. "But then the problem is to get a family that is willing to go into voluntary incarceration in our church because once they come in here because they can't leave until we get the court case solved and that might take 30 days it might take 60 days it might take three months—we don't know." That's how worried members of his congregation are about deportation— even going to the protection of a sanctuary church feels perilous since it means openly declaring your undocumented status. Many are just not going to do that. No one has asked for sanctuary yet—including Abarca and her kids from Mexico who are now without a dad and husband. But Pastor Morris is keeping busy all the same, finding lawyers for this community in dire straits, raising money to help families left behind when there is a detention or deportation and keeping on message about knowing your constitutional rights. And somehow, they have managed to keep another thing: a sense of humor.

As a neighborhood institution, it necessitates that congregational members and a social network of activists, organizations, and concerned residents be involved, providing opportunities for civic engagement to transpire.

Conceptualizing a house of worship as a "neighborhood institution" integrates it into the basic fabric of the community; if the community's residents are increasingly newcomers, this institution must respond and embrace them if it is to remain relevant (U. Schmidt & Johansen, 2016). To remain relevant in transitioning neighborhoods with increasingly higher numbers of immigrants, the institution must take its cues from them and their moral mission. Sanctuary houses of worship that enjoy institutional and ethical legitimacy are in a position to levy this into political capital, whereas a house of worship that caters only to its congregation and avoids community interaction is not.

Religious institutions have primarily responded to the unauthorized from a moral rather than a political standpoint (Openshaw, McLane, & Parkerson, 2015). Faith-based responses to those crossing the desert, including preventing deaths, bring mercy to those in tremendous need (Groody, 2017).

According to Professor Bryan Pham, a Jesuit priest and professor at Loyola Marymount University in Los Angeles, houses of worship wishing to assume a sanctuary designation are advised to consider at least three key critical points in their deliberations (Religious News Services, 2017):

1. There is no legal definition or standing for a "sanctuary," so housing an undocumented immigrant in a house of worship is a violation of federal law. 2. Congregations can't claim that harboring an undocumented immigrant is an expression of their First Amendment's guarantee of freedom of religion. 3. Claiming a house of worship as a "sanctuary" and housing people inside it could be a violation of local ordinances, which may give law enforcement officials probable cause to obtain a warrant for a search and possible arrests.

Sanctuary churches can have that label as a primary designation with the attention that this brings and still collaborate with other religious institutions for a variety of supportive roles (Glatzer & Carr-Lemke, 2016). Thinking of sanctuary churches and other organizations from a singular focused perspective may be too narrow, failing to take into account the grounding of these institutions within a broader social network of supporting institutions.

Houses of worship must embrace social justice values in guiding their views and actions toward newcomers. However, they cannot easily or automatically engage in political action regarding those who are undocumented without overcoming economic, legal, and institutional barriers to accomplishing this goal (Coddou, 2017; Eby et al., 2011). Religious practice, identity, and citizenship status are tied together when discussing the sanctuary movement throughout the world (Fiddian-Qasmiyeh, 2011).

The influence of local religious organizations can vary in sanctuary cities throughout the country (Cadge et al., 2013). Sun and Cadge (2013) undertook research in two New England cities—Danbury, Connecticut, and Portland, Maine—to study how these cities responded to new immigrants. They found that Portland relied heavily on existing social service organizations because the newcomers were labeled as refugees, whereas Danbury enlisted the support of religious organizations to augment the services provided by social service organizations because newcomers were labeled as undocumented. These findings lend credence to the important role that religious organizations must play in the case of those who are undocumented.

In addition, geographical entities, such as cities and towns, can be supportive of the values and principles guiding sanctuary sites without assuming the label of one. Such a perspective broadens the climate of receptivity, although it may be frustrating for advocates wishing for a more affirming embrace through the use of the term "sanctuary city" (Hoffman, 2016):

> Storm Lake, Iowa, isn't a "sanctuary city." Not if you ask Police Chief Mark Prosser, anyway. . . . But while some local governments pass official "sanctuary" policies and trumpet their status to the world, there are dozens—if not hundreds—of communities like Storm Lake choosing to quietly protect their undocumented residents because it simply makes sense. Storm Lake has a population of 14,000 representing 30 different nationalities—"We're the most diverse community in Iowa," Prosser boasted—and is home to an impressive array of ethnic restaurants and shops; its two packing plants employ migrants from around the world. Prosser holds outreach programs for different cultural groups and workshops to educate people about the U visa, which undocumented victims of domestic violence can obtain. His team never asks about immigration status at these events. "My impression is that 'sanctuary' has no real meaning, at least when we think of a city or a university," Shoba Wadhia, the director of the Immigrants' Rights Clinic at Penn State Law and a member of the American Immigration Lawyers Association, told me. "It's appealing to the degree that it unifies those who want to ensure that a place or policy is

pro-immigrant or protects immigrants, but I believe it's been so misconstrued and used by restrictionists that it may not be the best term to use." To avoid possible backlash, many local jurisdictions are avoiding using the term.

Houses of worship, such as those in the South without specific designations as sanctuary sites, can minimize the impact of immigration authorities, but this resistance can cover an entire spectrum from minimal to more organized, and significant, responses, illustrating a range of potential responses (Ehrkamp & Nagel, 2014). For instance, churches can initiate outreach and seek to bring in those who are undocumented without engaging in political action to make themselves sanctuary sites (Wickersham, 2013).

New destinations and immigrants are a fact of life in the United States, and this results in contact with new houses of worship, as well as tensions related to their presence (Ellis, Wright, & Townley, 2014). Although it is natural to place the historical presence of Mexicans in the Southwest and West, students of the history of Mexican people in the United States can trace their presence in the South to the early 20th century (Pierce, 2016). Mexicans have extended their reach into the Northeast to cities such as New York City, clearly a recent destination in their history of immigration (Nuño, 2013b).

New internal migration patterns have evolved during the past decade so that now Latinos are moving into neighborhoods of color that historically have not been destinations, raising the possibilities of new political alliances, as well as potential tensions as they compete for housing and employment (M. Hall & Stringfield, 2014). It also results in efforts to become part of established houses of worship, be they Catholic or Protestant, for instance.

New Latino immigration routes and destinations create the need for them to establish, or re-establish, formal or informal supportive networks. An inability to establish these supportive networks can compromise their health and safety when a need arises, such as in the case of intimate partner violence (Reina, Maldonado, & Lohman, 2013). Higher skill levels make newcomers, as in the case of Latinos in new destinations, more acceptable compared to those with low skill levels, providing them with greater options in connecting with established institutions (De Jong et al., 2017).

When the unauthorized go to new destinations, such as the New South (Nuevo South), they will not have the benefit of long-standing and established communities, including the requisite infrastructures from which to receive assistance, as in the case of Latinos, forcing them to rely on non-immigrant community institutions such as houses of worship. In addition, they will be challenged by the feeling that they do not belong (Ehrkamp & Nagel, 2014; Nagel & Ehrkamp, 2016).

When communities have strong religious traditions as in the case of Appalachia, they have been found to be more willing to provide needed material and spiritual support to newcomers by tapping religious biblical mandates and values of aiding the "poor and alien." However, provision of needed legal assistance in dealing with documented status is not provided (Means, 2015). Interestingly, a study on Latino interstate migration found that when states passed repressive legislation, this did not result in changes in migration patterns, which is counterintuitive (Ellis, Wright, & Townley, 2016).

It is appropriate to put a spotlight on the Catholic Church and its role in the sanctuary city movement. Religion plays a very important role in supporting those who are uprooted in their journey, making it easier for them to connect with their religious faiths upon entering the country and to receive services (Deck, 2015; Eppsteiner & Hagan, 2016). The provocative question of where Catholic churches stand on the provision of sanctuary can be raised considering the large percentage of undocumented Catholic Latinos. The question of the status of Latino Pentecostals in this movement has been previously posed (Duin, 2016). Evangelical churches are addressed later.

Although the Catholic Church may seem homogeneous to outsiders, this is not the case. There is tension in Catholic thought between the right to seek refuge and the right for a nation to control its borders (Marzen & Woodyard, 2016). Finding a balance between these two perspectives has been difficult, highlighting one dimension of the divide that exists among the Catholic leadership in the United States.

This observation is not meant to be provocative. Rather, its intent is to uplift a critical subject, in this case on Latinos but not limited to them, which finds its way into social, political, and theological discourse on those who are unauthorized and their right to find sanctuary in this country.

Pope Francis' statement that nations must strive to build bridges rather than walls was widely interpreted to be directed at then Republican presidential candidate Donald Trump. This signaled a stance on the Catholic Church's view of the displaced. The argument that is often made by those on the political right is that the Catholic Church's primary motivation for taking a pro-immigrant path, and supporting sanctuary cities, has more to do with gaining parishioners. The moral justification for embracing those who are undocumented is overlooked.

It is necessary to note that the United States Conference of Catholic Bishops (2017) has never condoned or condemned sanctuary cities, but prominent Catholic bishops have spoken out in favor of more compassionate immigration laws. The Archbishop of San Francisco and the Bishop of Austin, Texas, for instance, have spoken out in favor of sanctuary cities and immigrant rights. However, there is no unanimity on this stance.

Avoidance of the use of a sanctuary designation is not necessary restricted to law enforcement or elected officials, as noted by Father Friedrichsen and Reverend Valenti-Hein (Hoffman, 2016):

> Even leaders at Storm Lake's local churches, which often assist immigrants, opposed a formal "sanctuary" declaration. Father Tim Friedrichsen, the priest at St. Mary Catholic Church, boasted that he held "services in five languages, not even one in Latin," but worried that the term "sanctuary" was "a buzzword that creates more heat than light," and could "ratchet up outright opposition by people who want border control." And Reverend Charles Valenti-Hein of

Lakeside Presbyterian Church said Storm Lake "isn't interested in making a political statement" but wants to focus on its local community.

Washington, DC's Cardinal Wuerl also issued a caution on the use of the term "sanctuary" in reaching out to those who are unauthorized, by emphasizing the making of promises that the Church cannot keep (Zaumer, 2017):

Cardinal Donald Wuerl, leader of the Washington Archdiocese's 620,000 Catholics, said Thursday that the church's values compel it to oppose the deportation of people already living in the United States. But Wuerl expressed caution about the idea of churches acting as sanctuaries for those seeking to avoid deportation, as some congregations across the country have offered. "When we use the word sanctuary, we have to be very careful that we're not holding out false hope. We wouldn't want to say, 'Stay here, we'll protect you.'"

Chicago's Archbishop Cupich has taken a similar stance as Cardinal Wuert (Cherone, 2017). The subject of sanctuary and houses of worship, and no more so than when applied to the Catholic Church, will increasingly be raised throughout the nation, with the potential of regional differences based on local considerations. It is a subject that can be projected to take center stage if the Trump administration carries out its deportation goals and strategies (Evans & Shimron, 2016). Simpson (2015) provides a historical perspective and puts forth a right of center political argument that the sanctuary movement regarding Latinos has its origins in an undertaking by Catholic Charities, the United States Conference of Catholic Bishops (through its Catholic Campaign for Human Development), and the support for an open borders movement.

The historical avoidance of a sanctuary designation by the Catholic Church in California, a state with a large Latino population, has symbolically, practically, and dramatically changed in response to President Trump's policies to increase deportations (Fehely, 2017):

We've learned Catholic churches in the Bay Area's biggest city may soon shield immigrants from deportation under the Donald Trump administration. The Catholic Church in Santa Clara County is quietly lining up as many as 20 places of worship to act as potential safehouses for immigrants facing deportation under a Trump presidency. Father Jon Pedigo of the Dioceses of San Jose said, "We are not looking to make a political statement on sanctuary or anything like that. It's basically providing refuge, support, stability and safety for a family in need." The plan is part of a coordinated effort by churches, community organizations and local leaders in response to the election of Trump, who's advocated for an aggressive crackdown on illegal immigration. San Jose Mayor Sam Liccardo wants to relax some city regulations and make it easier for churches to provide sanctuary to immigrant families. Liccardo said, "What we're trying to do is simply get out of the way for those service providers—in this case churches and faith-based organizations—that have traditionally provided sanctuary."

This shift in policy would not be attempted without support from the Catholic Church's hierarchy, and possibly the Vatican. Furthermore, this embrace of a sanctuary designation brings much needed coordination with community organizations and elected officials, illustrating the political importance of being a sanctuary.

Sacramento's Bishop Sotohas also stated that the Catholic Church will provide sanctuary to those seeking aid from deportation (Maganini, 2017):

> If the Trump administration orders mass deportations, undocumented immigrants could take refuge in Catholic churches with the support of local parishioners, said Sacramento's Roman Catholic Bishop Jaime Soto on Ash Wednesday. Soto said he hoped "all the hysteria" over undocumented immigrants would result in comprehensive immigration reform before mass deportations. But in the event that undocumented immigrants start being rounded up en masse, "we have to be ready to respond if and when that happens," Soto said in his office on Broadway. Soto, whose diocese spans 1 million parishioners in 20 counties, cited precedent for churches providing sanctuary to immigrants.

It is no mistake that the Catholic leadership in California has come out so strongly in supporting a sanctuary movement, and it remains to be seen how this major institution will shape the movement in that state and throughout the country because of the immense social, economic, and political power that the Catholic Church wields. A moral stance is very difficult to fight politically.

Mainline Protestant churches have played a prominent role in the sanctuary city movement, but the same cannot be said for Latino evangelical churches, although the original sanctuary movement in the 1980s did have important participation from this segment (Espinosa, Elizondo, & Miranda, 2005). Where do Latino evangelical churches stand with regard to sanctuaries? That is a fair question. There is a growing Protestant movement among Latinos in the United States, and these churches will need to respond to demographic changes (J. Martinez, 2012; Mulder & Jonason, 2017; Mulder, Ramos, & Martí, 2017).

This growing membership has not translated into these Latino churches, as community institutions, entering the political fray on adopting sanctuary stances. Latino evangelical churches have a potential major constituency in those who are unauthorized, and they have advocated for the easing of immigration laws but have not played a major role in the sanctuary movement. In New Haven, Connecticut, there are churches, including a Latino Pentecostal church (Iglesia de Dios Pentecostal), that have declared themselves sanctuary churches, possibly signaling a national trend (E. Johnson, 2017).

The expanding influence of Pentecostals among Latinos has largely gone unnoticed, but this oversight can quickly be corrected if these new converts manage to shift these churches into an advocacy–political campaign seeking justice for undocumented members (A. Delgado, 2017; D. Ramirez, 2015). This question remains to be answered. The eventual answer will have profound implications for the sanctuary movement and other human rights and social justice movements impacting Latinos in the immediate and distant future.

Nontraditional Settings

To make matters more challenging, nontraditional settings, too, may be playing an influential role in serving those who are undocumented. These settings, which can be commercial establishments and social/home town clubs, for example, further expand the meaning, if not the official designation, of sanctuary (M. Delgado, 1997, 1999). Therefore, even in cities in which there is no sanctuary designation, there may be key community institutions playing important supportive roles for the unauthorized, taking the typical meaning of this term beyond the police not cooperating with immigration authorities.

An anti-Trump "sanctuary restaurant movement," which on the surface may seem odd but upon closer examination makes a great deal of sense, illustrates how organizations, in this case commercial, can also be sanctuary sites, which again can mostly be found in major urban areas such as New York City, Washington, DC, Denver, and Los Angeles (Bedard, 2017):

> Led by a legal group for restaurant workers and a "Latinx" advocacy organiza-
> tion, over 300 restaurants have joined the sanctuary effort, equal to the over 300
> sanctuary cities that refuse to cooperate with federal officials seeking to detain
> criminal illegals, the deportation target of both former President Obama and
> President Trump. "Sanctuary Restaurants, a joint project of ROC United and
> Presente.org, is proud to announce that it has surpassed 300 restaurants na-
> tionwide. Sanctuary Restaurants, an affirming project designed to welcome all,
> is not a legal distinction. Rather, it is a symbolic overture to restaurant workers,
> employers, and customers who seek a safe place," they said in a release. Unlike
> sanctuary cities who keep federal law enforcement at bay when seeking to de-
> tain illegals held in jails, the restaurants don't have any legal authority. Instead,
> the group aims to promote and protect diversity.

Their purpose, although without legal implications but nevertheless of great moral significance, is multifaceted, as noted in their statement of purpose:

> We stand by restaurant workers, owners, and consumers and respect their
> dignity, human rights, and contributions to our industry and our nation—
> including immigrants, refugees, people of all genders, faiths, races, abilities,
> and sexual orientations. We have zero tolerance for sexism, racism, and xen-
> ophobia. We believe that there is a place at the table for everyone. Sanctuary
> Restaurants is a joint project of the Restaurant Opportunities Centers (ROC)

United and Presente.org with the participation of thousands of workers, diners, and allies nationwide. Note: Sanctuary Restaurants is not a legal designation. We offer support and resources to workers, restaurants, and consumers to help create the inclusive and equitable world we want to see.

Readers can understand the central thrust of this statement and why a human rights and social justice stance is capable of bringing together organizations that normally would not work together in pursuit of a noble cause.

ORGANIZATIONAL TENSIONS

It would be lovely to end this chapter on a high note by just focusing on the important role that community organizations play in bringing to life what a sanctuary city is all about. Unfortunately, that would be unrealistic. The sanctuary movement is complex, and contentious, at the organizational level, in similar fashion to that found in communities, religious institutions, and the political world. Sanctuary cities and organizations assume a tremendous onus in responding to the needs and issues of the unauthorized with regard to failed national immigration policies (Martone et al., 2014). These added burdens can easily translate into community and organizational tensions.

Tensions, it must be emphasized, are not restricted to human service and activist organizations. They can be found within, and between, houses of worship. One house of worship that recently joined the movement is worth highlighting because it is the first Hindu temple (Shaanti Bhavan Mandir in Queens, New York) in the nation to declare itself a sanctuary, but not without first experiencing tension. Just as important, it brings attention to the religious institutions that are not part of this movement, even though the saliency of those who are undocumented is important among their membership. Reluctance to join this movement may not be the result of not caring but, rather, the result of concerns about the unwanted publicity associated with this designation.

The vast majority of houses of worship that have declared themselves sanctuaries are Christian or Jewish. In New York City, the New Sanctuary Coalition has 25 member organizations but no mosques, for example (Otterman, 2017):

> For mosques, the challenge of joining the movement has been particularly intense, given the persistence of suspicion about Islam nationally and the targeting of Muslims by law enforcement and immigration orders. In New York, the executive director of the Majlis Ash Shura, an umbrella organization of Muslim mosques and organizations, said that local mosques led by African-Americans and immigrants were rightfully wary of joining the movement. "The other imams feel that if they shelter a criminal, they could be treated by law as hiding a terrorist," Cheikh Ahmed Mbacke, the executive director, said. "They are very vulnerable and one of the biggest targets of law enforcement. It's not that easy for anyone to bring that heat on themselves." (p. A18)

Readers can understand that mosques and Hindu temples, for example, claiming sanctuary status takes on greater significance and corresponding greater risk compared to ubiquitous denomination houses of worship doing so.

Tensions can also be experienced between houses of worship, as in the case of New Haven, Connecticut, in this instance highlighting racial differences of opinion between Latino and African American congregations (Ricks, 2016):

> Fair Haven Pentecostal Pastor Hector Luis Otero said that the pastors of churches that serve the Hispanic community have been meeting to develop a protocol for how they will respond in the event that ICE restarts its raids. He also called out Rev. Kimber by name for his previous remarks. "It is preferred that the city of New Haven is a multi-ethnic community, enriched by the ethnic diversity," Otero said in Spanish, which was translated into English by an interpreter. "The city of New Haven has been a refuge for many. The city of New Haven has been a sanctuary city and has allowed our immigrant brethren to have an environment that respects their dignity regardless of their origin, political affiliation, or the color of their skin. We're once community comprised of Hispanics, African-Americans, Anglicans and Asians. We're one community."

The previous discussion did not address tensions that occur within houses of worship, which can easily be overlooked or completely lost in responding to external threats.

Human service administrators' attitudes toward newcomers, a key element in carrying out the functions of sanctuary cities, are positively shaped when organizations openly embrace, and value, services to these groups, including those who are unauthorized (Smith & Womack, 2016). Municipal administrators, too, are not exempt from this stance, as in the case of Arizona (Lucio, 2016). Administrators who hold the belief that the undocumented bring crime and problems will not favor paths for them to participate in municipal decision-making. In the case of cities, demographic changes caused by increases in the numbers of immigrants, both authorized and unauthorized, may cause organizations to adopt program goals counter to national immigration policies and that are easier to adopt.

Even when local law enforcement adopts a policy of not asking for proof of citizenship, as in sanctuary cities, there are exceptions within these departments, highlighting operationalizing the key factors of autonomy and discretion and the importance of a street-level bureaucracy perspective on policy implementation related to those who are undocumented (Armenta, 2016).

When local demographics change dramatically and there is organizational resistance to responding to these changes, covert efforts to reach those who are unauthorized will be undertaken at first. As time passes and there is greater embrace of newcomers, efforts can become more overt and political in focus. Competition for housing and employment at the bottom rung of the ladder will increase competition between those who are unauthorized and low-income and low-wealth residents occupying that strata, as has occurred in Los Angeles and Southern California (Adams, 2014; Kun & Pulido, 2013; Zamora, 2015). This competition can spill over into other spheres, including how organizational priorities and resources must be directed or redirected.

Contrary to what can be typically expected among Latino organizations, religious and non-religious, these types of organizations do not necessarily automatically support those who are unauthorized (Ecklund et al., 2013). Differences of opinion within these organizations can cause tension, and even open conflict, as to who should be avoided in assigning staff to work with the unauthorized. Concern about "dropping a dime," which is a very dated but vivid expression—that a call to ICE will occur—captures this form of tension.

Finally, any discussion of opposition to sanctuary designations would not be complete without attention to one often overlooked influential group (Goins-Phillips, 2017). Tensions can come from many different sources, including the newcomer community itself, which can pose serious challenges to this movement, as experienced in Maryland (Tavernise, 2017):

> In passionate testimony before country legislators, and in some tense debates with liberal neighbors, and intense debates with liberal neighbors born in the United states, legal immigrants argued that offering sanctuary to people who came to the country illegally devalued their own past struggles to gain citizenship. Some even felt it threatened their hard-won hold on the American dream. (p. A14)

It remains to be seen whether those organized to counter sanctuary designations actively enlist the support of those who are authorized to counterbalance charges of xenophobia. If they do, it promises to fracture the communities in which both groups live and to seriously undermine the ability of organizations to advance the sanctuary movement.

CONCLUSION

The sanctuary movement is similar to an expanding universe when we are willing to entertain that the universe is, in fact, expanding beyond conventional boundaries. Identifying, and even uplifting, sanctuary organizations beyond houses of worship and governmental entities brings a richer understanding of the importance of the sanctuary movement in the lives of countless individuals.

These organizations can have highly recognizable missions embracing those who are unauthorized; these institutions can also have an underground reputation because of political considerations and funding concerns. Furthermore, these organizations do not need civil rights or human service missions because nontraditional settings can fulfill this role within a community. In essence, an embrace of an expanding universe brings with it the rewards associated with extensive formal and informal resources devoted to aiding the unauthorized.

Chapter 8 concretizes a variety of values and theories into actual case examples that can help readers better understand three sanctuary cities and the paths they took to achieve the official status of sanctuary. Each of the case illustrations

(Boston, Los Angeles, and San Francisco) highlights similarities, as well as important differences. These case illustrations also provide readers with an appreciation of how historical, demographic, economic, and political forces came together, as if "a perfect storm," to help these cities achieve the distinction of becoming sanctuary cities or, in the case of Boston, a welcoming one.

Case Illustrations

Boston, Los Angeles, and San Francisco

INTRODUCTION

Case studies or illustrations have a special place in helping increase understanding of how social forces come together to create a phenomenon such as sanctuary cities (E. J. Brown, 2015; Silverman, 2016). Case studies have particular appeal when they help tell a "good" narrative of hope winning over despair, justice prevailing over injustice, and increase our understanding of a particular situation. Case studies arguably work best when a narrative renders a natural conclusion. It is quite challenging if the narrative is still unfolding, as in the case of the sanctuary movement.

I have always been very fond of case studies because they help in attempting to anticipate questions readers may have about the birth of a movement, and they put "meat on the bones" by presenting a cogent and coherent narrative. In essence, they aid in bringing key concepts to life in a way that theory and statistics cannot.

By this point, readers have been exposed to numerous facts, histories, stories, statistics, concepts, historical documents, and editorial comments, and the question arises as to how sanctuary cities come to be in particular locales throughout the country. Tracing their origins, and the "spark" that led to their creation, helps synthesize material to make a whole narrative come alive. It also helps us understand present-day or evolving developments.

There is a significant difference between a case study and a case illustration, which has to do with the depth of coverage. Regarding the former, an entire book can be written around one case, providing an incredible depth of detail and capturing elusive nuances. A case illustration is similar to a "miniature" case study, with many of the major sections but nowhere near the depth and detail. Using case illustrations allows an author to present multiple case examples, helping highlight similar themes and exceptions, while allowing space for nuanced interpretations.

Cities such as Boston, Houston, New York, Chicago, Los Angeles, New Orleans, and San Francisco have historically functioned as gateways for newcomers and serve as laboratories for best practices, and non-best practices, on how to integrate and safeguard newcomers' rights (Waters & Kasinitz, 2013). These and other cities have long histories of being the initial ports of entry, bringing a wealth of experience; it is no mistake that they have sanctuary city or other types of welcoming designations.

Miami, too, would fall into this category, but it recently elected to stop being a sanctuary city. This decision proved very troubling to me because I have visited that city on countless occasions throughout the years and have many friends and colleagues who make it their home. The pride that many of them shared in their city has been turned into shame, which is an experience on one wishes to have.

Three cities are the focus of this chapter. Any reader who has lived in or visited Boston, Los Angeles, or San Francisco will realize that it is difficult to imagine three more different cities in the United States. They differ with regard to history, size, status as national icons, climate, demographics, immigration histories, and the degree to which they have a national reputation regarding those who are undocumented. All three share the same distinction of either having a sanctuary or, in the case of Boston, a "welcoming city" designation. Boston, for all intents and purposes, is a sanctuary city. For example, it was on the list of cities that were threatened to have funds withheld by the Department of Justice (DeCosta-Klipa, 2017). Furthermore, each city's influence in this movement has been different, and it can be expected that these cities will play different roles in the future, both regionally and nationally.

Many of the key themes and considerations raised throughout previous chapters of this book are manifested in these cases. If we were to play word association with these cities, numerous responses would be recorded because of their privileged position in the nation's history regarding newcomers. I, in turn, have had the opportunity to write about various aspects of these cities throughout my career, and this effort from a sanctuary standpoint adds a different layer to my understanding.

I have elected to focus on two California cities rather than select a city in the South, such as New Orleans, which was the original intent. New Orleans was initially selected because it has developed a national, if not international, reputation for an embrace of differences and has a long history of being home to many different ethnic and racial groups. The city's history also carries over to welcoming of people not readily welcomed in other areas of the South. The history of the unauthorized in New Orleans can best be traced to the period post-Katrina, a flashpoint, during which the unauthorized Latino population grew significantly (Drever & Blue, 2011). They played an important role in rebuilding the city. Some of the major issues Latinos who are undocumented face in New Orleans are those common in other cities: (1) lack of access to banking, (2) social and economic insecurity, and (3) difficulty accessing public transportation and obtaining a driver's license (Drever & Blue, 2011).

I also debated including Chicago on this list, but I decided to focus on the two coasts. A city's history of arriving at a sanctuary designation brings unique, as well as common, forces to bear. Chicago, for example, started this journey on July 18, 1982, when a vote was taken by the Wellington Avenue Church to join the emerging sanctuary movement, making it the second house of worship to openly harbor those who were undocumented in the United States (Rumore, 2017). Soon afterward, the Chicago Religious Task Force on Central America emerged to act as a national clearinghouse on this movement. In addition, Mayor Harold Washington and a supportive city council took on the goal of making Chicago a safe city, and this eventually led to Chicago becoming a sanctuary city on March 29, 2006. Mayor Emanuel has continued to keep Chicago on the forefront of this movement.

I made the decision to include two California cities because of the current importance of this state in the sanctuary movement, whether we think of this movement as religious-led or an organic sociopolitical movement that parallels that of the New Sanctuary Movement with its religious overtones. For instance, California's criminal justice reforms reflect efforts to make this system more responsive to the rights of those who are undocumented, and other efforts, such as the following, can be expected in the immediate future, which can be copied by other states (Eagly, 2016):

(1) Require prosecutors to consider immigration penalties in plea bargaining; (2) change the state definition of "misdemeanor" from a maximum sentence of a year to 364 days; and (3) instruct law enforcement agencies to not hold immigrants for deportation purposes unless they are first convicted of serious crimes.

California became the first state in the country to declare itself a sanctuary state (the California Values Act), a significant distinction but not surprising. In late 2017, Governor Brown signed legislation (SB 54) making California a sanctuary state (Adler, 2017). This represents a major step forward for the sanctuary movement on various levels. First, the movement is now a sanctuary state and city movement, although towns, counties, and organizations can be a part of this movement. Second, the political symbolism of an entire state, and one of the political and economic size of California, cannot be lost on this author. Mind you, it does not mean that there was political unanimity in achieving this distinction. This stance will embolden other states and cities to take this move and will further politicize the divide between the federal government and states actively supporting this movement.

Predictably, President Trump responded negatively to California's embrace as a sanctuary state (Adler, 2017):

"The State of California has now codified a commitment to returning criminal aliens back onto our streets, which undermines public safety, national security, and law enforcement," Justice Department spokesman Devin O'Malley said in a statement. "Given the multiple high-profile incidents that have occurred in California in recent years, it is especially disappointing that state leaders have made it law to limit cooperation between local jurisdictions and immigration authorities attempting to keep Californians safe."

FRAMEWORK FOR DESCRIPTION AND ANALYSIS

This chapter combines information discussed previously with new information to present a short narrative of Boston, San Francisco, and Los Angeles in a manner that allows readers to develop an appreciation of these sanctuary cities, drawing conclusions about their similarities and differences. As noted previously, each city deserves its own book(s) in bringing together immigration history and current status in the sanctuary movement. Many forces came together to cause an embrace of the sanctuary city designation.

Each case illustration consists of six sections and a brief summary: (1) demographic overview of the general population and its unauthorized groups; (2) history as a destination for immigrants and unauthorized groups; (3) events leading up the influx of its unauthorized population; (4) an overview of its local representative government; (5) designation of sanctuary or welcoming city; and (6) present-day status. These sections are treated as discrete categories but with significant overlaps.

The sections provide a "snapshot" capturing central points and raise questions and considerations that will emerge in the future as the current presidential administration reacts to their acts of resistance from a legal and social perspective. It is hoped that readers will develop an even deeper appreciation of the significance of these three cities in this movement's history.

BOSTON

Boston has a long, distinguished, and, at times, tumultuous history regarding civil rights in this country. There is no denying its role in the founding of this nation and the continuing role it plays in helping shape narrative discourse on this subject (Wangsness, 2017). Boston's history regarding immigrants is part of the nation's heritage and the building of this country. It has been a shining light on a hill, as well as a symbol of intolerance and even hatred. In many ways, it parallels the experience of countless other cities throughout the country. The latest historical chapter is unfolding today as it moves forward as a welcoming city, and it is increasingly finding itself as a destination for those who are undocumented.

Boston does not garner the same level of national attention as its two California counterparts. It is relatively new to this movement, and it is not a "sanctuary" city but, rather, a "welcoming" city; however, one for all practical purposes, it functions as a sanctuary city. It is included in this chapter with two "official" sanctuary cities because there is a very thin line between these two designations, and its inclusion can provide insight into the many nuances involved in reaching out to those who are unauthorized. In addition, California wields prodigious influence in this movement compared to Massachusetts, and this context, including its economy, cannot be easily ignored.

Demographic Overview of the General Population and Its Unauthorized Groups

Few readers will automatically associate Boston with the national sanctuary city movement or its religious counterpart, the New Sanctuary Movement. It is relatively small in population size compared to Los Angeles, for example. However, its influence is potentially enhanced because some consider it the "Athens of America" due to the fact that it had an instrumental role in the birth of the nation and is home to a large number of colleges and universities—on a per capita basis, it leads the nation in this category. Based on its history and large number of institutions of higher education, it is in a unique perch regarding immigrants, including those who are unauthorized.

Boston has a population of approximately 667,000, of which 35,000 are undocumented, representing 5.5% of the city's population. The Greater Boston area is home to approximately 180,000 persons who are undocumented, making it the nation's 12th largest metropolitan area for the undocumented and representing 3.7% of the area's total population of 4.5 million residents (Rocheleu, 2017). Fifty-four percent of Boston's population is White, non-Latino, with a high percentage being of Irish and Italian heritage. Massachusetts is home to 8,000 of the nation's approximately 800,000 Dreamers (A. Johnson, 2017).

African American/Blacks represent 24.4% of Boston's population; Latinos represent 12.7%, with the vast majority being Catholic; and Asians comprise 8.9%. It is estimated that 10,000 persons who are undocumented are Irish. In essence, Boston is a minority–majority city when taking into account those who are undocumented, which is heavily of color but, again, with a sizable number with Irish heritage.

History as a Destination for Immigrants and Unauthorized Groups

Boston is one of the nation's oldest cities and has a long history as a destination for immigrants from Europe, most notably England, Ireland, and Italy. We often only think of the Irish and Italians as immigrants and forget that the English, too, were newcomers to this country. Consequently, it is not much of a stretch to think of Boston as a destination for immigrants, both authorized and unauthorized, and to consider them as being a vital segment of that city.

Boston's history is well grounded within Massachusetts history, for better or worse. For instance, Massachusetts governmental efforts to dictate who had a right to live in its territory have been traced back to 1637, when the General Court of Massachusetts ordered that all "aliens" in the colony required permission from the authorities to settle there. This probably marks the first "official" effort to restrict residency in the country. It is interesting that the term "alien" was used more than 380 years ago.

The Immigration Act of 1965, discussed in Chapter 2, is often referred to as a key factor in substantially changing Boston's demographic composition, with the percentage of foreign-born residents doubling from 1965 to 2010. This has brought increased diversity to the city and, some would argue, increased racial tensions that reached a peak during the 1970s busing crisis, ushering in a period that was unwelcoming to immigrants, regardless of their documented status. During the 1970s, Boston was marked by a rapid influx of people from Puerto Rico, Haiti, Cuba, Colombia, Honduras, and other countries in Latin America, with Latinos constituting less than 3% of its population. By 2000, they represented almost 15%.

Immigrants and Boston are intertwined by history (Widmer, 2017, p. K6):

> The story of democracy resembles an immigrant's tale, though we rarely think about it that way. Like many newcomers, the word was first received with hostility, and took decades to assimilate. But now, it's so much a part of our heritage that we can't envision ourselves without it. And it's New England as those fried clams.

The unauthorized have had a long, and continuous, presence here, with most of the early undocumented residents being Irish. It has been estimated that the Irish undocumented numbered 100,000 during the 1980s. It was also during the early 1980s that Central Americans, fleeing conflicts in their home countries, immigrated to the city and its surrounding cities, increasing the number of those who were undocumented to historic levels.

Events Leading Up to the Influx of Its Unauthorized Population

Tracing the "influx" of Boston's undocumented population is not as simple as it may first appear because there is no one incident, or spark, that stands out in significance as bringing this population here. In 2014, Democratic Mayor Walsh signed the Trust Act, which was passed unanimously by the city council and prohibits the Boston police from detaining anyone based solely on their immigration status, with the exception of when a criminal warrant is issued (Clause, 2017). This stance is the cornerstone of sanctuary cities.

Boston, and its immediate region, is highly dependent on immigrants and their children to sustain the economy (A. Johnston, 2017). The same can be said about Los Angeles but less so for San Francisco. It is not difficult to understand why Boston's climate, and I am not talking about its weather, makes the city attractive for absorbing those who are unauthorized to find employment and a way of life that is validating. Being in what is considered a very "progressive" state has also helped Boston sustain a leadership pro-immigrant role within the state and region.

An Overview of Its Local Representative Government

Not surprisingly, city hall, through the mayor and city council, is instrumental, as in other cities throughout all regions of the country, in implementing a sanctuary designation at a local governmental level. Pro-immigrant organizations, too, must not be overlooked, including religious institutions located within certain neighborhoods, representing a natural focal point due to their organized constituency.

The Democratic Party is alive and well in Boston and Massachusetts. Massachusetts has a long history of having Democratic congressional representatives and senators, with the exception of Senator Brown, who won a special election to fill the seat vacated by the death of Senator Ted Kennedy. It has a history of electing "progressive" Republican governors, and it currently has one in Governor Baker.

Designation of Welcoming City

Boston has never officially been designated a sanctuary city, although it is a "welcoming" city. Then why include it in this chapter?

I included Boston because it highlights the thin line between a "sanctuary city" and a "welcoming city," complicating our understanding of this movement (Encarnacao, 2016):

> "We are a welcoming city for all and are committed to fostering an environment where all members of our community have opportunities to contribute and thrive. Those are Boston's values and no policy will change them," [Mayor] Walsh said. The mayor's office said Boston police do not hold undocumented immigrants for deportation unless there is a warrant for them from the Immigration and Customs Enforcement (ICE), and that the city has no plans to change this practice. He added, "At this time, there are no official proposals to change any programs or funding from the federal government. Working with the Boston Police Department, we will continue our work to build trust in our communities because everyone who lives, works or visits our city deserves to feel safe and be protected." Officials in many Bay State communities have called for strengthening sanctuary city protections for immigrants in the wake of Trump's plans, including Somerville Mayor Joseph Curtatone—already the head of a sanctuary city—and City Councilor Tito Jackson, who has called for Boston to become a sanctuary city.

The geographical proximity to other cities with sanctuary designations (Cambridge and Somerville) creates a dimension different from that of Los Angeles and San Francisco, providing political support of congressional elected officials for these cities.

After Boston declared itself a welcoming city, its resolve to embrace this designation increased, and the Trump administration's immigration policies caused Boston's Mayor Walsh to publically articulate a strong pro-immigrant stance (Carswell, 2016b):

> The Democratic mayor is adopting a "wait and see approach" on the Trump administration's immigration policies but, in the meantime, has defiantly

pledged to maintain Boston's protections for the undocumented—regardless of the Republican president-elect's plans. "We defend and are going to defend people in the city—our friends, our neighbors, family members—from any efforts to exclude them from their rights here in the city of Boston. . . . Boston is a city of inclusion, welcoming diversity. We are a global city and we are going to stay that way. We are not going to stop being that city that respects immigrants, both documented and undocumented."

The mayor's stance signifies Boston's desire to legally, and politically, fight any federal efforts to require the city's active cooperation with immigration laws that are counter to the city's value base.

Present-Day Status

Boston currently remains a welcoming rather than sanctuary city. One can speculate as to why Boston is a welcoming rather than sanctuary city, and this is probably the result of the Catholic Church not taking a more forceful role in publicly supporting this movement, in similar fashion to what has happened in California, for instance. The Catholic Church has historically played a critical social and political role in Boston, although its reputation has been tarnished by child abuse scandals involving priests that have made national news. This does not mean that local Catholic churches are not reaching out to those in their membership who are unauthorized, however.

Boston is home to the New Sanctuary Movement, an important aspect often associated with sanctuary and welcoming cities, even though it is not a sanctuary city (http://www.bostonnewsanctuary.org). Its activities focus on education and advocacy:

> *Education*: We will educate ourselves about issues facing immigrants in our society and about the current movement. We will avail ourselves of resources from the New Sanctuary Movement and welcome the first-hand stories of immigrants themselves who have experienced injustice. We will renew our study of the sacred stories of migration and hospitality, injustice, and hope that already exist in our own faith traditions. Seeking also to educate our greater community, we will offer public forums on immigration.
>
> *Advocacy*: We understand that education alone brings no change if it does not lead to action. Therefore: We will actively and publicly work for comprehensive immigration reform in the United States. We call for an immediate moratorium on all raids and unjust deportations that cause the separation of families until such time as the broken system of immigration laws is fixed. We agree to include our names, our voices, and our selves (or representative members) in public events, various forms of media, and other appropriate venues. We will be a compassionate and persistent voice for justice for our immigrant brothers, sisters, and siblings.

As noted previously, the New Sanctuary Movement often consists of multiple organizations that are religious and non-religious in origin.

On September 24, 2017, the Bethel AME church, a historically African American/Black church with a long tradition of engaging in protest addressing the oppression of African Americans in this country, declared itself a "sanctuary" by giving shelter to an undocumented family from El Salvador that was facing deportation (Levenson, 2017). This makes it the second church in Massachusetts to declare itself a sanctuary and the country's first African American church to do so. Temple Nehar Shalom Community Synagogue in Boston is collaborating with Bethel AME to carry out this action.

The welcoming city status has not meant that ICE has pulled back in apprehending and deporting residents who are unauthorized. In Boston, ICE has been found to target courtrooms (local, state, and juvenile courthouses) to apprehend those who are unauthorized and appearing in court to face even minor charges. During the first 2 months of the current presidential administration, there were 444 arrests, or double the number during the first 2 months of 2016 (Cramer, 2017c). On October 16, 2017, a demonstration against a Guatemalan's deportation resulted in 18 arrests (Annear, 2017).

In 2017, following the lead of other cities such as Chicago and New York, Boston city government established the Greater Boston Immigrant Defense Fund ($1.4 million) to provide legal defense and education for newcomers, both documented and undocumented (Mascarenhas, 2017).

Summary

Boston's history with immigrants has continued to evolve during the past two centuries, and its designation as a welcoming city, rather than a sanctuary city, has marked a key stage in this evolution. Whether it takes the "plunge" and moves on to a sanctuary city remains to be seen.

The city's place in the history of this movement will largely rest on the eventual role that the Catholic Church plays and the many universities based there. Boston will either have a prominent place alongside Los Angeles and San Francisco or become a footnote in the history of the sanctuary movement.

SAN FRANCISCO

There are few cities in the country with the image and reputation that San Francisco possesses. Its unconventional history and the reputation it developed during the 1960s and 1970s as a haven for alternative thinking and lifestyles, in addition to its weather and beauty, stand out in its story. It is a national and international destination.

Being a destination for those who are undocumented can be compared to a beacon of light during a storm: It guides, provides hope, and provides direction during particularly trying and turbulent times. This reputation has a long history on the West Coast—one that has been enhanced by the latest developments pertaining to the unauthorized.

Demographic Overview of the General Population and Its Unauthorized Groups

In 2015, San Francisco had approximately 865,000 residents, of whom approximately 35,000 were unauthorized, representing 4% of the population, which is a very low percentage compared to that for Los Angeles.

The city has a minority–majority status, with White, non-Latinos accounting for 390,000 (45%), followed by Asians with 268,000 (33%), Latinos with 122,000 (14%), African American/Blacks with 53,000 (4.9%), a mix of two or more with 38,000 (4.4%), and American Indians with 4,000 (0.5%).

This demographic profile has served to bolster the city's resolve from political, economic, social, and even moral perspectives. Similar to Boston and Los Angeles, being a minority–majority city provides many political advantages in taking a pro-human rights stance, in addition to having the requisite organizations supporting newcomers, including houses of worship.

History as a Destination for Immigrants and Unauthorized Groups

Similar to Boston and Los Angeles, San Francisco is a gateway city with a long tradition of attracting Asians immigrants. Although there is a history of Asian immigrants settling in Boston and Los Angeles, San Francisco has an important role to play with regard to this community. San Francisco's Chinese New Year's Parade, for example, has a national and international reputation (Delgado, 2016a).

San Francisco has a unique history in this nation's immigration eras, and it continues to play a major role (Scott, 1998; R. Sullivan, 2016). Similar to several other coastal cities, San Francisco had a major influx of Chinese immigrants, primarily from southern China's Guangdong Province, between 1850 and the early 1900s (Jorae, 2009). Most initial immigrants were male of Hoisanese ethnicity who worked as miners on the transcontinental railroad and as mine workers and laborers during California's Gold Rush in the mid-1800s (Jorae, 2009). Due to racial discrimination, they were restricted from engaging in other types of employment, a familiar theme today because of documented status.

Events Leading Up to the Influx of Its Unauthorized Population

A modern historical review of those who are unauthorized in San Francisco can be traced to the 1980s, providing important parallels with other cities throughout the United States (McDede, 2017):

If you really want to understand the controversy of today, you might have to take a step inside an unlikely place: a church. Back in the early 1980s, Jose Artiga lived inside the Most Holy Redeemer Catholic Church in San Francisco's Castro District. That was after he fled El Salvador, when a death squad—a group of government backed assassins—came looking for him. "My sister came early Saturday morning as I was leaving the house I was staying at and told me, 'You've got to go, there is no time for questions, no time for investigations, you got to go,'" Artiga remembers. Artiga was not alone. Nearly a fifth of El Salvador's population fled the country's violent civil war. But the Reagan administration didn't want to admit that the Salvadoran government, an ally in the fight against communism, was also funding death squads. Artiga says the US government wanted to keep the violence under wraps. "More and more refugees were coming from El Salvador to the United States," Artiga says. "'As people were applying for political asylum, after a few years we realized that something like 99 percent of the applications were being denied.'" But that didn't stop the mass exodus. So, churches in the US stepped up, declaring themselves public sanctuaries. Church leaders offered to feed, shelter, and provide attorneys for the thousands fleeing violence.

Central America's political upheaval was largely responsible, as in the case of Los Angeles and Boston, for the initial mass influx of unauthorized people to San Francisco (Jonas & Rodríguez, 2015).

Unlike its sister city to the south, San Francisco did not experience a significant increase in undocumented Mexicans among its unauthorized community, although Mexican subgroups have made it to the city (Baquedano-López & Janetti, 2017). They found refuge in the Castro District, historic home to its Latino population, with established formal and informal support systems, including houses of worship.

An Overview of Its Local Representative Government

There are many obvious parallels with the local representative governments and the political party in charge in Boston and Los Angeles. Virtually all of San Francisco's elected officials are from the Democratic Party, and the city has a long tradition of electing representatives from this party.

The Democratic mayor and board of selectman play an influential role in shaping the city's response to federal efforts to curtail the activities welcoming immigrants, both documented and undocumented. This political party representation is similar to that of Boston and Los Angeles.

Designation of Sanctuary City

Similar to Los Angeles, San Francisco can trace its pro-undocumented stance to the 1980s. San Francisco initially declared itself a "City of Refuge" on October 28,

1986, and officially became a "sanctuary city" in 1989 (CBS SFBayArea, 2015), with the distinction of being the nation's first sanctuary city.

The move toward a sanctuary designation has been traced to San Francisco's response to the Reagan administration's policies toward Central America and its refusal to grant asylum to those fleeing the wars there, leading San Francisco to adopt policies usually associated with the sanctuary movement. The rationale put forth by one of the key authors of the sanctuary bill is as follows (Lagos, 2017):

It wasn't even as much that he loved immigrants, it was I think more a sense of, we need this type of policy because without it, we lose the trust and coopera-tion of the immigrant community that we are devoted to serve.

This reasoning highlights human rights/social justice values.

Mancini (2016) sets an excellent historical foundation for the convergence of various major social forces and organizations that led to the embrace of a sanc-tuary designation in San Francisco:

In the early 1980s the San Francisco Bay Area became one of the emerging centers of the U.S. sanctuary movement. Responding to the needs of an estimated 60,000–100,000 Central American refugees in the Bay Area, com-munity organizers employed by the San Francisco Catholic Archdiocese's Catholic Social Service (CSS-SF) and the Commission on Social Justice's Latin America Task Force (LATF) worked with religious leaders in over 65 churches, synagogues, and religious orders to educate them on the wars in Central America, the plight of refugees, and possible forms of communal action (in-cluding public sanctuary) to improve the situation. With the support of the San Francisco Archbishop John Quinn, the organizational space and resources of the Archdiocese were made available to sanctuary organizers to build an urgent action network of social workers, lawyers, health services providers, employers, and private family "sponsors" that addressed the life-sustaining needs of refugees. (p. 37)

Readers can see how major social, civic, and religious organizations came to-gether on a major social justice issue, with significant national and international ramifications (Culliton-González & Ingram, 2017).

Present-Day Status

San Francisco has maintained its status as a sanctuary city and will con-tinue to do so well into the future. History becomes a foundation or a heavy weight, depending on one's perspective, which cannot easily be dismissed, as demonstrated by the two other cities discussed in this chapter. Similar to Los Angeles, to reaffirm its identity as a sanctuary city, San Francisco has taken a defiant stance against the current presidential administration in embracing its residents who are undocumented, although as previously noted, this has not been accomplished without tension.

San Francisco arguably wields significantly more national public presence compared to Boston and Los Angeles; therefore, its actions regarding the sanctuary movement are significantly magnified, both positively and negatively. It instituted a lawsuit questioning efforts to cut federal funding, receiving more publicity than if another less media-worthy city performed the same task.

Conclusion

Regardless of readers' views of San Francisco—as a city, the "Golden Gate," or a haven for this country's "unwelcomed and unwashed"—there is little disputing that it is a major force with regard to immigration policy at the local level. Its population size is very small compared to that of its sister city to the south. Nevertheless, size may not matter after all, and San Francisco is such an example, with sheer determination wielding greater impact.

The city's historical legacy is unique, representing a solid foundation from which to undertake acts of courage against formidable forces. San Francisco's population is less than those of Los Angeles, Chicago, and New York. Its unique position in California and nationally, however, translates into influence beyond its population size.

LOS ANGELES

Los Angeles is playing a central role in today's sanctuary movement. It is rare that a week goes by without an event occurring in Los Angeles related to those who are unauthorized. Being part of California helps this city advance this human rights agenda.

Because California has one of the world's largest economies, what happens in that state is significant from both a national and an international perspective (Cherkaoui, 2016). If a city were to be designated the capital of the sanctuary city movement, Los Angeles would clearly win this honor. As I researched various cities for inclusion in this chapter, Los Angeles was at the top of my list from the beginning, and the more research I undertook, the more this position was reinforced because of its history in addressing immigrants.

Los Angeles and the state of California lead the nation in the sheer number of residents who are unauthorized. The size of this population, and its percentage of the total, in the city and the state is significant. In many ways, California sets the social and political tone for the country, and how it handles its unauthorized residents can also be expected to wield considerable influence throughout the nation.

California's Proposition 187, which eventually was found to be unconstitutional, and the election of President George W. Bush played influential roles in shifting statewide political affiliation, which was reinforced during the 2016 presidential election (Monogan & Doctor, 2016). Some observers believe that this proposition effectively made California a one political party state for at least a generation, facilitating it taking such a politically dramatic stance against current immigration policies.

Orange County, home to Los Angeles, has almost half of California's unauthorized population, with an estimated 1 million unauthorized residents, which is second only to the greater New York area with 1.2 million (Mejia, Carcamo, & Knoll, 2017). Not unexpectedly, California has 5 of 20 of the nation's largest metropolitan areas with residents who are unauthorized (Los Angeles and Orange County, 1 million; Riverside/San Bernardino, 250,000; San Francisco/Oakland, 240,000; San Diego/Carlsbad, 170,000; and San Jose/Sunnyvale, 120,000). California seems to be at the epicenter of the sanctuary city movement, and there are no indications that it will blink first in any confrontation with federal immigration authorities.

The Los Angeles Latino community understands the history of incarceration of its people and other groups of color, with those who are unauthorized being a significant part of this city's incarceration narrative. Hernández's (2017) book, *City of Inmates: Conquest, Rebellion, and the Rise of Human Caging in Los Angeles, 1771–1965*, details this history and its impact on the city's legacy, with implications for how this history has shaped the city's current response to arrest and deportation of its residents who are unauthorized.

Demographic Overview of the General Population and Its Unauthorized Groups

Immigration represents but one part of the equation, with emigration representing the other part; both parts are equally important in developing an understanding of what this migration means for two countries (Alarcón, Escala, & Odgers, 2016). California, in this case Los Angeles, becomes an instrumental part of the narrative, including the embrace of a new identity that introduces citizenship status.

Los Angeles is the nation's second largest city with approximately 4 million residents, behind New York but ahead of Chicago. It is estimated that approximately 47.5% of its residents are Latino, followed by White, non-Latinos (29.6%), Asians (10.7%), and African American/Blacks (9.8%), making it a minority–majority city, thus sharing this status with the other two cities discussed in this chapter.

As previously noted, California is home to almost one-fourth of the nation's total undocumented population, and it stands to reason that Los Angeles would have a large share. Los Angeles has an estimated 814,000 undocumented residents (Hayes & Hill, 2017), and it is home to the largest concentration of people of Mexican heritage outside of Mexico.

History as a Destination for Immigrants and Unauthorized Groups

The US geographic proximity to Mexico played an important role in the initial migration patterns of those crossing the southern border, and it is the reason why Los Angeles has been a prominent destination and also why their history in that city can be traced back to its founding (R. Wright & Ellis, 2016). It is impossible to separate Mexicans from Los Angeles history since its founding in 1781.

Los Angeles' proximity to the Mexican border and Mexico's history of once owning this territory have played critical roles in Los Angeles' embrace of its history and sanctuary designation. Those of Mexican descent make up approximately one-third of all Los Angeles residents.

Although the "repatriation" during the early 1930s, as addressed in Chapter 2, affected Mexicans throughout the country, it had a particularly hard impact on Los Angeles' Mexican community (Wagner, 2017):

> The raids . . . were vicious. With national concerns over the supposed burden that outsiders were putting on social welfare agencies, authorities targeted those Mexicans utilizing public resources. In Los Angeles . . . they had orderlies who gathered people [in the hospitals] and put them in stretchers on trucks and left them at the border. . . . The efforts were chaotic. The first raid in Los Angeles was in 1931—they surrounded La Placita Park near downtown L.A. . . . it was a heavily Latino area. They, literally, on a Sunday afternoon, rounded everyone up in the park that day, took them to train station and put them on a train that they had leased. These people were taken to Central Mexico to minimize their chances of crossing the border and coming back to the U.S.

These events shed a long shadow on this community, and stories have been passed down from generation to generation, making the potential of reliving history for this community very real and painful.

In 2006, California passed the Apology Act, considered a mea culpa, in an effort to publicly acknowledge that ignominious period in the state's history regarding how it treated its Mexican residents. There is a memorial in La Placita Park, site of one of the first raids in the state, as a marker to counter the shame experienced by this community (Wagner, 2017). This memorial site plays an important role in helping future generations understand their history in this city.

Events Leading Up to the Influx of Its Unauthorized Population

The 1910 Mexican Revolution resulted in political and economic dislocation of Mexicans causing a mass crossing of the border into the United States, with Los Angeles being a prime destination that has continued to this day in various degrees. The first massive upsurge to Los Angele occurred during the 1970s, although it had maintained itself as a destination for this population during prior years (Massey, 1986). The influx of unauthorized Mexicans to Los Angeles served to reaffirm the city's connection to Mexico (Waldinger, 1996).

The combination of an increased Latino population within the city and state set the stage for Proposition 187 (Calavita, 1996). Therefore, in similar fashion to San Francisco, Los Angeles received a number of Central Americans during the turbulent Central American era addressed throughout this book.

The largest proportion of undocumented people in Los Angeles originate from Mexico. There was a dramatic shift in the 1990s, which witnessed a surge of undocumented people from Guatemala and El Salvador due to disruptions in their native lands, as addressed in Chapter 2 (Hamilton & Chinchilla, 2001). This surge also occurred in Boston and other cities throughout the country.

An Overview of Its Local Representative Government

Local and national elected representatives heavily favor the Democratic Party. At the national level, California has two Democratic senators. House representatives, too, are Democratic. The Los Angeles mayor and city attorney are Democratic, and the city council consists of all Democrats. A *Los Angeles Times* article titled "Are Republicans Extinct in Los Angeles?" captures the status of the Republican Party (Nagourney, 2016).

Because the Democratic Party has a plurality regarding city and state national officials, the process of "bucking" federal policies meant to weaken the resolve at the local level is much easier. Such a plurality took a long time to evolve and take hold. It seems to be firmly entrenched within the politics of Los Angeles and the state of California, in addition to San Francisco, allowing these entities to take a defiant stance against the current presidential administration. As addressed previously, political party affiliation continues to heavily favor Democrats.

Designation of Sanctuary City

Both Los Angeles and San Francisco claim to be the nation's first city with a designation of being a sanctuary. Policies toward non-cooperation with ICE have been enacted without formally declaring themselves sanctuaries, and that is why there is a dispute concerning the "first" sanctuary city. Berkeley, California, would argue that it should be first because it designated itself a sanctuary city on November 8, 1971.

This sanctuary designation has taken on a "badge of courage" and been widely supported by residents, although not unanimously. The political support behind this movement has been reinforced with the recent increased involvement of the Catholic Church. The Catholic Church's stance, as noted in the discussion of Boston, cannot be minimized.

In January 2017, almost two-thirds (65%) of adults were in favor of "California state and local governments making their own policies and taking actions, separate from the federal government, to protect the legal rights of undocumented immigrants in California," with support breaking down along party lines: 80% of Democrats, 27% of Republicans, and 59% of independents favored this stance (Hayes & Hill, 2017). The two major political parties have contrasting views, with profound local and national implications.

Los Angeles has a long history of having churches offering those who are undocumented refuge and places to live, and efforts to find and support sanctuary homes, as addressed in Chapter 7, continue to this day (Maganini, 2017). This is a promising development because of the stability of this institution and the moral and political power that it wields in states such as California (Lipka, 2015):

> The face of Catholic America is changing. Today, immigrants make up a considerable share of Catholics, and many are Hispanic. At the same time, there has been a regional shift, from the Northeast (long home to a large percentage of the Catholic faithful) and Midwest to the Western and Southern parts of the U.S. . . . The share of US Catholics who are Hispanic has grown by 5 percentage points since 2007 (from 29% to 34%), while the percentage of all U.S. adults who are Hispanic has grown by 3 points (from 12% to 15%). And the share of Catholics who are Hispanic is likely to continue to grow; among Catholic millennials, as many are Hispanic (46%) as are white (43%).

California's national connections can rally critical financial, social, and political support for the undocumented. The Latino parishioner share of the Catholic Church has strong regional influence, particularly in certain regions of the country, helping it to spur an embrace of a sanctuary city designation.

Regarding California, its percentage of Latino Catholics (67%) is second only to that of Texas (72%). Such a high percentage of Catholics is bound to exert considerable direct or indirect social and political pressure on that institution to be repressive and advocate for this community (Cuevas, 2017). This Catholicism trend is long term and can be traced back almost 50 years to the 1970s, so it is not new, which bodes well for this community (Mossaad & Mather, 2008).

Present-Day Status

Los Angeles, similar to its sister city to the north, continues to embrace its sanctuary designation, and as evidenced by the list and range of activities emanating from this city, it remains in active resistance, with a highly public national role. This does not mean that ICE efforts to apprehend and deport those who are undocumented cannot extend to those engaged in serving their community, as in the case of street vendors, for example (Rosario, 2017). Los Angeles, as in the rest of the country, has experienced an upsurge in the number of arrests of undocumented people, with criminal and without criminal records. Having a sanctuary city designation does not translate into a "keep-away" strategy by ICE.

Considerable political criticism has been directed at Los Angeles because of its stance, and the Catholic Church has not escaped this criticism. Los Angeles Archbishop Jose Gomez noted in response to a criticism of the Catholic Church taking such an affirming stance on unauthorized Latinos that it has done so to build its declining membership and increase its coffers (as quoted in Cuevas, 2017):

> Well, it makes me sad to hear that. All my years working in South Los Angeles, working with immigrants, it never once crossed my mind to help another

human being just so that I would have somebody else in my church. We are not here really to serve the church; we're here to serve the world, to serve the people, especially those who are suffering. And we certainly respect the laws of our country and our borders and the right of a country to form borders. But in any way we can, we also have to help those who are in need. And that's not partisan, not left or right. It's the Gospel. It goes back to who we are. We can't ignore the suffering of the people around us. Because then we are less human, we're less Christian. And we are breaking that covenant we have with each other.

Readers may question whether the Catholic Church's status in taking a leading role in this national movement can be expected to expand or diminish in the immediate future. I see no slowing down of this momentum anytime soon. In fact, I expect this effort to escalate in new and exciting ways, influencing other cities throughout the nation as the moral dimensions continue to grow in importance.

The internal demographic, social, economic, religious, and political forces have deep roots, and there is no indication that they will weaken in the near or distant future pertaining to the unauthorized in their midst. When combined with a historical legacy and geographical location, it is a formula that increases the chances that Los Angeles will be a force to be reckoned with in the immediate future, helping shape local and state responses to regressive national immigration policies.

Summary

Los Angeles is playing an influential role in reaching out to those who are unauthorized in a variety of ways, including playing a significant role in the legal arena. These efforts have sought to engage a wide sector of its population, with the latest efforts focused on providing safe houses. Furthermore, because of its major film and entertainment industry, Los Angeles can play an even greater influential role by sponsoring documentaries and films focused on those who are unauthorized.

Los Angeles will also continue to make national news as it persists in carrying out a mission of protecting the unauthorized from federal officials intent on carrying out deportation orders. This stance will endear this city, as well as cast it as a target for federal authorities wishing to make an example of it. If we think of the sanctuary movement as having deep roots in this city, it is easy to understand the broad reach of this movement and the challenges that federal authorities will face in carrying out anti-sanctuary city sanctions.

CONCLUSION

Reducing the histories and responses to those who are undocumented in three cities to several thousand words seems "unholy." Their positions in the sanctuary movement make them stars in an ever-expanding galaxy, to use a celestial metaphor. To continue with this metaphor, when the universe will stop expanding remains to be seen. If we conceptualize the three cities discussed in this chapter as stars, yet of different sizes and brightness, their brilliance will cast a wide reach.

The process of arriving at a sanctuary city designation was never smooth in the cases of these cities. For example, Boston never even claimed this status but, for all intents and purposes, functions as one and is treated by federal authorities as one. The attention garnered due to a sanctuary city designation has put these cities in the national spotlight for potential retribution from the Trump administration, the Department of Homeland Security, and the Department of Justice.

These cities have redoubled their efforts to expand the services provided to those who are unauthorized, particularly in the case of Los Angeles, and have publicly stated this aim. The Catholic Church has played a pivotal, and more active, role in Los Angeles and San Francisco compared to Boston, although this is open to debate.

This chapter served to bring together various types and sources of information and presented a narrative regarding the birth and growth of the sanctuary movement in three significant cities and two regions of the country, although the "actual" birthplace of this movement is debatable, with Berkeley, California, also seeking claim to this distinction. These three sites bring to the forefront both similar and different sets of dynamics that have influenced the evolution of the sanctuary city movement, and they will have roles to play in the future when attempts to quell this movement take further hold.

SECTION 3

Where to Now?

Section 3 consists of two chapters and is devoted to bringing some "closure" in this book on a movement that seems to have no end from a moral, social, and legal standpoint, with many twists, turns, and surprises in the immediate future. Fifty years from now, social historians will look back at this movement and make a determination of its place in US history. I believe that this movement will stand out as critical in helping shift the nation's narrative toward those who are unauthorized, much as the social movement in the 1970s influenced the ending of the Vietnam War. The sanctuary city movement will be much more than a footnote during the Trump presidency.

9

Supporting the Sanctuary City Movement

INTRODUCTION

Supporting the sanctuary movement takes on great importance during the Trump administration. This support transpires in subtle as well as highly public ways. Public awareness of sanctuary cities has increased significantly, from a small segment of the United States to national and international recognition, and it promises to increase as this movement receives greater media attention (Owusu-Sarfo, 2016).

This widening recognition signifies how this movement has tapped essential core elements, or the rare nerve, of this democracy and how human rights have taken center stage or been reinforced, as the case may be, in the consciousness of the country. This bodes well for this movement, but it also places a target on it as the anti-immigrant forces gather strength and view sanctuaries as a serious national threat, as did the anti-war movement during the Vietnam War in the 1960s and 1970s.

For those new to this movement, it introduces valuable political and financial resources; it also has potential to cause tension and conflict related to strategies and tactics that are often part of achieving a sanctuary designation. Some communities would rather not seek this type of publicity while de facto being sanctuaries without this "seal of approval." Social movements are never smooth change efforts, without experiencing tensions, hard feelings, setbacks, and casualties along the way toward achieving social justice.

Several themes stand out and are worthy of specific focus in this chapter, with attention paid to ways in which to foster this movement's progress in the immediate future. Those privileged enough to read this book are in a position to contribute to this human rights and social justice issue. The nature of the contribution that people can make to this human rights and social justice issue depends on what "hat" they wear and the activities they perform. This chapter focuses on community residents, religious leaders, human service providers, elected officials, academics, and community events. There are countless other roles and activities, and these are not mutually exclusive.

It must be emphasized that there are numerous activities that bring groups together in pursuit of a common agenda. The undertaking of rights education campaigns, for instance, brings neighborhood institutions, concerned residents who are citizens, lawyers, and the children of the unauthorized together to teach and learn about their rights (Allen, 2017). These efforts have proliferated throughout the country, providing possibilities for engaging concerned residents and professionals in pursuit of a justice agenda.

An underlying chapter theme of this quest is to engender compassion and empathy for a group whose members are very limited in sharing their narratives and who are often ignored, misunderstood, or the subject of innuendos and lies (Shuford, 2017). There is no question that they are in desperate need of allies. Compassion and empathy can be rooted in moral, ethical, or social concerns. Regardless of the source, they serve as a foundation for engagement in this cause.

A lack of compassion, and even a total overlooking of the plight of those who are undocumented within our midst, is quite disturbing from a moral and ethical perspective, but this stance takes on even greater significance when this silence occurs in religious institutions (Kammer et al., 2017):

> In the face of this negative public discourse about immigrants and the issue of immigration, there is a perception of a notable lack of a compassionate response from many faith leaders. Consequently, anti-immigrant politicians and some media are able to set the terms of the debate and to dominate the conversation through the use of negative and offensive stereotypes. (p. 4)

These roles and efforts are conceptualized as falling into discrete categories. However, nothing could be further from the truth. The categories used are meant to focus on individuals and activities, but in reality, these activities involve many different permutations and combinations, with local circumstances dictating the "best" approach to enlisting overt and covert support in this movement.

ROLES AND ACTIVITIES OF THOSE INVOLVED IN THE SANCTUARY CITY MOVEMENT

Community Residents

It is easy to focus exclusively on religious leaders, elected politicians, activists, and key government-appointed personnel in supporting this movement. However, this movement is not possible without "ordinary" residents. The Los Angeles example of residents turning their homes into sanctuaries stands out as symbolic and practical support that they can provide to this movement. Although there may be many who are not in a position to actually convert their homes, these individuals can help others do so.

Leaders without bases of support will be ineffective, and that is where community residents enter into the discussion on how to support this movement (Annese, Moyhinan, & Slattery, 2017). Community members can provide material support, participate in mass demonstrations, and write letters and make telephone calls to elected officials in support of the sanctuary movement (Loth, 2017). The concept of "participatory citizenship" comes to mind when people engage in campaigns such as the sanctuary movement (LeCompte & Blevins, 2016).

It is important to keep in mind that community residents shop, work, worship, play, and interact in numerous social circles and are in positions to further the central message of the sanctuary movement. In many ways, these resident educational campaigns are far more effective in changing public attitudes compared to the mass media. "Ordinary" people doing "ordinary" things can result in "extraordinary" changes within communities. It is worth emphasizing that engaging local residents can go beyond the "usual" suspects of well-known activists and human service providers. The housing of families that are undocumented in houses of worship can also be an opportunity to enlist local carpenters, plumbers, painters, and others in the cause.

Enlisting and preparing residents to actively engage in assisting the undocumented holds much promise. In Austin, Texas, for example, a grassroots initiative (Sanctuary in the Streets) has been developed to train and enlist residents to form a physical barrier between ICE agents and those they seek to apprehend for deportation. The moment ICE announces its presence at their door, a call can be made to have one or more US citizens arrive and block the door and to observe and record the arrest, helping to ensure that rights are not violated (Dart & Pilkington, 2017).

There are many other forms of initiatives that support sanctuary sites. One example is New York City's Funders' Collaborative on Youth Organizing, which sponsored a webinar on utilizing the concept of sanctuary to organize at the community level in support of highly marginalized groups, including those who are unauthorized.

Community demonstrations wield tremendous influence within and outside of communities. So much goes into a mass demonstration, providing opportunities for civic engagement across a community regardless of citizenship status and age (Fiorito & Nicholls, 2016). Event organizers can be community leaders, residents, elected officials, and so on, making these events true community events. When these demonstrations are successful, those involved in the planning do not mind the effort required to provide the logistical and material support that the events require. Furthermore, these events require considerable mobilization of human capital, with people needed to meet all requirements and time constraints, creating social capital (bonding and bridging) in the process.

Finally, use of local media sources targeting the Latino community can be an effective outlet for counter-narratives by providing support and information to local undocumented residents. Spanish radio programming opens up tremendous possibilities for reaching out to a group that is rarely addressed in mainstream media (Castañeda, 2016). Although these efforts fall under the category of human service providers, they are not limited to them. Disseminating information about sanctuary activities in other communities throughout the nation can be combined with providing information to the local broadcast area.

Religious Leaders

As noted previously, there are essentially two sanctuary movements occurring simultaneously. One has a deep religious and moral basis (the New Sanctuary Movement), and the other is focused on governments (the sanctuary city movement). Urban houses of worship and their religious leaders are in a propitious position to not only address the spiritual needs of their communities but also educate them in pursuit of social justice (D. W. Brown, 2016). Religious leaders are not relegated to participating solely on the religious institutional side of this movement.

In a book published approximately 20 years ago but still very relevant today as we focus on the sanctuary movement, Harper (1999) identified a series of vital signs of urban-based houses of worship, with two standing out in relevance:

(1) In city centers where congregations are vital and growing, church members and pastors are engaging in community-building in the neighborhoods; (2) as churches become more and more involved with social justice work, they have also become more politically aware and involved.

Religious leaders are playing significant roles in both movements, although due to their moral stance, they are playing a greater role in the New Sanctuary Movement. Religious leaders hold prominent positions within their communities, and they have a role to play in advancing an immigrant rights agenda within or outside of the sanctuary movement (Coddou, 2016).

Religious leaders can be influential in shaping the discourse on a moral and affirming level, which is essential in seeking positive change regarding those who are undocumented (Kammer et al., 2017):

Much of the uncivil and dehumanizing language on immigration is rooted in deep-seated fears and knowledge gaps about immigrants and immigration. This negative public discourse obscures the complex conditions that lead people to undertake this perilous migration, as well as the moral dilemmas this phenomenon poses to our country. Some of these fears behind the discourse need to be acknowledged, while others are unfounded and should be challenged. Faith leaders are well positioned to counter negative discourse and to address the many "gaps in understanding" surrounding immigration. (p. 3)

Religious leaders can lead their congregations in engaging in difficult conversations as an important step in raising consciousness and moving forward with a moral and human rights campaign focused on the rights of the undocumented. How these discussions are framed takes on significance (Boryczka & Gudelunas, 2016):

When framed in terms of religion and local experience, a more positive and empathetic discussion of immigration emerges. Alternatively, when participants discussed immigration in terms of government or institutional frame, a qualitatively more negative dialogue develops. Further, our research identifies tensions that arise for parishioners when priests introduce political issues directly into religious services.

Religious leaders in sanctuary houses of worship have a high spiritual and moral profile, and they play an instrumental role in aiding those who are unauthorized within their neighborhoods. Those at institutions that are not in sanctuary sites can still play a range of roles, including informing congregations about the unauthorized through sermons, informing them of events in which they may participate, and obtaining financial and material donations to be given to organizations helping this group.

Missions focused on the unauthorized can be established to help galvanize various types and levels of membership support. Finally, giving testimony at public hearings can also be a role that religious leaders can play in reinforcing the moral and human rights aspects of sanctuary movements. This testimony brings a national or international issue to the local level, particularly when covered by the media.

Human Service Providers

Human service providers are in a unique position to reach out, educate, and serve the unauthorized, either within the organizations that employ them or outside of these structures. Their knowledge of resources and the law places them in a propitious position to aid those seeking refuge in houses of worship or to put them into contact institutions that help those who are undocumented. As addressed previously, librarians can provide a wide range of services to advance the movement and aid residents who are undocumented, including creating affirming and welcoming libraries (Flock, 2017).

Fears of deportation have severely restricted the social navigation of the unauthorized, and this has been largely experienced in places such as food pantries and health clinics (Cramer, 2017a). Concerted effort to help mitigate their fears is an important action that can be taken by both institutions and individuals.

Civic engagement is a topic well recognized in this country but rarely applied to those who are undocumented. Civic engagement projects can be developed to aid and engage the undocumented community. The undocumented also have a right to contribute in an organized activities and can even join the military.

Human service providers can develop civic engagement initiatives focused on undocumented residents (Pohl, Garcia, & Emeka, 2016). These efforts effectively uplift the often invisible contributions that these residents make to their communities, as well as provide a viable avenue for this group to engage and feel safe.

Elected Officials

Elected officials are representative leaders of their communities. Thus, they enjoy consumer legitimacy to articulate and make policies to ensure that sanctuary cities fulfill their mission (Rathord, 2016). These leaders are in a position to help marshal community discourse and action on behalf of those who are unauthorized, including ICE arrests and deportations. Unlike human service leaders, who often function as community leaders, elected officials can be voted out of office.

Elected officials are also members of national organizations, such as the National Council of Mayors and the National Association of Latino Elected and Appointed Officials, and can move these national organizations to take a stance that brings national media attention to this cause.

Academics

It is appropriate to include in this chapter a focus on academics. We have a robust role to play in this movement through our teaching, advising students, scholarship, civic engagement, and research. All of these aspects can come together to shed light on the importance of this movement for those who are undocumented, their communities and cities, and the nation as a whole, and institutions of higher learning have a role to play in this movement, too.

Those of us in the academy are in a position to undertake research and publish on this movement and the importance of providing a counter-narrative of those who are undocumented being criminals. Academics in communities with significant numbers of the undocumented can actively tap their voices in our scholarship. Mind you, I am not saying that academics should be writing books. Fortunately, we have many different outlets for our scholarship through articles, conferences, research awards, and contract reports, in addition to our teaching and advising.

It would be foolhardy to think of the unauthorized as being "out there" and not within the institutions in which we work. For example, social work education must address the needs of students who are unauthorized and are in a precarious position while in school and upon graduation and entering the workforce (Loya et al., 2016). Those of us who focus our research on urban communities must endeavor to either bring specific attention to this group or include it in our research, making sure that the voices of its members are not subsumed in our reporting.

We can also volunteer, donate money, and sign appropriate petitions, along with putting pressure on our respective institutions to take public stances on this subject. Bringing our presence to this movement serves to encourage others to do so, and thus influencing current and future generations.

Community-Focused Efforts

It is appropriate to end this chapter by discussing events that can be community sponsored and go beyond mass demonstrations. The key actors identified in this chapter can exist in isolation. Community events can bring people together and bring an added, and possibly more important, potential contribution to the sanctuary movement.

Initiating or sponsoring community events such as music concerts, slam poetry readings, art exhibitions, plays, and other creative activities also engage residents, interested providers, and elected officials, for example, opening up an avenue for cooperation and participation across all groups interested in this cause (Delgado, 2016a; Khoir, Du, & Koronios, 2015; Lornell & Rasmussen, 2016; J. Sullivan, 2017). These events can also provide education and services that enhance the well-being of the participants (Bakri et al., 2014; Campano, Ghiso, & Welch, 2016; Villa-Torres, Fleming, & Barrington, 2015).

Efforts to capture and maintain event archives takes on great significance for the history of this movement within these communities. Photovoice, for instance, can be used to document participants' experiences and to develop albums and exhibitions of these narratives that not only inform the general public but also empower the participants in the process (Delgado, 2015; Streng et al., 2004). These exhibitions can be digitized and shared with other communities, and they can be housed in local libraries for future retrievals, serving as an important historical record for future generations.

CONCLUSION

This chapter highlighted several major themes that can be drawn from the literature and the case studies presented in Chapter 8. There are no "neat" strategies that can be put forth that will be effective throughout the country. Those of us fortunate enough to be in sanctuary sites will find it much easier to support this movement; those of us in non-affirming sites will have fewer options to get involved. No one is located in a site where there is nothing he or she cannot do to help someone who is unauthorized and the sanctuary movement.

Options for support and involvement are plentiful and can be tailored according to how salient the issues of those who are undocumented and sanctuary cities are in our personal and professional lives. Readers can engage and disengage depending on personal and professional demands. Chapter 10 focuses on reflections and predications for the future of this movement; only time will tell how accurate these predictions will be.

10

The Evolution of a National Discourse on the Sanctuary Cities Movement

INTRODUCTION

The sanctuary movement story is evolving, and its final chapter has yet to be written. This movement's narrative is exciting, hopeful, tension filled, and even tumultuous. The movement is anything but boring or dying. Its intensity has a potential to transform the nation, with its reach limited only by our imagination and political will. This final chapter provides me with a chance to share some parting words. Although a book, in similar fashion to a painting, is never truly finished, there are deadlines that bind an author who finally has to let go, as is the case here.

The 13 themes presented in this chapter are treated as separate entities and are best viewed as highly interrelated. These themes have deep historical roots while still playing significant social and political roles in current national narratives, including in countries such as Mexico, which has steadfast refused to "pay for the wall." The prose used in this chapter differs from that of previous chapters, although there are occasional references or quotes interspersed throughout. This writing style is purposeful for conveying my deep feelings about this subject, personally and professionally.

AN EVOLVING ISSUE OF TREMENDOUS NATIONAL IMPORTANCE

The subject of citizenship status, as noted at the beginning of this book, can be considered "dynamic," which is a term that captures an issue that refuses to stand still. Mind you, I am far from a journalist seeking to break or chase a big story. Rather, I am an academic who wants to focus on telling a compelling story about issues with current relevance to my profession, although also relevant to other helping professions.

As this book unfolded, it seemed as if no week went by that I was not watching a newscast or reading a newspaper article(s) on the subject (Shear,

2017). One way of capturing a moving object was to first ground it histori-cally, providing a foundation from which to make observations, conclusions, and predictions.

This chapter touches upon "unfolding" events with significance for the sanctuary movement and this nation's anti-unauthorized stance as encapsulated by President Trump's "transactional" style of governing. Evolving events regarding the undo-cumented are an integral part of this presidential administration, and any book waiting for the waters to calm down to be written may go unwritten because the wa-ters will not calm down to allow academics to pause, analyze, and predict the future.

In mid-2017, a leaked Department of Homeland Security memo outlined a plan to speed up hiring of 5,000 border agents. A number of shortcuts are proposed to facilitate hires because they typically take 10 months from start to finish, including relaxing hiring standards on Spanish language competencies, removing polygraph tests, and curtailing physical fitness tests (Nixon, 2017d; Yee & Nixon, 2017). Whether, and how, this policy evolves is unknown at this time. The groundwork has been laid for expediting hiring of personnel, in-cluding judges, to move on a promise by President Trump to create an "im-migration force" to carry out his vision. The further militarization of this nation's border patrol marches on, no pun intended. The dramatic increases in deportations stand as a testament to how efforts to expedite deportations are succeeding.

In April 2017, there was a highly publicized trip to Nogales, Arizona (approxi-mately 70 miles south of Tucson on the US–Mexico border), by Attorney General Sessions, which was intended to keep a national focus on those who are undocu-mented. It is considered out of the ordinary to have the Attorney General make such a trip, which is usually done by the Secretary of Homeland Security. An announcement was made that there would be an addition of 50 immigration judges in fiscal year 2017 and 75 in fiscal year 2018, representing an concerted attempt to increase the processing of the unauthorized. It remains to be seen to what extent this makes a significant dent in the backlog, which is estimated to number 500,000.

This trip to the Arizona–Mexico border did not address local concerns. For ex-ample, no effort was made to speak with local humanitarian organizations and the casualties of those attempting to cross the border. Furthermore, it did not address contradictions in proposed policies and funding (Stern, 2017):

> One thing Sessions didn't talk about was the State Criminal Alien Assistance Program, which reimburses county sheriffs' offices and the state for the incar-ceration and medical costs of border crossers and illegal-immigrant criminals. Trump's budget outline released last month zeroed out SCAAP funding, which alarmed sheriffs of border counties.

There was call for the filing of felony criminal charges for those who are unau-thorized, with the language used by Secretary Sessions indicative of a sustained federal effort to criminalize this group (Neuhauser, 2017):

The attorney general did make clear that a primary goal is deterrence. He issued what are perhaps the Trump administration's strongest statements yet on immigration since the president was on the campaign trail, vowing to "take our stand against this filth" of criminal gangs and declaring the nation's southwest border "ground zero in this fight."

Although President Trump has spoken about deporting the 2 to 3 million undocumented persons who are criminals, this number is false. "Operation New Dawn" represents one of the latest ICE initiatives to target transnational gangs (Bellafante, 2017). Its primary goal is to reduce gang-related violence. The chances of achieving this goal rest with a close relationship between residents and the police, which is compromised when there is distrust. There are an estimated 1.9 million non-citizen immigrants who have been convicted of crimes, but this number includes those who are unauthorized and authorized in this country; 820,000 are unauthorized with a range of criminal offenses, not all of which are violence related (Casselman, 2016).

The establishment of the Department of Homeland Security Victims of Immigration Crime Engagement (VOICE) is a public relations effort to counteract pro-immigrant sentiments by shedding light on the victims of crime committed by "illegals" (Nakamora, 2017): "Trump's spotlight on the victims' families has sparked an outcry among those who charge the president is exaggerating the risks to sow public fear to make his proposals more politically expedient." There is an acknowledgment on both sides of the debate that public relations will play an increasingly important role in shaping future narratives and actions (Nixon & Robbins, 2017; Yee, 2017d).

The discussion of detention centers addressed previously, and to which I return later in this chapter, set the stage for initiatives that will have jails playing an even more significant role in the detention of the unauthorized. The role of jails in the deportation process is not new and can be traced back 15 years. They have historically had a detailed protocol to follow when dealing with undocumented prisoners with regard to language capacities, most notably concerning Spanish: These prisoners have an advocate assigned to them when attending hearings, access to health care, and other requirements.

A renewed emphasis on jails playing a role with the apprehended who are unauthorized resulted in a relaxing of protocols, making it more attractive for local law enforcement to make their jails available. Currently, it is estimated that 10% of the undocumented in facilities are held by ICE, with 50% being held in privatized prisons.

In April 2017, there was another leaked internal Department of Homeland Security memo, which may not come to fruition but clearly is an indicator of current thinking into how the deportations will be addressed in the near future (Dickerson, 2017a): Those incarcerated due to citizen status will be subjected to the same conditions as individuals incarcerated for crimes usually associated with felony imprisonment. One can see important constitutional issues emerging with regard to the rights of those who are unauthorized.

For every action there is an equal and opposite reaction. Deporting those who are undocumented, and even DACAs, impacts this country and the countries to which they are deported, possibly causing instability there, which can foster revolution and thus open the door to socialism and communism. A globalized society is subject to globalized trends. Although the numbers of how many undocumented people will be deported get tossed around quite freely, it is important to not lose sight of the lives and narratives attached to them.

Certain regions of the country and states have been very active in proposing or enacting immigration laws that are pro or against immigrants, and not all are predicable along political party lines. In Illinois, for example, Republican Governor Rauner has expressed a desire to sign an immigrant friendly bill (Chokshi, 2017).

It is fitting to end this section with yet another "evolving" action relating to an executive order to terminate federal funding to sanctuary cities. Not unexpectedly, the Trump administration's efforts at cutting federal grants to sanctuary cities have been temporarily stalled by a district judge in San Francisco. The legal appeal of this district judge's temporary stay will be heard by the US Court of Appeals for the Ninth Circuit Court (Baker, 2017; Yee, 2017b). President Trump put forth a rationale that has been echoed by legal activists and scholars on this point (Anderson, 2017): "The judge wrote that federal funding that 'bears no meaningful relationship to immigration enforcement cannot be threatened merely because a jurisdiction chooses an immigration enforcement strategy of which the president disapproves'" (p. A1). In June 2017, the House of Representatives passed a bill, which has to be taken up by the Senate, seeking termination of federal funding and is subject to constitutional challenges (Huetteman & Kulish, 2017).

The following statement issued by the United States Council of Mayors (2017) grounds the sanctuary movement within the current political climate and efforts by the presidential administration to enforce immigration laws within cities:

Washington, D.C.—U.S. Conference of Mayors CEO and Executive Director Tom Cochran issued the following statement on today's ruling of the U.S. District Court for the Northern District of California: The nation's mayors applaud today's decision by the U.S. District Court for the Northern District of California which granted San Francisco and Santa Clara County's motion for a nationwide preliminary injunction, thus enjoining nationwide the provisions in the interior enforcement executive order applying to sanctuary jurisdictions. We stand with San Francisco Mayor Ed Lee and the leaders of other local governments who have challenged the provisions in the executive order. The Court found that the Counties demonstrated that they are likely to succeed on their claim that the Executive Order purports to wield powers exclusive to Congress and violates the Tenth and Fifth Amendments. Today's decision comes just hours after a meeting the Conference of Mayors had with

Attorney General Jeff Sessions in which the mayors and police chief present were told that the definition of a sanctuary city is based on compliance with 8 U.S.C. 1373. The Conference has long opposed the withholding of funds from so-called "sanctuary cities," which, of course, is a political term not a legal one. In partnership with police chiefs, mayors have strong reservations about any efforts, either through executive action or legislation to deny federal funds to cities that aim to build trusting and supportive relations with immigrant communities.

This organization, representing the nation's mayors, is but one of many that can be expected to weigh in with reactions to attempts at imposing sanctions on sanctuary cities. As more organizations join, the political backlash further expands, making it more difficult to push a national anti-immigrant agenda.

Governors are actively weighing in for, and against, sanctuary cities within their states. Texas and Mississippi, for example, are anti-sanctuary states, but Virginia's governor vetoed such a measure (Sacchetti, 2017):

> The governor of Texas is poised to sign a sweeping bill that would outlaw sanctuary jurisdictions in the state and impose costly fines and even jail time on officials who refuse to cooperate with U.S. immigration agents. It makes clear that local law enforcement officers may ask people they detain about their immigration status, a line of questioning that critics say should be reserved for federal immigration agents.... The legislation would be the country's most significant crackdown so far on sanctuary cities, which in general refuse to hold immigrants who have been arrested for local crimes past their release date so that Immigration and Customs Enforcement can take them into federal custody and try to deport them.

Texas Governor Abbott was true to his word and signed a bill (SB 4) on May 8, 2017, which has been referred to as the nation's strictest anti-immigrant bill since the passage of Arizona's' infamous SB 1070 (Fernandez & Montgomery, 2017; Weber, 2017).

The passage of SB 4 had immediate and potential long-term consequences, with pro-immigrants engaging in protest and others leaving the state (Hoffman & Weissert, 2017):

> But even as some vowed to fight, others have begun to flee the state. Their ranks are still too small to quantify, but a large exodus—similar to what occurred in Arizona—could have a profound effect on the Texas economy. . . . Some are abandoning Texas for more liberal states, where they feel safer—even if it means relinquishing lives they've spent years building.

Texas has been spotlighted as an anti-sanctuary city state, counteracting California, and this view was supported by President Trump's newly appointed Secretary of Homeland Security (PBS, 2017):

President Donald Trump's former deputy White House chief of staff, Nielsen was confirmed by the Senate last week. She wasted little time visiting Austin, where Travis County Sheriff Sally Hernandez once promised not to comply with some "detainers," or federal requests to hold for possible deportation people who were already jailed on non-immigration charges.

DETENTION CENTERS AS PRISONS

In 2017, there were more than 200 detention centers, and this number is bound to increase if deportation policies unfold as planned. During World War II, 120,000 Japanese Americans, including women, children, and older adults, were imprisoned in 10 internment camps in the United States. This "internment" or "imprisonment" period also claimed other causalities. For example, 900 Native Alaskans were sent to internment camps, and this has largely gone unnoticed. Undocumented families, too, can be detained in similar camps until deportation. It remains to be seen whether the imagery of having children and grandparents imprisoned can withstand intense national and international opinion.

These "centers" have the potential to become a major international embarrassment, if not shame, for the nation. Total institutions have a history of becoming a world unto themselves, where rules do exist but can be implemented according to the leadership of these institutions. Oversight is often minimal because these institutions house people whom society considers unworthy. The potential for neglect and abuse is rampant, with untreated or poorly treated illness and death being the result. One only has to turn to the histories of mental hospitals, juvenile detention centers, and prisons, for example, to see how the "best of intentions" went astray.

Readers can disagree with this prognostication, and I hope I am wrong. This is an issue that I do not have a vested interest in being right about. Predicting into the future is best left to those with the power to see the future. I have never been fond of being asked to predict the future, unless it relates to demographic patterns. This topic is of sufficient importance to violate this rule.

There are ample scholarly references attesting to abuses having occurred in detention camps, both private and public. "Privatizing" this movement is not going to prevent violation of rights. Rather, it will mark the continued criminalization of this group of people and introduce a chapter in the nation's history of immigration that future generations will read about and react to in shame, in similar fashion to how readers reacted to the material covered in Chapter 2 and throughout this book.

UNAUTHORIZED NARRATIVES

Each of us has a story to tell. Many readers probably work in fields in which narratives are an essential part of their work. I like to believe that we have narratives, but so do organizations and communities. Our narratives may share many similarities with those of immigrants, too, with stories of struggle, sadness, victories, and resiliency. These stories, including our own, are rarely sought and shared.

The story of immigrants is in a perpetual state of being told if we pause to listen. There is never one simple story that unites all forces that led to uprootment and re-location to this country. There is never a story that can be told in a prescribed lim-ited period of time either. That makes the telling of stories much more difficult to accomplish. The fact that this is arduous does not mean that we should not strive to achieve this goal. Narratives can build bridges within communities, nation-ally, and internationally, creating opportunities for shared efforts at addressing the rights of the undocumented, as well as those who are here with requisite govern-mental permission (Fernandez, 2017b; Muraszkiewicz, 2016). The media have an immense role to play in sharing these stories nationally and internationally.

IMMIGRATION CONTEXT

Immigration is a phenomenon that is as old as history itself, and it is a part of future history, too. Mobility has been an integral part of the human experience. We move from place to place in search of a better existence, and sometimes that means crossing national boundaries. For some of us, it is done in search of an ed-ucation; for others, it means better employment, career opportunities, or health care. Yet, for others, it is a search for safety. Both the context leading to the motiva-tion to move and the context in which we settle in are essential in understanding who we are. The same applies to understanding immigration across borders, and more so for those who elect to do so against all odds.

A greater understanding of the role and influence of context is essential in helping develop laws and policies in this arena. Immigration researchers and policymakers have a vested interest in understanding how immigrant contexts shape outcomes for three very important reasons (Gelatt, Bernstein, & Koball, 2015):

> First, researchers and policymakers seeking to evaluate the costs and benefits of passing state or local (referred to in this brief as "local" unless otherwise specified) immigration legislation want to know whether policies achieve their intended objectives, which may include expelling unauthorized immigrants from an area, improving the local economy, or supporting the educational attainment of children of immigrants, among other goals, and whether there are unanticipated costs and benefits of passing local immigra-tion legislation. Second, researchers interested in immigrant integration—the social, civic, educational, and economic outcomes of immigrants and their children—are interested in how local immigrant contexts shape inte-gration trajectories. Third, political scientists want to understand how local economic and demographic factors, political parties, individual attributes of legislators, and national conversations shape local politics as measured through public opinion or passage of local policies. (pp. 1–2)

One, two, or all three of these reasons may resonate with readers, regardless of political position on immigration, because of how contextual forces shape experiences, both positive and negative. All three have saliency among human service providers and social activists.

BROADENING THE DEBATE ON THOSE WHO ARE UNAUTHORIZED

The "immigration debate" has exclusively focused on one side of the border, emphasizing the need to arrest and deport, while paying no attention to what happens to the deported. The political, rather than the humanitarian, perspective has dominated this discourse, resulting in an incomplete picture of a very complex social issue.

Mexico is generating its own public relations campaign to counteract the deportations occurring in the United States (Malkin, 2017a):

Mexico's president dashed to the airport to greet a planeload of deportees. The education minister rushed to the Texas border to meet Mexicans being kicked out of the United States. Mexico City's labor secretary is urging companies to hire migrants who abruptly find themselves sent back home. "Unlike what's happening in the United States, this is 'your home,'" the labor secretary, Amalia Garcia, told deportees in the audience at a recent event in the city's jobs programs. (p. 1)

Although efforts at meeting the needs of Mexican deportees are noteworthy, similar efforts at aiding deportees who are non-Mexican, and facing incredible challenges in returning to their native countries, have not occurred. Their trip to their countries of origin—most likely El Salvador, Guatemala, or Honduras—is perilous and without rewards waiting for them. It is important to remember that they left for very good reasons, which often involved personal safety.

Those eventually deported who are not Mexicans are doomed to face "social death," finding themselves on the margins of Mexico's society, particularly in cases in which they came to the United States as children or young adults and spent most of their lives in this country, and experiencing difficulty relating to life south of the border (Ybarra & Peña, 2017). They are placed in vulnerable positions that further exploitation. They, too, are casualties in a war that generates innumerable casualties. Helping professionals and communities will be called upon to pick up the pieces on both sides of the border.

On a final note, this nation's toxic political climate impacts those who are unauthorized, serving to discourage others from coming (Semple, 2017):

Inside the United states, the Trump administration has cast a broader enforcement net, including reversing Obama-era rules that put a priority on arresting serious criminals and mostly left other undocumented immigrants alone. Arrests of immigrants living illegally in the United States has soared, with the biggest increase coming among those migrants without criminal records. The shift has spawn a new sense of fear among undocumented immigrants in the United States. In turn, they have sent a warning back to relatives and friends in their homelands. Don't come. (p. A7)

HELPING PROFESSIONS AT THE TABLE ON IMMIGRATION AND THE UNAUTHORIZED

Helping professions are strategically located throughout the nation's major urban centers to address the needs of immigrants, specifically those who are undocumented. The historical beginnings of the social work profession include the settlement house movement (Padilla et al., 2008):

> Social workers have always been at the forefront of work with immigration. From our profession's earliest days working with immigrants at the Hull House in Chicago to the current immigrant debate, our commitment to social justice has driven our service and policy decisions regarding immigration. Our values have not changed, neither have some of the more divisive and destructive aspects of the immigration debate. (p. 5)

The following stance by S. Jones et al. (2015), although specifically addressing social work, can easily apply to other professions that have social justice as a central tenet; it states that it is important to fight against the country's nativist sentiments that are increasingly being vocalized and acted upon through local legislation:

> The consequences for the profession of social work are also striking. The rise of anti-immigrant policies as well as nativist sentiment pose serious challenges both to the social work profession as a whole, and to individual social workers.... On one hand, ethical obligations to clients underscore the importance of social justice training in social work education and practice.... On the other hand, punitive anti-immigrant social policies pose a serious threat and a significant dilemma for social workers' social justice orientation. Such policies often require social workers to collaborate with the state through the punitive action of restricting social services and, at worst, identifying and thereby criminalizing undocumented persons. (p. 53)

Social workers, religious personnel, and other helping professions often have social justice as a central goal, whether conceptualized as an ethical or a moral imperative. All facets of these professions must rally in pursing justice for groups that are marginalized because they cannot vote yet pay taxes, Social Security, and contribute to the Medicare Trust Fund, in addition to making nonmonetary contributions to their communities, cities, and society.

Undocumented youth in the country (Dreamers) illustrate how harnessing their political power to achieve important social and political rights and assuming an influential role in immigrant rights, including the designation of sanctuary cities, wield tremendous potential (Nicholls, 2014). Tapping youth energy and determination in this movement can have the same impact that the 2006 demonstrations had on a national scale (Delgado, 2016b).

THE RELIGIOUS BASES OF THE SANCTUARY CITY MOVEMENT

I cannot help but conclude that the future of the sanctuary city movement will, and should, have a moral basis for its existence. My reasoning is informed by four considerations based on the short history of this movement and its unfolding:

1. Politically, it will be much more difficult to take a hard line against the sanctuary city movement if an ecumenical basis (Catholic, Protestants, Jews, and Muslims) for this movement is actively sought. Crossing conventional religious lines has always been a key indicator of the ethical legitimacy of any social justice movement. In this case, it would make it much more difficult for the Trump administration, or any other presidential administration, to question the moral purpose of this rights movement. Arresting religious leaders and concerned citizens of all ages and backgrounds does not make for good policy or good press.
2. Economically, houses of worship possess resources through their leadership and congregations that can be marshaled in support of campaigns targeting the election of candidates who are pro-immigrant. These institutions are in a position to financially support the basic needs of the undocumented.
3. Religious institutions provide physical structures that can accommodate families and therefore, from a very practical perspective, can carry out functions that are difficult in homes or community organizations.
4. Houses of worship have the communication capability to spread the central message of human rights through local, national, and international media, informing and encouraging support of those who are unauthorized in a manner that few other institutions can. Helping to counteract false media reports takes on great significance in this movement's effort to present a much needed counter-narrative.

It remains to be seen whether immigration reform, if and when it occurs, will unite and mobilize Latino pastors, for example, to politically engage their congregations to help shape this issue at the local and national levels (Martínez, 2016). If this coalition comes to fruition, there is no telling how far the movement will go in accomplishing its goals.

Victories are occurring, as in the case of Philadelphia (Goodstein, 2017)

Mr. Flores walked out the church for good, a rare winner among the tens of thousands of undocumented immigrants who fought battles over deportation this year. . . . He was promised a special type of visa given to victims of crime who assist the police. But even so, Mr. Flore's freedom gives the growing sanctuary movement, organized by houses of worship across the country to protect undocumented immigrants, a small victory in the face of a widespread federal crackdown. (p. A17)

Incidentally, during the week of October 9–13, 2017, churches in Raleigh, North Carolina, Meriden, Connecticut, and Highland Park, New Jersey, started to offer sanctuary to a total of four persons.

DACA (DREAMERS) AND A NATION AT WAR WITH ITSELF

Dreamers have an extensive base of support. An estimated 80% of voters, including 72% of Republicans, believe that the children of those who are unauthorized should be allowed to remain in the country (Linskey, 2017). This support has spurred well-financed and multifaceted efforts to aid them (Jordan, 2017e).

The impact of ending Deferred Action for Childhood Arrivals (DACA) will be extensive throughout the country (Reif, 2017). For example, Harris County, Texas (Houston), would be expected to lose 28,000 residents and $1.6 billion annually in local gross domestic product (*Boston Globe* Editorial, 2017). Hurricane Harvey's economic impact on this county will be even greater if Dreamers are taken out of the economy. Furthermore, ending DACA will put those in the military at risk for deportation (R. M. Gates, 2017).

Donald Trump promised on the campaign trial that the children of the undocumented would not be deported from the country. On June 16, 2017, President Trump signed an executive order extending protections for those who arrived in this country as children, representing an important victory for Dreamers and their communities (Shear & Yee, 2017). This decision changed, however. On September 5, 2017, President Trump rescinded DACA, leaving it to Congress to find a solution for these 800,000 people; this, not surprisingly, has been challenged in the courts by 15 states and Washington, DC (Burns & Yee, 2017). On October 5, 2017, an arbitrary deadline, Dreamers renewed their protections for the last time if no legislation is passed granting them some form of permanent status (Jordan, 2017b). Incidentally, in early 2018, a federal district judge issued an injunction that stopped the Trump administration from not issuing DACA renewals (D. Gonzalez, 2018).

I think about potential urban unrest occurring throughout the nation, the bringing in of the National Guard, and a country on the verge of civil war if Dreamers are deported in a highly visible manner. I do not make this statement lightly. Readers may recoil at this statement. Undocumented parents and their children are integral parts of this nation's major cities (Jordan, 2017a). Frustrations associated with other social issues will combine with these deportations to cause urban unrest.

Students of "urban unrest" will understand why I have made this statement. Urban demonstrations throughout the nation's major cities led to political pressures to establish the DACA program through an executive action by

President Obama. Urban unrest can be minimized if these raids transpire during winter months in northern cities, and I am not being facetious. If these raids occur during the summer months, it taps into all of the social factors that have historically led to urban riots—several days of 90-degree heat and 90% humidity, a history of oppression, and an incident that serves as a match to ignite a fire. Imagine the "Black Lives Matter" movement coming together with the "Brown Lives Matter" movement across the country (Palmer, 2017).

The argument will be put forth that "Blue Lives Matter" and that "All Lives Matter," too. The potential convergence of these two movements with other human rights movement cannot be put down without major national discord in the streets and in major institutions—governmental, private, and religious. My counter-argument is that it is true that all lives matter. Some lives, however, matter more than others. After all, we are all equal, but some of us are more equal than others, as the saying goes. Human rights is about humans, and those who are unauthorized, putting aside all the labels we use to describe them, are first and foremost humans, with all of the strengths and foibles human beings possess.

Readers will be the ultimate judge of the chance of this situation materializing in the near future and tearing apart the country as the Vietnam War did during the 1960s and early 1970s. Ironically, that was about a war overseas and in a country very few of us have ever visited or could locate on a map. This war will take place within our geographical boundaries in the nation's cities and, therefore, on our doorsteps, and it will be much more difficult to ignore. Citizenship journalists will join their professional colleagues to help ensure that these struggles remain in the national consciousness.

An estimated 21,000 people were deported during the first few months of President Trump's presidency, representing an increase from 16,000 during the same period the year before. One of the latest deportees was a DACA person (23-year-old Juan Manuel Montes Bojorquez), whose case has resulted in a legal suit against the federal government (S. Schmidt, 2017a). The case, which was randomly assigned, is scheduled to be heard before Judge Gonzalo Curiel, the same judge made famous by then candidate Trump's vitriol because he was Mexican and passing judgment on the Trump University lawsuit, which was eventually settled out of court for a $25 million judgment (S. Schmidt, 2017b).

Efforts are underway to increase the number of arrests and deportations in sanctuary sites throughout the country. In early fall 2017, 50 Massachusetts unauthorized residents were arrested (Fox, 2017). These efforts have tended to focus on those with criminal convictions. It remains to be seen how expansive these efforts will be in the future.

Delayed mail has resulted in DACA renewals being denied, as in the case of Jose in Chicago, who mailed his renewal 3 weeks early and by certified mail. His is just one of a countless number of such cases, bringing an added dimension to the precarious state these individuals face, putting them at the mercy of the mail system (Robbins, 2017d). A decision was made, however, to allow late applicants to resubmit their applications if they could provide proof that they had previously mailed these in a timely manner (Robbins, 2017e).

Finally, although technically not a DACA topic, abortion is a subject that involves undocumented youth. The interjection of abortion, as in the case of two undocumented teenagers in US shelters, further exacerbates the highly charged subject of immigration (Astor, 2017; Yee, 2017j). As a result, this issue promises to expand the political battlefield against those who are undocumented.

COMING OUT OR STAYING HIDDEN?

The term "coming out" has historically been used by individuals who have hidden their sexual orientation or gender identity to loved ones and the world. So much emotion and symbolism are attached to this term. It signifies an empowerment of these individuals to own their identity and make a social and political statement as a consequence, which can easily translate into active resistance to efforts to silence them. This term is increasingly being used by those who are unauthorized to achieve similar outcomes by declaring their presence, national belonging, humanity, and their intent to be an integral part of this country's future, as well as playing an active role in changing the oppressive circumstances that led to their going underground (Enriquez & Saguy, 2016; Villazor, 2013).

It would be irresponsible not to raise the fears that those who are unauthorized are experiencing with the increased threat of deportation (D. Gonzalez, 2017). Activists and allies will be called upon to take a more active stance because fears within this community will interfere with its members' ability to "come out" and engage in civil protest.

CRIMINALIZATION IS ALIVE AND WELL

Unfortunately, the theme of criminalization permeates much of the past and current narratives regarding those who are unauthorized and sanctuary cities. Historically, casting them as a criminal class has made it easier for society to put them aside and fear them at the same time. The same be true today.

Crimes committed by those who are unauthorized have been the primary rationale for forcing sanctuary sites to comply with ICE requirements (Savage, 2017):

> The agency cited the rising murder rate in Chicago and cast blame for gang murders in New York on what it labeled a "soft on crime" stance. It also complained that after the recent arrests of 11 members of the MS-13 Salvadoran street gang, the deputy police chief of Santa Cruz, Calif., had stressed that the raid was unrelated to immigration instead of "warning other MS-13 members that they would be next." (p. A10)

MS-13 is widely considered to play a minor role in immigrant-related violence (Herndon, 2017). Ironically, New York City calls itself the "safest big city in America" and has near historic lows in major crime rates (M. Schultz, 2017).

Criminalizing the undocumented generates public opinion in support of punishing sanctuary cities, and it remains to be seen how it becomes a political campaign issue in states with high numbers of residents who are undocumented, as happened in the 2017 New Jersey and Virginia governor races, for example (J. Martin, 2017).

On April 21, 2017, Attorney General Sessions sent a letter to the following nine cities and counties requiring them to prove they are cooperating with ICE by June 30, 2017, continuing to carry out the threat of terminating federal grant funding from the Department of Justice: Boston, Chicago and Cook County, Clark County (Nevada), Miami–Dade County, Milwaukee, New Orleans, New York, Philadelphia, and San Francisco (Associated Press, 2017b; Gurman, 2017; Yee & Ruiz, 2017).

Federal effort to implement this order was found to be unconstitutional by US District Judge Leinenweber on September 11, 2017, representing a temporary legal defeat, which will be appealed (Babwin, 2017). On November 20, 2017, a federal judge (US District Court Judge William Orrick), in responding to a San Francisco and Santa Clara lawsuit, delivered a significant setback to President Trump's efforts to cut federal funding to sanctuary cities by issuing a permanent injunction (Thanawala, 2017).

Although the second effort at revising a travel ban by the Trump administration may ultimately be judged constitutional, legal efforts to punish sanctuary cities may not (Parloff, 2017):

> The same cannot be said of the sanctuary-cities order, which appears to offend the principles of separation of powers, due process, and interpretations of both the Tenth Amendment (establishing that the federal government only has powers specifically delegated to it by the Constitution) and limits on Congress's spending power that have been mainly championed by conservative justices—including President Trump's own claimed judicial hero, Antonin Scalia.

Those who are unauthorized are not criminalized in sanctuary cities. Although some do commit serious crimes, there is wide recognition that these are the exceptions rather than the rule. This stance allows them to feel that they are judged as human beings and by the actions that they take. A cloud does not hang over their heads, and their children can experience *orgullo* (pride) in their lives.

A HUMAN RIGHTS ISSUE HAS BECOME PARTISAN AND A POLITICAL FOOTBALL—UNINTENDED CONSEQUENCES

Human life, regardless of citizenship status, should not be viewed from a politically partisan perspective. However, that is exactly what has occurred in developing an understanding of how sanctuary cities emerge, and this issue takes on the status of a political football, with one side (Democrats, with some exceptions) representing the visiting team, and the other side (Republicans, with some exceptions) representing the "home" team. This divide is integral to the sanctuary city movement, with exceptions.

The case studies and the literature on past and current efforts to achieve a sanctuary designation highlight the importance of elected officials in embracing or resisting this movement. Again, sanctuary status invariably unfolds in cities with strong Democratic Party traditions and extensive histories of having immigrants. As immigrants move to new destinations within the United States, communities without such histories may find themselves with increasing numbers of immigrants, and not all of them undocumented.

Last, the threat of deportation has had unintended consequences in cases in which prosecutors are considering plea deals with those who are undocumented or with a legal status that can impact their citizenship quest if convicted of certain crimes, and are facing trial to avoid having them deported (Yee, 2017f). This has resulted in local jurisdictions potentially coming into conflict with federal authorities by reflecting local sociopolitical circumstances. Recent efforts to arrest and deport MS-13 gang members have resulted in a decrease in crime reported to the police because of fears of being deported upon going to the police (Lieberman, 2017). Furthermore, it has enhanced the reputation of this gang, helping its recruitment efforts. These unintended consequences have generally gone unreported but have immense implications for day-to-day life in these communities.

"THE WALL": NEED WE SAY MORE?

In early 2017, Congress passed a budget reconciliation bill extending the nation's budget to the end of the 2017 fiscal year. Key concessions by the Republican-led House of Representatives and Senate excluded funding for the building of the "wall" with Mexico and defunding sanctuary cities (Nixon, 2017b). In typical political speak, the wall and defunding sanctuary cities have been kicked down the road and, in the case of the wall, framed as enhanced "border security," dropping the highly symbolic use of the "wall." The wall, if eventually built, will extend the current wall in the Rio Grande Valley and replace existing fences in El Paso, Texas, and San Diego, California.

It remains to be seen whether this "major" project will ever see fruition in future congressional budget battles (Rappeport, 2017). In summer 2017, the US Army Corps of Engineers started preliminary preparations for expanding the wall with Mexico in El Paso and Grande Valley, Texas; Santa Teresa, New Mexico; and Calexico and San Diego, California (Nixon, 2017f).

The wall has a much greater symbolic value for current anti-immigration sentiments throughout the country because although it will make entering the country more difficult, and fewer will want to do so, human creativity and drive to survive are bound to prevail for immigrants attempting to cross the border. The wall is not within the confines of an infrastructure initiative many in this country favored during the last presidential campaign.

"A ROSE BY ANY OTHER NAME WOULD SMELL AS SWEET"

It is appropriate to end this chapter and book with a quote by Shakespeare: "A rose by any other name would smell as sweet." Arriving at a label that is sufficiently extensive to capture a social phenomenon, which seems to be expanding at record speed, but with sufficiently delineated boundaries that allows an in-depth discussion with a common embrace of the parameters is a challenge for me. The naming of this phenomenon does not solve the challenge, and that is the case in point with sanctuary cities.

Each sanctuary site, officially or unofficially designated, has a story to tell us that enriches and informs our lives as it relates to immigration but also personally since we are all immigrants, with the exceptions noted previously. Fortunately, there are significant efforts to bring these stories to life. Movies of those who are undocumented must follow suit to provide much needed visuals to reinforce central messages and life lessons (Peeren, 2014).

Concern about maintaining gains accomplished throughout the years has been a key motivator in seeking an official designation as a sanctuary city, as in the case of Los Angeles, where there has been a long-time policy not to cooperate with immigration authorities. San Francisco, too, has a long history with an official designation, and it has even instituted a lawsuit against President Trump challenging his threats to cut federal funding as unconstitutional.

A sanctuary designation has evolved from a narrow focus on law enforcement–immigration control cooperation to a meaning that is far greater, involving instrumental (concrete assistance), expressive (emotional support and feelings of safety and being valued), and informational (information related to new immigration raids, plans, and resources) services. Some sites are providing all of the assistance normally associated with a sanctuary designation but are doing so without embracing this designation; other sites with the designation also provide services, but these may be limited in scope and depth. Are these places any less significant in the movement than their "official" counterparts?

I believe the answer to this question is no. The official designation does create important political capital. There are certain immigrant organizations undertaking very important work with the unauthorized. Some of these organizations may even have official state designation. The same forces that led to the creation of state offices in select states focused on immigrants and refugees are also operative in the creation of sanctuary city designations (de Graauw, 2015).

These state offices have played influential roles within their respective states by providing needed positive narratives about those who are unauthorized and also providing leadership on this and other issues related to newcomers. The coming together of sympathetic elected officials, key stakeholders, community organizations, public opinion, and a growing concern related to social justice and newcomers should not seem surprising.

San Diego is providing the assortment of services associated with sanctuary cities. Therein lies one of the problems with the looseness of a sanctuary designation. San Diego has not undergone an official process through its city council and mayor and, therefore, is not a "sanctuary city." However, for all intents and purposes, it functions as one with said designation (Stewart, 2017). Many of those who follow this movement would be surprised to learn that it is not a sanctuary city (Libby, 2017):

> Plenty of websites have compiled lists of sanctuary cities, and San Diego lands on many of them. But the mayor's office has said San Diego is not one. Mayor Kevin Faulconer's staff told City News Service in 2015 that despite San Diego being listed as a sanctuary city on various online resources, there's no specific law or policy making it one—and that the city does work cooperatively with federal immigration authorities. Faulconer vowed in his 2015 State of the City address to support comprehensive immigration reform, which should include a path to citizenship. The City Council unanimously supported any plan that included that. Faulconer's criticism of Trump's border rhetoric more recently, however, has centered on commerce and trade rather than immigration policy.

Readers may not care whether cities such as San Diego have obtained an official designation that has the ringing endorsement of major elected leaders, even though it helps clear up any confusion concerning the degree of cooperation local law enforcement can have with ICE. After all, "A rose by any other name would smell as sweet."

CONCLUSION

The sanctuary city debate is really a proxy for a much broader, and complex, debate about the nation's future to regulate who can "officially" be part of this country. It is also about the speed at which this country's racial composition is changing and becoming browner. This racial dimension is much more difficult to address. The nation, too, is growing grayer as its population continues to age, and it is growing browner as its Latino and Asian populations continue to increase. The convergence of these powerful forces has placed sanctuary cities in the national spotlight.

The sanctuary city movement is a work in progress, and that is perfectly acceptable. Are there tensions? Sure, and any social movement worth its weight in salt would have tensions and possibly also experience internal conflicts. I fully expect, and embrace, many books being written on this movement, and that means that it has maintained relevance. I do not believe that a pathway to citizenship will emerge with a corresponding decrease in political opposition to it anytime soon. However, a struggle worth fighting for means that it is a struggle with life-changing consequences for countless people, and in this case, those with a contribution to make this country even greater today than ever.

The human rights and social justice aspects of those who are unauthorized will continue to grow in influence in the immediate future or at least until the next

presidential election. I sincerely hope that readers are better equipped to anticipate, as well as understand, national events as they unfold and that they are better
equipped to respond with, and on behave of, those who are unauthorized in this
country, whose only crime is seeking a better life for themselves and their loved
ones and advancing the dream inspirited in the Statue of Liberty poem at the beginning of this book.

REFERENCES

A blow to Salvadorans—and the Mass. economy [Editorial]. (2018, January 10). *The Boston Globe*, p. A11.

A-Wan, I., Baquero, B., Cowan, K., Daniel-Ulloa, J., LeBron, A., Lopez, W. D., . . . Temrowski, O. (2017). *The first two community ID programs in the Midwest: Organizing, education, and community health in Johnson County IA and Washtenaw, MI*. https://mospace.umsystem.edu/xmlui/handle/10355/60961

Abraham, E. (2011). Transfiguring the Tenth Amendment from a shield into a sword? A discussion of San Francisco's sanctuary ordinance & its implications for federalism. *Children's Legal Rights Journal, 31*, 1.

Abrams, K. R. (2016). Contentious citizenship: Undocumented activism in the Not 1 More Deportation campaign. *Berkeley La Raza Law Journal, 26*, 46.

Abrego, L. J. (2015). Immigration law and immigrants' lived experiences. In A. Sarat & P. Ewick (Eds.), *The handbook of law and society* (pp. 258–272). New York, NY: Wiley.

Acitelli, T. (2017, February 22). Sanctuary cities in Massachusetts grow in number with Newton vote. *CurbedBoston*. https://boston.curbed.com/2017/2/22/14695092/sanctuary-cities-massachusetts

Ackerman, A. R., & Furman, R. (2013a). *The criminalization of immigration: Contexts and consequences*. Durham, NC: Carolina Academic Press.

Ackerman, A. R., & Furman, R. (2013b). The criminalization of immigration and the privatization of the immigration detention: Implications for justice. *Contemporary Justice Review, 16*(2), 251–263.

Ackerman, A. R., Sacks, M., & Furman, R. (2014). The new penology revisited: The criminalization of immigration as a pacification strategy. *Justice Policy Journal, 11*(1), 1–20.

Adams, T. J. (2014). Immigration politics, service labor, and the problem of the undocumented worker in southern California. In M. Halter, M. S. Johnson, K. P. Viens, & C. E. Wright (Eds.), *What's new about the "new" immigration?* (pp. 265–288). New York, NY: Palgrave Macmillan.

Adjei-Kontoh, H. (2017, January 31). Workers strike to protest Trump. *Green Left Weekly, 15*(1123).

Adler, B. (2017, October 5). *California governor signs "sanctuary state bill."* National Public Radio. https://www.npr.org/sections/thetwo-way/2017/10/05/555920658/california-governor-signs-sanctuary-state-bill

Agren, D., & Stanglin, D. (2017, February 22). Mexico says no to Trump's new deportation rules. *USA Today*. https://www.usatoday.com/story/news/world/2017/02/22/foriegn-minister-mexico-immigrations-proposals/98252710

Aguilar, J. (2017, February 16). A week after Austin ICE raids, immigrants and their supporters march in protest. *The Texas Tribune*. https://www.texastribune.org/tribpedia/sanctuary-cities

Aguirre, A., Jr. (2012). Arizona's SB1070, Latino immigrants and the framing of anti-immigrant policies. *Latino Studies, 10*(3), 385–394.

Ahmed, A. (2017a, November 20). Haunted by loss, and chasing ghost in Mexico. *The New York Times*, pp. A1, A6–A7.

Ahmed, A. (2017b, August 4). The deadliest town in Mexico's deadliest year. *The New York Times*, pp. A1, A8.

Ahn, I. (2013a). The democratic inclusion of the other and the case of Arizona immigration law: Habermas, Derrida, and a Christian ethical response. *Journal of Church and State, 55*(3), 527–552.

Ahn, I. (2013b). *Religious ethics and migration: Doing justice to undocumented workers*. New York, NY: Routledge.

Ahn, I., Chiu, A., & O'Neill, W. (2013). "And you welcomed me?" *CrossCurrents, 63*(3), 303–322.

Akincigil, A., Mayers, R. S., & Fulghum, F. H. (2011). Emergency room use by undocumented Mexican immigrants. *Journal of Sociology & Social Welfare, 38,* 33.

Alarcón, R., Escala, L., & Odgers, O. (2016). *Making Los Angeles home: The integration of Mexican immigrants in the United States*. Berkeley, CA: University of California Press.

Allen, E. (2017, April 29). Teen immigrants learn about rights: Group prepares students facing risk of deportation. *The Boston Globe*, p. 3.

Almendral, A. (2017, June 5). On the run from Duterte's drug crackdown. *The New York Times*, p. A4.

Alvarez, L. (2017, May 21). 58,000 Haitians in U.S. may lose safeguard granted after earthquake. *The New York Times*, p. 17.

Alvarez, P. (2017, January 25). Donald Trump targets sanctuary cities. *The Atlantic*. https://www.theatlantic.com/politics/archive/2017/01/trump-crack-down-sanctuary-city/514427

Amaral, E. F. (2016). *Introduction to demography*. http://www.ernestoamaral.com/docs/rand-dem16/Slides01.pdf

American Association of Geographers. (2017, February 7). *Boston: Geography in a sanctuary city*. http://news.aag.org/2017/02/boston-geography-in-a-sanctuary-city

American Civil Liberties Union. (2017). *Resources: Sanctuary cities*. https://aclum.org/our-work/aclum-issues/immigrants-rights/resources-sanctuary-cities

American Immigration Council. (2012, October 24). *Public education for immigrant students: Understanding Plyler v. Doe*. https://www.americanimmigrationcouncil.org/research/plyler-v-doe-public-education-immigrant-students

American Immigration Council. (2016, August 10). *Did my family really come here "illegally"?* https://www.americanimmigrationcouncil.org/research/did-my-family-really-come-legally-todays-immigration-laws-created-a-new-reality

Ameringer, C. F., & Liebert, S. (2017). Free clinics as safety net providers for Hispanic immigrants. *Public Administration Review, 77*(2), 310–311.

Amuedo-Dorantes, C., Puttitanun, T., & Martinez-Donate, A. (2013a). Tougher immigration measures increase fears of deportation, but do not change future migration plans. *LSE American Politics and Policy*. http://eprints.lse.ac.uk/58378

Amuedo-Dorantes, C., Puttitanun, T., & Martinez-Donate, A. P. (2013b). How do tougher immigration measures affect unauthorized immigrants? *Demography, 50*(3), 1067–1091.

Anderson, D. (2017, April 26). Plan to withhold sanctuary cities' funding blocked. *The Boston Globe*, pp. A1, A9.

Andrews, C., & Caron, C. (2016). *Long term disaster recovery planning in urban centers: The role of land tenure and housing in reducing vulnerability*. Washington, DC: The World Bank. https://www.researchgate.net/profile/Cynthia_Caron2/publication/296195730_Long_Term_Disaster_Recovery_Planning_in_Urban_Centers_The_Role_of_Land_Tenure_and_Housing_in_Reducing_Vulnerability/links/56d32d9408ae4d8d64a77 613.pdf

Annear, S. (2017, October 17). 18 arrested at protest of Guatemalan's deportation. *The Boston Globe*, p. B4.

Annese, J., Moyhinan, E., & Slattery, D. (2017, February 11). Hundreds of pro-immigration activists march to support NYC as sanctuary city. *Daily News*. http://www.nydailynews.com/new-york/manhattan/pro-immigration-activists-march-support-nyc-sanctuary-city-article-1.2970071

Apollonio, D., Lochner, T., & Heddens, M. (2013). Immigration and prosecutorial discretion. *California Journal of Politics and Policy, 5*(2), 232–251.

Appold, K. (2015). Treatment challenges. *Hospitalist, 2015*(12).

Arbona, C., Olvera, N., Rodriguez, N., Hagan, J., Linares, A., & Wiesner, M. (2010). Acculturative stress among documented and undocumented Latino immigrants in the United States. *Hispanic Journal of Behavioral Sciences, 32*(3), 362–384.

Arias, A., & Milian, C. (2013). US Central Americans: Representations, agency and communities. *Latino Studies, 11*(2), 131–149.

Armacost, B. E. (2016). "Sanctuary" laws: The new immigration federalism. *Michigan State Law Review, 2016*(5).

Armenta, A. (2016). Between public service and social control: Policing dilemmas in the era of immigration enforcement. *Social Problems, 63*(1), 111–126.

Armenta, A., & Alvarez, I. (2017). Policing immigrants or policing immigration? Understanding local law enforcement participation in immigration control. *Sociology Compass, 11*(2).

Arriaga, F. (2017). Relationships between the public and crimmigration entities in North Carolina: A 287(g) program focus. *Sociology of Race and Ethnicity, 3*(3), 417–431.

Arriola, E. R. (2015). Queer, undocumented, and sitting in an immigration detention center: A post-Obergefell reflection. *UMKC Law Review, 84*, 617.

As Houston rebuilds, it will need Dreamers [Editorial]. (2017, September 1). *The Boston Globe*, p. A8.

Associated Press. (2017a, April 11). Sessions outlines border enforcement. *The New York Times*. https://www.nytimes.com/aponline/2017/04/11/us/ap-us-border-tour-sessions-the-latest.html?_r=0

Associated Press. (2017b, April 21). Justice Department threatens sanctuary cities in immigration fights. *The New York Times*. http://www.foxnews.com/politics/2017/04/21/justice-dept-threatens-sanctuary-cities-in-immigration-fight.html

Astor, M. (2017, December 19). 2 undocumented teenagers in U.S. shelters must be allowed abortions, judge rules. *The New York Times*, p. A15.

Auchter, J. (2013). Border monuments: Memory, counter-memory, and (b)ordering practices along the US–Mexico border. *Review of International Studies, 39*(2), 291–311.

Avalos, H. (2016). Diasporas "R" us: Attitudes toward Immigrants in the Bible. In F. F. Flannery & R. A. Werline (Eds.), *The Bible in political debate: What does it really say?* (pp. 33–45). Oxford, UK: Bloomsbury.

Avera, L. (2016). *The Bracero Program: A historical perspective on the perpetuation of isolated labor markets in south Texas.* http://discoverarchive.vanderbilt.edu/handle/1803/8346

Ayón, C., & Philbin, S. P. (2017). "Tú no eres de aquí": Latino children's experiences of institutional and interpersonal discrimination and microaggressions. *Social Work Research, 41*(1), 19–30.

Aysa-Lastra, M., & Cachón, L. (Eds.). (2015). *Immigrant vulnerability and resilience. Comparative perspectives on Latin American immigrants during the Great Recession.* New York, NY: Springer.

Babwin, D. (2017, September 16). Sessions suffers legal defeat on sanctuary cities. *The Boston Globe*, p. 11.

Bagelman, J. (2013). Sanctuary: A politics of ease? *Alternatives, 38*(1), 49–62.

Bagelman, J. (2016). *Sanctuary city: A suspended state.* New York, NY: Springer.

Bailey, J. (2013). *"Tener exito": Stories of self-efficacy from undocumented Latinos in the pursuit of higher education.* Ann Arbor, MI: ProQuest.

Baker, P. (2017, April 27). Trump pledges to defend executive order on sanctuary cities. *The New York Times*, p. A19.

Bakri, A. F., Zaman, N. Q., Kamarudin, H., & Amin, N. M. (2014). Reviving the physical and cultural attributes of ethnic enclave: A conservation approach. *Procedia—Social and Behavioral Sciences, 153*, 341–348.

Balch, A. (2016a). *Immigration and the state: Fear, greed and hospitality.* London, UK: Palgrave Macmillan.

Balch, A. (2016b). *Attrition by enforcement. Immigration and the state.* London, UK: Palgrave Macmillan.

Balderrama, F. E., & Rodriguez, R. (2006). *Decade of betrayal: Mexican repatriation in the 1930s.* Albuquerque, NM: University of New Mexico Press.

Balkaran, S. (2017, January 23). An open letter on behalf of undocumented immigrants. *The Huffington Post.* http://www.huffingtonpost.com/entry/an-open-letter-on-behalf-of-undocumented-immigrants_us_5885210de4b08f5134b6222e

Baquedano-López, P., & Janetti, G. B. (2017). The Maya diaspora Yucatan–San Francisco. In S. Salas & P. R. Portes (Eds.), *US Latinization: Education and the new Latino south* (pp. 161–185). Albany, NY: State University of New York Press.

Barajas, M. (2015, March 18). Stop calling Houston a "sanctuary city." *Houston Press.* http://www.houstonpress.com/news/stop-calling-houston-a-sanctuary-city-6729418

Barboza, G., Dominguez, S., Siller, L., & Montalva, M. (2017). Citizenship, fear and support for the criminalization of immigration: Contextualizing Mexican Americans' attitudes about the role of law enforcement. *Policing, 40*(2).

Barenboim, D. (2016). The specter of surveillance: Navigating "illegality" and indigeneity among Maya migrants in the San Francisco Bay Area. *PoLAR: Political and Legal Anthropology Review, 39*(1), 79–94.

Barragan, J. (2017, April 16). Poll: Texans oppose border wall and sanctuary cities, think immigrants help more than they hurt. Dallas

News.   (https://www.dallasnews.com/news/immigration/2017/04/18/
poll-texans-oppose-border-wall-sanctuary-citiesthink-immigrants-help-hurt)

Barrera, A. G., & Krogstad, M. (2017, March 2). *What we know about illegal immigration from Mexico*. Washington, DC: Pew Research Center.

Barreto, M., Segura, G. M., Bergman, E., Damore, D., & Pantoha, A. (2014). The Prop 187 effect: The politics of immigration and lessons from California. In M. Barreto & G. M. Segura (Eds.), *Latino America: How America's most dynamic population is poised to transform the politics of the nation* (pp. 173–188). New York, NY: Public Affairs.

Bassano, D. (2016). *Fight and flight: The Central America human rights movement in the United States in the 1980s*. Newcastle Upon Tyne, UK: Cambridge Scholars Publishing.

Bauder, H. (2016a). Possibilities of urban belonging. *Antipode, 48*(2), 252–271.

Bauder, H. (2016b). Domicile citizenship, migration and the city. In H. Bauder & C. Matheis (Eds.), *Migration policy and practice* (pp. 79–99). New York, NY: Palgrave Macmillan.

Bauder, H. (2017). Sanctuary cities: Policies and practices in international perspective. *International Migration, 55*(2), 174–187.

Bayor, R. H. (Ed.). (2016). *The Oxford handbook of American immigration and ethnicity*. New York, NY: Oxford University Press.

Becerra, D. (2012). The impact of anti-immigration policies and perceived discrimination in the United States on migration intentions among Mexican adolescents. *International Migration, 50*(4), 20–32.

Becerra, D. (2016). Anti-immigration policies and fear of deportation: A human rights issue. *Journal of Human Rights and Social Work, 1*(3), 109–119.

Becerra, D., Androff, D. K., Ayon, C., & Castillo, J. T. (2012). Fear vs. facts: Examining the economic impact of undocumented immigrants in the US. *Journal of Sociology & Social Welfare, 39*, 111.

Becerra, D., & Kiehne, E. (2016). Assessing the relationship between remittance receipt and migration intentions among Mexican adolescents living along the US–Mexico border. *Norteamérica, 11*(2), 7–30.

Bedard, P. (2017, February 24). 300 "sanctuary restaurants" join 300 "sanctuary cities." *Washington Examiner*. http://www.washingtonexaminer.com/300-sanctuary-restaurants-join-300-sanctuary-cities/article/2615663

Bell, K. W. (2010). *The sanctuary movement: How broken immigration policies affect cities*. Chicago, IL: Author.

Bellafante, G. (2017, May 21). Stepped-up immigration raids, but gang violence persists. *The New York Times*, p. 26.

Bennett, B. (2017, February 4). Not just "bad hombres": Trump is targeting 8 million people for deportation. *Los Angeles Times*. http://www.latimes.com/politics/la-na-pol-trump-deportations-20170204-story.html

Berardi, G. K. (2014). The changing nature of Colorado immigration laws: 2006–2013. *Journal of Social Science for Policy Implications, 2*(4), 1–29.

Berenson, T. (2017, August 28). Undocumented immigrants may get less time to make their case. *Time*, p. 12.

Berg, O., & Schwenken, H. (2013). Masking, blurring, replacing: Can the undocumented migrant have a face in film? In C. Bischoff, F. Falk, & S. Kafeshy (Eds.), *Images of illegalized immigration: Towards a critical iconology of politics* (pp. 111–127). London, UK: Transcription Publishers.

Bergeron, C. (2013). *Going to the back of the line: A primer on lines, visa categories, and wait times.* Washington, DC: Migration Policy Institute.

Berlinger, N., & Raghavan, R. (2013). The ethics of advocacy for undocumented patients. *Hastings Center Report, 43*(1), 14–17.

Bernal, R. (2017, March 1). Remittances to Mexico are on the rise. *The Hill.* http://thehill. com/latino/321869-remittances-to-mexico-are-on-the-rise

Bhatt, C. (2012). *Secularism and conflicts about rights.* London School of Economics Research Online. http://eprints.lse.ac.uk/46733/1/Secularism%20and%20 conflicts%20about%20rights(lsero).pdf

Bhimji, F. (2010). Struggles, urban citizenship, and belonging: The experience of undocumented street vendors and food truck owners in Los Angeles. *Urban Anthropology and Studies of Cultural Systems and World Economic Development, 39*(4), 455–492.

Bhimji, F. (2014). Undocumented immigrants' performances and claims of urban citizenship in Los Angeles. *Journal of Intercultural Studies, 35*(1), 18–33.

Bhuyan, R. (2011). *Negotiating social rights and social membership on the frontlines of service delivery to migrants with precarious status.* University of Toronto. https://www. researchgate.net/profile/Rupaleem_Bhuyan/publication/267218649_Negotiating_ Social_Rights_and_Social_Membership_on_the_Frontlines_of_Service_Delivery_ to_Migrants_with_Precarious_Status/links/5608960908ae8e08c0946306.pdf

Bilke, C. (2009). Divided we stand, united we fall: A public policy analysis of sanctuary cities' role in the illegal immigration debate. *Indiana Law Review, 42,* 165.

Bishop, M. (2015, October 23). Why are immigrant mothers wearing ankle monitors? *Latino USA.* http://latinousa.org/2015/10/23/why-are-immigrant-mothers-wearing-ankle-monitors

Bloch, K. R. (2016). "It is just sickening": Emotions and discourse in an anti-immigrant discussion forum. *Sociological Focus, 49*(4), 257–270.

Bloemraad, I., & Gleeson, S. (2012). Making the case for organizational presence: Civic inclusion, access to resources, and formal community organizations. In M. P. Smith & M. MacQuarrie (Eds.), *Remaking urban citizenship: Organizations, institutions, and the right to the city* (pp. 109–134). New Brunswick, NJ: Transactions Publishers.

Bloemraad, I., Silva, F., & Voss, K. (2016). Rights, economics, or family? Frame resonance, political ideology, and the immigrant rights movement. *Social Forces, 94*(4), 1647–1674.

Bloemraad, I., Voss, K., & Silva, F. (2014). *Framing the immigrant movement as about rights, family, or economics: Which appeals resonate and for whom?* (Working Paper No. 112-14). Berkeley, CA: University of California Berkeley, Institute for Research and Labor Employment.

Boccagni, P. (2017). *Migration and the search for home.* New York, NY: Palgrave Macmillan.

Born, B. (2017, January 25). Pittsburgh public schools declares itself "sanctuary." *Pittsburgh Post-Gazette.* http://www.post-gazette.com/news/education/2017/ 01/25/Pittsburgh-Public-Schools-declares-itself-sanctuary-campus/stories/ 201701250214

Boryczka, J. M., & Gudelunas, D. (2016). *Strangers as Neighbors Toolkit: One parish one community—A guide for engaging United States in difficult dialogues.* Fairfield University. http://digitalcommons.fairfield.edu/strangersasneighbors-pubs/5

Boscarino, T. (2017, January 30). Is Detroit a sanctuary city? Depends upon who you ask. *Model D*. http://www.modeldmedia.com/features/detroit-sanctuary-city-013017. aspx

Bosworth, M. (2016). Border criminology: How migration is changing criminal justice. In M. Bosworth, C. Hoyle, & L. Zedner (Eds.), *Changing contours of criminal justice* (pp. 213–227). New York, NY: Oxford University Press.

Brannon, I., & Albright, L. (2016). *Immigration's impact on the Texas economy*. Texas Public Policy Foundation. http://www.texaspolicy.com/library/doclib/Immigration-s-Impact-on-the-Texas-Economy.pdf

Bronk, C., & González-Aréchiga, B. (2011). Mexico–United States border security: From a bilateral to a truly binational policy process. *Latin American Policy, 2*(2), 152–181.

Brown, D. W. (2016). *Assumptions of the Tea Party movement*. New York, NY: Palgrave Macmillan.

Brown, E. J. (2015). Models of transformative learning for social justice: Comparative case studies of non-formal development education in Britain and Spain. *Compare: A Journal of Comparative and International Education, 45*(1), 141–162.

Brown, H. E., Jones, J. A., & Dow, T. (2016). Unity in the struggle: Immigration and the South's emerging civil rights consensus. *Law and Contemporary Problems, 79*, 5–27.

Burciaga, E. M. (2016). *The Latino undocumented 1.5-generation: Navigating belonging in new and old destinations* Doctoral dissertation, University of California, Irvine, CA.

Burghart, D., & Zeskind, L. (2012). *Beyond FAIR: The decline of the established anti-immigrant organizations and the rise of Tea Party nativism.*. Seattle, WA: Institute for Research & Education on Human Rights.

Burke, F. (2017). *A land apart: The Southwest and the nation in the twentieth century*. Tucson, AZ: University of Arizona Press.

Burki, S. J. (2017). Demographic changes. In S. J. Burki (Ed.), *Rising powers and global governance* (pp. 183–193). New York, NY: Palgrave Macmillan.

Burnett, J. (2015, October 24). *For Irish illegally in the U.S., a life locked in place, hoping for change*. National Public Radio.http://www.npr.org/2015/10/24/451213832/for-irish-illegally-in-u-s-a-life-locked-in-place-hoping-for-change

Burns, A., & Johnson, K. (2017, November 5). Poised to control west coast, democrats envision "blue wall." *The New York Times*, pp. 1, 18.

Burns, A. & Yee, V. (2017, September 7). Second chance for "dreamers" seen in court. *The New York Times*, pp. A1, A16.

Burridge, A. (2016). From the desert to the courtroom. In P. Mudu & S. Chattopadhyay (Eds.), *Migration, squatting and radical autonomy: Resistance and destabilization of racist regulatory policies and B/ordering mechanisms* (pp. 35–38). New York, NY: Routledge.

Byrne, J., & Dardick, H. (2017, August 7). Emanuel sues Trump's Justice Department over sanctuary city policy. *Chicago Tribune*. http://www.chicagotribune.com/news/local/politics/ct-rahm-emanuel-donald-trump-lawsuit-met-0808-2-20170807-story. html

Cabaniss, E. (2016, April 26). Pulling back the curtain examining the backstage gendered dynamics of storytelling in the undocumented youth movement. *Journal of Contemporary Ethnography*.

Cade, J. A. (2013). Policing the immigration police: ICE prosecutorial discretion and the Fourth Amendment. *Columbia Law Review Sidebar, 113*, 180–203.

Cadge, W., Levitt, P., Jaworsky, B. N., & Clevenger, C. (2013). Religious dimensions of contexts of reception: Comparing two New England cities. *International Migration, 51*(3), 84–98.

Cadman, D. (2014). *How a finely tuned system of checks and balances has been effectively dismantled.* Center for Immigration Studies. http://cis.org/sites/cis.org/files/cadman-asylum.pdf

Calavita, K. (1996). The new politics of immigration: "Balanced-budget conservatism" and the symbolism of Proposition 187. *Social Problems, 43*(3), 284–305.

Caldwell, A. A. (2017, May 10). In review, US digs for evidence of Haitian immigrant crimes. *The Boston Globe*, p. A9.

Calvo, A. M. M. M., & Sanchez, J. B. (2016). *Hospitality in American literature and culture: Spaces, bodies, borders.* New York, NY: Routledge.

Cameron, D. (2017, January 25). How sanctuary cities work, and how Trump's executive order might affect them. *The Washington Post.* https://www.washingtonpost.com/graphics/national/sanctuary-cities

Caminero-Santangelo, M. (2012). The voice of the voiceless. In R. Lippert & S. Rehaag (Eds.), *Sanctuary practices in international perspectives: Migration, citizenship and social movements* (pp. 90–104). New York, NY: Routledge.

Caminero-Santangelo, M. (2016). *Documenting the undocumented.* Gainesville, FL: University Press of Florida.

Campano, G., Ghiso, M. P., & Welch, B. J. (2016). *Partnering with immigrant communities: Action through literacy.* New York, NY: Teachers College Press.

Campbell, K. M. (2012). Humanitarian aid is never a crime? The politics of immigration enforcement and the provision of sanctuary. *Syracuse Law Review, 63*, 71.

Campbell, W. S. (2008). Lessons in resilience: Undocumented Mexican women in South Carolina. *Affilia, 23*(3), 231–241.

Campos, V. (2014). *Restoring the right to drive: Re-licensing the undocumented community in California.* https://www.oxy.edu/sites/default/files/assets/UEP/Comps/2014/Campus,Violeta_Restoring%20the%20Right%20to%20Drive.pdf

Campsen, G. E., III. (2013). Preemption and *United States v. South Carolina*: Undermining our nation's border and the Constitution's border between state and federal sovereignty. *South Carolina Law Review, 65*, 901.

Capps, R., Fix, M., & Zong, J. (2016). *A profile of US children with unauthorized immigrant parents.* Washington, DC: Migration Policy Institute.

Carcamo, C. (2017, February 11). BART rail system may designate itself a "sanctuary in transit." *Los Angeles Times.* http://www.latimes.com/local/california/la-me-bart-may-become-immigration-sanctuary-20170211-story.html

Carens, J. (2013). *The ethics of immigration.* New York, NY: Oxford University Press.

Carroll, M. (2016, November 30). Sanctuary cities insist they'll stand alone. *U.S. News and World Report.* https://www.usnews.com/news/national-news/articles/2016-11-30/sanctuary-cities-insist-theyll-stand-strong

Carroll, R., Respaut, R., & Sullivan, A. (2017, January 26). *Top 10 U.S. sanctuary cites face roughly $2.27 in cuts by Trump policy.* Reuters. https://www.reuters.com/article/us-usa-trump-sanctuarycities-idUSKBN1592V9

Carson, A. P. (2017). Justice for noncitizens: A case for reforming the immigration legal system. *VA Engage Journal, 5*(1), 4.

Carswell, S. (2016a, November 18). Undocumented Irish in U.S. live in fear of Trump's resolve. *The Irish Times*. https://www.irishtimes.com/news/world/us/undocumented-irish-in-us-live-in-fear-of-trump-s-resolve-1.2873549

Carswell, S. (2016b, November 26). Boston mayor vows to defend undocumented Irish. *The Irish Times*. http://www.irishtimes.com/news/world/us/boston-mayor-vows-to-defend- undocumented-irish-1.2884048

Carter, D. B., & Poast, P. (2017). Why do states build walls? Political economy, security, and border stability. *Journal of Conflict Resolution, 61*(2), 239–270.

Casey, E. S., & Watkins, M. (2014). *Up against the wall: Re-imagining the US–Mexico border*. Austin, TX: University of Texas Press.

Casselman, B. (2016, November 14). There aren't 2 to 3 million undocumented immigrants with criminal records for Trump deport. *FiveThirtyEight*. https://fivethirtyeight.com/features/there-arent-2-to-3-million-undocumented-immigrants-with-criminal-records-for-trump-to-deport

Castañeda, M. (2016). Altering the US soundscape through Latina/o community radio. In M. E. Cepeda. (Ed.), *The Routledge Companion to Latina/o Media* [ebook]. New York: Routledge.

Castillo, A. (2017). US–Mexico relations are officially off-the-wall. *Eureka Street, 27*(2), 59–61.

CBS New York. (2017, March 28). *City leaders defy White House threat on "sanctuary city" policies*. http://newyork.cbslocal.com/2017/03/28/city-leaders-defy-white-house-threat-on-sanctuary-cities-policies

CBS News. (2017, January 26). *What is a sanctuary city? And what happens now?* http://www.cbsnews.com/news/what-is-a-sanctuary-city-and-what-happens-now

CBS SFBayArea. (2015, January 8). *Timeline: How San Francisco became a sanctuary city for undocumented immigrants*. http://sanfrancisco.cbslocal.com/2015/07/08/timeline-how-san-francisco-became-a-sanctuary-city-for-undocumented-immigrants

Cebula, R. J. (2016). Give me sanctuary! The impact of personal freedom afforded by sanctuary cities on the 2010 undocumented immigrant settlement pattern within the US, 2SLS estimates. *Journal of Economics and Finance, 40*(4), 792–802.

Chacón, J. M. (2012). Overcriminalizing immigration. *Journal of Criminal Law and Criminology, 102*, 613.

Chacón, J. M. (2017). Privatized immigration enforcement. *Harvard Civil Rights–Civil Liberties Law Review, 57*, 2–45. http://harvardcrcl.org/wp-content/uploads/2017/02/Chacon.pdf

Chand, D. E., & Schreckhise, W. D. (2015). Secure communities and community values: Local context and discretionary immigration law enforcement. *Journal of Ethnic and Migration Studies, 41*(10), 1621–1643.

Chappell, B. (2017, March 30). *Seattle sues Trump administration over "sanctuary city" threat: The two-way*. National Public Radio. http://www.npr.org/sections/thetwo-way/2017/03/30/522030259/seattle-sues-trump-administration-over-sanctuary-city-threat

Chauvin, S., & Garcés-Mascareñas, B. (2014). Becoming less illegal: Deservingness frames and undocumented migrant incorporation. *Sociology Compass, 8*(4), 422–432.

Chavez, L. R. (2012a). *Shadowed lives: Undocumented immigrants in American society*. Belmont, CA: Wadsworth.

Chavez, L. R. (2012b). Undocumented immigrants and their use of medical services in Orange County, California. *Social Science & Medicine, 74*(6), 887–893.

Chavez, L. R. (2013). *The Latino threat: Constructing immigrants, citizens, and the nation.* Palo Alto, CA: Stanford University Press.

Chávez, S. (2011). Navigating the US–Mexico border: The crossing strategies of undocumented workers in Tijuana, Mexico. *Ethnic and Racial Studies, 34*(8), 1320–1337.

Cházaro, A. (2012). Rolling back the tide: Challenging the criminalization of immigrants in Washington state. *Seattle Journal of Social Justice, 11,* 127.

Chen, M. (2016, March 14). Undocumented immigrants contribute over $11 billion to our economy each year. *The Nation.* https://www.thenation.com/article/undocumented-immigrants-contribute-over-11-billion-to-our-economy-each-year

Chen, M. H. (2015). Trust in immigration enforcement: State noncooperation and sanctuary cities after secure communities. *Chicago–Kent Law Review, 91.*

Cherkaoui, M. (2016). *Donald Trump's presidency: New dawn or dooms day?* http://studies.aljazeera.net/mritems/Documents/2016/11/27/4c187850fb4f4171931543d81bb0d103_100.pdf

Cherone, H. (2017, February 28). *Cardinal Cupich: No immigration agents in Catholic churches without warrants.* DNA Info. https://www.dnainfo.com/chicago/20170228/mt-greenwood/cupich-no-immigration-agents-catholic-churches-without-warrants

Chokshi, N. (2017, August 8). In Trump era, states are shifting focus to immigration laws. *The New York Times,* p. A11.

Chomsky, A. (2014). *Undocumented: How immigration became illegal.* Boston, MA: Beacon Press.

Christina, G. (2017). What can we do? *The Humanist, 77*(2), 34–35.

Ciancio, A. (2016). *The impact of immigration policies on local enforcement, crime and policing efficiency.* https://www.dropbox.com/s/p4ncwaift8tkz89/CIANCIO_jmp.pdf?dl=0

Cisneros, A. S. (2017). *Latino identity and political attitudes.* New York, NY: Springer.

Clause, K. S. (2017, February 17). *Everyone is missing the point about sanctuary cities.* http://www.bostonmagazine.com/news/blog/2017/02/17/boston-sanctuary-cities-287g-agreements

Cleaveland, C. (2010). "We are not criminals": Social work advocacy and unauthorized migrants. *Social Work, 55*(1), 74–81.

Clevenger, C., Derr, A. S., Cadge, W., & Curran, S. (2014). How do social service providers view recent immigrants? Perspectives from Portland, Maine, and Olympia, Washington. *Journal of Immigrant & Refugee Studies, 12*(1), 67–86.

Cobas, J. A., Duany, J., & Feagin, J. R. (2015). *How the United States racializes Latinos: White hegemony and its consequences.* New York, NY: Routledge.

Coddou, M. (2016). An institutional approach to collective action: Evidence from faith-based Latino mobilization in the 2006 immigrant rights protests. *Social Problems, 63*(1), 127–150.

Coddou, M. (2017). Sanctified mobilization: How political activists manage institutional boundaries in faith-based organizing for immigrant rights. In B. Wejnert & P. Parigi (Eds.), *On the cross road of polity, political elites and mobilization* (pp. 25–65). Bingley, UK: Emerald Group.

Cohen, P. (2017, May 30). In rural Iowa, a future rests on immigrants. *The New York Times,* pp. A1, A12.

Cohn, D'V., Passel, J. S., & Gonzalez-Barrera, A. (2017, December 7). *Rise in U.S. immigrants from El Salvador, Guatemala and Honduras outpaces growth from elsewhere.* Washington, DC: Pew Research Center.

Coleman, M. (2007). Immigration geopolitics beyond the Mexico–US border. *Antipode, 39*(1), 54–76.

Coleman, M., & Kocher, A. (2011). Detention, deportation, and devolution and immigrant incapacitation in the U.S., post 9-11. *Geographical Journal, 177*(3), 228–237.

Coleman, M., & Stuesse, A. (2014). Policing borders, policing bodies: The territorial and biopolitical roots of US immigration control. In R. Jones & C. Johnson (Eds.), *Placing the border in everyday life* (pp. 33–65). New York, NY: Routledge.

Collingwood, L., & El-Khatib, S. (2016). *Gimme shelter: The myth and reality of the American sanctuary city.* http://www.collingwoodresearch.com/uploads/8/3/6/0/8360930/shelter_nopols.pdf

Comino, S., Mastrobuoni, G., & Nicolò, A. (2016). *Silence of the innocents: Illegal immigrants' underreporting of crime and their victimization.* https://papers.ssrn.com/sol3/papers.cfm?abstract_id=2861091

Commonwealth Institute. (2015). *Undocumented, but not untaxed.* http://www.thecommonwealthinstitute.org/wp-content/uploads/2016/01/Tax-Contributions-of-Undocumented-Immigrants-2015_V1.pdf

Conn, S. (2014). *Americans against the city: Anti-urbanism in the twentieth century.* New York, NY: Oxford University Press.

Cooke, A., & Kemeny, T. (2016). *Urban immigrant diversity and inclusive institutions* (US Census Bureau Center for Economic Studies Paper No. CES-WP-16-07). Washington, DC: US Census Bureau.

Cooper, T. (2015). Welcome the stranger or seal the borders? Conflicting religious responses to migrants. In S. D. Brunn (Ed.), *The changing world religion map* (pp. 3053–3073). Dordrecht, the Netherlands: Springer.

Correa, J. G. (2013). "After 9/11 everything changed": Re-formations of state violence in everyday life on the US–Mexico border. *Cultural Dynamics, 25*(1), 99–119.

Correa-Cabrera, G., Garrett, T., & Keck, M. (2014). Administrative surveillance and fear: Implications for US–Mexico border relations and governance. *European Review of Latin American and Caribbean Studies, 96,* 35–53.

Correal, A., & Semple, K. (2017, September 1). As Texans battened hatches, migrants saw their shot across border. *The New York Times,* p. A15.

Corrigall-Brown, C. (2013). Participation in social movements. In D. A. Snow & D. della Porta (Eds.), *The Wiley–Blackwell encyclopedia of social and political movements.* New York, NY: Wiley.

Corsi, J. R. (2016, November 16). 1 main reason U.S. border wall hasn't been built. *WorldNetDaily.* http://www.wnd.com/2016/11/1-main-reason-u-s-border-wall-hasnt-been-built

Costantini, C. (2011, December 21). Municipal ID cards given to undocumented immigrants in cities across the US with success. *Huffington Post.* http://www.huffingtonpost.com/2011/10/21/municipal-id-cards-undocumented-immigrants_n_1024412.html

Coté-Boucher, K. (2014). Bordering citizenship in "an open and generous society": The criminalization of migration in Canada. In S. Pickering & J. Ham (Eds.), *The Routledge handbook on crime and international migration* (pp. 75–90). London, UK: Routledge.

Coutin, S. B. (1993). *The culture of protest: Religious activism and the U.S. sanctuary movement (conflict and social change).* Boulder, CO: Westview.

Coutin, S. B., & Vogel, E. (2016). Migrant narratives and ethnographic tropes: Navigating tragedy, creating possibilities. *Journal of Contemporary Ethnography, 45*(6), 631–644.

Cowell, A. (2017, November 15). Grim list illuminates plight of refugees. *The New York Times*, p. A10.

Cramer, M. (2017a, April 27). Deportation fears create gaps in care: Fewer visitors to food pantries, health clinics. *The Boston Globe*, pp. A1, A11.

Cramer, M. (2017b, May 23). Haitians are given reprieve, for now. *The Boston Globe*, pp. B1, B4.

Cramer, M. (2017c, June 16). Jump in arrests by ICE raises concerns. *The Boston Globe*, pp. A1, A9.

Crawford, E. R. (2017). When boundaries around the "secret" are tested: A school community response to the policing of undocumented immigrants. *Education and Urban Society, 50*(2), 155–182.

Crimaldi, L. (2017, October 22). Welcome signs. *The Boston Globe*, pp. B1, B14.

Crossley, C. (2017, March 31). *Offering sanctuary is nothing new, and neither are the emotions behind it.* WGBH. http://news.wgbh.org/2017/03/31/local-news/offering-sanctuary-nothing-new-and-neither-are-emotions-behind-it

Cruz, G. T. (2016). Christian mission and ministry in the context of contemporary migration. *International Journal of Practical Theology, 20*(2), 242–260.

Cuevas, S. (2017, February 28). *L.A. Catholic leaders resist trump immigration crackdowns.* KQED News. https://ww2.kqed.org/news/2017/02/28/l-a-catholic-leaders-resist-trump-immigration-crackdowns

Culliton-González, K., & Ingram, J. C. (2017). *Sanctuary, safety and community: Tools for protecting immigrants through local democracy.* https://works.bepress.com/katherine_culliton/19

Daiute, C. (2017). Narrating refuge. *Europe's Journal of Psychology, 13*(1), 1. https://www.ncbi.nlm.nih.gov/pmc/articles/PMC5342307

Darling, J. (2010). A city of sanctuary: The relational re-imagining of Sheffield's asylum politics. *Transactions of the Institute of British Geographers, 35*(1), 125–140.

Darling, J. (2014). From hospitality to presence. *Peace Review, 26*(2), 162–169.

Darling, J. (2016). Forced migration and the city: Irregularity, informality, and the politics of presence. *Progress in Human Geography, 41*(2), 178–198.

Darling, J., & Squire, V. (2012). Everyday enactments of sanctuary. In R. Lippert & S. Rehaag (Eds.), *Sanctuary practices in international perspectives: Migration, citizenship and social movements* (pp. 191–204). New York, NY: Routledge.

Dart, T., & Pilkington, E. (2017, February 14). Austin sanctuary network: Grassroots leadership. *The Guardian*. https://grassrootsleadership.org/tags/austin-sanctuary-network

Davey, M. (2017, February 27). He's a local pillar. Now he could be deported: A Midwestern town rallies to rescue an immigrant. *The New York Times*, pp. A1, A10.

Davidson, F. M., Sours, T., & Moll, R. L. (2016). Demography, identity and the 2016 presidential election. *The Geography Teacher, 13*(3), 106–111.

Davidson, M. (1998). *Convictions of the hearth: Jim Corbett and the sanctuary movement.* Tucson, AZ: University of Arizona Press.

Davidson, M. J. (2014). Sanctuary: A modern legal anachronism. *Capital University Law Review, 42*, 583.

Davila, A., & Saenz, R. (1990). The effect of maquiladora employment on the monthly flow of Mexican undocumented immigration to the US, 1978–1982. *International Migration Review, 24*, 96–107.

Davis, J. H., & Savage, C. (2017, March 28). White House to sanctuary cities: Shield the undocumented and lose police funding. *The New York Times*, p. A19.

Daza, V. (2017, March 6). Local libraries are true immigrant sanctuaries. *The Daily News.* http://www.nydailynews.com/opinion/local-libraries-true-immigrant-sanctuaries-article-1.2989829

de Graauw, E. (2014). Municipal ID cards for undocumented immigrants: Local bureaucratic membership in a federal system. *Politics & Society, 42*(3), 309–330.

de Graauw, E. (2015). Rolling out the welcome mat: State and city immigrant affairs offices in the United States. *IdeAs, 6.* https://ideas.revues.org/1293

de Graauw, E., & Bloemraad, I. (2017). Working together: Building successful policy and program partnerships for immigrant integration. *Journal on Migration and Human Security, 5*(1).

de Graauw, E., & Vermeulen, F. (2016). Cities and the politics of immigrant integration: A comparison of Berlin, Amsterdam, New York City, and San Francisco. *Journal of Ethnic and Migration Studies, 42*(6), 989–1012.

De Jong, G. F., Graefe, D., Galvan, C., & Hasanali, S. H. (2017). Unemployment and immigrant receptivity climate in established and newly emerging destination areas. *Population Research and Policy Review, 36*(2), 157–180.

de la Torre, M. A. (2016). *The US immigration crisis: Toward an ethics of place* (Vol. 27). Eugene, OR: Wipf &Stock.

de la Vega, S. L., & Steigenga, T. (2013). Facing immigration fears: A constructive local approach to day labor, community, and integration. *Journal on Migration and Human Security, 1*, 1–16.

De León, J. (2013). Undocumented migration, use wear, and the materiality of habitual suffering in the Sonoran Desert. *Journal of Material Culture, 18*(4), 321–345.

Deck, A. F. (2015). Latino migration and the transformation of USA Catholicism: Framing the question. *Perspectiva Teológica, 46*(128), 89. http://www.faje.edu.br/periodicos/index.php/perspectiva/article/view/2949

DeCosta-Klipa, N. (2017, March 21). Boston and 4 other Massachusetts cities included in ICE's first sanctuary cities list. *Boston.com.* https://www.boston.com/news/politics/2017/03/21/boston-and-4-other-massachusetts-cities-included-on-ices-first-sanctuary-city-list

del Hierro, M. (2016). Mojado. In I. D. Ruiz & R. Sanchez (Eds.), *Decolonizing rhetoric and composition studies* (pp. 169–181). New York, NY: Palgrave Macmillan.

Delgado, A. (2017). The sanctuary movement: Historical & contemporary uses. *AmeriQuests, 13*(1).

Delgado, M. (1997). Role of Latina-owned beauty parlors in a Latino community. *Social Work, 42*(5), 445–453.

Delgado, M. (1999). *Social work practice in nontraditional urban settings.* New York: Oxford University Press.

Delgado, M. (2011). *Latino small businesses and the American dream: Community social work and economic and social development.* New York, NY: Columbia University Press.

Delgado, M. (2015). *Urban youth and photovoice: Visual ethnography in action.* New York, NY: Oxford University Press.

Delgado, M. (2016a). *Celebrating urban community life: Fairs, festivals, parades, and community practice.* Toronto, CN: University of Toronto Press.

Delgado, M. (2016b). *Community practice and urban youth: Social justice service-learning and civic engagement.* New York, NY: Routledge.

Delgado, M. (2017). *Social work with Latinos: Social, economic, political, and cultural perspectives* (2nd ed.). New York, NY: Oxford University Press.

Democracy Now. (2005, April 5). *Vigilantes or civilian border patrol? A debate on the Minuteman Project.* http://www.democracynow.org

Derby, J. (2015). *Everyday illegal: When policies undermine immigrant families.* Berkeley, CA: University of California Press.

DeStefano, J., Jr. (2016). Cities and immigration reform: National policy from the bottom up. In R. Brescia & J. T. Marsall (Eds.), *How cities will save the world: Urban innovation in the face of population flows, climate change and economic inequality* (pp. 137–157). New York, NY: Routledge.

Díaz-Barriga, M., & Dorsey, M. (2016). Anthropology, art, and the US–Mexico border wall. *Anthropology News, 57*(5), e69–e70.

Diaz-Edelman, M. D. (2014). *Working together: Multicultural collaboration in the interfaith immigrant rights movement.* Doctoral dissertation, Boston University, Boston, MA.

DiCamillo, M. (2017). *Release #2017-02: Californians hold divided and partisan views about sanctuary cities; This contrasts with bipartisan support for providing undocumented immigrants a pathway to citizenship and opposition to building the US–Mexico wall.* Berkeley Institute of Governmental Studies Poll.

Dick, H. P. (2011). Making immigrants illegal in small-town USA. *Journal of Linguistic Anthropology, 21*(Suppl. 1), E35–E55.

Dickerson, C. (2017a, April 14). Plan would limit protections for immigrants held in jails. *The New York Times,* pp. A1, A12.

Dickerson, C. (2017b, December 26). In west Texas, a mystery on the border. *The New York Times,* p. A11.

Dickerson, C., & Jordan, M. (2017, May 4). They came for asylum, but were shown the door. *The New York Times,* p. A9.

Dickerson, C., & Stevens, M. (2017, December 1). In case invoked by Trump, Mexican man is acquitted in death of California women. *The New York Times,* p. A18.

DiGrazia, J. (2014). Individual protest participation in the United States: Conventional and unconventional activism. *Social Science Quarterly, 95*(1), 111–131.

Dinan, S. (2016, June 14). Illegal immigrants who overstay visas almost never caught, feds admit. *The Washington Times.* https://www.washingtontimes.com/news/2016/jun/14/illegal-immigrants-who-overstay-visas-almost-never

Dinan, S. (2017a, January 18). Congress looks to punish "sanctuary campus" colleges that protect illegal immigrants. *The Washington Times.* https://www.washingtontimes.com/news/2017/jan/18/congress-looks-punish-sanctuary-campus-colleges

Dinan, S. (2017b, February 27). Deportation agency ignored 1.6 million visa overstays under Obama. *The Washington Times.* https://www.washingtontimes.com/news/2017/feb/27/deportation-agency-ignored-16-million-visa-oversta

Dingeman, K., Arzhayev, Y., Ayala, C., Bermudez, E., Padama, L., & Tena-Chávez, L. (2017). Neglected, protected, ejected: Latin American women caught by crimmigration. *Feminist Criminology, 12*(3), 293–314.

Dingeman-Cerda, K., Burciaga, E. M., & Martinez, L. M. (2016). Neither sinners nor saints: Complicating the discourse of noncitizen deservingness. *Association of Mexican American Educators Journal, 9*(3) 199–227.

DiPazza, A. (2017, March 2). *NC bill withholds state funding from immigration sanctuary cities.* Fox 8 News. http://myfox8.com/2017/03/02/nc-bill-withholds-state-funding-from-immigration-sanctuary-cities

Ditlmann, R. K., & Lagunes, P. (2014). The (identification) cards you are dealt: Biased treatment of Anglos and Latinos using municipal-issued versus unofficial ID cards. *Political Psychology, 35*(4), 539–555.

Donelson, A. J., & Esparza, A. X. (2016). *The colonias reader: Economy, housing and public health in US–Mexico border colonias.* Tucson, AZ: University of Arizona Press.

Donnatelli, J. (2017, February 27). Trump just made life hell for undocumented immigrants. *Los Angeles Magazine.* http://www.lamag.com/culturefiles/trump-crackdown-undocumented-immigrants

Donnermeyer, J. F. (2016). The other side of agricultural crime. In M. Hall, T. Wyatt, N. South, A. Nurse, G. Potter, & J. Maher. (Eds.), *Greening criminology in the 21st century: Contemporary debates and future directions in the study of environmental harm* (pp. 147–161). New York, NY: Routledge.

Dorsey, M. E., & Diaz-Barriga, M. (2010). Beyond surveillance and moonscapes: An alternative imaginary of the US–Mexico border wall. *Visual Anthropology Review, 26*(2), 128–135.

Douglas, K. M., & Sáenz, R. (2013). The criminalization of immigrants & the immigration–industrial complex. *Daedalus, 142*(3), 199–227.

Drever, A. I., & Blue, S. A. (2011). Surviving sin papeles in post-Katrina New Orleans: An exploration of the challenges facing undocumented Latino immigrants in new and re-emerging Latino destinations. *Population, Space and Place, 17*(1), 89–102.

Duin, J. (2016, November, 25). Offering sanctuary: The church/immigration story that's not going away. *GetReligion.* https://www.getreligion.org/getreligion/2016/11/23/offering-sanctuary-the-churchimmigration-story-thats-not-going-away

Durand, J., Massey, D. S., & Pren, K. A. (2016). Double disadvantage unauthorized Mexicans in the US labor market. *Annals of the American Academy of Political and Social Science, 666*(1), 78–90.

Durst, N. J., & Wegmann, J. (2017). Informal housing in the United States. *International Journal of Urban and Regional Research, 41*(2), 282–297. http://onlinelibrary.wiley.com/doi/10.1111/1468-2427.12444/full

Eagly, I. V. (2016). Criminal justice reform in an age of immigration enforcement: Solutions from California. *New Criminal Law Review, 20,* 12. (UCLA School of Law, Public Law Research Paper No. 16-53)

Eaton, S. E. (2016). *Integration nation: Immigrants, refugees, and America at its best.* New York, NY: The New Press.

Eby, J., Iverson, E., Smyers, J., & Kekic, E. (2011). The faith community's role in refugee resettlement in the United States. *Journal of Refugee Studies, 24*(3), 586–605.

Ecklund, E. H., Davila, C., Emerson, M. O., Kye, S., & Chan, E. (2013). Motivating civic engagement: In-group versus out-group service orientations among Mexican Americans in religious and nonreligious organizations. *Sociology of Religion, 74*(3), 370–391.

Efstratios, L., Anastasios, M., & Anastasios, K. (2014). Return migration: Evidence from a reception country with a short migration history. *European Urban and Regional Studies, 21*(2), 161–174.

Ehrkamp, P., & Nagel, C. (2014). "Under the radar": Undocumented immigrants, Christian faith communities, and the precarious spaces of welcome in the US South. *Annals of the Association of American Geographers, 104*(2), 319–328.

Eleftheriou-Smith, L.-M. (2017, 21). Montreal becomes "sanctuary city" for undocumented immigrants. *Independent*. http://www.independent.co.uk/news/world/americas/montreal-sanctuary-city-undocumented-immigrants-canada-quebec-ontario-toronto-london-hamilton-mayor-a7591266.html

Ellis, M., Wright, R., & Townley, M. (2014). The allure of new immigrant destinations and the great recession in the United States. *International Migration Review, 48*(1), 3–33. https://www.ncbi.nlm.nih.gov/pmc/articles/PMC4002044

Ellis, M., Wright, R., & Townley, M. (2016). State-scale immigration enforcement and Latino interstate migration in the United States. *Annals of the American Association of Geographers, 106*(4), 891–908.

Emanuel, G. (2017, March 6). *Bathing in the Baptistery: The history of sanctuary churches*. WGBH News Boston. http://news.wgbh.org/2017/03/06/how-we-live/bathing-baptistery-history-sanctuary-churches

Encarnacao, J. (2016, November 14). Walsh: Boston "welcoming," but no sanctuary plans. *Boston Herald*. http://www.bostonherald.com/news/local_coverage/herald_bulldog/2016/11/walsh_boston_welcoming_but_no_sanctuary_city_plans

Enriquez, L. E., & Saguy, A. C. (2016). Coming out of the shadows: Harnessing a cultural schema to advance the undocumented immigrant youth movement. *American Journal of Cultural Sociology, 4*(1), 107–130.

Epps, D., & Furman, R. (2016). The "alien other": A culture of dehumanizing immigrants in the United States. *Social Work & Society, 14*(2). http://socwork.net/sws/article/view/485/990

Eppsteiner, H. S., & Hagan, J. (2016). Religion as psychological, spiritual, and social support in the migration undertaking. In J. B. Saunders, E. Fiddian-Oasmiyeh, & S. Snyder (Eds.), *Intersections of religion and migration* (pp. 49–70). New York, NY: Palgrave Macmillan.

Esaki, N., Benamati, J., Yanosy, S., Middleton, J., Hopson, L., Hummer, V., & Bloom, S. (2013). The sanctuary model: Theoretical framework. *Families in Society, 94*(2), 87–95.

Escobar, M. D. (2016). *Captivity beyond prisons: Criminalization experiences of Latina (im)migrants*. Austin, TX: University of Texas Press.

Espinosa, G., Elizondo, V. P., & Miranda, J. (2005). *Latino religions and civic activism in the United States*. New York, NY: Oxford University Press.

Estep, K. (2016). Constructing a language problem status-based power devaluation and the threat of immigrant inclusion. *Sociological Perspectives, 60*(3), 437–458. http://journals.sagepub.com/doi/abs/10.1177/0731121416638367

Estrada, E. P., Ebert, K., & Lore, M. H. (2016). Apathy and antipathy: Media coverage of restrictive immigration legislation and the maintenance of symbolic boundaries. *Sociological Forum, 31*(3), 555–576.

Evans, E. E., & Shimron, Y. (2016, November 16). "Sanctuary churches" vow to shield immigrants from Trump crackdown. *National Catholic Reporter*. https://www.ncronline.org/news/politics/sanctuary-churches-vow-shield-immigrants-trump-crackdown

Ewing, W. A., Martínez, D. E., & Rumbaut, R. G. (2015, July). *The criminalization of immigration in the United States* [Special report]. Washington, DC: American Immigration Council.

Executive order: Enhancing public safety in the interior of the United States. (2017). https://www.immigrantjustice.org/sites/default/files/content-type/research-item/documents/2017-01/EOInteriorEnforcementAnnotated2017_01_27FINAL.pdf

Fabri, M. (2016). *Refugee resettlement: A core humanitarian value.* http://www.mercymidatlantic.org/PDF/Refugee_Resettlement-Dr.%20Mary%20Fabri-A_Core_Humanitarian_Value.pdf

Falcón, S. (2016). "National security" and the violation of women: Militarized border rape at the US–Mexico border. In A. Braithwaite & C. M. Orr (Eds.), *Everyday Women's and Gender Studies: Introductory Concepts* (pp. 227–237). New York, NY: Routledge.

Fan, M. D. (2013). The case for crimmigration reform. *North Carolina Law Review, 92*(1), 75–148.

Farley, R. (2011, May 16). Obama says the border fence is "now basically complete." *Politifact.* http://www.politifact.com/truth-o-meter/statements/2011/may/16/barack-obama/obama-says-border-fence-now-basically-complete

Farris, E. M., & Holman, M. R. (2016). All politics is local? County sheriffs and localized policies of immigration enforcement. *Political Research Quarterly, 70*(1), 142–154. http://journals.sagepub.com/doi/abs/10.1177/1065912916680035

Fehely, D. (2017, January 10). *San Jose Catholic churches may serve as sanctuaries for immigrants.* CBS SFBayArea . http://sanfrancisco.cbslocal.com/2017/01/10/san-jose-catholic-churches-may-serve-as-sanctuaries-for-immigrants-under-trump

Fernández, A., & Rodriguez, R. A. (2017, February 6). Undocumented immigrants and access to health care. *JAMA Internal Medicine, 177*(4), 536–537. http://jamanetwork.com/journals/jamainternalmedicine/article-abstract/2601076

Fernandez, M. (2017a, May 5). A northbound path, marked by more and more bodies. *The New York Times*, pp. A1, A22.

Fernandez, M. (2017b, May 5). Poignant paper trail from the border. *The New York Times*, p. A2.

Fernandez, M., & Montgomery, D. (2017, May 10). With measures banning "sanctuary cities," Texas pushes further to right. *The New York Times*, p. A15.

Ferreti, G. (2016). *Let's empty the clip: State-level immigration restriction and community resistance.* Doctoral dissertation, University of Texas, Austin, TX.

Fialho, C. M. (2016). Let us in: An argument for the right to visitation in US immigration detention. In M. J. Guia, R. Koulish, & V. Mitsilegas (Eds.), *Immigration detention, risk and human rights* (pp. 251–278). New York, NY: Springer.

Fiddian-Qasmiyeh, E. (2011). Introduction: Faith-based humanitarianism in contexts of forced displacement. *Journal of Refugee Studies, 24*(3), 429–439.

Filomeno, F. A. (2017a). The migration–development nexus in local immigration policy: Baltimore City and the Hispanic diaspora. *Urban Affairs Review, 53*(1), 102–137.

Filomeno, F. A. (2017b). *Theories of local immigration policy.* New York, NY: Springer.

Finkelman, P. (2014). Coping with a new yellow peril: Japanese immigration, the gentlemen's agreement, and the coming of World War II. *West Virginia Law Review, 117,* 1409.

Fiorito, T. R., & Nicholls, W. J. (2016). Silencing to give voice: Backstage preparations in the undocumented youth movement in Los Angeles. *Qualitative Sociology, 39*(3), 287–308.

Fisher, M., & Taub, A. (2017, October 29). Mexico's record violence is a crisis 20 years in the making. *The New York Times*, p. 16.

Fisher, S. (2016, September–October). Getting immigrants out of detention is very profitable. *Mother Jones*. https://www.motherjones.com/politics/2016/09/immigration-detainees-bond-ankle-monitors-libre

Fleischaker, J. (2017, February 17). *Librarians across the country protest, resist, and persist.* Melville House. https://www.mhpbooks.com/librarians-across-the-country-protest-resist-and-persist

Fleischman, J. M., Kendell, A. E., Eggers, C. C., & Fulginiti, L. C. (2017). Undocumented border crosser deaths in Arizona: Expanding intrastate collaborative efforts in identification. *Journal of Forensic Sciences, 62*(2), 840–849.

Fletcher, J. (2017). Space-naming: The sanctuary movement and the role of institution identity [Commentary]. *AmeriQuests* 13(1).

Flock, E. (2017, February 13). *Why these librarians are protesting Trump's executive orders.* PBS. http://www.pbs.org/newshour/art/librarians-protesting-trumps-executive-orders

Flores, A. (2017, January 25). Trump to publish weekly list of crimes committed by immigrants in sanctuary cities. *Buzzfeed*. https://www.buzzfeed.com/adolfoflores/trump-to-publish-weekly-list-of-crimes-committed-by-undocume?utm_term=.ifEW0E7Rr#.bqm6nvwdR

Flores, E. (2017, February 17). *Sanctuary schools marked by Monarch butterfly.* NBC Chicago. http://www.nbcchicago.com/news/local/Sanctuary-Schools-to-be-Marked-By-Yellow-Butterfly-in-Chicago-414139563.html

Flores, L. A. (2016). *Seeing through murals. Boom: A Journal of California, 6*(4), 16–27.

Flores-Macías, G. A. (2017, February 27). *Trump's mass deportations have hidden costs.* CNBC. http://www.cnbc.com/2017/02/27/trumps-mass-deporations-have-hidden-costs.html

Foley, N. (2014). *Mexicans in the making of America.* Cambridge, MA: Belknap.

Foner, N. (2000). *From Ellis Island to JFK: New York's two great waves of immigration.* New Haven, CT: Yale University Press.

Ford, A. M. (2016). *Life on hold: Central American women's experiences of US immigrant detention.* Doctoral dissertation, University of Texas, Austin, TX.

Fox, J. C. (2017, September 29). 50 immigrants arrested in Mass. as US cracks down. *The Boston Globe*, pp. A1, A7.

Fox, J. C. (2018, January 14). Salvadorans have many fears, few options. *The Boston Globe*, pp. B1, B4.

Fredriksen-Goldsen, K. (2016). Aging out in the queer community: Silence to sanctuary to activism in faith communities. *Generations, 40*(2), 30–33.

Freeland, G. (2010). Negotiating place, space and borders: The new sanctuary movement. *Latino Studies, 8*(4), 485–508.

Friedman, G. R. (2017, February 15). Oregon lawmakers push to repeal sanctuary state designation, make English the official language. *The Oregonian*. http://www.oregonlive.com/politics/index.ssf/2017/02/oregon_lawmakers_push_to_repea.html

Fuentes, E. H., & Pérez, M. A. (2016). Our stories are our sanctuary: Testimonio as a sacred space of belonging. *Association of Mexican American Educators Journal, 10*(2).

Fuller, S. (2016). *The US–Mexico border in American Cold War film: Romance, revolution, and regulation.* New York, NY: Springer.

Furman, R., Ackerman, A., Sanchez, M., & Epps, D. (2015). Immigration detention centers: Implications for social work. *Smith College Studies in Social Work, 85*(2), 146–158.

Furman, R., Sanchez, M., Ackerman, A., & Ung, T. (2015). The immigration detention center as a transnational problem: Implications for international social work. *International Social Work, 58*(6), 813–818. http://journals.sagepub.com/doi/abs/10.1177/0020872813500803

Gallet, W. (2017). Practical theology and contemporary social issues. *Pointers: Bulletin of the Christian Research Association, 27*(1), 6.

Gallo, S. (2016). Humor in father–daughter immigration narratives of resistance. *Anthropology & Education Quarterly, 47*(3), 279–296.

Gamso, N. (2014). Illiberal promises: Two texts on immigration and moral debt. *WSQ: Women's Studies Quarterly, 42*(1), 235–241.

Garcia, B. (2016). Theory and social work practice with immigrant populations. In J. D. Fernando Chang-Muy & E. P. Congress (Eds.), *Social work with immigrants and refugees: Legal issues, clinical skills, and advocacy* (pp. 87–108). New York, NY: Springer.

García, J. R. (1981). *Operation Wetback: The mass deportation of Mexican undocumented workers in 1954.* Westport, CT: Praeger.

García Hernández, C. C. (2017a). Immigration imprisonment's failures. *Immigration and Nationality Law Review, 36,* 47. (University of Denver Legal Studies Research Paper No. 17-02)

Garcia Hernandez, C. C. (2017b, November 27). Keep ICE arrests out of courts. *The New York Times*, p. A23.

Gardinar, D. (2016, August 31). Phoenix council Oks ID cards for undocumented immigrants. *AZ Central.* http://www.azcentral.com/story/news/local/phoenix/2016/08/31/phoenix-city-council-id-cards-undocumented/89613748

Gardner, T. G. (2014). The promise and peril of the anti-commandeering rule in the homeland security era: Immigrant sanctuary as an illustrative case. *St. Louis University Public Law Review, 34,* 313.

Gast, M. J., & Okamoto, D. G. (2016). Moral or civic ties? Deservingness and engagement among undocumented Latinas in non-profit organisations. *Journal of Ethnic and Migration Studies, 42*(12), 2013–2030.

Gates, A. B. (2017). "No one will speak for us": Empowering undocumented immigrant women through policy advocacy. *Journal of Community Practice, 25*(1), 5–28.

Gates, R. M. (2017, November 9). Don't dishonor immigrants. *The New York Times*, p. A25.

Gelatt, J., Bernstein, H., & Koball, H. (2015). *Uniting the patchwork: Measuring state and local contexts.* Washington, DC: Urban Institute.

Geraghty, J. (2017, January 27). The first sanctuary city surrenders! *National Review.* http://www.nationalreview.com/morning-jolt/444332/sanctuary-city-surrender-media-accountability-deathstroke-comics

Germano, R. (2014). Unauthorized immigrants paid $100 billion into Social Security over last decade. *Vice News.* https://news.vice.com/article/unauthorized-immigrants-paid-100-billion-into-social-security-over-last-decade

Giagnoni, S. (2017). *Here we may rest: Alabama immigrants in the age of HB 56.* Montgomery, AL: New South Books.

Gillespie, P. (2017, January 25). *Trump threatens Mexico's biggest cash source.* CNN. http://money.cnn.com/2017/01/25/news/economy/mexico-remittances-trump

Gilman, D. L. (2016). *To loose the bonds: The deceptive promise of freedom from pre-trial immigration detention*. University of Texas Law, Public Law Research Paper No. 644. https://papers.ssrn.com/sol3/papers.cfm?abstract_id=2737416

Glatzer, M., & Carr-Lemke, T. (2016). Accompanying the stranger in a context of political impasse and constraints: New sanctuary movement Philadelphia. In J. Dominguez-Mujica (Ed.), *Global change and human mobility* (pp. 183–202). New York, NY: Springer.

Gleeson, S. (2012). *Conflicting commitments: The politics of enforcing immigrant worker rights in San Jose and Houston*. Ithaca, NY: Cornell University Press.

Gleeson, S., & Gonzales, R. G. (2012). When do papers matter? An institutional analysis of undocumented life in the United States. *International Migration, 50*(4), 1–19.

Goins-Phillips, T. (2017, May 9). *Maryland Democrats are surprised legal immigrants oppose sanctuary city policies*. The Blaze. http://www.theblaze.com/news/2017/05/09/maryland-democrats-are-surprised-legal-immigrants-oppose-sanctuary-city-policies

Golash-Boza, T. M. (2015). *Immigration nation: Raids, detentions, and deportations in post-9/11 America*. New York, NY: Routledge.

Goldstein, J., & Weiser, B. (2017, October 7). A murderous drug lord partners with the U.S. *The New York Times*, pp. A1, A6.

Gomberg-Muñoz, R. (2015). The punishment/el castigo: Undocumented Latinos and US immigration processing. *Journal of Ethnic and Migration Studies, 41*(14), 2235–2252.

Gomberg-Muñoz, R. (2016a). Hardship politics: The strategic sharing of migration stories. *Journal of Contemporary Ethnography, 45*(6), 741–764.

Gomberg-Muñoz, R. (2016b). The Juárez Wives Club: Gendered citizenship and US immigration law. *American Ethnologist, 43*(2), 339–352.

Gomez, A. (2016, January 19). Nearly 500,000 foreigners overstayed visas in 2015. *USA Today*. http://www.usatoday.com/story/news/2016/01/19/immigration-visa-overstays-department-of-homeland-security-report/79026708

Gomez, R. (2016). Vulnerability and information practices among (undocumented) Latino migrants. *Electronic Journal of Information Systems in Developing Countries, 75*(1), 1–43.

Gómez Cervantes, A., Menjívar, C., & Staples, W. G. (2017). "Humane" immigration enforcement and Latina immigrants in the detention complex. *Feminist Criminology, 12*(3), 269–292.

Gonzalez, B., Collingwood, L., & El-Khatib, S. (2017). *The politics of refuge: Sanctuary cities, crime, and undocumented immigration*. http://www.collingwoodresearch.com/uploads/8/3/6/0/8360930/shelter_nopols_blind_final_rev_313.pdf

Gonzalez, B. F. (2014). *The undocumented threat: Beliefs, policy preferences, and the politics of immigration*. Doctoral dissertation, University of Washington, Seattle, WA.

Gonzalez, D. (2017, November 27). Without so much as a hug, a father is detained for deportation. *The New York Times*, p. A21.

Gonzalez, D. (2018, January 13). Federal government begins accepting DACA renewals following court order. *The Republic*. http://www.king5.com/article/news/nation-world/federal-government-begins-accepting-daca-renewals-following-court-order/507-507868233

González, E. R. (2017). *Latino city: Urban planning, politics, and the grassroots*. New York, NY: Routledge.

Gonzalez-Barrera, A., & Krogstad, J. M. (2017, March 2). *What we know about illegal immigration from Mexico*. Washington, DC: Pew Research Center.

Goo, S. K. (2015, August 24). *What Americans want to do about illegal immigration*. Washington, DC: Pew Research Center.

Goodstein, L. (2017, October 12). Immigrant father shielded from deportation by a Philadelphia church walks free. *The New York Times*, p. A17.

Gorman, C. S. (2017). Redefining refugees: Interpretive control and the bordering work of legal categorization in US asylum law. *Political Geography, 58,* 36–45.

Goth, B. (2017, February 3). Mayor: Phoenix can't be a sanctuary city. *USA Today*. https://www.usatoday.com/story/news/nation-now/2017/02/03/mayor-phoenix-cant-sanctuary-city/97432814

Goth, B. R. (2013). *Tucson's sanctuary movement: A living history of its founders and their work on the US–Mexico border today*. PhD thesis, University of Arizona, Tucson, AZ.

Gramlich, J., & Bialik, K. (2017, April 10). *Immigration offenses make up a growing share of federal arrests*. Washington, DC: Pew Research Center.

Gratton, B., & Merchant, E. (2013). Immigration, repatriation, and deportation: The Mexican-origin population in the United States, 1920–1950. *International Migration Review, 47*(4), 944–975.

Gravelle, M., Ellermann, A., & Dauvergne, C. (2012). Studying migration governance from the bottom-up. In B. Anderson, M. J. Gibney, & E. Paletti (Eds.), *The social, political and historical contours of deportation* (pp. 59–77). New York, NY: Springer.

Gray, M. J. (2016). Cities of refuge. *Tikkun, 31*(2), 52–53.

Gray, N. A., Boucher, N. A., Kuchibhatla, M., & Johnson, K. S. (2017, February 6). Hospice access for undocumented immigrants. *JAMA Internal Medicine, 177*(4), 579–580. http://jamanetwork.com/journals/jamainternalmedicine/article-abstract/2601077

Gregorin, J. L. (2015). Hidden beneath the waves of immigration debate: San Francisco's sanctuary ordinance. *Liberty University Law Review, 6*(1), 7.

Griffith, B., & Vaughan, J. (2017, March 27). *Maps: Sanctuary cities, counties, and states*. http://cis.org/Sanctuary-Cities-Map

Groody, D. G. (2017). Migration, mercy, and mission: Faith based responses and the US–Mexico border. *Journal of Catholic Social Thought, 14*(1), 123–140.

Gruberg, S. (2014, June 10). *LGBT undocumented immigrants face an increased risk of hate violence*. Center for American Progress. https://www.americanprogress.org/issues/immigration/news/2014/06/10/91233/lgbt-undocumented-immigrants-face-an-increased-risk-of-hate-violence

Guerlain, M. A., & Campbell, C. (2016). From sanctuaries to prefigurative social change: Creating health-enabling spaces in East London community gardens. *Journal of Social and Political Psychology, 4*(1), 220–237.

Guerra, C. (2017, November 7). Uncertain future: Nearly 8,000 immigrants in Massachusetts face possible deportation. *The Boston Globe*, pp. B1, B4.

Guerra, C. (2018, January 11). At rally, children plead for protecting parents. *The Boston Globe*, pp. B1, B9.

Gui, X., Forbat, J., Nardi, B., & Stokols, D. (2016). Use of information and communication technology among street drifters in Los Angeles. *First Monday, 21*(9). http://www.firstmonday.dk/ojs/index.php/fm/article/view/6813/5623

Gulbas, L. E., Zayas, L. H., Yoon, H., Szlyk, H., Aguilar-Gaxiola, S., & Natera, G. (2016). Deportation experiences and depression among US citizen-children with undocumented Mexican parents. *Child: Care, Health and Development, 42*(2), 220–230.

Gupta, M. D. (2014). "Don't deport our daddies": Gendering state deportation practices and immigrant organizing. *Gender & Society, 28*(1), 83–109.

Gurman, S. (2017, April 22). Sanctuary cities threatened with loss of federal grant money. *The Washington Post.* https://www.usnews.com/news/politics/articles/2017-04-22/sanctuary-cities-threatened-with-loss-of-federal-grant-money

Gutiérrez, D. (2016). Protecting America's borders and the undocumented immigrant dilemma. In R. H. Bayor (Ed.), *The Oxford handbook of American immigration and ethnicity* (pp. 124–142). New York, NY: Oxford University Press.

Gutierrez, L. N. (2015). *(Re)framing the immigrant narrative: Exploring testimonios that counter the essentialized image of (un)documented people in the discourses of contemporary US rhetoric.* Doctoral dissertation, Indiana University of Pennsylvania, Indiana, PA.

Guttentag, L. (2012). Discrimination, preemption, and Arizona's immigration law: A broader view. *Stanford Law Review Online, 65*, 1.

Guzmán, R. A. (2013). *From the politics of citizenship to citizenship as politics: On universal citizenship, nation, and the figure of the undocumented immigrant.* PhD dissertation, University of Arizona, Tucson, AZ.

Guzmán, R. A. (2016). Criminalization at the edge of the eventual site: Undocumented immigration, mass incarceration, and universal citizenship. *Theory & Event, 19*(2). https://muse.jhu.edu/article/614368/summary

Haas, B. M. (2017). Citizens-in-waiting, deportees-in-waiting: Power, temporality, and suffering in the US asylum system. *Ethos, 45*(1), 75–97.

Haensel, K., & Garcia-Zamor, J. C. (2016). History and challenges of US immigration policymaking. *Journal of Public Administration and Governance, 6*(4), 139–149.

Haines, D. W. (2015, November 25). *Learning from our past: The refugee experience in the United States.* Washington, DC: American Immigration Council. https://www.americanimmigrationcouncil.org/research/refugee-experience-united-states

Hale, J. N. (2014, June 24). The forgotten story of the Freedom Schools. *The Atlantic.* https://www.theatlantic.com/education/archive/2014/06/the-depressing-legacy-of-freedom-schools/373490

Hall, J., & Wang, S. (2017, February 1). *Graham Hudson, Idil Atak, Michele Manocchi & Charity-Ann Hannan* (RCIS Working Paper No. 2017).

Hall, M., & Stringfield, J. (2014). Undocumented migration and the residential segregation of Mexicans in new destinations. *Social Science Research, 47*, 61–78.

Hamel, M. B., Young, M. J., & Lehmann, L. S. (2014). Undocumented injustice? Medical repatriation and the ends of health care. *New England Journal of Medicine, 370*(7), 669–673.

Hamilton, N., & Chinchilla, N. S. (2001). *Seeking community in a global city: Guatemalans and Salvadorans in Los Angeles.* Philadelphia, PA: Temple University Press.

Hannan, C. A., & Bauder, H. (2015). *Towards a sanctuary province.* https://www.ryerson.ca/content/dam/rcis/documents/RCIS_WP_Hannan_Bauder_No_2015_3.pdf

Hardina, D. (2014). Deferred action, immigration, and social work: What should social workers know? *Journal of Policy Practice, 13*(1), 30–44.

Hardy, M. (2017, August 14). Texas naturalists also see a border wall as a threat. *The New York Times*, p. A14.

Harper, N. (1999). *Urban churches, vital signs: Beyond charity toward justice.* Grand Rapids, MI: Eerdmans.

Harrison, J. L., & Lloyd, S. E. (2012). Illegality at work: Deportability and the productive new era of immigration enforcement. *Antipode, 44*(2), 365–385.

Hartelius, E. J. (2016). "Undocumented and unafraid"? Challenging the bureaucratic paradigm. *Communication and Critical/Cultural Studies, 13*(2), 130–149.

Hayes, J., & Hill, L. (2017, March). *Undocumented Immigrants in California.* Public Policy Institute of California. http://video.ppic.org/content/pubs/jtf/JTF_UndocumentedImmigrantsJTF.pdf

Hayoun, M. (2017, February 15). *What happens during a deportation raid in the U.S.A.* Aljazeera. http://www.aljazeera.com/indepth/features/2017/02/immigration-deportation-raid-170214213550603.html

Healey, B. (2017, April 3). Yes, they pay taxes: Billons flow to federal, state treasuries from undocumented workers. *The Boston Globe*, pp. B9–B10.

Healy, J. (2017, August 13). Loving and leaving America: Stay, hide, "self-deport"? Facing hard choices in the heartland. *The New York Times*, pp.1, 16–17.

Hedrick, J. (2011a). *Welcoming the huddled masses: Sanctuary policies in American cities.* https://cpb-us-east-1-juc1ugur1qwqqqo4.stackpathdns.com/blogs.rice.edu/dist/2/493/files/2011/03/SWPSA2011_Hedrick_Sanctuary.pdf

Hedrick, J. (2011b). *The diffusion of sanctuary policies in American cities.* Paper presented at the annual meeting of the Western Political Science Association.

Held, M. L. (2017). A study of remittances to Mexico and Central America: Characteristics and perspectives of immigrants. *International Journal of Social Welfare, 26*(1), 75–85. http://onlinelibrary.wiley.com/doi/10.1111/ijsw.12225/full

Hemish, M. (2017, February 28). United States: Trump attacks met with growing unity. *Green Left Weekly, 15*(1127).

Henderson, S. W. (2016). I pity the poor immigrant: Stigma and immigration. In R. Parekh & E. W. Childs (Eds.), *Stigma and prejudice* (pp. 227–245). New York, NY: Springer.

Here, J. (2016, April 25). Operation Wetback revisited. *The New Republic.* https://newrepublic.com/article/132988/operation-wetback-revisited

Hernández, A. E. J. (2017). *International migration and crisis.* New York, NY: Springer.

Hernandez, C. C. G. (2017). Abolishing immigration prisons. *Boston University Law Review, 97*, 245.

Hernandez, H. (2015). *An interpretative phenomenological analysis of the identity of un-documented Mexican-origin adolescents living in California.* Doctoral dissertation, The Wright Institute, Berkeley, CA.

Hernández, K. L. (2006). The crimes and consequences of illegal immigration: A cross-border examination of Operation Wetback, 1943 to 1954. *Western Historical Quarterly, 37*(4), 421–444.

Hernández, K. L. (2010). *Migra! A history of the US border patrol* (Vol. 29). Berkeley, CA: University of California Press.

Hernández, K. L. (2017). *City of inmates: Conquest, rebellion, and the rise of human caging in Los Angeles, 1771-1965.* Chapel Hill, NC: University of North Carolina Press.

Herndon, A. W. (2017, October 11). Rhetoric on gang violence disputed: Despite White House focus, MS-13 isn't a major factor, many criminologists say. *The Boston Globe*, pp. A1, A9.

Hester, T. (2015). Deportability and the carceral state. *Journal of American History, 102*(1), 141–151.

Heyer, K. E. (2016). The promise of a pilgrim church. In S. Synder, J. Ralston, & A. M. Brazal (Eds.), *Church in an age of global migration* (pp. 83–98). New York, NY: Palgrave Macmillan.

Hing, B. O. (2012a). Immigration sanctuary policies: Constitutional and representative of good policing and good public policy. *UC Irvine Law Review, 2,* 247–312. (University of San Francisco Law Research Paper No. 2012-03)

Hing, B. O. (2012b). *Defining America: Through immigration policy.* Philadelphia, PA: Temple University Press.

Hing, B. O. (2015). Ethics, morality, and disruption of US immigration laws. *Kansas Law Review, 63,* 981–1044. (University of San Francisco Law Research Paper No. 2015-09)

Hintjens, H., & Pouri, A. (2014). Toward cities of safety and sanctuary. *Peace Review, 26*(2), 218–224.

Hirschfeld Davis, J., & Steinhauer, J. (2017, February 27). Trump's soft spot for the Dreamers alienates immigration hard-liners in his base. *The New York Times*, p. A10.

Hoffman, M. (2016, December 15). *This small town is helping undocumented immigrants, but don't call it a "sanctuary city."* Vice. https://www.vice.com/en_us/article/sanctuary-cities-complicated-politics-small-towns

Hoffman, M. (2017, April 21). In Texas, a fight over how to detain families. *The Boston Globe*, p. A12.

Hoffman, M., & Weissert, W. (2017, May 30). Tension about immigration boils over in Texas. *The Boston Globe*, p. A2.

Hondagneu-Sotelo, P. (2017). At home in inner-city immigrant community gardens. *Journal of Housing and the Built Environment, 32*(1), 13–28.

Hoover, M. (2013). *Undocumented migration, the Fourteenth Amendment and the enduring battle over who counts.* PhD thesis, DePaul University, Chicago, IL.

Hopkins, D. J., Mummolo, J., Esses, V. M., Kaiser, C. R., Marrow, H. B., & McDermott, M. (2016). Out of context: The absence of geographic variation in US immigrants' perceptions of discrimination. *Politics, Groups, and Identities, 4*(3), 363–392.

Housel, J., Saxen, C., & Wahlrab, T. (2016). Experiencing intentional recognition: Welcoming immigrants in Dayton, Ohio. *Urban Studies, 55*(2), 384–405. http://journals.sagepub.com/doi/abs/10.1177/0042098016653724

Houston, S. D. (2016). Sacred squatting. In P. Mudu & S. Chattopadhyay (Eds.), *Migration, squatting and radical autonomy: Resistance and destabilization of racist regulatory policies and b/ordering mechanisms* (pp. 183–188). New York, NY: Routledge.

Houston, S. D., & Lawrence-Weilmann, O. (2016). The model migrant and multiculturalism: Analyzing neoliberal logics in US sanctuary legislation. In H. Bauder & C. Matheis (Eds.), *Migration policy and practice* (pp. 101–126). New York, NY: Palgrave Macmillan.

Houston, S. D., & Morse, C. (2017). The ordinary and extraordinary: Producing migrant inclusion and exclusion in US sanctuary movements. *Studies in Social Justice, 11*(1), 27–47.

Howrasteh, A. (2017, January 24). *A tax on remittances won't pay for a border wall.* The Cato Institute. https://www.cato.org/blog/tax-remittances-wont-pay-border-wall

Hsi Lee, E. Y. (2016, March 24). *Being an undocumented Black immigrant in America is a "lonely experience."* ThinkProgress. https://thinkprogress.org/being-an-undocumented-black-immigrant-in-america-is-a-lonely-experience-8f90e946374c#.boesgl1rb

Huang, X., & Liu, C. Y. (2016). Welcoming cities immigration policy at the local government level. *Urban Affairs Review, 54*(1), 3–32.

Hudson, G., Atak, I., & Hannan, C. A. (2016). *(No) Access To: A pilot study on sanctuary city policy in Toronto, Canada.* Ryerson Centre for Immigration and Settlement Working Paper Series, 2017/1.

Huetteman, E., & Kulish, N. (2017, June 30). House passes 2 strict immigration bills, at president's urging. *The New York Times*, p. A19.

Hummel, D. (2016). Immigrant-friendly and unfriendly cities: Impacts on the presence of a foreign-born population and city crime. *Journal of International Migration and Integration, 17*(4), 1211–1230.

Hyman, L. & Iskander, N. (2016, November 16). What the mass deportation might look like. *Slate.* http://www.slate.com/articles/news_and_politics/history/2016/11/donald_trump_mass_deportation_and_the_tragic_history_of_operation_wetback.html

Irons, M. (2017, January 27). What is a sanctuary city? *The Boston Globe.* https://www.bostonglobe.com/metro/2017/01/27/what-sanctuary-city/8mXFmc9TZUPZhBZhn1Mi6H/story.html

Iten, A. E., Jacobs, E. A., Lahiff, M., & Fernández, A. (2014). Undocumented immigration status and diabetes care among Mexican immigrants in two immigration "sanctuary" areas. *Journal of Immigrant and Minority Health, 16*(2), 229–238.

Jaggers, J., Gabbard, W. J., & Jaggers, S. J. (2014). The devolution of US immigration policy: An examination of the history and future of immigration policy. *Journal of Policy Practice, 13*(1), 3–15.

Jamison, E. C. (2016). State-based immigration efforts and internally displaced persons (IDPs): An experiment in Alabama. In H. Bauder & C. Matheis (Eds.), *Migration Policy and Practice* (pp. 149–174). New York, NY: Palgrave Macmillan.

Jaworsky, B. N. (2015). Mobilising for immigrant rights online: Performing "American" national identity through symbols of civic-economic participation. *Journal of Intercultural Studies, 36*(5), 579–599.

Jaworsky, B. N. (2016a). *Debating immigration. The boundaries of belonging.* New York, NY: Springer.

Jaworsky, B. N. (2016b). Evaluating values. In B. N. Jaworsky (Ed.), *The boundaries of belonging: Online work of immigration-related social movement organizations* (pp. 171–225). New York, NY: Springer.

Jenkins, J. (2017, April 4). *Nation's largest Jewish denomination encourages congregations to protect undocumented.* ThinkProgress. https://thinkprogress.org/nations-largest-jewish-denomination-encourages-congregations-to-protect-undocumented-immigrants-da309634624a

Johnson, A. (2017, June 17). Immigrant advocates' relief mixed with fear. *The Boston Globe*, pp. 1, 5.

Johnson, D. L. (2017). *Social inequality, economic decline, and plutocracy.* New York, NY: Springer.

Johnson, E. (2017, April 27). New Haven churches to be sanctuary for undocumented immigrants. *Yale News.* http://yaledailynews.com/blog/2017/04/27/new-haven-churches-to-be-sanctuary-for-undocumented-immigrants

Johnson, K. R. (2012). Immigration and civil rights: Is the "new" Birmingham the same as the "old" Birmingham. *William & Mary Bill of Rights Journal, 21,* 367.

Johnson, K. R. (2014). Racial profiling in the war on drugs meets the immigration removal process: The case of *Moncrieffe v. Holder. University of Michigan Journal of Law Reform, 48*(4), 967.

Johnson, K. R., & Ingram, J. E. C. (2012). Anatomy of a modern-day lynching: The relationship between hate crimes against Latina/os and the debate over immigration reform. *North Carolina Law Review, 91,* 1613.

Johnson, L. (2015). Material interventions on the US–Mexico border: Investigating a sited politics of migrant solidarity. *Antipode, 47*(5), 1243–1260.

Johnston, K. (2017, May 18). Immigrants vital to Boston economy, MIT study says. *The Boston Globe,* p. B13.

Jonas, S., & Rodríguez, N. (2015). *Guatemala–US migration: Transforming regions.* Austin, TX: University of Texas Press.

Jones, B. (2016, April 15). *Americans' views of immigrants marked by widening partisan, generational divides.* Washington, DC: Pew Research Center.

Jones, H., Gunaratnam, Y., Bhattacharyya, G., Davies, W., Dhaliwal, S., Forkert, K., ... Saltus, R. (2017). *Go home? The politics of immigration controversies.* Manchester, UK: University of Manchester Press.

Jones, R. (2014). Border wars: Narratives and images of the US–Mexico border on TV. In R. Jones & C. Johnson (Eds.), *Placing the border in everyday life* (pp. 185–204). New York, NY: Routledge.

Jones, S., Furman, R., Loya, M., Ackerman, A. R., Negi, N., Epps, D., & Mondragon, G. (2015). The rise of anti-immigrant policies: An analysis of three state laws and implications for social work. *Intersectionalities, 3*(1), 39–61.

Jones-Correa, M., & De Graauw, E. (2013a). Looking back to see ahead: Unanticipated changes in immigration from 1986 to the present and their implications for American politics today. *Annual Review of Political Science, 16,* 209–230.

Jones-Correa, M., & de Graauw, E. (2013b). The illegality trap: The politics of immigration & the lens of illegality. *Dædalus, 142*(3), 185–198.

Jönsson, J. H. (2014). Local reactions to global problems: Undocumented immigrants and social work. *British Journal of Social Work, 44*(Suppl. 1), i35–i52.

Jorae, W. R. (2009). *The children of Chinatown: Growing up Chinese American in San Francisco, 1850–1920.* Chapel Hill, NC: University of North Carolina Press.

Jordan, M. (2017a, May 12). 7 years after arrest and outcry, young woman again faces deportation. *The New York Times,* p. A10.

Jordan, M. (2017b, October 2). "Dreamers" scramble to renew their protections one last time. *The New York Times,* p. A12.

Jordan, M. (2017c, October 28). Future uncertain, a surge for citizenship. *The New York Times,* p. A9.

Jordan, M. (2017d, November 21). Haitians to lose path to stay in US: Protected status ends in mid-July 2019. *The Boston Globe,* pp. A1, A9.

Jordan, M. (2017e, December 8). "Dreamers," in jeopardy get support from range of stars and businesses. *The New York Times*, p. A20.

Jordan, M. (2017f, December 19). 15 years after deportation, marine is free to return. *The New York Times*, p. A18.

Jordan, M. (2018, January 9), U.S. eliminates a protected visa for Salvadorans. *The New York Times*, pp. A1, A14.

Joseph, T. D. (2016). What health care reform means for immigrants: Comparing the Affordable Care Act and Massachusetts health reforms. *Journal of Health Politics, Policy and Law 41*(1), 101–116.

Jovanovic, M. A. (2017). *How to normatively theorize immigration? Demographic politics in a constitutional democracy.* https://papers.ssrn.com/sol3/papers.cfm?abstract_id=2915381

Joyner, B. P., & Voss, D. C. (2017). *Deep dive: Sanctuary cities.* Lincoln, Nebraska: Golden Rule Omnimedia.

Joyner, K. (2016). *Arresting immigrants: Unemployment and immigration enforcement in the decade following the September 11 terrorist attacks.* https://www.bgsu.edu/content/dam/BGSU/college-of-arts-and-sciences/center-for-family-and-demographic-research/documents/working-papers/2016/WP-2016-07-Joyner-Arresting-Immigrants.pdf

Kammer, F., Weishar, S., Williams, P. J., Edwards, A. C. W. P., Mata, M., & Salvatierra, A. (2017). *Recovering the human face of immigration in the US South.* Gainesville, FL: University of Florida, Center for Latin American Studies. http://www.latam.ufl.edu/media/latamufledu/website-pdfs/Recovering-human-face-0317-Final.pdf

Kanno-Youngs, Z., Calvert, S., & Gay, M. (2017, January 4). New York City major crimes fall to lowest recorded level. *The Wall Street Journal.* https://www.wsj.com/articles/new-york-city-crime-rate-falls-to-lowest-recorded-level-1483543802

Kanstroom, D. (2003). Criminalizing the undocumented: Ironic boundaries of the post-September 11th "Pale of Law." *North Carolina Journal of International Law & Commercial Regulation, 29,* 639.

Kanstroom, D., & Chicco, J. (2015). The forgotten deported: A declaration on the rights of expelled and deported persons. *New York University Journal of International Law & Policy, 47,* 537.

Karthick Ramakrishnan, S., & Colbern, A. (2015). *The "California package": Immigrant integration and the evolving nature of state citizenship.* http://policymatters.ucr.edu/wp-content/uploads/2015/06/pmatters-vol6-3-state-citizenship.pdf

Katiya, Y., & Reid, C. (2012). Urban neoliberalism and the right to the city alliance. In E. Shragge, A. Choudry, & J. Hanley (Eds.), *Organize! Building from the local for global justice* (pp. 291–304). Oakland, CA: PM Press

Kawashima, M. (2017). New immigrants and the "underclass." In M. Kawashima (Ed.), *American history, race and the struggle for equality* (pp. 143–163). New York, NY: Springer.

Kelley, A., Riggleman, K., Clara, I., & Navarro, A. E. (2017). Determining the need for social work practice in a public library. *Journal of Community Practice, 25*(1), 112–125.

Kemeny, T., & Cooke, A. (2017). Urban immigrant diversity and inclusive institutions. *Economic Geography, 93,* 267–291.

Kendall, E. C. (2014). Sanctuary in the 21st century: The unique asylum exception to the extradition rule. *Michigan State International Law Review, 23,* 153.

Kennedy, P. J. F. (2016). *A nation of immigrants*. Pickle Partners.

Kent Fitzsimons, J. (2017). "Hospitality now!" From meeting migrant needs to rethinking contemporary urban dwelling—A critical review of two studio experiments. In M. Couceiro de Costa, F. P. Lages, & C. de Costa (Eds.), *Architectural research addressing societal challenges* (pp. 439–446). Boca Raton, FL: CRC Press.

Khoir, S., Du, J. T., & Koronios, A. (2015). Information sharing in community associations: Asian immigrants' experiences. *Proceedings of the Association for Information Science and Technology, 52*(1), 1–4.

Kim, E. C. (2009). "Mama's family": Fictive kinship and undocumented immigrant restaurant workers. *Ethnography, 10*(4), 497–513.

Kincaid, C. (2015, July 28). *The Catholic Church & sanctuary cities*. http://www.worldviewweekend.com/news/article/catholic-church-sanctuary-cities

Kincaid, J. D. (2016). The rational basis of irrational politics: Examining the great Texas political shift to the right. *Politics & Society, 44*(4), 525–550.

King5 News. (2017, February 1). *Mayor asks city council to not declare Tacoma sanctuary city*. http://www.king5.com/news/local/tacoma/mayor-asks-city-council-to-not-declare-tacoma-a-sanctuary-city/395224991

Kipton, D. (2016, November 10). How to weather the Trump administration: Head to the library. *Los Angeles Times*. http://www.latimes.com/books/jacketcopy/la-ca-jc-kipen-essay-20161110-story.html

Kiss, T., & Asgari, S. (2015). A case study of personal experiences of undocumented Eastern European immigrants living in the United States. *Journal of Identity and Migration Studies, 9*(2), 42–61.

Kline, N. (2017). Pathogenic policy: Immigrant policing, fear, and parallel medical systems in the US South. *Medical Anthropology, 36*(4), 396–410.

Knight, N. (2017, February 21). Day without immigrants strikes shake US. *Green Left Weekly, 15*(1126).

Koca, B. T. (2016). New social movements: "Refugees welcome UK." *European Scientific Journal, 12*(2).

Koh, J. L. (2017). Removal in the shadows of immigration court. *Southern California Law Review, 90*, 181.

Kopan, K. (2017, January 25). *What are sanctuary cities, and can we defund them?* CNN. http://www.cnn.com/2017/01/25/politics/sanctuary-cities-explained

Kotin, S., Dyrness, G. R., & Irazábal, C. (2011). Immigration and integration: Religious and political activism for/with immigrants in Los Angeles. *Progress in Development Studies, 11*(4), 263–284.

Kotlowitz, A. (2016, November 23). The limits of sanctuary cities. *The New Yorker*. https://www.newyorker.com/news/news-desk/the-limits-of-sanctuary-cities

Koulish, R. (2016). Sovereign bias, crimmigration, and risk. In M. J. Guia, R. Koulish, & V. Mitsulegas (Eds.), *Immigration detention, risk and human rights* (pp. 1–12). New York, NY: Springer.

Krasner, C. (n.d.). *History of the border fence*. https://organpipehistory.com/border/history-of-th-border-fence

Krogstad, J. M. (2016, February 11). *5 facts about Mexico and immigration to the U.S.* Washington, DC: Pew Research Center.

Krogstad, J. M., & Keegan, M. (2014, June 14). *From Germany to Mexico: How America's source of immigrants has changed over a century*. Washington, DC: Pew Research Center.

Krogstad, J. M., & Lopez, M. H. (2016, November 29). *Hillary Clinton won Latino vote but fell below 2012 support for Obama.* Washington, DC: Pew Research Center.

Krogstad, J. M., Lopez, M. H., Lopez, G., Passel, J. S., & Patten, E. (2016, January 19). *The changing Latino electorate in 2016.* Washington, DC: Pew Research Center.

KTLA5. (2017, February 24). *In Los Angeles, underground network is readying homes to hide undocumented im7migrants.* http://ktla.com/2017/02/24/in-los-angeles-underground-network-is-readying-homes-to-hide-undocumented-immigrants

Kubrin, C. E. (2014). Secure or insecure communities? *Criminology & Public Policy, 13*(2), 323–338.

Kubrin, C. E., Zatz, M. S., & Martinez, R. (Eds.). (2012). *Punishing immigrants: Policy, politics, and injustice.* New York, NY: New York University Press.

Kulish, N. (2017a, April 25). Hard-liners on immigration, now in high places. *The New York Times,* pp. A1, A13.

Kulish, N. (2017b, June 14). Expecting handshake, getting handcuffs instead. *The New York Times,* p. A10.

Kulish, N., Dickerson, C., & Nixon, R. (2017, February 26). Agents discover a new freedom on deportations. *The New York Times,* pp. A1, A20.

Kulish, N., Dickerson, C., & Robbins, L. (2017, February 11). Reports of raids shake undocumented immigrants. *The New York Times.* https://www.bostonglobe.com/news/politics/2017/02/11/reports-raids-shake-undocumented-immigrants/9fbVXvETjJEiZz1A8oqibM/story.html

Kun, J., & Pulido, L. (2013). *Black and Brown in Los Angeles: Beyond conflict and coalition.* Berkeley, CA: University of California Press.

Kurashige, L. (2016). *Two faces of exclusion: The untold history of anti-Asian racism in the United States.* Charlotte, NC: University of North Carolina Press.

Lagos, M. (2017, April 6). *Long history of sanctuary laws, debate in San Francisco.* KQED News. https://ww2.kqed.org/news/2017/04/06/long-history-of-sanctuary-laws-debate-in-san-francisco

Lagunes, P. F. (2011). Documenting the undocumented: A review of the United States' first municipal ID program. *Harvard Journal of Hispanic Policy, 24,* 43–64.

Lakoff, G., & Ferguson, S. (2017). *The framing of immigration.* http://afrolatinoproject.org/2007/09/24/the-framing-of-immigration-5

Laman, J. (2015). *Revisiting the sanctuary city: Citizenship or abjection? Spotlighting the case of Toronto.* http://cerlac.info.yorku.ca/files/2016/06/John-Laman.pdf

Lamphear, G., Furman, R., & Epps, D. (Eds.). (2016). *The immigrant other: Lived experiences in a transnational world.* New York, NY: Columbia University Press.

Langerbein, H. (2009). Great blunders? The Great Wall of China, the Berlin Wall, and the proposed United States/Mexico border fence. *The History Teacher, 43*(1), 9–29.

Lasch, C. N. (2012). Federal immigration detainers after *Arizona v. United States. Loyola of Los Angeles Law Review, 46,* 629.

Lasch, C. N. (2016). Sanctuary cities and dog-whistle politics. *New England Journal on Criminal and Civil Confinement, 42*(2), 159.

Lauby, F. (2016). Leaving the "perfect DREAMer" behind? Narratives and mobilization in immigration reform. *Social Movement Studies, 15*(4), 374–387.

Lauer, C. (2017, March 25). Immigrants find sanctuary in growing Austin church network. *US News & World Report.* https://www.usnews.com/news/best-states/texas/articles/2017-03-25/immigrants-find-sanctuary-in-growing-austin-church-network

Lawrence, M. A. (2015). Humanities: Building sanctuary: The movement to support Vietnam War resisters in Canada, 1965–1973 [Book review]. *University of Toronto Quarterly, 84*(3), 255–257.

Le Bot, Y. (2016). The emergence of the migrant subject. In H. Lustiger-Thaler (Ed.), *Reimagining social movements: From collectives to individuals* [ebook]. New York, NY: Routledge.

Lechner, F. J. (2017). "Land of liberty": The American governmental exception. *The American Exception, 2,* 61–117.

LeCompte, K., & Blevins, B. (2016). Participatory citizenship. In C. Wright-Maley & T. Davis (Eds.), *Teaching for democracy in an age of economic disparity* (pp. 163–177). New York, NY: Routledge.

Lee, E. Y. H (2017, April 18). *Three services that immigrants are too afraid to access now that Trump is president.* ThinkProgress. https://thinkprogress.org/immigrants-afraid-deportation-services-5936361b4b90

Lee, J. C., Omri, R., & Preston, J. (2017, February 6). What are sanctuary cities? *The New York Times.* https://www.nytimes.com/interactive/2016/09/02/us/sanctuary-cities.html

Leitner, H., & Strunk, C. (2014). Spaces of immigrant advocacy and liberal democratic citizenship. *Annals of the Association of American Geographers, 104*(2), 348–356.

Leonard, S. (2017). Left foot forward. *Dissent, 64*(1), 10–11.

Levenson, M. (2017, September 26). A church's sanctuary: Bethel AME shelters immigrant facing deportation. *The Boston Globe,* pp. A1, A6.

Levin, J. M. (2013). *Planning the undocumented city: Unauthorized immigrants and planners in the 21st century.* https://smartech.gatech.edu/handle/1853/48759

Lewis, E., & Peri, G. (2014). *Immigration and the economy of cities and regions* (No. w20428). Washington, DC: National Bureau of Economic Research.

Lewis, P. G., Provine, D. M., Varsanyi, M. W., & Decker, S. H. (2012). Why do (some) city police departments enforce federal immigration law? Political, demographic, and organizational influences on local choices. *Journal of Public Administration Research and Theory, 23*(1), 1–25.

Leyro, S. P. (2017). *The fear factor: Exploring the impact of the vulnerability to deportation on immigrants' lives.* Doctoral dissertation, City University of New York, New York, NY.

Libby, S. (2017, January, 25). Is San Diego a sanctuary city and what does that even mean? *The Gist.* http://www.voiceofsandiego.org/topics/news/san-diego-sanctuary-city-even-mean

Libertarian Party. (2017, January 27). *Libertarians condemn Mayor Gimenez's sanctuary city repeal and vow to fight back.* http://www.lpmdade.org/blog/libertarians-condemn-mayor-gimenezs-sanctuary-city-repeal-and-vow-to-fight-back

Lieberman, D. (2017, July 28). *MS-13 members: Trump makes the gang stronger.* CNN. http://www.cnn.com/2017/07/28/us/ms-13-gang-long-island-trump/index.html

Linskey, A. (2017, September 1). Deadline looms for migrant decision. *The Boston Globe,* pp. A1, A4.

Lipka, M. (2015, September 14). *A closer look at Catholic America.* Washington, DC: Pew Research Center.

Litemind (n.d.). *Put yourself in any mental state with a mental sanctuary.* https://litemind.com/mental-sanctuary

Lombard, M. (2014). Constructing ordinary places: Place-making in urban informal settlements in Mexico. *Progress in Planning, 94*, 1–53.

Longazel, J. G. (2013). Moral panic as racial degradation ceremony: Racial stratification and the local-level backlash against Latino/a immigrants. *Punishment & Society, 15*(1), 96–119.

Lopez, G., & Patten, E. (2017, September 8). *Key facts about Asian Americans, a diverse and growing population.* Washington, DC: Pew Research Center.

Lopez, M. H., & Gonzalez-Barrera, A. (2013, October 3). *Latino views of illegal immigration's impact on their community improve.* Washington, DC: Pew Research Center.

Lopez, W. D., Kruger, D. J., Delva, J., Llanes, M., Ledón, C., Waller, A., . . . Israel, B. (2017). Health Implications of an immigration raid: Findings from a Latino community in the Midwestern United States. *Journal of Immigrant and Minority Health, 19*(3), 702–708.

Lorber, B. (2013). Creating sanctuary faith-based activism for migrant justice. *Tikkun, 28*(3), 41–45.

Lorentzen, L. A. (Ed.). (2014). *Hidden lives and human rights in the United States: Understanding the controversies and tragedies of undocumented immigration* [3 vols.]. Santa Barbara, CA: ABC-CLIO.

Lornell, K., & Rasmussen, A. K. (Eds.). (2016). *The music of multicultural America: Performance, identity, and community in the United States.* Oxford, MS: University Press of Mississippi.

Loth, R. (2017, March 6). "Sanctuary cities" have the law on their side. *The Boston Globe.* https://www.bostonglobe.com/opinion/2017/03/06/sanctuary-cities-have-law-their-side/AAmVsF94Jw2IXATCOXv9PN/story.html

Low, N. (2013). *Planning politics & state.* New York, NY: Routledge.

Loya, M., Jones, S., Sun, H., & Furman, R. (2017). Silent struggles—The plight of undocumented students in social work education. *Global Social Welfare, 4*(4), 199–207.

Lucio, J. D. (2016). Public administrators and noncitizens. *Administration & Society, 48*(7), 831–850.

Lugo-Lugo, C. R., & Bloodsworth-Lugo, M. K. (2014). "Anchor/terror babies" and Latina bodies: Immigration rhetoric in the 21st century and the feminization of terrorism. *Journal of Interdisciplinary Feminist Thought, 8*(1), 1.

Lundberg, A., & Strange, M. (2016). Who provides the conditions for human life? Sanctuary movements in Sweden as both contesting and working with state agencies. *Politics, 37*(3), 347–362.

Lybecker, D. L., McBeth, M. K., Husmann, M. A., & Pelikan, N. (2015). Do new media support new policy narratives? The social construction of the US–Mexico border on YouTube. *Policy & Internet, 7*(4), 497–525.

Lyons, C. J., Vélez, M. B., & Santoro, W. A. (2013). Neighborhood immigration, violence, and city-level immigrant political opportunities. *American Sociological Review, 78*(4), 604–632.

Lyons, C. J., Vélez, M. B., & Santoro, W. A. (2014, October 15). The protective influence of neighborhood immigration on violence is strongest in cities that are more open to immigrants. *LSE American Politics and Policy.* http://eprints.lse.ac.uk/58300

Macia, L. (2016). Experiences of discrimination in an emerging Latina/o community. *PoLAR: Political and Legal Anthropology Review, 39*(1), 110–126.

Macías-Rojas, P. (2016). *From deportation to prison: The politics of immigration enforcement in post-civil rights America.* New York, NY: New York University Press.

Maganini, S. (2017, March 1). Bishop Jamie Soto says Sacramento Catholic Church could provide refuge to immigrants. *The Sacramento Bee.* http://www.sacbee.com/news/local/article135865728.html

Majka, T., & Longazel, J. (2017). Becoming welcoming: Organizational collaboration and immigrant integration in Dayton, Ohio. *Public Integrity, 19,* 151–163.

Maldonado, C. Z., Rodriguez, R. M., Torres, J. R., Flores, Y. S., & Lovato, L. M. (2013). Fear of discovery among Latino immigrants presenting to the emergency department. *Academic Emergency Medicine, 20*(2), 155–161.

Malkin, E. (2017a, April 16). In a shift, deportees find "open arms" in Mexico. *The New York Times,* pp. 1, 4.

Malkin, E. (2017b, May 21). Pain of deportation swells when children are left behind. *The New York Times,* p. 8.

Mancina, P. (2016). *In the spirit of sanctuary: Sanctuary-city policy advocacy and the production of sanctuary-power in San Francisco, California.* Doctoral dissertation, Vanderbilt University, Nashville, TN.

Marfleet, P. (2011). Understanding "sanctuary": Faith and traditions of asylum. *Journal of Refugee Studies, 24*(3), 440–455.

Markowitz, P. L. (2015). Undocumented no more: The power of state citizenship. *Stanford Law Review, 67,* 869.

Marquardt, M., Steigenga, T., Williams, P., & Vásquez, M. (2013). *Living" illegal": The human face of unauthorized immigration.* New York, NY: The New Press.

Martin, J. (2017, November 7). Trump's agenda moves to fore as a race tightens in Virginia. *The New York Times,* p. A10.

Martin, P. (2017). Trump and US immigration policy. *California Agriculture, 71*(1), 15–17.

Martinez, B. J. (2017). *The dialectics of the community: Mexican production of death.* Doctoral dissertation, University of Arkansas, Fayetteville, AR.

Martinez, D., & Slack, J. (2013). What part of "illegal" don't you understand? The social consequences of criminalizing unauthorized Mexican migrants in the United States. *Social & Legal Studies, 22*(4), 535–551.

Martinez, D. E. (2016). Migrant deaths in the Sonora Desert: Evidence of unsuccessful border militarization efforts from southern Arizona. In R. Rubio-Goldsmith, C. Fernandez, J. K. Finch, & A. Masterson-Algar (Eds.), *Migrant deaths in the Arizona desert: La vida no vale nada* (pp. 97–119). Tucson, AZ: Arizona State University.

Martinez, J. (2012). *The Latino church: The religious scene in Latino Los Angeles.* Los Angeles, CA: University of Southern California, Center for Religion and Civic Culture.

Martínez, J. F. (2016). *Walk with the people: Latino ministry in the United States.* Eugene, OR: Wipf & Stock.

Martinez, K. (2015, April 14). *Drownings in Rio Grande increase after US Border Patrol expansion.* World Socialist Web Site. https://www.wsws.org/en/articles/2015/04/14/immi-a14.html

Martinez, O. L., Martinez, C., & Sontag, D. (2016, November 20). Killers on a shoestring: Inside the gangs of El Salvador. *The New York Times.* https://www.nytimes.com/2016/11/21/world/americas/el-salvador-drugs-gang-ms-13.html?_r=1

Martinez, R. O. (2016). The impact of neoliberalism on Latinos. *Latino Studies, 14*(1), 11–32.

Martínez-De-Castro, C. (2015). *Statement of the National Council of La Raza.* Washington, DC: National Council of La Raza.

Martone, J., Zimmerman, D., Vidal de Haymes, M., & Lorentzen, L. (2014). Immigrant integration through mediating social institutions: Issues and strategies. *Journal of Community Practice, 22*(3), 299–323.

Marzen, C. G., & Woodyard, W. (2016). Catholic social teaching, the right to immigrate, and the right to regulate borders: A proposed solution for comprehensive immigration reform based upon Catholic social principles. *San Diego Law Review, 53*(4).

Mascarenhas, N. (2017, September 15). Boston creates defense fund for immigrants, refugees. *The Boston Globe*, p. B4.

Massey, D. S. (1986). The social organization of Mexican migration to the United States. *Annals of the American Academy of Political and Social Science, 487*(1), 102–113.

Massey, D. S., Durand, J., & Pren, K. A. (2014). Explaining undocumented migration to the US. *International Migration Review, 48*(4), 1028–1061.

Massey, D. S., Durand, J., & Pren, K. A. (2015). Border enforcement and return migration by documented and undocumented Mexicans. *Journal of Ethnic and Migration Studies, 41*(7), 1015–1040.

Massey, D. S., & Pren, K. A. (2012). Origins of the new Latino underclass. *Race and Social Problems, 4*(1), 5–17.

Massey, D. S., Rugh, J. S., & Pren, K. A. (2010). The geography of undocumented Mexican migration. *Mexican Studies/Estudios Mexicanos, 26*(1), 129–152.

Mather, L. (2016). Is law inside or out? And why does it matter? *Flinders Law Journal, 18*(2), 183–211.

Matias, G. (2016). *Citizenship as a human right*. New York, NY: Palgrave Macmillan.

Mazzei, P., & Hanks, D. (2017a, January 17). Anger erupts after Miami–Dade mayor ends "sanctuary" policy. *Miami Herald Tribune*. http://www.miamiherald.com/news/local/community/miami-dade/article129149809.html

Mazzei, P., & Hanks, D. (2017b, February 17). Fearing Trump, commission drops Miami–Dade's "sanctuary" protections. *Miami Herald Tribune*. http://www.miamiherald.com/news/local/community/miami-dade/article133413384.html

McCann, J. A., Nishikawa Chávez, K. A., Plasencia, M., & Otawka, H. (2016). The changing contours of the immigrant rights protest movement in the United States: Who demonstrates now? *The Forum, 14*(2), 169–190.

McCorkle, W. D., & Bailey, B. (2016). UN human rights violations here at home? The plight of undocumented and DACA students in South Carolina, USA. *Journal of International Social Studies, 6*(1), 161–167.

McDede, H. (2017, March 6). *Hey area: A history of San Francisco's contested sanctuary city status*. KALW. http://kalw.org/post/hey-area-history-san-franciscos-contested-sanctuary-city-status#stream/0

McDonald, T. T. (2017, February 9). Jersey City council unanimously supports sanctuary city order. *The Jersey Journal*. http://www.nj.com/hudson/index.ssf/2017/02/jersey_city_council_unanimously_supports_sanctuary.html

McElmurry, S., Kerr, J., Brown, T. C., Zamora, L., & Center, B. P. (2016). *Balancing priorities: Immigration, national security, and public safety*. Chicago, IL: Bipartisan Policy Center.

McEwen, M. M., Boyle, J. S., & Messias, D. K. H. (2015). Undocumentedness and public policy: The impact on communities, individuals, and families along the Arizona/Sonora border. *Nursing Outlook, 63*(1), 77–85.

McGuire, R. H. (2013). Steel walls and picket fences: Rematerializing the US–Mexican border in Ambos Nogales. *American Anthropologist, 115*(3), 466–480.

McKinley, J. (2009, June 12). San Francisco at crossroads over immigration. *The New York Times*. http://www.nytimes.com/2009/06/13/us/13sanctuary.html

McLaughlin, M. W., Irby, M. A., & Langman, J. (1994). *Urban sanctuaries: Neighborhood organizations in the lives and futures of inner-city youth*. San Francisco, CA: Jossey-Bass.

McNevin, A. (2017). Learning to live with irregular migration: Towards a more ambitious debate on the politics of "the problem." *Citizenship Studies, 21*(3), 255–274.

McThomas, M. (2016). *Performing citizenship: Undocumented migrants in the United States*. New York, NY: Routledge.

McWilliams, C., Meier, M. S., & García, A. M. (2016). *North from Mexico: The Spanish-speaking people of the United States*. Santa Barbara, CA: ABC-CLIO.

Means, B. (2015). *Sanctuary in southern Appalachia: Faith and Hispanic immigrant integration into Appalachian communities*. Doctoral dissertation, Appalachian State University, Boone, NC.

Meckler, L., & Peterson, K. (2017, April 21). Border lawmakers balk at Donald Trump's wall request. *Wall Street Journal*. https://www.wsj.com/articles/border-lawmakers-balk-at-donald-trumps-wall-request-1492802294

Medina, J. (2017a, April 30). Too scared to report abuse: For fear of being deported. *The New York Times*, pp. A1, A21.

Medina, J. (2017b, December 2). California resolute in sanctuary status as a heated case ends. *The New York Times*, p. A9.

Medina, J., & Bidgood, J. (2017, April 11). California moves to become "sanctuary state" and other cities look to follow. *The New York Times*, p. A15. https://www.nytimes.com/2017/04/10/us/sanctuary-states-immigration.html?hpw&rref=us&action=click&pgtype=Homepage&module=well-region&region=bottom-well&WT.nav=bottom-well

Medina, J., & Yee, V. (2017, May 2). On May Day, marchers fight for myriad goals. *The New York Times*, p. A13.

Mejia, B., Carcamo, C., & Knoll, C. (2017, February 9). L.A., Orange Counties are home to 1 million immigrants who are in the country illegally. *Los Angeles Times*. http://www.latimes.com/local/lanow/la-me-illegal-immigration-los-angeles-20170208-story.html

Mena Robles, J., & Gomberg-Muñoz, R. (2016). Activism after DACA: Lessons from Chicago's Immigrant Youth Justice League. *North American Dialogue, 19*(1), 46–54.

Menchaca, M. (2011). *Naturalizing Mexican immigrants: A Texas history*. Austin, TX: University of Texas Press.

Menjívar, C. (2016). Immigrant criminalization in law and the media: Effects on Latino immigrant workers' identities in Arizona. *American Behavioral Scientist, 60*(5–6), 597–616.

Menjívar, C., & Abrego, L. (2012). Legal violence: Immigration law and the lives of Central American immigrants. *American Journal of Sociology, 117*(5).

Menjívar, C., & Kanstroom, D. (Eds.). (2013). *Constructing immigrant "illegality": Critiques, experiences, and responses*. New York, NY: Cambridge University Press.

Merolla, J., Ramakrishnan, S. K., & Haynes, C. (2013). "Illegal," "undocumented," or "unauthorized": Equivalency frames, issue frames, and public opinion on immigration. *Perspectives on Politics, 11*(3), 789–807.

Michalowski, R., & Hardy, L. (2014). Victimizing the undocumented. In D. L. Rothe & D. Kauzlarich (Eds.), *Towards a victimology of state crime* (pp. 87–109). New York, NY: Routledge.

Migration Policy Institute. (2016). *Profile of the unauthorized population: United States.* http://www.migrationpolicy.org/data/unauthorized-immigrant-population/state/US

Miguel, A. (2016). *The US immigration crisis: Toward an ethics of place* (Vol. 27). Eugene, OR: Wipf & Stock.

Milivojevic, S., Segrave, M., & Pickering, S. (2016). The limits of migration-related human rights. In L. Weber, E. Fishwick, & M. Marmo (Eds.), *The Routledge international handbook of criminology and human rights* (pp. 291–300). New York, NY: Routledge.

Miller, T. (2016). Border patrol capitalism: On the US–Mexico border, the border security industry grows alongside the expanding militarization of the drug wars. *NACLA Report on the Americas, 48*(2), 150–156.

Miroff, N. (2017a, November 7). Immigrants await government ruling on protected status. *The Boston Globe*, p. A2.

Miroff, N. (2017b, December 6). Mexico border arrests down sharply, statistics show. *The Boston Globe*, p. A7.

Miroff, N. (2018). ICE hits 7-Eleven in nationwide raids. *The Boston Globe*, p. A11.

Mironova, O. (2017). *Counterpublic spaces and movement-building.* http://www.metropolitiques.eu/Counterpublic-Spaces-and-Movement.html

Mollenkopf, J., & Pastor, M. (2013). *Struggling over strangers or receiving with resilience? The metropolitics of immigrant integration.* Working paper by the MacArthur Foundation Network on Building Resilient Regions, University of California, Berkeley, Berkeley, CA.

Mollenkopf, J., & Pastor, M. (Eds.). (2016). *Unsettled Americans: Metropolitan context and civic leadership for immigrant integration.* Ithaca, NY: Cornell University Press.

Møller, P. (2014). Restoring law and (racial) order to the old dominion: White dreams and new federalism in anti-immigrant legislation. *Cultural Studies, 28*(5–6), 869–910.

Moloney, D. M. (2012). *National insecurities: Immigrants and U.S. deportation policy since 1882.* Chapel Hill, NC: University of North Carolina Press.

Mondragon, I. (2016). *Addressing the impact of deportation on citizen children and their undocumented parents.* Monterey Bay, CA: California State University, Monterey Bay.

Monogan, J. E., & Doctor, A. C. (2016). Immigration politics and partisan realignment: California, Texas, and the 1994 election. *State Politics & Policy Quarterly, 17*(1), 3–23. http://journals.sagepub.com/doi/abs/10.1177/1532440016645655

Montgomery, D., & Fernandez, M. (2017, May 2). Texas immigration bill draws protesters. *The New York Times*, p. A13.

Morales, D. I. (2016). Undocumented migrants as new (and peaceful) American revolutionaries. *Duke Journal of Constitutional Law & Public Policy, 12*(1) (Civil Rights Symposium). https://papers.ssrn.com/sol3/papers.cfm?abstract_id=2878269

Morello, C., & Lazo, L. (2012, July 24). Baltimore puts out welcome mat for immigrants, hoping to stop population decline. *The Washington Post.* http://www.globaldetroit.com/wp-content/uploads/2014/10/www-washingtonpost-com.pdf

Moreno, D. (2014). *Undocumented transgenders fear getting sent back home where they were discriminated.* Master's thesis, City of New York University, New York, NY.

Mossaad, N., & Mather, M. (2008). *Immigration gives Catholicism a boost in the United States.* Washington, DC: Population Resource Bureau.

Mousin, C. B. (2016). You were told to love the immigrant, but what if the story never happened? Hospitality and United States immigration law. *Vincentian Heritage Journal, 33*(1), Article 8.

Muchow, A. (2017, April 10). *Exploring the unintended consequences of local immigration enforcement: Evidence from Los Angeles County*. Paper presented at the APPAM California Regional Student Conference. https://appam.confex.com/appam/sc17ca/webprogram/Paper20471.html

Mulder, M. T., & Jonason, A. (2017). White Evangelical congregations in cities and suburbs: Social engagement, geography, diffusion, and disembeddedness. *City & Society, 29*(1), 104–126.

Mulder, M. T., Ramos, A. I., & Martí, G. (2017). *Latino Protestants in America: Growing and diverse*. Lanham, MD: Rowman & Littlefield.

Mummolo, J. (2016). *The perceptual side effects of government action: The case of police militarization*. Palo Alto, CA: Stanford University. http://web.stanford.edu/~jmummolo/mummolo_jmp.pdf

Muñoz, S., Espino, M. M., & Antrop-Gonzalez, R. (2014). Creating counter-spaces of resistance and sanctuaries of learning and teaching: An analysis of Freedom University. *Teachers College Record, 116*(7), 1–32.

Muraszkiewicz, J. (2016). *Depoliticising migration: Global governance and international migration narratives*. New York, NY: Oxford University Press.

Myers, C., & Colwell, M. (2012). *Our god is undocumented: Biblical faith and immigrant justice*. New York, NY: Orbis Books.

Nagel, C., & Ehrkamp, P. (2016). Deserving welcome? Immigrants, Christian faith communities, and the contentious politics of belonging in the US South. *Antipode, 48*(4), 1040–1058.

Nagourney, A. (2016, December 7). The next class of California political leaders. *The New York Times*. https://www.nytimes.com/interactive/2016/12/07/us/politics/07californiapolitics.html

Nagourney, A. (2017, April 23). California's downpours wash away a homeless colony. *The New York Times*, p. 16.

Nagourney, A., & Martin, J. (2017, June 2). California is at the core of the Democrats' fight to take back the house. *The New York Times*, p. A18.

Nail, T. (2015). Migrant cosmopolitanism. *Public Affairs Quarterly, 29*(2), 187–200.

Nail, T. (2016). *Theory of the border*. New York, NY: Oxford University Press.

Nakamora, D. (2017, February 28). Trump calls for creation of an office to support victims of crimes by illegal immigrants. *The Washington Post*. https://www.washingtonpost.com/politics/2017/live-updates/trump-white-house/real-time-fact-checking-and-analysis-of-trumps-address-to-congress/trump-calls-for-creation-of-office-to-support-victims-of-crimes-by-illegal-immigrants/?utm_term=.43b1cde5d0db

National Academies of Sciences, Engineering, and Medicine and Committee on Population. (2016). *The integration of immigrants into American society*. Washington, DC: National Academies Press.

National Immigration Law Center. (2017, February 24). *Sanctuary city toolkit*. https://www.nilc.org/issues/immigration-enforcement/sanctuary-city-toolkit

Nazario, S. (2017, October 29). Who gets to stay? *The New York Times* (Sunday Review), pp. 1, 4–5.

Negrón-Gonzales, G. (2016). Unlawful entry: Civil disobedience and the undocumented youth movement. In J. Conner & S. M. Rosen (Eds.), *Contemporary youth activism: Advancing social justice in the United States* (pp. 271–288). Santa Barbara, CA: Praeger.

Nessel, L. A., & Anello, F. R. (2016). *Deportation without representation: The access-to-justice crisis facing New Jersey's immigrant families*. South Orange, NJ: Seton Hall Law Center for Social Justice. https://papers.ssrn.com/sol3/papers.cfm?abstract_id=2805525

Neuhauser, A. (2017, April 11). Sessions mandates felony prosecutions for immigration violations: "This is the Trump era." *U.S. News & World Report*. https://www.usnews.com/news/national-news/articles/2017-04-11/sessions-mandates-felony-prosecutions-for-immigration-violations

Newcomer, S. N., & Puzio, K. (2016). Cultivando confianza: A bilingual community of practice negotiates restrictive language policies. *International Journal of Bilingual Education and Bilingualism, 19*(4), 347–369.

Ngai, M. (2017). A call for sanctuary. *Dissent, 64*(1), 16–19.

Ngai, M. M. (2014). *Impossible subjects: Illegal aliens and the making of modern America*. Princeton, NJ: Princeton University Press.

Nguyen, (2014, August 15). 5 terrifying facts about undocumented Asian Americans. *The Huffington Post*. http://www.huffingtonpost.com/sahra-vang-nguyen/5-terrifying-facts-about-_b_5670005.html

Nicholls, W. J. (2013). Making undocumented immigrants into a legitimate political subject: Theoretical observations from the United States and France. *Theory, Culture & Society, 30*(3), 82–107.

Nicholls, W. J. (2014). From political opportunities to niche-openings: The dilemmas of mobilizing for immigrant rights in inhospitable environments. *Theory and Society, 43*(1), 23–49.

Nicholls, W. J., & Uitermark, J. (2016). Migrant cities: Place, power, and voice in the era of super diversity. *Journal of Ethnic and Migration Studies, 42*(6), 877–892.

Nicholls, W. J., Uitermark, J., & van Haperen, S. (2016). The networked grassroots: How radicals outflanked reformists in the United States' immigrant rights movement. *Journal of Ethnic and Migration Studies, 42*(6), 1036–1054.

Nienass, B., & Délano, A. (2016). Deaths, visibility, and the politics of dissensus at the US–Mexico border. In A. Oberprantacher & A. Siclodi (Eds.), *Subjectivation in political theory and contemporary practices* (pp. 287–304). New York, NY: Palgrave Macmillan.

Nieto-Gomez, R. (2014). Walls, sensors and drones: Technology and surveillance on the US–Mexico border. In E. Vallet (Ed.), *Borders, fences and walls: States of insecurity* (pp. 191–209). Burlington, VT: Ashgate.

Niles, E. (2017, February 18). Truthdiggers of the week: Sanctuary churches, havens for the undocumented. *Truthdig*. http://www.truthdig.com/report/item/truthdigger_of_the_week_sanctuary_churches_undocumented_immigrants_20170218

Nix, N. A. (2016). Urban gardening practices and culture. In E. Hodges Synder, K. McIvor, & S. Brown (Eds.), *Sowing seeds in the city* (pp. 89–100). Dordrecht, the Netherlands: Springer.

Nixon, R. (2016, January 1). U.S. doesn't know how many foreigners overstay visas. *The New York Times*. https://www.nytimes.com/2016/01/02/us/politics/us-doesnt-know-how-many-foreign-visitors-overstay-visas.html?_r=0

Nixon, R. (2017a, April 19). On Rio Grande, patrolling the border on four legs. *The New York Times*, pp. A14–A15.

Nixon, R. (2017b, May 4). Immigration proposals "conspicuously absent" from budget bill. *The New York Times*, p. A12.

Nixon, R. (2017c, May 8). Trump's border wall faces a barrier in Texas: Lawsuits by landowners. *The New York Times*, p. A17.

Nixon, R. (2017d, May 21). Story of a rogue agent clouds efforts to ease border patrol expansion. *The New York Times*, p. A21.

Nixon, R. (2017e, October 27). Border wall prototypes unveiled, but obstacles remain for Trump's plan. *The New York Times*, p. A16.

Nixon, R. (2017f, July 19). Laying groundwork for a border wall. *The New York Times*, p. A16.

Nixon, R. (2017g, May 23). 629,000 overstayed U.S. visas last year, report says. *The New York Times*, p. A19.

Nixon, R. (2017h, December 6). U.S. says fall in arrests shows border crackdown is working. *The New York Times*, p. A16.

Nixon, R., & Robbins, L. (2017, April 27). ICE office aids victims of crimes by aliens. *The New York Times*, p. A19.

Norton, A. (2017). The king's new body. *Theory & Event, 20*(1), 116–126.

Nuño, L. F. (2013a). Police, public safety, and race-neutral discourse. *Sociology Compass, 7*(6), 471–486.

Nuño, L. F. (2013b). Mexicans in New York City. *Societies Without Borders, 8*(1), 80–101.

Obinna, D. N. (2014). The challenges of American legal permanent residency for family- and employment-based petitioners. *Migration and Development, 3*(2), 272–284.

Ochoa, L. (2016). Documenting the undocumented: Testimonios as a humanizing pedagogy. *Association of Mexican American Educators Journal, 10*(2), 49–64.

O'Gorman, E., Salmon, N., & Murphy, C. A. (2016). Schools as sanctuaries: A systematic review of contextual factors which contribute to student retention in alternative education. *International Journal of Inclusive Education, 20*(5), 536–551.

Ohio Jobs & Justice PAC. (2017). *The original list of Sanctuary Cities, USA.* http://www.ojjpac.org/sanctuary.asp

Olayo-Méndez, A., Haymes, S. N., & Vidal de Haymes, M. (2014). Mexican migration-corridor hospitality. *Peace Review, 26*(2), 209–217.

O'Leary, A. O. (2016). "Con el peso en la frente": A gendered look at the human and economic costs on migration on the U.S.–Mexico border. In R. Rubio-Goldsmith, C. Fernandez, J. K. Finch, & A. Masterson-Algar (Eds.), *Migrant deaths in the Arizona desert: La vida no vale nada* (pp. 69–93). Tucson, AZ: Arizona State University.

Oomen, B., & Baumgärtel, M. (2014). Human rights cities. In A. Mihr & M. Gibney (Eds.), *The Sage handbook of human rights* (pp. 709–729). London, UK: Sage.

Openshaw, L., McLane, A., & Parkerson, S. (2015). *Faith-based support for undocumented immigrant families.* http://www.nacsw.org/Convention/OpenshawLFaithBasedFINAL.pdf

Orner, P. (2015). *Underground America: Narratives of undocumented lives.* San Francisco, CA: McSweeney's Books.

O'Toole, F. (2017, March 17). Green beer and rank hypocrisy. *The New York Times*, p. A25.

Otterman, S. (2017, May 8). Hindu temple in Queens joins sanctuary movement. *The New York Times*, p. A18.

Owusu-Sarfo, K. (2016). *Deconstructing public discourse on undocumented immigration in the United States in the twenty first century.* Doctoral dissertation, Nova Southeastern University, Davie, FL.

Padilla, Y. C., Shapiro, E. R., Fernández-Castro, M. D., & Faulkner, M. (2008). An urgent call to social workers. *Social Work, 53*(1), 5–8.

Page, K. R., & Polk, S. (2017). Chilling effect? Post-election health care use by undocumented and mixed-status families. *New England Journal of Medicine, 376*(12), e20.

Palidda, S. (Ed.). (2016). *Racial criminalization of migrants in the 21st century.* New York, NY: Routledge.

Pallares, A. (2014). *Family activism: Immigrant struggles and the politics of noncitizenship.* New Brunswick, NJ: Rutgers University Press.

Palmer, B. J. (2017). The crossroads: Being Black, immigrant, and undocumented in the era of #Black Lives Matter. *Georgetown Journal of Law & Modern Critical Race Perspectives, 9,* 99.

Papademetriou, D. G., & Banulescu-Bogdan, N. (2016). *Understanding and addressing public anxiety about immigration.* Washington, DC: Migration Policy Institute.

Papazian, S. (2011). Secure communities, sanctuary laws, and local enforcement of immigration law: The story of Los Angeles. *Southern California Review of Law and Social Justice, 21,* 283.

Park, J., & Norpoth, H. (2016). Policy popularity: The Arizona immigration law. *Electoral Studies, 44,* 15–25.

Parker, C. (2017, June 10). Intense debate on immigrants. *The Boston Globe,* p. 5.

Parks, B. O., Peters, E. D., Porterfield, C., Winston, D., & Anderson, B. E. (2016). Border migrant deaths and the Pima County medical examiner's office. In R. Rubio-Goldsmth, C. Fernandez, J. K. Finch, & A. Masterson-Algar (Eds.), *Migrant deaths in the Arizona desert: La vida no vale nada* (pp. 120–131). Tucson, AZ: University of Arizona.

Parloff, R. (2017, April 11). The sanctuary-cities executive order is Trump's next legal train wreck. *New Yorker.* http://nymag.com/daily/intelligencer/2017/04/the-sanctuary-cities-order-is-trumps-next-legal-train-wreck.html

Parrado, E. A., & Flippen, C. A. (2016). The departed deportations and out-migration among Latino immigrants in North Carolina after the Great Recession. *Annals of the American Academy of Political and Social Science, 666*(1), 131–147.

Parveen, R. (2017). *Recipes and songs.* New York, NY: Springer.

Passel, J. S., & Cohn, D'V. (2016, November 17). *Children of unauthorized immigrants make up rising share of K–12 students.* Washington, DC: Pew Research Center.

Passel, J. S., & Cohn, D'V. (2017a, February 9). *Most U.S. unauthorized immigrants live in just 20 metro area.* Washington, DC: Pew Research Center.

Passel, J. S., & Cohn, D'V. (2017b, April 28). *As Mexican share declined, U.S. unauthorized immigrant population fell in 2015 below recession level.* Washington, DC: Pew Research Center.

Pastor, M. (2016). Latinos and the new American majority. *Dissent, 63*(3), 55–63.

Patel, S., & Baptist, C. (2012). Editorial: Documenting by the undocumented. *Environment and Urbanization, 24*(1), 3–12. http://journals.sagepub.com/doi/full/10.1177/0956247812438364

Pateman, J., & Williment, K. (2013). *Developing community-led public libraries: Evidence from the UK and Canada.* New York, NY: Routledge.

Patler, C., & Gonzales, R. G. (2015). Framing citizenship: Media coverage of anti-deportation cases led by undocumented immigrant youth organisations. *Journal of Ethnic and Migration Studies, 41*(9), 1453–1474.

Paulumbo, G., & Ahmed, A. (2018, January 10). El Salvador feels the weight of Washington shaping its fate. *The New York Times*, p. A15.

Payan, T., & De la Garza, E. (Eds.). (2014). *Undecided nation: Political gridlock and the immigration crisis* (Vol. 6). New York, NY: Springer.

PBS. (2017, December 12). *Homeland Security chief says other states should emulate Texas ban on sanctuary cities*. https://www.pbs.org/newshour/nation/homeland-security-chief-says-other-states-should-emulate-texas-ban-on-sanctuary-cities

Peeren, E. (2014). *The spectral metaphor*. New York, NY: Palgrave Macmillan.

Pérez Huber, L. (2017). Healing images and narratives: Undocumented Chicana/Latina pedagogies of resistance. *Journal of Latinos and Education, 16*(4), 374–389.

Perla, H., Jr. (2017). *Sandinista Nicaragua's resistance to US coercion: Revolutionary deterrence in asymmetric conflict*. New York, NY: Cambridge University Press.

Perla, H., Jr., & Coutin, S. B. (2012). Legacies and origins of the 1980s US–Central American sanctuary movement. In R. Lippert & S. Rehaag (Eds.), *Sanctuary practices in international perspectives: Migration, citizenship* (pp. 73–90). New York, NY: Routledge.

Peters, M. A., & Besley, T. (2015). The refugee crisis and the right to political asylum. *Educational Philosophy and Theory, 47*(14–15), 1367–1374.

Pew Research Center. (2016, August 31). *Remittance flows worldwide in 2015*. Washington, DC: Author.

Phelan, H. (2017). "Let us say yes . . .": Music, the stranger and hospitality. *Public Voices, 9*(1), 113–124.

Philbin, S. P., & Ayón, C. (2016). Luchamos por nuestros hijos: Latino immigrant parents strive to protect their children from the deleterious effects of anti-immigration policies. *Children and Youth Services Review, 63*, 128–135.

Phillips, K. (2017, November 16). The story behind this powerful photo of deported military veterans saluting the American flag. *The Washington Post*. https://www.washingtonpost.com/news/checkpoint/wp/2017/11/16/the-story-behind-this-powerful-photo-of-deported-military-veterans-saluting-the-american-flag/?utm_term=.952bf8b48842

Pierce, M. (2016). Corazón De Dixie: Mexicanos in the US South since 1910. *The Arkansas Historical Quarterly, 75*(2), 172.

Pirie, S. H. (2013). The origins of a political trial: The sanctuary movement and political justice. *Yale Journal of Law & the Humanities, 2*(2), 7.

Piven, F. F., & Cloward, R. A. (1971). *Regulating the poor: The functions of public welfare*. New York, NY: Pantheon.

Pohl, B. E., Jr., Garcia, V., & Emeka, T. (2016). Latino civic and social engagement. *Journal of Family Strengths, 16*(1), 2. http://digitalcommons.library.tmc.edu/cgi/viewcontent.cgi?article=1313&context=jfs

Poputa, M. (2016). Going places, blending spaces. *British and American Studies, 22*, 89. https://www.questia.com/library/journal/1P3-4111335891/going-places-blending-spaces

Porter, E. (2017, October 25). A policy as good for farms as locusts. *The New York Times*, pp. B1–B2.

Porter, M. (2017). Prepare for potential changes in handling of key legal, civil rights issues on campus. *Campus Legal Advisor, 17*(7), 1–3.

Portes, A., Fernández-Kelly, P., & Light, D. (2012). Life on the edge: Immigrants confront the American health system. *Ethnic and Racial Studies, 35*(1), 3–22.

Portes, A., & Rumbaut, R. G. (2014). *Immigrant America: A portrait* (4th ed.). Berkeley, CA: University of California Press.

Post, D. (2017, March 30). Let's call them "constitutional cities," not "sanctuary cities," okay? *The Washington Post.* https://www.washingtonpost.com/news/volokh-conspiracy/wp/2017/03/30/lets-call-them-constitutional-cities-not-sanctuary-cities-okay/?utm_term=.ea873ee119eb

Preston, J. (2013). Ailing Midwestern cities extend a welcoming hand to immigrants. *The New York Times.* http://www.fosterglobal.com/news/ailing_midwestern_cities10062013.pdf

Price, M., & Breese, D. (2016). Unintended return: US deportations and the fractious politics of mobility for Latinos. *Annals of the American Association of Geographers, 106*(2), 366–376.

Price, P. L. (2012). Race and ethnicity Latino/a immigrants and emerging geographies of race and place in the USA. *Progress in Human Geography, 36*(6), 800–809.

Prieto, G. (2016). Opportunity, threat, and tactics: Collaboration and confrontation by Latino immigrant challengers. In L. E. Hancock (Ed.), *Narratives of identity in social movements, conflicts and change* (pp. 123–154). Bingley, UK: Emerald Group.

Provine, D. M., & Varsanyi, M. W. (2012). Scaled down: Perspectives on state and local creation and enforcement of immigration law: Introduction to the special issue of *Law & Policy. Law & Policy, 34*(2), 105–112.

Provine, D. M., Varsanyi, M. W., Lewis, P. G., & Decker, S. H. (2016). *Policing immigrants: Local law enforcement on the front lines.* Chicago, IL: University of Chicago Press.

Quesada, J. (2011). No soy welferero: Undocumented Latino laborers in the crosshairs of legitimation maneuvers. *Medical Anthropology, 30*(4), 386–408.

Quesada, J., Arreola, S., Kral, A., Khoury, S., Organista, K. C., & Worby, P. (2014). "As good as it gets": Undocumented Latino day laborers negotiating discrimination in San Francisco and Berkeley, California, USA. *City & Society, 26*(1), 29–50.

Rabben, L. (2011). *Give refuge to the stranger: The past, present, and future of sanctuary.* Oakland, CA: Left Coast Press.

Rabben, L. (2016). *Sanctuary and asylum: A social and political history.* Seattle, WA: University of Washington Press.

Rajaram, P. K. (2015). Common marginalizations: Neoliberalism, undocumented migrants and other surplus populations. *Migration, Mobility, & Displacement, 1*(1). http://mmduvic.ca/index.php/mmd/article/view/13288

Ralston, J. (2016). Gathered from all nations. In S. Synder, A. M. Brazal, & J. Ralston (Eds.), *Church in an age of global migration* (pp. 35–50). New York, NY: Palgrave Macmillan.

Ramakrishnan, K., & Colbern, A. (2015). *The "California package" of immigrant integration and the evolving nature of state citizenship.* Los Angeles, CA: UCLA, Institute for Research on Labor and Immigration.

Ramey, D. M. (2013). Immigrant revitalization and neighborhood violent crime in established and new destination cities. *Social Forces, 92*(2), 597–629.

Ramirez, D. (2015). *Migrating faith: Pentecostalism in the United States and Mexico in the twentieth century.* Chapel Hill, NC: University of North Carolina Press.

Ramirez, M., III, Argueta, N. L., Castro, Y., Pérez, R., & Dawson, D. B. (2016). The relation of drug trafficking fears and cultural identity to attitudes toward Mexican immigrants in five south Texas communities. *Journal of Borderlands Studies, 31*(1), 91–105.

Rana, S. (2014). Response: Immigration law's new frontiers. *Ohio State Law Journal Furthermore, 75,* 19.

Rappeport, A. (2017, May 19). Trump seeks $2.6 billion for border in budget. *The New York Times,* p. 13.

Rathord, S. (2016, December 2). Here are the sanctuary cities ready to resist Trump's deportation threats. *Mother Jones.* http://www.motherjones.com/politics/2016/11/sanctuary-city-immigration-federal-deportation-trump-threats-budget

Ravuri, E. D. (2014). Return migration predictors for undocumented Mexican immigrants living in Dallas. *Social Science Journal, 51*(1), 35–43.

Real Vision. (2014, August 14). *The history of illegal immigration in the United States.* http://www.abc.net.au/radionational/programs/rearvision/the-history-of-illegal-immigration-in-the-united-states/5678670

Reddon, E. (2016, November 15). Growing movement calls on universities to limit their cooperation with federal immigration. *Inside Higher Ed.* https://www.insidehighered.com/news/2016/11/15/growing-movement-calls-universities-limit-their-cooperation-federal-immigration

Reed-Sandoval, A. (2016). Locating the injustice of undocumented migrant oppression. *Journal of Social Philosophy, 47*(4), 374–398.

Reif, R. (2017, September 1). Trump shouldn't repeal DACA. *The Boston Globe,* p. A8.

Reina, A. S., Maldonado, M. M., & Lohman, B. J. (2013). Undocumented Latina networks and responses to domestic violence in a new immigrant gateway: Toward a place-specific analysis. *Violence Against Women, 19*(12), 1472–1497.

Reineke, R. (2016). Los desparecidoes de la frontera (The disappeared on the border). In R. Rubio-Goldsmith, C. Fernandez, J. K. Finch, & A. Masterson-Algar (Eds.), *Migrant deaths in the Arizona desert: La vida no vale nada* (pp. 132–149). Tucson, AZ: Arizona State University.

Religious News Services. (2017, March 24). Church worldwide: Sanctuary for the undocumented comes with legal consequences. *The Banner.* http://thebanner.org/news/2017/03/church-worldwide-sanctuary-for-the-undocumented-comes-with-legal-consequences

Resnik, J. (2016). *"Within its jurisdiction": Moving boundaries, people, and the law of migration.* Yale Law School, Public Law Research Paper No. 580.

Ricks, M. (2016, December 14). Rally affirms sanctuary city status. *New Haven Independent.* http://www.newhavenindependent.org/index.php/archives/entry/immigration_rally2

Ridgley, J. (2008). Cities of refuge: Immigration enforcement, police, and the insurgent genealogies of citizenship in U.S. sanctuary cities. *Urban Geography, 29*(1), 53–77.

Ridgley, J. (2012). The city as a sanctuary in the United States. In R. Lippert & S. Rehaag (Eds.), *Sanctuary practices in international perspectives: Migration, citizenship and social movements* (pp. 219–231). New York, NY: Routledge.

Rios, E. (2017, January 27). The first big fight over sanctuary cities pits a Latino sheriff against Texas' governor. *Mother Jones.* http://www.motherjones.com/politics/2017/01/texas-greg-abbott-austin-sanctuary-city-immigration

Ríos, V. (2014). Security issues and immigration flows: Drug-violence refugees, the new Mexican immigrants. *Latin American Research Review, 49*(3), 3. http://viridianarios.com/wp-content/uploads/2014/05/RiosV2014_LARR2014_SecurityImmigration.pdf

Ríos, V., & Shirk, D. A. (2011). *Drug violence in Mexico: Data and analysis through 2010.* Trans-Border Institute, University of San Diego.

Riosmena, F. (2016). Guatemala–US migration: Transforming regions. *Contemporary Sociology, 45*(4), 462–464.

Rissler, G. E. (2016). Varied responsiveness to immigrant community growth among local governments: Evidence from the Richmond, Virginia, metropolitan area. *State and Local Government Review, 48*(1), 30–41.

Robbins, L. (2017a, February 23). Police fear Trump's orders may handcuff their effort to fight gangs. *The New York Times*, p. A14.

Robbins, L. (2017b, May 11). Surge pricing for migrants heading north ends in penalty for a taxi owner. *The New York Times*, p. A22.

Robbins, L. (2017c, July 19). For the undocumented, a broken headlight can lead to deportation. *The New York Times*, p. A21.

Robbins, L. (2017d, November 11). Mail is late, and DACA renewals are denied: Deportation fears after Chicago delays. *The New York Times*, p. A18.

Robbins, L. (2017e, November 17). In reversal, immigration agency will consider delayed DACA requests. *The New York Times*, p. A22.

Robbins, L., & Correal, A. (2017, January 17). Immigrants stay home, and their absence reverberates. *The New York Times*, p. A10.

Roberts, B., Menjívar, C., & Rodríguez, N. P. (2017). *Deportation and return in a border-restricted world.* New York, NY: Springer.

Rocheleu, M. (2017, February 17). Greater Boston home to 180,000 undocumented immigrants, report says. *The Boston Globe.* https://www.bostonglobe.com/metro/2017/02/17/greater-boston-home-undocumented-immigrants-report-finds/dFVIV8Qf3HjsxVeFYEgbAP/story.html

Rocco, R. (2016). Disposable subjects: The racial normativity of neoliberalism and Latino immigrants. *Latino Studies, 14*(1), 99–117.

Rodgers, B. (2017, February 15). Undocumented immigrants voice fears of possible mass deportations. *VOA News.* http://www.voanews.com/a/undocumented-immigrants-voice-fears-of-possible-mass-deportations/3724648.html

Rodríguez, N. P., & Hagan, J. (2016). US polices to restrict immigration. In N. P. Rodriguez & J. Hagan (Eds.), *Migration in an era of restriction and recession* (pp. 27–38). New York, NY: Springer.

Rodriguez, S., & Sider, R. (2013). *Christians at the border: Immigration, the Church, and the Bible* (2nd ed.). Grand Rapids, MI: Baker Academic.

Rogin, M. P. (1975). *Fathers & children: Andrew Jackson and the subjugation of the American Indian.* New York, NY: Vintage Books.

Romero, M. (2011). Constructing Mexican immigrant women as a threat to American families. *International Journal of Sociology of the Family, 37*(1), 49–68.

Romero, S. (2017, September 15). Motel 6 employees in Arizona tipped off immigration officers about guests. *The New York Times*, p. A12.

Romero, S., & Jordan, M. (2017, August 30). An uneasy time for immigrants, and then the rain began to fall. *The New York Times*, pp. A1, A16.

Rongerude, J., & Sandoval, G. F. (2016). From the table to the street: Strategies for building a more inclusive collaborative process. In R. D. Margerum & C. J. Robinson (Eds.), *The challenges of collaboration in environmental governance: Barriers and responses* (pp. 317–336). Northampton, MA: Elger.

Rosario, R. (2017, February 2). Los Angeles is refusing to arrest undocumented street vendors. *VIBE*. http://www.vibe.com/2017/02/los-angeles-protects-undocumented

Rosas, A. E. (2015). Pathways to legalization: Undocumented Mexican immigrants in the US/Mexico borderlands, 1942–1956. *Kalfou, 2*(2). https://tupjournals.temple.edu/index.php/kalfou/article/view/67

Rosas, G. (2015). The border thickens: In-securing communities after IRCA. *International Migration, 54*(2). http://onlinelibrary.wiley.com/doi/10.1111/imig.12198/pdf

Rosenberg, E. (2017, March 31). More tourists, a few tears and plenty of soul- searching. *The New York Times*, p. A20.

Rosenbloom, R. E. (2013). The citizenship line: Rethinking immigration exceptionalism. *Boston College Law Review, 54*(5), 1965–2024. (Northeastern University School of Law Research Paper No. 143-2013)

Rosenblum, M. R., & Meissner, D. (2014). *The deportation dilemma: Reconciling tough and humane enforcement*. Washington, DC: Migration Policy Institute.

Ross, J. (2015, July 8). 6 things to know about sanctuary cities. *The Washington Post*. https://www.washingtonpost.com/news/the-fix/wp/2015/07/08/4-big-things-to-know-about-sanctuary-cities-and-illegal-immigration/?utm_term=.7250029ad17c

Roth, B. J., & Allard, S. W. (2016). (Re)defining access to Latino immigrant-serving organizations: Evidence from Los Angeles, Chicago, and Washington, DC. *Journal of the Society for Social Work and Research, 7*(4), 729–753.

Roth, B. J., Sichling, F., & Brake, A. (2016). Recentering our tendencies: Immigrant youth development and the importance of context in social work research. *Journal of Human Behavior in the Social Environment, 26*(6), 509–520.

Rubenstein, D. S., & Gulasekaram, P. (2017). Immigration exceptionalism. *Northwestern University Law Review, 111*(3)

Rubesin, H. (2016). The stories we share: Reflections on a community-based art exhibit displaying work by refugees and immigrants. *Journal of Applied Arts & Health, 7*(2), 159–174.

Rubio-Goldsmith, R., Fernandez, C., Finch, J. K., & Masterson-Algar, A. (Eds.). (2016). *Migrant deaths in the Arizona desert: La vida no vale nada*. Tucson, AZ: Arizona State University.

Ruddell, L. S., Champion, W. T., & Norris, D. (2011). The ethical dilemma of local ordinances that purport to deport illegal aliens. *University of Detroit Mercy Law Review, 89*, 299.

Ruiz Marrujo, O. T. (2014). Undocumented families in times of deportation at the San Diego–Tijuana border. *Journal of Borderlands Studies, 29*(4), 391–403.

Rumbaut, R. G., Ewing, W., & Martinez, D. (2015). *The criminalization of immigration in the United States*. Washington, DC: American Immigration Council, Immigration Policy Center.

Rumore, K. (2017, September 15). Chicago's history as a sanctuary city. *Chicago Tribune*. http://www.chicagotribune.com/news/ct-chicago-sanctuary-history-htmlstory.html

Russell, D. (2017). The shadow immigration system. *North Carolina Central Law Review, 39*, 109.

Ryan, G. (2017, February 8). Goodwin Proctor targets Trump order in new-sanctuary order. *Boston Business Journal.* http://www.bizjournals.com/boston/news/2017/02/08/goodwin-targets-trump-order-in-new-sanctuary-city.html

Ryer, P. (2014). Immigration and its effects. *Latin American Research Review, 49*(3), 277–286.

Sacchetti, M. (2017, May 4). Texas governor poised to sign nation's harshest anti-sanctuary bill. *The Washington Post.* https://www.washingtonpost.com/local/social-issues/texas-governor-poised-to-sign-nations-harshest-anti-sanctuary-bill/2017/05/04/c9c6ddf0-30dc-11e7-9dec-764dc781686f_story.html?utm_term=.37d0db08cb1e

Sadowski-Smith, C. (2014). The centrality of the Canada–US border for hemispheric studies of the Americas. *Forum for Inter-American Research, 7*(3), 20–40. http://www.uni-bielefeld.de/cias/fiar/pdf/073/FIAR073-20-40-Sadowski-Smith.pdf

Saillant, C. (2012). LA council approves ID cards for city residents. *The Los Angeles Times.* http://www.fosterquan.com/news/la_id_cards11072012.pdf

Sampaio, A. (2016). Latin@ voters stand poised to reshape the US electoral map in the wake of Donald Trump's racist presidential campaign. *NACLA Report on the Americas, 48*(3), 221–228.

Sanchez, G. (2017). Beyond the matrix of oppression: Reframing human smuggling through instersectionality-informed approaches. *Theoretical Criminology, 21*(1), 46–56.

Sanders, L., Martinez, R., Harner, M., Harner, M., Horner, P., & Delva, J. (2013). Grassroots responsiveness to human rights abuse: History of the Washtenaw Interfaith Coalition for Immigrant Rights. *Social Work, 58*(2), 117–125.

Sandoval-García, C. (2017). *Exclusion and forced migration in Central America: No more walls.* New York, NY: Springer.

Santos, F. (2017, June 17). Border patrol agents raid camp in Arizona desert run by aid organization. *The New York Times,* p. A17.

Sassen, S. (2013). When the center no longer holds: Cities as frontier zones. *Cities, 34,* 67–70.

Saunders, J., Lim, N., & Prosnitz, D. (2014). *Enforcing immigration law at the state and local levels: A public policy dilemma* (Vol. 273). Santa Monica, CA: RAND.

Saunders, L. (2017, February 9). Libraries as sanctuary spaces. *Somerville Patch.* http://patch.com/massachusetts/somerville/libraries-sanctuary-spaces

Savage, C. (2017, April 22). Justice Dept. warns cities to comply on migrants. *The New York Times,* p. A10.

Schewel, B. (2016). The moral relevance of borders: Transcendence and the ethics of migration. In J. B. Saunders, E. Fiddian-Qasmiyeh, & S. Snyder (Eds.), *Intersections of religion and migration* (pp. 241–257). New York, NY: Palgrave Macmillan.

Schmid, A. P. (2016). *Links between terrorism and migration.* The Hague, the Netherlands: International Centre for Counter Terrorism—The Hague. https://www.icct.nl/wp-content/uploads/2016/05/Alex-P.-Schmid-Links-between-Terrorism-and-Migration.pdf

Schmid, C. L. (2017). The past is ever present: Transnationalism old and new—Italian and Mexican immigrants in the US. *International Migration, 55*(3), 20–37.

Schmidt, S. (2017a, April 20). First "dreamer" deported since Trump election. *The Boston Globe,* p. A2.

Schmidt, S. (2017b, April 21). Judge Trump rapped gets a key case. *The Boston Globe*, p. A12.

Schmidt, Susan. (2017). "They need to give us a voice": Lessons from listening to unaccompanied Central American and Mexican children on helping children like themselves. *Journal on Migration and Human Security, 5*(1).

Schmidt, U., & Johansen, K. H. (2016). Theological anthropologies in a neighbourhood church. In E.-M. Becker, J. Dietrich, & B. K. Holm (Eds.), *Theological encounters with anthropology* (pp. 379–401). Bristol, CT: Vandenhoeck & Ruprecht.

Schoen, J. W. (2016, April 5). *Would Trump's plan to stop remittances to Mexico work?* NBC News. http://www.nbcnews.com/business/business-news/would-trump-s-plan-stop-remittances-mexico-work-n551211

Schoen, J. W. (2017, February 24). *Trumps' deportation plan could cost half a trillion dollars.* CNBC. http://www.cnbc.com/2017/02/24/trumps-deportation-plan-could-cost-half-a-trillion-dollars.html

Schrag, P. (2010, September 13). *The unwanted: Immigration and nativism in America.* Washington, DC: American Immigration Council. https://www.americanimmigrationcouncil.org/research/unwanted-immigration-and-nativism-america

Schulte, E., & Bon, D. (2017). People rise up, block US airports. *Green Left Weekly, 13*(1124).

Schultz, M. (2017, April 23). Sessions praises NYPD after calling city "soft on crime." *New York Post.* http://nypost.com/2017/04/23/sessions-praises-nypd-after-calling-city-soft-on-crime/?link=mktw

Schütze, S. (2016). *Constructing transnational political spaces.* New York, NY: Palgrave Macmillan.

Schwiertz, H. (2016, July). *With or without papers–We will always be illegal: The movement of undocumented youth beyond citizenship and legislation.* Paper presented at the Third ISA Forum of Sociology, July 10–14, 2016.

Scott, A. J. (1998). *The city: Los Angeles and urban theory at the end of the twentieth century.* Berkeley, CA: University of California Press.

Segal, U. A. (2000). *A framework for immigration: Asians in the United States.* New York, NY: Columbia University Press.

Seif, H. (2014). "Coming out of the shadows" and "undocuqueer": Undocumented immigrants transforming sexuality discourse and activism. *Journal of Language and Sexuality, 3*(1), 87–120.

Selbourne, M. (2017, February 11). Hundreds of undocumented immigrants arrested. *The Hill.* http://thehill.com/homenews/319075-hundreds-of-undocumented-immigrants-arrested-report

Seltzer, L. F. (2016). Outrage meets outrageousness: The populist logic behind Trump's surprising popularity. *Journal of Psychohistory, 44*(1), 73–84.

Semple, K. (2017, July 4). Fearful migrants stop short of U.S. *The New York Times,* pp. A1, A7.

Sen, R. (2009). Back of the house, front of the house: What a campaign to organize New York restaurant workers tells us about immigrant integration. *National Civic Review, 98*(1), 43–51.

Shaikh, A., & Kauppi, C. (2010). Deconstructing resilience: Myriad conceptualizations and interpretations. *International Journal of Arts and Sciences, 3*(15), 155–176.

Sharpless, R. A. (2016). "Immigrants are not criminals": Respectability, immigration reform, and hyperincarceration. *Houston Law Review, 53,* 691.

Shaw, J. (2015). Illegal immigration figures in New York. *Newsmax.* http://www.newsmax.com/FastFeatures/illegal-immigration-New-York/2015/09/24/id/693135

Shear, M. D. (2017, October 9). Trump demands tighter borders for deal on DACA. *The New York Times,* pp. A1, A14.

Shear, M. D., & Nixon, R. (2017, February 22). More immigrants face deportation under new rules. *The New York Times,* pp. A1, A12.

Shear, M. D., & Yee, V. (2017, June 17). "Dreamers" to stay in U.S. for now, but their long-term fate is unclear. *The New York Times,* p. A17.

Shepard, E. A. (2016). *The emerging "immigrant-friendly" city: How and why cities frame themselves as welcoming places to immigrants.* Master's thesis, University of Vermont, Burlington, VT.

Sheppard, B. (2017). Huge women's marches stare down Trump's attacks. *Green Left Weekly, 15*(1123).

Sherman, A. (2017, February 3). Trump wall will not fix path most undocumented arrived in Florida overstaying visas. *Miami Herald.* http://www.miamiherald.com/news/politics-government/article130594224.html

Shuford, J. (2017). The compassion of "compassionate migration." In S. W. Bender & W. F. Arrocha (Eds.), *Compassionate migration and regional policy in the Americas* (pp. 217–236). New York, NY: Palgrave Macmillan.

Sidney, M. (2014a). Settling in: A comparison of local immigrant organizations in the United States and Canada. *International Journal of Canadian Studies, 49,* 105–134.

Sidney, M. (2014b). Outsiders/insiders: How local immigrant organisations contest the exclusion of undocumented immigrants in the US. In H. Schwenken, S. Russ, & S. Ruß-Sattar (Eds.), *New border and citizenship politics* (pp. 103–122). New York, NY: Palgrave Macmillan.

Silverman, D. (Ed.). (2016). *Qualitative research.* Thousand Oaks, CA: Sage.

Simes, J. T., & Waters, M. C. (2014). The politics of immigration and crime. In S. M. Bucerius & M. H. Tonry (Eds.), *The Oxford handbook of ethnicity, crime, and immigration* (pp. 476–478). New York, NY: Oxford University Press.

Simpson, J. (2015). *The red–green axis: Refugees, immigration and the agenda to erase America.* Washington, DC: Center for Security Policy Press.

Singer, A., Svajlenka, N. P., & Wilson, J. H. (2015). *Local insights from DACA for implementing future programs for unauthorized immigrants.* Washington, DC: Brookings Institute.

Singh, K. D. (2016, September 22). India is the fastest-growing source of new illegal immigrants to the U.S. *The Wall Street Journal.* http://blogs.wsj.com/indiarealtime/2016/09/22/india-is-the-fastest-growing-source-of-new-illegal-immigrants-to-the-u-s

Siskin, A. (2015). *Alien removals and returns: Overview and trends.* Congressional Research Service. https://fas.org/sgp/crs/homesec/R43892.pdf

Skiba, K. (2017, March 31). Spicer ties Chicago's sanctuary city status to city's gang, violence problem. *Chicago Tribune.* http://www.chicagotribune.com/news/local/politics/ct-chicago-sanctuary-city-lose-federal-dollars-met-0331-20170331-story.html

Slack, J., Martínez, D. E., Lee, A. E., & Whiteford, S. (2016). The geography of border militarization: Violence, death and health in Mexico and the United States. *Journal of Latin American Geography, 15*(1), 7–32.

Slack, J., Martínez, D. E., Whiteford, S., & Peiffer, E. (2013, March). *In the shadow of the wall: Family separation, immigration enforcement and security.* Tucson, AZ: The Center for Latin American Studies, University of Arizona.

Slack, M. R. (2013). Ignoring the lessons of history: How the open borders myth led to repeated patterns in state and local immigration control. *Journal of Civil Rights and Economic Development, 27,* 467.

Smith, B. D., & Womack, B. G. (2016). Human service administrators' attitudes toward immigration: Shaped by community and organizational context? *Human Service Organizations: Management, Leadership & Governance, 40*(1), 6–21.

Smith, M. (2017, August 8). Sessions scolds Chicago for suing over "sanctuary" threat. *The New York Times,* p. A11.

Smith, M. E., Engquist, A., Carvajal, C., Johnston-Zimmerman, K., Algara, M., Gilliland, B., . . . Young, A. (2015). Neighborhood formation in semi-urban settlements. *Journal of Urbanism, 8*(2), 173–198.

Smith, R. (2014, January). *Are cities the new settlements? Local government policies to welcome immigrants.* Paper presented at the Society for Social Work and Research 18th Annual Conference: Research for Social Change: Addressing Local and Global Challenges.

Snyder, S. (2011). Un/settling angels: Faith-based organizations and asylum-seeking in the UK. *Journal of Refugee Studies, 24*(3), 565–585.

Snyder, S. (2015). Looking through the bars: Immigration detention and the ethics of mysticism. *Journal of the Society of Christian Ethics, 35*(1), 167–187.

Snyder, S. (2016). "La mano zurda with a heart in its palm": Mystical activism as a response to the trauma of immigration detention. In S. N. Arel & S. Rambo (Eds.), *Posttraumatic public theology* (pp. 217–240). New York, NY: Springer.

Sohoni, D., & Mendez, J. B. (2014). Defining immigrant newcomers in new destinations: Symbolic boundaries in Williamsburg, Virginia. *Ethnic and Racial Studies, 37*(3), 496–516.

Sowards, S. K., & Pineda, R. D. (2013). Immigrant narratives and popular culture in the United States: Border spectacle, unmotivated sympathies, and individualized responsibilities. *Western Journal of Communication, 77*(1), 72–91.

Spener, D. (2014). The lexicon of clandestine migration on the Mexico–US border. *Aztlán: A Journal of Chicano Studies, 39*(1), 71–104.

Squire, V. (2011). From community cohesion to mobile solidarities: The City of Sanctuary network and the Strangers into Citizens campaign. *Political Studies, 59*(2), 290–307.

Srikantiah, J. (2017). Resistance and immigrants' rights. *Stanford Journal of Civil Rights & Civil Liberties, 13,* 5.

Stansfield, R. (2014). Safer cities: A macro-level analysis of recent immigration, Hispanic-owned businesses, and crime rates in the United States. *Journal of Urban Affairs, 36*(3), 503–518.

Staudt, K., & Coronado, I. (2016). *Fronteras no mas: Toward social justice at the US–Mexican border.* New York, NY: Springer.

Steil, J. P., & Vasi, I. B. (2014). The new immigration contestation: Social movements and local immigration policy making in the United States, 2000–2011. *American Journal of Sociology, 119*(4), 1104–1155.

Stemple, K. (2017, August 6). Flaws seen as asylum in Mexico is strained. *The New York Times,* p. 9.

Stern, R. (2017, April 11). U.S. Attorney General Jeff Sessions delivers remarks on border security and immigration. *Phoenix New Times*. http://www.phoenixnewtimes.com/news/us-attorney-general-jeff-sessions-delivers-remarks-on-border-security-and-immigration-in-nogales-arizona-9228298

Stevens, M. (2017, May 6). Rape charges to be dropped against students in case cited by White House. *New York Times*, p. A10.

Stewart, J. (2017, April 16). Mayor; San Diego police won't be immigration officers. *The San Diego Union-Tribune*. http://www.sandiegouniontribune.com/news/politics/sd-me-faulconer-immigration-20170317-story.html

Stinson, P. M. (2017, February, 10). Crime stats should inform the public. Trump is misusing them to scare us instead. *The Washington Post*. https://www.washingtonpost.com/posteverything/wp/2017/02/10/crime-stats-should-inform-the-public-trump-is-misusing-them-to-scare-us-instead

Stockman, F., & Goodman, J. D. (2017, February 25). Immigration policies pose conflict for police in "sanctuary cities." *The New York Times*, p. A10.

Stodder, S. (2017, March 31). Why I changed my mind on "sanctuary cities." *Politico*. http://www.politico.com/agenda/story/2017/03/changed-position-sanctuary-cities-trump-000386

Stoltz Chinchilla, N., Hamilton, N., & Loucky, J. (2009). The sanctuary movement and Central American activism in Los Angeles. *Latin American Perspectives, 36*(6), 101–126.

Streng, J. M., Rhodes, S., Ayala, G., Eng, E., Arceo, R., & Phipps, S. (2004). Realidad Latina: Latino adolescents, their school, and a university use photovoice to examine and address the influence of immigration. *Journal of Interprofessional care, 18*(4), 403–415.

Strunk, C., & Leitner, H. (2013). Resisting federal–local immigration enforcement partnerships: Redefining "secure communities" and public safety. *Territory, Politics, Governance, 1*(1), 62–85.

Stuesse, A., & Coleman, M. (2014). Automobility, immobility, altermobility: Surviving and resisting the intensification of immigrant policing. *City & Society, 26*(1), 51–72.

Stupi, E. K., Chiricos, T., & Gertz, M. (2016). Perceived criminal threat from undocumented immigrants: Antecedents and consequences for policy preferences. *Justice Quarterly, 33*(2), 239–266.

Su, R. (2013). The promise and peril of cities and immigration policy. *Harvard Law & Policy Review, 7*, 299.

Suárez, L. (2016). Liberty at the cost of constitutional protections: Undocumented immigrants and Fourth Amendment rights. *University of Miami Inter-American Law Review, 48*, 153.

Sullivan, E., & Olmedo, C. (2015). Informality on the urban periphery: Housing conditions and self-help strategies in Texas informal subdivisions. *Urban Studies, 52*(6), 1037–1052. http://journals.sagepub.com/doi/abs/10.1177/0042098014533733

Sullivan, J. (2017, April 29). Time to raise their voices. *The Boston Globe* (Goodlife Section), pp. 1, 4.

Sullivan, R. (2016). *Street level: Los Angeles in the twenty-first century*. New York, NY: Routledge.

Suls, R. (2017, February 24). *Most Americans continue to oppose U.S. border wall*. Washington, DC: Pew Research Center.

Sun, K. C. Y., & Cadge, W. (2013). How do organizations respond to new immigrants? Comparing two New England cities. *Journal of Immigrant & Refugee Studies, 11*(2), 157–177.

Sundberg, J. (2015). The state of exception and the imperial way of life in the United States–Mexico borderlands. *Environment and Planning D: Society and Space, 33*(2), 209–228.

Tallet, O. P. (2017, February 8). "Mi casa es su casa": Houston mayor on "sanctuary cities." *Houston Chronicle.* http://www.houstonchronicle.com/lifestyle/calle-houston/article/Sylvester-Turner-on-Houston-and-the-attack-on-10918281.php?t=b679052047438d9cbb

Tamez, M. (2012). The Texas–Mexico border wall and Ndé memory. In J. M. Loyd, M. Mitchelson, & A. Burridge (Eds.), *Beyond walls and cages: Prisons, borders, and global crisis* (pp. 57–73). Athens, GA: University of Georgia Press.

Tanaka, K. (2014). Advanced marginalization and re-criminalization of undocumented workers in the US. In R. E. Rinehart, K. N. Barbour, & C. C. Pope (Eds.), *Ethnographic worldviews* (pp. 39–48). Dordrecht, the Netherlands: Springer.

Tavernise, S. (2017, May 10). The immigrants who oppose sanctuary. *The New York Times*, pp. A14–A15.

Taylor, C. (2016). *Immigrants, undocumented: Criminalization.* Brighton, UK: University of Sussex.

Taylor, M. A., Decker, S. H., Provine, D. M., Lewis, P. G., & Varsanyi, M. W. (2014). Illegal immigration and local policing. In M. D. Reisig & R. J. KaneIllegal (Eds.), *The Oxford handbook on polic and policing* (pp. 409–429). New York, NY: Oxford University Press.

Teixeira, G. H. (2016). Who wants to go to Arizona? A brief survey of criminalization of immigration law in the US context. In M. J. Guia & R. Koulish (Eds.), *Immigration detention, risk and human rights* (pp. 279–293). Dordrecht, the Netherlands; Springer.

Tejada, K. (2016). Activists and philanthropists: Understanding the political habitus of Salvadorans in the DC metro area. *Interface: A Journal on Social Movements, 8*(1). 97–116.

Terrio, S. J. (2015). *Whose child am I? Unaccompanied, undocumented children in US immigration custody.* Berkeley, CA: University of California Press.

Thanawala, S. (2017, November 20). Federal judge permanently block's Trump executive order to cut funding to sanctuary cities. *Chicago Tribune.* http://www.chicagotribune.com/news/immigration/ct-trump-sanctuary-cities-funding-ruling-20171120-story.html

Tharoor, I. (2016, November 18). Trump victory has Ireland worried about its undocumented immigrants in the U.S. *The Washington Post.* https://www.washingtonpost.com/news/worldviews/wp/2016/11/18/trump-victory-has-ireland-worried-about-its-illegal-immigrants-in-u-s/?utm_term=.356fa2824d1f

The New York Times Editorial Board. (2017a, September 1). Blocking a bad immigration law in Texas. *The New York Times*, p. A20.

The New York Times Editorial Board. (2017b, November 20). Let the Haitians stay. *The New York Times*, p. A22.

The New York Times Editorial Board. (2018, January 13). So much for the beacon of hope. *The New York Times*, p. A18.

Theodore, N., & Habans, R. (2016). Policing immigrant communities: Latino perceptions of police involvement in immigration enforcement. *Journal of Ethnic and Migration Studies, 42*(6), 970–988.

Thi Nguyen, M. (2014). *When local law enforcement officers become immigration agents, communities suffer.* USApp-American Politics and Policy Blog. http://eprints.lse.ac.uk/61204

Thompson, C. D., Jr. (2015). *Border odyssey: Travels along the US/Mexico divide.* Austin, TX: University of Texas Press.

Tidwell, N. (2013). Fragmenting the community: Immigration enforcement and the unintended consequences of local police non-cooperation policies. *St. John's Law Review, 88*(1).

Timberlake, J. M., & Williams, R. H. (2012). Stereotypes of US immigrants from four global regions. *Social Science Quarterly, 93*(4), 867–890.

Tirman, J. (2015). *Dream chasers: Immigration and the American backlash.* Cambridge, MA: MIT Press.

Tobin, R. W. (2016). *Hospitality and the immigration crisis.* Eutopias. https://escholarship.org/uc/item/62v21327

Tomsho, R. (1987). *The American sanctuary movement.* Austin, TX: Texas Monthly Press.

Torre Cantalapiedra, E. (2016). Explaining state and local anti-immigrant policies in the United States: The case of Arizona's SB 1070. *Migraciones Internacionales, 8*(3), 37–63.

Torres, N. I. (2015). *Walls of indifference: Immigration and the militarization of the US–Mexico border.* New York, NY: Routledge.

Toussaint, N. G. (2013). *The metropolitan dimensions of United States immigration policy: A theoretical and comparative analysis.* Doctoral dissertation, Portland State University, Portland, OR.

Tramonte, L. (2011). *Debunking the myth of "sanctuary cities": Community policing policies protect American communities.* Washington, DC: Immigration Policy Center.

Tsai, J. H. C. (2009). Chinese immigrant restaurant workers' injury and illness experiences. *Archives of Environmental & Occupational Health, 64*(2), 107–114.

Tsiklauri, G. (2017). Overview of the United States immigration policy. *Journal of Humanities, 5*(2), 70–73.

Tsutsui, K., & Smith, J. (2017). *Human rights and social movements: From the boomerang pattern to a sandwich effect.* http://d-scholarship.pitt.edu/31005/1/Tsutsui%20 and%20Smith%20Human%20Rights%20and%20Social%20Movements%20Fin%20 Submitted%20Version.pdf

Turkewitz, J., & Heisler, T. (2017, May 6). Somewhere to shelter, but nowhere to run. *The New York Times*, p. A11.

Ugwu, R. (2017, November 2). A.C.L.U. sues over detention of immigrant. *The New York Times*, p. A10.

Uitermark, J., & Nicholls, W. (2012). How local networks shape a global movement: Comparing Occupy in Amsterdam and Los Angeles. *Social Movement Studies, 11*(3–4), 295–301.

Uneasy neighbors: A brief history of Mexican–U.S. migration. (2007, May–June). *Harvard Magazine.* http://harvardmagazine.com/2007/05/uneasy-neighbors-a-brief-html

United States Conference of Catholic Bishops. (2017). *Sanctuary cities.* http://justiceforimmigrants.org/2016site/wp-content/uploads/2017/01/sanctuary-cities.pdf

United States Council of Mayors. (2017). *Statement by the USCM CEO & Executive Director Tom Cochran on national injunction of executive order.* https://www. usmayors.org/2017/04/25/statement-by-uscm-ceo-executive-director-tom-cochran-on-nationwide-injunction-of-sanctuary-cities-provisions-in-interior-enforcement-executive-order/

Urbana, J. A. N. (2014). *Illegal: Reflections of an undocumented immigrant.* Urbana, IL: University of Illinois Press.

Urrea, L. A. (2015). Foreword. In P. Orner (Ed.), *Underground America: Narratives of undocumented lives* (pp. 1–4). San Francisco, CA: McSweeney's.

US Department of Homeland Security. (2012). *Yearbook of immigration statistics.* Washington, DC: Author.

Van den Berg, E., & Oomen, B. M. (2014). Towards a decentralization of human rights: The rise of human rights cities. In T. Van Lindert & D. Lettinga (Eds.), *The future of human rights in an urban world: Exploring opportunities, threats and challenges* (pp. 11–16). Amsterdam, the Netherlands: Amnesty International.

Van Horn, T. (2016). Criminalizing brown bodies. http://s3.amazonaws.com/academia.edu.documents/45312149/Van_Horn_Capstone_1.pdf?AWSAccessKeyId =AKIAIWOWYYGZ2Y53UL3A&Expires=1491788871&Signature=wvCAdZEN MI2q%2F09U9q4FTwWsXvI%3D&response-content-disposition=inline%3B%20 filename%3DCriminalizing_Brown_Bodies_Framing_the_D.pdf

Vargas, R., & McHarris, P. (2017). Race and state in city police spending growth: 1980 to 2010. *Sociology of Race and Ethnicity, 3*(1), 96–112.

Varzally, A. (2017). Reflections on the racial turn in immigration history. *Journal of American Ethnic History, 36*(2), 62–71.

Vasquez, M. A. (2014). From colonialism to neo-liberal capitalism: Latino/a immigrants in the US and the new biopolitics. *JCRT: Journal for Cultural and Religious Theory, 13*(1), 83–84.

Vaughan, J. M. (2015). *Number of sanctuaries and criminal releases still growing.* Washington, DC: Center for Immigration Studies.

Vaughn, J. (2016, December 14). *Sanctuary cities continue to obstruct enforcement, threaten public safety.* Center for Immigration Studies. http://cis.org/ Sanctuary-Cities-Map

Velásquez, E. R. (2017). Are undocumented migrants illegal? *Peace Review, 29*(1), 104–111.

Velasquez, R. J. (2016). The mass incarceration of undocumented Latinos/as in the prison–immigration industrial complex. In S. Egharevba (Ed.), *Police brutality, racial profiling, and discrimination in the criminal justice system* (pp. 274–294). Hershey, PA: ICE Global.

Vennochi, J. (2017, September 28). Sessions' anti-immigrant obsession. *The Boston Globe,* p. A15.

Villa-Torres, L., Fleming, P. J., & Barrington, C. (2015). Engaging men as promotores de salud: Perceptions of community health workers among Latino men in North Carolina. *Journal of Community Health, 40*(1), 167–174.

Villarruel, K. L. (1986). The Underground Railroad and the sanctuary movement: A comparison of history, litigation, and values. *Southern California Law Review, 60,* 1429.

Villazor, R. C. (2010). Sanctuary Cities and Local Citizenship. Fordham Urb. LJ, 37, 573.

Villazor, R. C. (2013). The undocumented closet. *North Carolina Law Review, 1.*(UC Davis Legal Studies Research Paper No. 357)

Villegas, F. J. (2017). "Access without fear!": Reconceptualizing "access" to schooling for undocumented students in Toronto. *Critical Sociology, 43*(7–8), 1179–1195. http://journals.sagepub.com/doi/abs/10.1177/0896920516677352

Viser, M. (2017, November 26). Rules shifted abruptly, and fear rushed in. *The Boston Globe,* pp. A1, A12–A13.

Vitiello, D. (2014). The politics of place in immigrant and receiving communities. In M. Halterm, M. S. Johnson, K. P. Viens, & C. E. Wright (Eds.), *What's new about the "new" immigration?* (pp. 83–110). New York, NY: Palgrave Macmillan.

Voekel, P. (2016). Organizing for freedom. *NACLA Report on the Americas, 48*(1), 68–78.

Vrasti, W., & Dayal, S. (2016). Cityzenship: Rightful presence and the urban commons. *Citizenship Studies, 20*(8), 994–1011.

Vysotsky, S., & Madfis, E. (2016). Uniting the right: Anti-immigration, organizing, and the legitimation of extreme racist organizations. *Journal of Hate Studies, 12*(1), 129–151.

Waasdorp, J., & Pahladsingh, A. (2017). Expulsion or imprisonment? Criminal law sanctions for breaching an entry ban in the light of crimmigration law. *Bergen Journal of Criminal Law & Criminal Justice, 4*(2), 247–266.

Wagner, A. (2017, March 6). America's forgotten history of illegal deportations. *The Atlantic.* https://www.theatlantic.com/politics/archive/2017/03/americas-brutal-forgotten-history-of-illegal-deportations/517971

Waldinger, R. (1996). From Ellis Island to LAX: Immigrant prospects in the American city. *International Migration Review, 30*(94), 1078–1086.

Walker, K. E. (2014). Immigration, local policy, and national identity in the suburban United States. *Urban Geography, 35*(4), 508–529.

Wallace, S. J. (2014). Papers please: State-level anti-immigrant legislation in the wake of Arizona's SB 1070. *Political Science Quarterly, 129*(2), 261–291.

Wang, H. L. (2017, February 27). *Breaking down the nearly 11 million unauthorized immigrants in the U.S.* National Public Radio. http://www.npr.org/2017/02/22/516695433/breaking-down-the-nearly-11-million-unauthorized-immigrants-in-the-u-s

Wang, X. (2012). Undocumented immigrants as perceived criminal threat: A test of the minority threat perspective. *Criminology, 50*(3), 743–776.

Wangsness, L. (2017, February 21). Congregations in Mass. preparing to shelter immigrants. *The Boston Globe.* https://www.bostonglobe.com/metro/2017/02/20/sanctuary-congregations-preparing-shelter-immigrants/Hgat97Ke2d3eItbDlgNI4H/story.html

Waslin, M. (2016, September 21). *What is the economic cost of deporting all undocumented immigrants?* American Immigration Council. http://immigrationimpact.com/2016/09/21/economic-cost-deporting-undocumented-immigrants

Waters, M. C., & Kasinitz, P. (2013). Immigrants in New York City: Reaping the benefits of continuous immigration. *Daedalus, 142*(3), 92–106.

Watson, S. (2015). The criminalization of human and humanitarian smuggling. *Migration, Mobility, & Displacement, 1*(1), 27–41. https://journals.uvic.ca/index.php/mmd/article/view/13273/4410

Weber, P. J. (2017, May 9). Texas police chief rips "sanctuary cities" law. *The Boston Globe,* p. A5.

Weffer, S. (2013). Immigration, protest, and social movements. In D. A. Snow & D. della Porta (Eds.), *The Wiley-Blackwell encyclopedia of social and political movements* (pp. 119–135). New York, NY: Wiley.

Weissman, D. M. (2016). The federalization of racism and nativist hostility: Local immigration enforcement in North Carolina. In D. L. Leal & N. P. Rodriguez (Eds.), *Migration in an era of restriction and recession* (pp. 99–115). Dordrecht, the Netherlands: Springer.

Welch, B. J. (2016). Beautiful walls: Reclaiming urban space through mural making. *Penn GSE Perspectives on Urban Education, 13*(1), 81–85.

Wells, K. (2017). What does a Republican government with Donald Trump as president of the USA mean for children, youth and families? *Children's Geographies, 15*(4), 491–497.

Werman, M. (2016, March 26). *The sanctuary church movement is on the rise again in California*. Public Radio International. https://www.pri.org/stories/2016-03-21/sanctuary-church-movement-rise-again-california

Wexelbaum, R. (2016). The library as safe space. In S. S. Hines & K. M. Crowe (Eds.), *The future of library space* (pp. 37–78). Bingley, UK: Emerald Group.

Wickersham, M. E. (2013). Parables and politics: Clergy attitudes toward illegal immigration in Alabama. *Hispanic Journal of Behavioral Sciences, 35*(3), 336–353.

Widmer, T. (2017, July 9). Democracy's immigrant story. *The Boston Globe*, p. K6.

Wiebe, V. (2016). *The immigration hotel. Rutgers Law Review, 68,* 1673. https://poseidon01.ssrn.com/delivery.php?ID=380124069122108089091005064122066081059089022064027023064107066125083026119004007123033062000029047123108124078073090120009027058071007053078071065085066004101095064050012092100100074114123066023114026069087117111106812409806712011810011806700206609&EXT=pdf

Wilkins, J. (2017, January 25). After border wall, will "overstayed visas" be next? *The San Diego Union-Tribune*. http://www.sandiegouniontribune.com/news/immigration/sd-me-visa-overstay-20170125-story.html

Williams, K. M., & Hannon, L. (2016). Immigrant rights in a deep south city. *Du Bois Review: Social Science Research on Race, 13*(1), 139–157.

Wilson, C. E. (2011). Immigrant nonprofit organizations and the fight for comprehensive immigration reform. *Nonprofit Policy Forum, 2*(2). https://www.degruyter.com/downloadpdf/j/npf.2011.2.issue-2/2154-3348.1025/2154-3348.1025.pdf

Wilson, C. E. (2013a). Collaboration of nonprofit organizations with local government for immigrant language acquisition. *Nonprofit and Voluntary Sector Quarterly, 42*(5), 963–984.

Wilson, C. E. (2013b). Language access policies in Philadelphia: Municipal directives and nonprofit collaboration. *Nonprofit and Voluntary Sector Quarterly, 42*(5), 963–984. http://journals.sagepub.com/doi/abs/10.1177/0899764012461400

Wilson, P. (2016, October 6). Immigrant officials use technology to track illegal immigrants. *North Carolina Journal of Law and Technology, 19.* http://ncjolt.org/immigrations-officials-use-technology

Wilson, R. (2017, March 30). Seattle sues Trump administration over sanctuary city ban. *The Hill.* http://thehill.com/homenews/state-watch/326481-seattle-sues-trump-admin-over-sanctuary-city-ban

Winders, J. (2016). Immigration and the 2016 election. *Southeastern Geographer, 56*(3), 291–296.

Winsor, M. (2017, May 12). *Undocumented mother granted temporary stay on deportation after 86 days in sanctuary.* ABC News. http://abcnews.go.com/US/undocumented-mother-granted-temporary-stay-deportation-86-days/story?id= 47370279

Wogan, P. (2017). *Corner-store dreams and the 2008 financial crisis: A true story about risk, entrepreneurship, immigration, and Latino-Anglo friendship.* New York, NY: Springer.

Wolgin, P. E. (2015, August 19). How much would it cost to deport all undocumented immigrants? *Newsweek.* http://www.newsweek.com/how-much-would-it-cost-deport-all-undocumented-immigrants-364316

Wong, R. S. C., Wong, P. Y., Chen, J. Y., & Chan, L. C. (2016). Reflective space: The medical library as a mindfulness sanctuary. In A. Peterkin & P. Brett-MacLean (Eds.), *Keeping reflection fresh: A practical guide for clinical educators* (pp. 17–37). Kent, OH: Kent State University Press.

Wong, T. K., & Kosnac, H. (2017). Does the legalization of undocumented immigrants in the US encourage unauthorized immigration from Mexico? An empirical analysis of the moral hazard of legalization. *International Migration, 55*(2), 159–173.

Woude, M. A., Leun, J. P., & Nijland, J. A. A. (2014). Crimmigration in the Netherlands. *Law & Social Inquiry, 39*(3), 560–579.

Wright, C. (2016). *Con job: How Democrats gave us crime, sanctuary cities, abortion profiteering, and racial division.* Washington, DC: Regnery.

Wright, R., & Ellis, M. (2016). Perspectives on migration theory: Geography. In M. J. White (Ed.), *International handbook of migration and population distribution* (pp. 11–30). Dordrecht, the Netherlands: Springer.

Wright, S. (2017). *Standing on holy ground: Responding to the call for sanctuary.* http://www.mercymidatlantic.org/PDF/Responding_to_the_Call_for_Sanctuary-Education_for_Justice.pdf

Ybarra, M., & Peña, I. L. (2017). "We don't need money, we need to be together": Forced transnationality in deportation's afterlives. *Geopolitics, 22*(1), 34–50.

Ybarra, V. D., Sanchez, L. M., & Sanchez, G. R. (2016). Anti-immigrant anxieties in state policy: The Great Recession and punitive immigration policy in the American states, 2005–2012. *State Politics & Policy Quarterly, 16*(3), 313–339.

Yan, H., & Simon, D. (2017, December 1). *Katie Steinle death: Garcia Zarate acquitted of homicide.* CNN. http://www.cnn.com/2017/11/30/us/kate-steinle-murder-trial-verdict/index.html

Yao-Kouame, K. P. C. H. (2016). *Understanding the crisis of undocumented minors from Central America coming to the USA: A case study in Mecklenburg County, North Carolina.* Doctoral dissertation, University of North Carolina at Charlotte, Charlotte, NC.

Yee, V. (2017a, February 23). Migrants hide, fearing capture on "any corner." *The New York Times,* pp. A1, A14.

Yee, V. (2017a, April 26). Trump can't withhold funding to sanctuary cities, judge rules. *The New York Times,* pp. A1, A16.

Yee, V. (2017b, May 6). Many ask for asylum, but it's rarely granted. *The New York Times,* p. A15.

Yee, V. (2017c, June 26). From deep grief, a solid bond with Trump on border policy. *The New York Times*, pp. A1, A18.

Yee, V. (2017d, July 5). Immigration arrests stun Iraqis who fled over Christian faith. *The New York Times*, pp. A1, A12.

Yee, V. (2017e, August 1). Deal with prosecutor to avoid a "life sentence of deportation." *The New York Times*, pp. A1, A15.

Yee, V. (2017f, October 28). US nursed an undocumented girl, 10: Now it may deport her. *The New York Times*, p. A13.

Yee, V. (2017g, November 26). As arrests surge, immigrants fear even driving. *The New York Times*, pp. 1, 18.

Yee, V. (2017h, December 22). Thousands of federal inmates are in the US illegally, administration says. *The New York Times*, p. A14.

Yee, V. (2017i, December 23). Despite a rape, the US fought a girl's abortion. *The New York Times*, p. A15.

Yee, V. (2018, January 14). Trump's jabs echo attitudes. *The New York Times*, pp. 1, 22.

Yee, V., & Nixon, R. (2017, April 13). Memo tells of US plan to speed up border hires. *The New York Times*, p. A15.

Yee, V. & Ruiz, R. R. (2017, May 23). Sessions narrows order against sanctuary cities. *The New York Times*, p. A19.

Yukich, G. (2013a). *One family under God: Immigration politics and progressive religion in America*. New York, NY: Oxford University Press.

Yukich, G. (2013b). Constructing the model immigrant: Movement strategy and immigrant deservingness in the new sanctuary movement. *Social Problems, 60*(3), 302–320.

Zallman, L., Woolhandler, S., Himmelstein, D., Bor, D., & McCormick, D. (2013). Immigrants contributed an estimated $115.2 billion more to the Medicare Trust Fund than they took out in 2002–09. *Health Affairs, 32*(6), 1153–1160.

Zaman, T. (2016). *Islamic traditions of refuge in the crises of Iraq and Syria*. New York, NY: Palgrave Macmillan.

Zamora, S. (2015). Black and Brown in Los Angeles: Beyond conflict and coalition. *Ethnic and Racial Studies, 38*(8), 1473–1475.

Zatz, M. S., & Smith, H. (2012). Immigration, crime, and victimization: Rhetoric and reality. *Annual Review of Law and Social Science, 8*, 141–159.

Zaun, N., Roos, C., & Gülzau, F. (2016). Circumventing deadlock through venue-shopping: Why there is more than just talk in US immigration politics in times of economic crisis. *Journal of Ethnic and Migration Studies, 42*(10), 1590–1609.

Zauzmer, J. (2017, March 2). Cardinal Wuerl voices Catholic support for immigrants but urges caution about sanctuary. *The Washington Post*. https://www.washingtonpost.com/news/acts-of-faith/wp/2017/03/02/cardinal-wuerl-voices-catholic-support-for-immigrants-but-urges-caution-about-sanctuary-churches/?utm_term=.3d05430616d8

Zayas, L. (2015). *Forgotten citizens: Deportation, children, and the making of American exiles and orphans*. New York, NY: Oxford University Press.

Zepeda-Millán, C. (2016). Weapons of the (not so) weak: Immigrant mass mobilization in the US South. *Critical Sociology, 42*(2), 269–287.

Ziegler-McPherson, C. A. (2017). *Selling America: Immigration promotion and the settlement of the American continent, 1607–1914*. Santa Barbara, CA: ABC-CLIO.

Zimmer, K. (2017, February 14). *Houses of worship sign up to house undocumented immigrants during raids*. DNA Info. https://www.dnainfo.com/new-york/20170214/union-square/sanctuary-movement-undocumented-immigrants

Zorn, J. (2014). "No border, no nation, stop deportation": Protest against immigration control as empowerment. *Critical and Radical Social Work, 2*(2), 175–192.

Zucker, N. L., & Zucker, N. F. (2016). *Desperate crossings: Seeking refuge in America.* New York, NY: Routledge.

INDEX